Uzbekistan

the Bradt Travel Guide

Sophie Ibbotson

Updated by
Tim Burford

edition
3

www.bradtguides.c

Bradt Travel Guides Ltd, UK
The Globe Pequot Press Inc, USA

D1428353

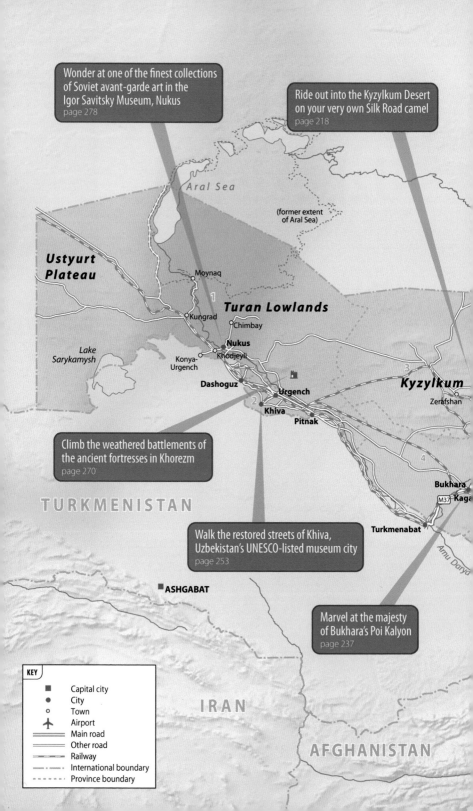

Wonder at one of the finest collections of Soviet avant-garde art in the Igor Savitsky Museum, Nukus
page 278

Ride out into the Kyzylkum Desert on your very own Silk Road camel
page 218

Aral Sea

(former extent of Aral Sea)

Ustyurt Plateau

Moynaq

1

Turan Lowlands

Kungrad

Chimbay

Lake Sarykamysh

Nukus
Khodjeyli

Konya-Urgench

3

Kyzylkum

Dashoguz

Urgench

Zerafshan

2

Khiva

Pitnak

4

Climb the weathered battlements of the ancient fortresses in Khorezm
page 270

Bukhara

M37 Kaga

TURKMENISTAN

Turkmenabat

Walk the restored streets of Khiva, Uzbekistan's UNESCO-listed museum city
page 253

Amu Darya

■ ASHGABAT

Marvel at the majesty of Bukhara's Poi Kalyon
page 237

IRAN

AFGHANISTAN

KEY

■   Capital city
●   City
○   Town
✈   Airport
Main road
Other road
Railway
International boundary
Province boundary

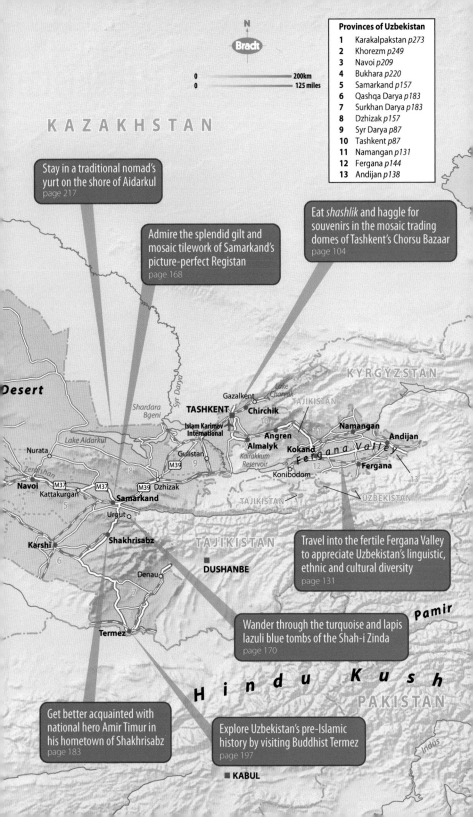

N

Bradt

0 ——— 200km
0 ——— 125 miles

Provinces of Uzbekistan

1	Karakalpakstan	p273
2	Khorezm	p249
3	Navoi	p209
4	Bukhara	p220
5	Samarkand	p157
6	Qashqa Darya	p183
7	Surkhan Darya	p183
8	Dzhizak	p157
9	Syr Darya	p87
10	Tashkent	p87
11	Namangan	p131
12	Fergana	p144
13	Andijan	p138

KAZAKHSTAN

Stay in a traditional nomad's
yurt on the shore of Aidarkul
page 217

Admire the splendid gilt and
mosaic tilework of Samarkand's
picture-perfect Registan
page 168

Eat *shashlik* and haggle for
souvenirs in the mosaic trading
domes of Tashkent's Chorsu Bazaar
page 104

KYRGYZSTAN

Desert

Shardara
Bgeni

Syr Darya

Gazalkent

Lake
Charyak

TAJIKISTAN

TASHKENT
Chirchik
10

Islam Karimov
International

Angren
Almalyk
Kokand
Kairakkum
Reservoir
Konibodom

Namangan

Andijan

Fergana Valley

11

12

Fergana

13

UZBEKISTAN

Nurata

Lake Aidarkul

Zerafshan

Navoi
M37

Kattakurgan

M37

M37

M39

Dzhizak

Gulistan
M39
9

8

5

Samarkand

Urgut

TAJIKISTAN

Karshi

Shakhrisabz

6

Denau

7

DUSHANBE

Travel into the fertile Fergana Valley
to appreciate Uzbekistan's linguistic,
ethnic and cultural diversity
page 131

Pamir

Wander through the turquoise and lapis
lazuli blue tombs of the Shah-i Zinda
page 170

Termez

Hindu Kush

PAKISTAN

Get better acquainted with
national hero Amir Timur in
his hometown of Shakhrisabz
page 183

Explore Uzbekistan's pre-Islamic
history by visiting Buddhist Termez
page 197

KABUL

Indus

Uzbekistan
Don't miss...

Museum City
The Ichon Qala – the central walled city of Khiva – is stuffed with mosques, madrasas and mausoleums
(J/S) page 260

Camel trekking
Get to know your Bactrian camel while riding across the sands of the Kyzylkum Desert
(ME) page 218

Islamic architecture

The Registan in Samarkand is one of the world's greatest examples of medieval Islamic architecture

(EA/D) page 168

Traditional style

Uzbekistan is famous for its wonderful silk carpets, with their tight weave, smooth finish and rich colours

(SS) page 76

Khorezm fortresses

The Ayaz Qala fortress is part of UNESCO's Golden Ring of Ancient Khorezm

(SD/S) page 270

Uzbekistan in colour

above No trip to Samarkand is complete without visiting the Shah-i Zinda, a magnificent collection of medieval tiled tombs (M/S) page 170

left The gilded interior of the Tilla Kari Madrasa reveals the incredible wealth of these Islamic schools (SS) page 169

below The Mir-i Arab Madrasa has been an important Islamic educational institution for nearly 500 years (ME) page 239

above left Ismail Samani, founder of the Samanid dynasty, is buried at this place of pilgrimage in Bukhara (AL/S) page 237

above right The khans of Kokand were great patrons of the arts, as shown by the Khudayar Khan Palace (EF/D) page 153

right The stations of the Tashkent metro are beautifully decorated; each has an individual theme (LBP/S) page 95

below Most of Tashkent's mosques have been repeatedly destroyed by earthquakes — the Juma (Friday) Mosque was largely rebuilt in the 1990s in a peculiarly Russian style (L/S) page 109

TRAVEL THE UNKNOWN

Follow the

SILK ROAD

through Uzbekistan, neighbouring Stans, Iran, Caucasus, China & Turkey

 www.traveltheunknown.com/silk

 UK: 020 7183 6371 | US: 1 800 604 6024

WINNER
BRITISH
TRAVEL
AWARDS
2018

9854
ATOL
PROTECTED

AUTHOR

Sophie Ibbotson is Uzbekistan's Tourism Ambassador to the UK. She has had a professional interest in central Asia since 2008, working in the region as a consultant for public- and private-sector clients including government ministries and the World Bank. Sophie is the founder of Maximum Exposure Ltd, Business and Economics Advisor at Scarmans, and a member of council at the Royal Society for Asian Affairs (w rsaa.org.uk).

UPDATER

This edition has been updated by **Tim Burford**, who has spent almost 30 years writing guidebooks, many to destinations in the post-Soviet sphere, including Romania, Poland, Ukraine, Georgia, Armenia, Dresden and Bratislava. Uzbekistan, therefore, felt familiar from the outset. He says: 'I really don't speak Russian (or Uzbek) and I don't eat meat, so there are challenges, but it's all good fun! The Uzbeks are wonderful people, and in the main Silk Road cities

such as Samarkand and Bukhara many younger people now speak English. The infrastructure is also improving rapidly, especially with new railway lines and high-speed trains, and the political and social systems are becoming much less restrictive. There's lots of scope for outdoor adventure, so that's something I hope we see more of in the future.' Tim studied languages at Oxford and has now written nine guides for Bradt.

PUBLISHER'S FOREWORD

Adrian Phillips, Managing Director

Reckon writing a guidebook to a country on the Silk Road must be the most romantic job around? Think again. The authors describe their visit to Chorsu Bazaar as the 'first and only place we've seen the boot of a Lada stacked with decapitated cow heads' and they admit that camels are 'invariably smelly and jolly uncomfortable to ride'. This is a guidebook that tells it as it is. But that means too that it tells of a country where spring brings a riot of colourful flowers in mountain pastures, where summer offers starry skies and nights spent in yurts, where traditional festivals are things of thrilling pomp and circumstance – and where a toilet stop in a carpet shop can lead to an invitation to a family wedding!

Third edition published January 2020
First published 2013
Bradt Travel Guides Ltd
31a High Street, Chesham, Buckinghamshire, HP5 1BW, England
www.bradtguides.com
Print edition published in the USA by The Globe Pequot Press Inc,
PO Box 480, Guilford, Connecticut 06437-0480

Photographs Adam Balogh (AB); DOCA Tours: Oybek Ostanov (OO/DT); Dreamstime.com: David Prudek (DP/D), Elizaveta Kharicheva (EK/D), Enrico Mariotti (EM/D), Eranicle (E/D), Evgeniy Agarkov (EA/D), Evgeniy Fesenko (EF/D), Mattiaath (M/D), Muzaffar Mahkamov (MM/D), Radist (R/D); Gettyimages.com: Marc Dozier (MD/G); Laurent Nilles @societyofexploration (LN); Maximum Exposure Ltd (ME); Shutterstock.com: Anatolijs Laicans (AL/S), Evgeniy Agarkov (EA/S), javarman (j/S), Limpopo (L/S), Lukas Bischoff Photograph (LBP/S), Marina Rich (MR/S), MehmetO (M/S), posztos (p/S), RelisaGranovskaya (R/S), Sergey Dzyuba (SD/S); Superstock.com (SS); Wikimedia Commons: ChanOJ (C/W)
Front cover Gur-i Amir (MD/G)
Back cover Market sellers (LN); foothills of Uzbekistan (SS)
Title page Lake Charvak (EA/S); Tilla Kari (SS); craft market (LN)

Maps David McCutcheon FBCart.S

Typeset by D & N Publishing, Baydon, Wiltshire, www.dataworks.co.in and Ian Spick, Bradt Travel Guides Ltd
Production managed by Jellyfish Print Solutions; printed in India
Digital conversion by www.dataworks.co.in

Acknowledgements

ACKNOWLEDGMENTS FOR THE THIRD EDITION Thanks above all to Oybek Ostanov (DOCA Tours) and Hakim Makhmudov (Uzbekistan Airways). Thanks also to Ravshan (Gulnara Guesthouse, Tashkent), Rafael Zinurov (Topchan Hostel, Tashkent), Pavel (Art Hostel, Tashkent), Azamat Giyasov (Amir Khan Hostel, Tashkent), Oybek (Mirzo Guesthouse, Tashkent), Chris and Alice Allan (HM Embassy, Tashkent), Nargiza Khamraeva (Minzifa Boutique Hotel, Bukhara), Komil Kadirov (Komil Bukhara Boutique Hotel, Bukhara), Muhabbat Shukurullaeva (Hotel Fayz, Urgench), Hélène Pelosse (Hélène Oasis, Bukhara), Jaloladdin Matkarimov (Meros B&B, Khiva), David Pearce (Friends of Nukus Museum) and, of course, to Sophie Ibbotson and all at Bradt Travel Guides – especially Carys Homer.

Thanks to Cédric Barret, Carl and Hester Dijkstra, M Downs, Sarai Franklin, Lara Koopen, Jane Law, Daniel Majchrowicz, Paul Sommerfeld, Petra Valkova and Arlo Werkhoven for reader updates.

ACKNOWLEDGEMENTS FOR THE PREVIOUS EDITIONS *Sophie Ibbotson*
I would like to express huge thanks to the staff at the Embassy of Uzbekistan in London and Uzbekistan Airways for their ongoing support. The previous editions of this guide would not have been possible without the hard work of Max Lovell-Hoare, Ainura Temiralieva, Jack Barkley-Smith, John Newby, Georgina Suttie, Svetlana Rakhimova, and Steph Adams. Bijan Omrani, Bryn Kewley, and Ben Tavener also provided invaluable input.

UPDATER'S STORY

I started out writing guidebooks to eastern Europe and then moved further east to Ukraine, Georgia and Armenia, so updating Bradt's *Uzbekistan* seemed like a logical extension – and indeed much of the post-Soviet background was very familiar. But at the same time, this is Asia – this is the Silk Road! There was much that was new and thrilling, and I'm very grateful to have been offered the opportunity to work on this guide. It was already excellent, but a lot of work was needed to bring it into the post-Karimov era – I hope I've managed that successfully.

Contents

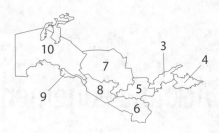

LIST OF MAPS

Introduction

In his 1913 poem *The Golden Road to Samarkand*, each of James Elroy Flecker's characters describes in vivid detail moonlit cities, the heat of the winds, shadows cast on the sands, and the silent air of the desert. The reader is swept along in their timeless caravan, sharing in the atmospheric journey, and, like the merchants, gives scarcely a thought for the women left behind, ignored completely, as everyone's attention is utterly transfixed by the destination of which they dream.

Uzbekistan captures the imagination like almost nowhere else. The country is virtually synonymous with the Silk Road, and three of the greatest Silk Road cities – Samarkand, Bukhara and Khiva – all fall on Uzbek soil. The people, ideas and goods that travelled east to west, and, indeed, west to east, have left indelible marks on Uzbekistan's landscape, its culture and the genetic make-up of its people, creating a diverse destination with layer upon layer of competing (but entwined) identities.

It is a country with a rich, fascinating past, and its long-settled history has left numerous physical remains, making it far more tangible than in neighbouring Kazakhstan or Kyrgyzstan, where nomadism was the norm. The country has been continually inhabited since Neanderthal man first walked across the steppe and took refuge in the Gissar Mountains south of Samarkand. His Stone Age descendants carved their marks in caves, and by the 1st millennium BC Iranian nomads had settled the grassy plains, planted crops and built rudimentary irrigation channels. In their wake came wave after wave of invaders: Scythians, Achaemenids, Greeks, Arabs and Mongols. Each group built palaces, fortresses and places of worship and of trade, attempting to eclipse both physically and in public memory whatever had been there before.

The constant cycle of construction and destruction has had a significant impact on what we see in Uzbekistan today. The buildings that survive, and which make the striking skylines of each and every city, are not necessarily the most modern or the mostly strongly constructed: they are the ones which, by dint of good fortune, have avoided both the attentions of marauding hordes and equally destructive natural disasters. Well into the 20th century the Soviets were levelling ancient buildings to make way for architecture that was, in its aesthetics and its function, better in keeping with their ideology. To a lesser extent, the same is also true of the post-independence period. Restoration projects, some more sympathetic than others, have raised medieval buildings like phoenixes from the ashes, though how much of their appearance is original and how much should be attributed to artistic licence, a modern architect or a politician's idealised vision of the past, is always open to debate. City-wide beautification projects, such as the one that occured in Shakhrisabz, are especially controversial.

Man's impact, past and present, on the natural environment, as well as on the urban landscape, is clear in Uzbekistan, too. The taming of the Amu Darya and Syr Darya rivers and the construction of canals, dams and other irrigation methods have made it possible to farm huge swathes of land that naturally could not support crops. The country's lucrative cotton crop especially depends on man's manipulation of nature. Interfering in this manner is not without its dangers, however, and in the race to cultivate more and more land, to produce ever-greater quantities of cotton, the ecosystem has become disturbingly unbalanced: the Aral Sea has already retreated beyond the level from which it is thought to be recoverable; stretches of once fertile land are turning to desert; and even greater areas are increasingly saline and/or toxic, heavily polluted with industrial waste and chemical pesticides.

In many ways, Uzbekistan is at a crossroads. This applies, as it has always done, in a physical sense, as the country lies in the heart of Eurasia: Europe and Iran are to the west; Russia is to the north; China is to the east; and Afghanistan and the Indian subcontinent spread out southwards. But it is also true culturally, economically and politically. Almost three decades after the fall of the Soviet Union, Uzbekistan is no longer a bedfellow of Moscow, but neither has it been able properly to integrate with markets and potential allies in the West. If any country is the beneficiary of this economic and political power vacuum, it is China, who is now Uzbekistan's biggest investor; but even so, the Chinese are still viewed by the Uzbeks with suspicion. Unlike in Africa and other resource-rich regions, the Chinese have not had it all their way in Uzbekistan, with local firms, and government regulations, keeping them in check.

History has shown that Uzbekistan is at its greatest when it has a symbiotic relationship with its neighbours, when people, ideas and goods flow back and forth, enriching society. After a period of relative isolationism, it is returning to the world stage. Since 2016, the country has grown in confidence and influence, actively courting foreign governments, businesses and tourists to visit, collaborate, trade and share the finest aspects of their respective societies for mutual benefit.

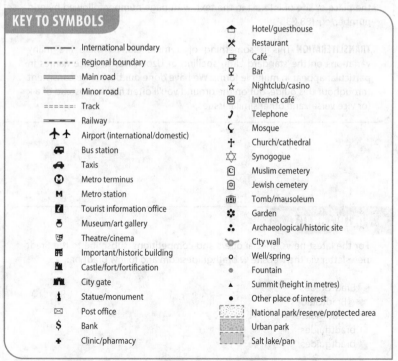

KEY TO SYMBOLS

International boundary	Hotel/guesthouse
Regional boundary	Restaurant
Main road	Café
Minor road	Bar
Track	Nightclub/casino
Railway	Internet café
Airport (international/domestic)	Telephone
Bus station	Mosque
Taxis	Church/cathedral
Metro terminus	Synagogue
Metro station	Muslim cemetery
Tourist information office	Jewish cemetery
Museum/art gallery	Tomb/mausoleum
Theatre/cinema	Garden
Important/historic building	Archaeological/historic site
Castle/fort/fortification	City wall
City gate	Well/spring
Statue/monument	Fountain
Post office	Summit (height in metres)
Bank	Other place of interest
Clinic/pharmacy	National park/reserve/protected area
	Urban park
	Salt lake/pan

AUTHOR'S FAVOURITES Finding genuinely characterful accommodation or that unmissable off-the-beaten-track café can be difficult, so the author has chosen a few of his favourite places throughout the country to point you in the right direction. These 'author's favourites' are marked with an ✳.

PRICES

Price codes Throughout this guide we have used price codes to indicate the cost of those places to stay and eat listed. For a key to these price codes, see page 71 for accommodation and page 72 for restaurants.

Prices in this guide Although Uzbekistan's official currency is the Uzbek som, prices (for accommodation in particular) are widely quoted in US dollars, which is seen as more stable and consistent. We have therefore quoted prices in US dollars throughout this guide.

MAPS

Keys and symbols Maps include alphabetical keys covering the locations of those places to stay, eat or drink that are featured in the book. Note that regional maps may not show all hotels and restaurants in the area: other establishments may be located in towns shown on the map.

Grids and grid references Several maps use gridlines to allow easy location of sites. Map grid references are listed in square brackets after the name of the place or site of interest in the text, with page number followed by grid number, eg: [88 C3].

TRANSLITERATION This is something of a minefield, as there are many variations on the standard Latin spelling of Uzbek words; place names in particular appear in multiple forms. We have done our best to be consistent throughout this guide, but on the ground you'll often find a q instead of a k (or vice versa), and other similar issues.

For the latest news, special offers and competitions, subscribe to the Bradt newsletter via the website **w** bradtguides.com and follow Bradt on:

- 🅕 BradtGuides
- 🐦 @BradtGuides
- 📷 @bradtguides
- 🅟 bradtguides
- ▶ bradtguides

Part One

GENERAL INFORMATION

Location Landlocked in the heart of central Asia

Neighbouring countries Afghanistan, Kazakhstan, Kyrgyzstan, Tajikistan and Turkmenistan

Area 447,400km^2 (172,700 square miles)

Climate Extreme continental

Status Republic

Population 32.59 million (November 2018)

Life expectancy 72.3 years (male 69.7, female 75.0)

Capital Tashkent (population 2.5 million)

Other main towns Andijan, Bukhara, Nukus, Samarkand

Major exports Cotton, jute, minerals (notably copper, lead, zinc, tungsten, uranium and gold), chemicals, fertiliser, leather and natural gas

GDP (PPP) US$222.3 billion; GDP (PPP) per capita US$7,000 (2017)

Official language Uzbek. Russian and Tajik are also widely used.

Religion Islam (90% of the population), Russian Orthodox

Currency Uzbek som (UZS)

Exchange rate £1 = UZS11,694; US$1 = UZS9,396; €1 = UZS10,372 (September 2019)

National airline Uzbekistan Airways

International telephone code +998

Time UTC (GMT) +5

Electric voltage 220AC (50Hz)

Weights and measures Metric

Flag Three horizontal stripes of light blue, white and green, with thin red stripes in between each colour. There is a crescent moon and 12 stars in the top left-hand corner.

National anthem 'O'zbekiston Respublikasining Davlat Madhiyasi' (Opening lines: 'My sunny free land, happiness and salvation to your people, You are a warmhearted companion to your friends!)

National sports *Kupkari* (a game played between two teams, using a goat's carcass to score points), *kurash* (traditional wrestling), football, judo, boxing and tae kwon do

Public holidays 1–2 January (New Year's Day), 14 January (Day of Defenders of the Motherland), 8 March (International Women's Day), 21 March (Navruz, the Persian New Year), 9 May (Remembrance Day), 1 September (Independence Day), 1 October (Teachers' Day), 8 December (Constitution Day)

1

Background Information

GEOGRAPHY

Viewed from the air, Uzbekistan is a striking patchwork of colours, with vast stretches of arid desert in the west giving way to jade-green stripes along rivers and in the fertile Fergana Valley. The seams of snow-capped Tian Shan Mountains mark the country's southern and eastern borders, their glacial meltwater the lifeblood of the plains.

At 447,400km² in size, the country is equivalent in area to Spain or California. It measures 1,425km from its western to eastern borders, and 930km from north to south. Uzbekistan is one of only two double-landlocked countries (ie: landlocked countries completely surrounded by other landlocked countries) in the world, the other being Liechtenstein.

The **physical environment** is diverse, ranging from the flat, arid deserts that cover almost 80% of the country's territory, to the eastern mountain peaks that rise up to 4,643m (15,233ft) above sea level.

Water resources are unevenly distributed, with many irrigation channels spreading it more widely. The two largest rivers are the Amu Darya (known to the ancient Greeks as the Oxus) and the Syr Darya (the Jaxartes; see box, below), both of which originate in the mountains of Kyrgyzstan and Tajikistan. In addition, the Zerafshan flows out of Tajikistan, near Samarkand and Bukhara,

THE SYR DARYA

Known to the ancient Greeks as the Jaxartes on account of its colour (from the Persian *yakhsha arta*, meaning 'great pearly river'), the Syr Darya became famous in the classical world as the site where Alexander the Great fought the Scythians in 329BC at the Battle of Jaxartes. Subsequent Islamic writings from the medieval period suggest that the Syr Darya is one of four rivers whose common source lies in Paradise. The others are the Amu Darya (the Oxus), the Nile and the Euphrates.

In reality, the Syr Darya rises from headstreams in the Tian Shan Mountains of Kyrgyzstan and flows 2,212km (1,374 miles) west, passing briefly through Uzbekistan and then into the deserts of Kazakhstan. Its water flow is around 37km³ a year, which would naturally finally drain into the Aral Sea. However, the diversion of the Syr Darya's water into a network of canals is one of the main reasons for the environmental disaster that is the shrinking of the Aral Sea (see box, page 10). So much water is used for cotton irrigation (and lost due to evaporation and leakage from poorly maintained channels) that the river runs dry long before reaching its natural end.

and into the Amu Darya. Much of the ill-fated Aral Sea (see box, page 10) was once within Uzbek territory; Lake Sarygamysh, on the border with Turkmenistan and Lake Aidarkul, near the Kazakh border, were created accidentally by Soviet irrigation projects.

CLIMATE

Uzbekistan has an extreme continental climate owing to its location at the centre of the Eurasian landmass. The hottest period, known as the *chillya*, is from late June to mid-August, when temperatures frequently reach 40°C or even higher (it is a dry heat, so not as unbearable as you might think). **Autumn** is warm and pleasant, and the bazaars are full of fruit and vegetables. In **winter** (beginning in late October on the steppe and December in the south, and generally lasting into March), temperatures may fall to -15°C in the cities and as low as -30°C in the steppe and mountains, with limited precipitation. The average snowfall nationwide is 5cm, rising to 10–12cm in the foothills. **Spring**, from March to June, is another good time to visit – it will be warm with some rain.

Much of Uzbekistan is arid and has little **rainfall**. Humidity is generally low and annual rainfall is typically 100–200mm, stunting the growth of crops and other flora during the summer months. There is some regional variation, however, as the far south of the country has a more tropical climate (complete with higher levels of humidity and rainfall), and the annual rainfall in the mountains can be as much as 900mm.

NATURAL HISTORY AND CONSERVATION

GEOLOGY Uzbekistan lies on several geological fault lines. Its proximity to the Tian Shan and Pamir-Alay ranges, the Kyzylkum and Karakum deserts, and the Kazakh steppe has given the country rich and diverse geological resources, but also made it prone to earthquakes. Uzbekistan's mineral wealth was first comprehensively surveyed during the Soviet period, but is still underexploited (see box, page 9). The country is known to have significant deposits of precious metals and uranium, as well as coal, hydrocarbons and construction materials.

The downside of Uzbekistan's geology is the constant threat of earthquakes, many of which emanate from the densely populated Fergana Valley. Although the 5.1-magnitude 1966 Tashkent earthquake (see box, page 119) is the best known, it is by no means an isolated incident. A 6.1-magnitude quake on the Uzbek–Kyrgyz border killed 14 people in 2011, and smaller quakes (4.0–5.0 on the Richter scale) hit parts of the country on an almost monthly basis.

PALEONTOLOGY Uzbekistan has a rich fossil record, both of plant life and of dinosaurs. The most important specimens to date come from the Cretaceous period (145 million to 66 million years ago) and have been uncovered at the Dzharakuduk site in the Kyzylkum Desert.

Excavations at the site, which began in the 1970s, have revealed abundant remains of a very diverse biota including both mammals and dinosaurs. Large vertebrate remains were collected, as was sediment that could then be processed for microvertebrate remains. Well-preserved dinosaur bones and teeth have all been unearthed, from sauropods and even central Asia's first-known ceratopsid. The discoveries at Dzharakuduk significantly contribute to our understanding of faunal evolution in the northern hemisphere during the Cretaceous period. The oldest

Uzbekistan has two major national parks, both of which are legally protected biosphere reserves with a wealth of indigenous wildlife and glorious, untouched landscapes.

The **Ugam-Chatkal National Park** (page 128) is close to Tashkent, on the spurs of the western Tian Shan Mountains. Contained within its 570km² of territory are mountain steppe and forest, alpine meadow, river valleys and floodplains. It includes the Chimgan ski resort (page 129) and the peak of Great Chimgan (3,309m). The park was founded in 1947 and designated a UNESCO biosphere reserve in 1978.

Ugam-Chatkal supports more than 1,100 species of plant including grasses, wild fruit trees and juniper forests. They provide food for 230 species of bird, of which wild turkey and mountain partridge are particularly numerous. The rarer golden eagle and bearded vulture soar periodically overhead.

The park also has 44 species of mammal. Patient visitors (preferably armed with binoculars) can expect to see wild ram, mountain goat and Siberian roe deer; wild boar, stone marten and red marmot are also present in large numbers. Brown bears and wolves are found in the Pskem Valley, and there are Turkestan lynx and even snow leopards in remoter areas.

Uzbekistan's oldest protected area is the **Zaamin National Park** (page 181), created in 1926 as the Guralsh Nature Preserve. It encompasses 156km² of rolling hills and mountains in the Kulsoy, Guralsh, Baikungur and Aldashmansoy river valleys near Dzhizak.

The park was created to preserve unique mountain-pines ecosystems. The main asset of the reserve is the *Archa* (Central Asian juniper), which reaches 18m in height. Some of the junipers in the reserve are nearly 1,000 years old. Rowan, currant, dog rose, barberry, St John's wort and origanum also feature among the park's 700+ plant species.

Fauna in the park include 150 species of bird and reptile and 40 species of mammal, the highlights of which are white-claw bear, lynx, wild boar and porcupines.

Also important are the **Lower Amu Darya Biosphere Reserve** and the **Amu Darya State Nature Reserve**, both protecting riparian forest along the Amu Darya River; known as tugay, 90% of this important habitat has been lost. Three hanguls (Bukhara red deer) were moved in 1976 (when they were close to extinction) to the LADBR, where their population now numbers 850, with over 1,000 elsewhere in Uzbekistan and the neighbouring countries. Other species protected here include the Amu Darya pheasant, various endemic fish and plants such as wild liquorice; wetlands in the Amu Darya delta are important stopping-off points for migrating waterfowl, and goitred gazelle can be found in the desert. On the other hand, no tigers have been seen between the Amu Darya and Syr Darya rivers since 1970.

hominid remains in Uzbekistan, the bones and teeth of *Homo erectus* (formerly known as Pithecanthropus), date back around 1.5 million years. In 1938, the remains of a young male from the Middle Palaeolithic period (300,000 to 40,000 years ago) were discovered in the Teshik Tash cave in the Gissar Mountains south of Samarkand. Known as the Teshik Tash Boy, he was buried with five pairs of ibex horns, possibly in an early funeral rite. Though assumed to be Neanderthal, there was little hope of telling as the bones were in such poor condition. It was not until the advent of DNA testing (and this too was tricky as fossils don't contain much DNA) that scientists were able to confirm that the genetic material was 98% the same as Neanderthal material discovered elsewhere. When combined with a similar discovery in the Denisov cave in Siberia, the Teshik Tash Boy showed that Neanderthal man ranged far further east than previously thought.

FLORA It is said that the green of Uzbekistan's flag represents nature, and the state emblem depicts the bright sun shining above a valley in bloom, with wheat and cotton crops clearly visible.

Given that Uzbekistan has more than 3,700 species of plant, 20% of which are endemic, it's unsurprising they've been unable to select a single national flower. Sweetbriar, Juno iris, hollyhock, filipendula, forget-me-not, patchouli, clary sage, safflower, helianthus and petunia all grow in large numbers, creating a riot of colour in spring and summertime. There are a significant number of vascular plants unique to Uzbekistan, of which the most notable are *Iris hippolyti*, *Iris capnoides*, *Allium haneltii*, *Dianthus uzbekistanicus* and various members of the tulip family such as *Tulipa butkovii*, *T. uzbekistanica*, *T. batalinii* and *T. clusiana*.

The majority of Uzbekistan's flora is found in the **mountains**, although only 30% of the high peaks are covered with plants and this is mainly tipchak, which is somewhere between a grass and a herb, and common across central Asia. In the

BIRDING IN UZBEKISTAN   *Steve Rooke (w sunbirdtours.co.uk)*

The rich variety of habitats found within Uzbekistan make it a wonderful country for birdwatching, a pastime made a lot easier with the publication of the field guide *The Birds of Central Asia* by Christopher Helm in 2012. The birds visitors will encounter vary according to the time of year, with May perhaps the best time to see breeding and migrant species. However, even the winter months have their rewards with flocks of waxwing and black-throated thrush visiting from their breeding ground further afield.

Even among the parks and wooded areas of verdant **Tashkent** you can find hobby, European nightjar, white-winged woodpecker and golden oriole, and at night hear the distinctive sonar-like 'ping' of the Eurasian scops owl. The common myna is a relatively recent colonist to the region but can now be found everywhere throughout the country. During spring migration almost anything can turn up in the city parks, with species such as Blyth's reed warbler and scarlet rosefinch particularly common.

The **hills and mountains** of Uzbekistan are rich in birds and those looking for a day excursion from Tashkent should visit the area around Chimgan (page 129). One special feature of Uzbekistan's birdlife is the sprinkling of Himalayan species that creep into the Tian Shan Mountains, and around Chimgan you can see three of these – the large blue whistling thrush and brown dipper, found near fast-running water, and the rufous-naped tit, which favours mature juniper. Large raptors often seen here and in other hilly areas include both Himalayan and Eurasian griffon vultures, cinereous (black) vulture, and the mighty lammergeier or bearded vulture, while in May it's not unusual to see large migrating flocks of both European and Oriental honey buzzards.

South of Samarkand on the road to Timur's birthplace, Shakhrisabz, the rocky hills are covered in scrub and hawthorn bushes and offer some fantastic middle ranges dog-rose and other bushes grow, but it is in the lower mountains where a wide variety of deciduous trees and bushes may be found. The main plants in this area are fir trees, the timber of which is highly valued – some of which are more than a thousand years old (mulberry trees up to 2,200 years old can also be found here). Beside these, deciduous trees like maple, hawthorn, wild apple, pistachio, walnut, birch, poplar and cherry are widespread, as are honeysuckle, barberry, dog-rose, meadow-sweet and bushes of wild grape.

Grasses are also diverse. Herbs such as Muscat sage, rhubarb, tulip and Pskem onion (a precious herb used for medical purposes) grow profusely. The most valuable wood species – *Archa* (central Asian juniper) – can be found in the lower mountains. In the vast, low plains along the river valleys, wooden, bushy, grassy plants, such as sedges and hawthorn, are well developed. On the sub-mountainous plains, the landscape is characterised by grass; there are no trees, but barberry bushes, dog roses, and honeysuckle grow along water courses. The high foothills feature dry steppes with sparse grass on bare earth.

The **desert plants** are particularly interesting as they protect the soil from being blown away by constant desert winds and are well adjusted to poor soil and conditions of drought by having no leaves (or only very tiny ones). Much of the Ustyurt Plateau is covered with saxaul (small, dry shrubs found in southwest and central Asia). The black saxaul is the only plant that can grow in saline areas, and although it grows quickly, it is short-lived; it is a source of food for desert animals including sheep and camel.

birding. Red-headed bunting are everywhere, and special birds up here include white-throated robin and barred, Upcher's and eastern Orphean warblers, with lesser grey and isabelline shrikes common. Fanatical birders will seek out the monotone Hume's short-toed lark, but perhaps more obvious will be European bee-eater, flocks of pink-and-black rose-coloured starling, and dapper pied wheatear. Although Samarkand City is not as green as Tashkent, it still has its birds, notably the large brown-and-white alpine swifts screaming around the old buildings such as the Bibi Khanum mosque. This species, along with the smaller common swift, has become scarcer in recent years as better restoration removes its nesting holes.

In and around the city of **Bukhara** you will find Eurasian collared and laughing doves, while smaller birds include tree sparrow and pied bushchat. A short ride from the town takes you to the wetlands surrounding Lake Tadykol, where reed beds are alive with clamorous reed warbler, bearded tit and citrine wagtail, while careful searching of the bushes may reveal bluethroat. Travelling east from Bukhara across the Kyzylkum Desert, roadside birds include beautiful Wedgwood-blue European roller and vivid blue-cheeked bee-eater, which can be very common in places, while the shy MacQueen's bustard can be very hard to find despite its size. This vast expanse is home to the 'poster bird' of Uzbekistan: the remarkable Pander's ground jay. One of four species of ground jay in the world, it is found only here and in some very remote parts of Kazakhstan, and the road to Khiva is without doubt the best place on the planet to see it. A striking thrush-sized pale-grey bird with distinctive black-and-white wings, it can often be spotted perched on a saxaul bush or telegraph pole, or racing over a sand dune.

FAUNA Uzbekistan's diverse natural habitats host all manner of wildlife, many species of which are indigenous or endemic. The most iconic of these is surely the rare snow leopard.

In desert areas, common **mammals** include wolf, jackal and fox. Here, animals need to be quick to survive, and have therefore evolved with longer legs than their counterparts in Europe and elsewhere. This is particularly true of the deer. In the mountains bordering Kyrgyzstan and Tajikistan you'll see wild goat and boar, mountain sheep, lynx, Bukhara red deer, Alpine ibex, and maybe even the endangered saiga antelope or elusive snow leopard. The western Tian Shan is one of the most ecologically clean regions in the world, and its fauna remains as abundant as it was thousands of years ago with up to 44 species of mammal, including the white-claw bear, in the Pskem Valley.

Reptiles are also abundant in deserts, where species include the roundhead lizard, steppe agama and the 1.6m-long monitor lizard. The threatened central Asian cobra is still found in the Karshi Desert, and the saygak and four-striped runner (an eastern rat snake) can be seen across the Ustyurt Plateau.

Insects found only in Uzbekistan include butterflies (*Hyponephele murzini* and *Melitaea permuta*), grasshopper (*Conophyma turkestanicum*), a long-horned beetle (*Psilotarsus turkestanicus*) and a chalcidoid wasp (*Entedon tobiasi*). Other endemic invertebrates include jumping spiders (*Yllenus tamdybulak* and *Yllenus bucharensis*), tree-trunk spider (*Hersiliola esyunini*) and a 4cm-long scorpion (*Orthochirus feti*).

Almost as diverse are the species of **fish**. There are more than 60 types of river fish in the country, including Amudarya trout, European perch, northern pike, Turkestan sculpin roach and barbel, as well as a species of loach (*Dzihunia ilan*) found only in Uzbekistan. Sadly, owing to the destruction of the Aral Sea, the once-common Aral salmon is now extinct here.

The most interesting of the 368 species of **bird** found here are detailed in the box on page 6, but you'll certainly see many doves, magpies and the common myna in the towns, and maybe even the national bird, the white stork.

According to the *Fifth National Report of the Republic of Uzbekistan on Conservation of Biodiversity*, compiled in 2015, the country is home to various **threatened species** including Strauch's toad, the slender-billed curlew, sociable lapwing, snow leopard and saiga. In 2019, BirdLife listed 19 endangered bird species in Uzbekistan.

CONSERVATION ISSUES

Pollution Large-scale use of chemical fertilisers and pesticides in cotton cultivation, inefficient irrigation and poor drainage has led to highly saline and contaminated **water** being pumped back into the soil. The use of chemicals in agriculture is now up to eight times higher than it was in the Soviet period, and high levels of industrial pollutants (including oil and phenol) are also released into the Amu Darya. A government report, updated in 2016, suggested that half the country's population resided in areas suffering from severe water pollution, and that only a quarter of houses outside Tashkent have proper sewers.

Environmental mismanagement has also caused significant levels of **air pollution**. Salt and dust storms and the spraying of pesticides have led to severe degradation of air quality in rural areas, while in the cities, factories and cars are belching out fumes. Fewer than half of factory smokestacks have adequate filtration devices, and none has the capacity to filter gaseous emissions. In addition, a high percentage of existing filters are defective or out of operation.

MINING IN UZBEKISTAN

Uzbekistan has massive mineral reserves, notably of gold, uranium and copper, and the mining industry could one day dominate the economy, reducing Uzbekistan's need to produce relatively low-value items such as cotton. However, it is rather less developed than one might expect – this is partly due to a 'brain drain' of skilled professionals leaving the country to work in better-paid jobs elsewhere, but it's more to do with the actions of the Karimov government. Within six months of independence it had set up a joint venture with American company Newmont Mining to exploit the Muruntau gold mine in the Kyzylkum Desert (a huge hole measuring 3.35km long, 2.5km wide and 560m deep – the world's fifth-deepest open-pit mine); this functioned well for almost 13 years, contributing more than US$500 million to the state budget, but in 2006 the company was presented with a demand for US$48 million in back taxes. A legal dispute led to the government taking control of the mine in 2007 and Newmont accepting a settlement of just US$80 million. Naturally, foreign investors were reluctant after this to put their money into Uzbekistan, but the new Mirziyoyev government has changed course and the mining industry is set to expand greatly.

The two main mining companies are Navoi Mining and Metallurgical Company (NMMC), which produces gold and uranium, and Almalyk Mining and Metallurgical Company (AMMC; partly owned by the Uzbek-born Russian oligarch Alisher Usmanov), which accounts for 20% of the country's gold production, 90% of its silver production and also has a monopoly on copper mining. NMMC plans to increase Muruntau's output by 30% to 71 tonnes per year, to open three new gold mines in the centre of the country, and to increase uranium production by 40% to 3,300 tonnes per year. AMMC plans to double its gold production from 18 to 34 tonnes per year by 2025 (notably by opening new mines near Angren and elsewhere in the Tashkent region).

There are also about 30,000 private gold-miners in Uzbekistan – these operate illegally but have thus far been left alone by the authorities. Many of the gold deposits are close to the surface, so expensive equipment is not needed to reach them.

Uzbekistan produced 100 tonnes of gold in 2017, making it the world's ninth-largest producer; this commodity was the country's second-largest earner of foreign currency, accounting for almost 9% of GDP. Production is expected to increase to 130 tonnes per year by 2025. As for uranium, NMMC produced an estimated 2,400 tonnes in 2017, making Uzbekistan the world's seventh-largest producer. And there are plans for big new tungsten mines in the Samarkand region, which would produce up to 6% of global output, making Uzbekistan the world's third-largest producer.

Air pollution data for Tashkent, Fergana and Olmaliq, updated in 2016, show all three cities exceeding recommended levels of nitrous dioxide and particulates. Furthermore, in February 2018, air pollution in Tashkent and other industrial cities was reported to be 2.7 times the permitted levels. High levels of heavy metals have also been recorded, particularly around Tashkent. Visitors will notice that it's still more or less compulsory for shops to hand out multiple plastic bags, and there's no recycling.

THE ARAL SEA

The Aral Sea, which means 'Sea of Islands' in reference to the 1,534 islands it once contained, was previously one of the world's four largest lakes, with an area of 68,000km² (26,300 square miles), straddling the border between Kazakhstan and Uzbekistan.

In a period of just 60 years, however, it has declined to just 10% of its former size, with the remaining waters toxic and extremely saline. The retreat of the sea has also caused noticeable localised climate change, and those who once depended on fishing for their livelihood have quite literally been left high and dry. Scientists have called the shrinking of the Aral Sea, now just 41,000km², 'one of the planet's worst environmental disasters'.

The sea's decline began in the 1960s when Soviet bureaucrats decided to divert the waters of the Amu Darya and Syr Darya rivers to irrigate water-intensive crops such as cotton and melons. The irrigation canals were poorly constructed, however, with as much as 75% of the water leaking out or evaporating before it reached the crops. Even today, only 12% of Uzbekistan's irrigation canals are waterproofed.

Deprived of its water supply, the Aral Sea began to shrink. In the 1960s the water level fell at a rate of 20cm a year. This rate tripled in the 1970s, and by the 1980s the water level was dropping by, on average, 90cm annually. The quantity of water being diverted for irrigation continued to increase too, despite its obvious impact on the sea; by 1991 no water at all was reaching the sea from the Amu Darya.

Following independence, Uzbekistan continued the Soviet irrigation policies and the agricultural focus on cotton production, despite its unsustainability (see box, page 24). Monoculture and soil depletion required ever higher quantities of artificial fertiliser, with the run-off further increasing the chemical levels in the sea.

The increase in salinity and pollution had wiped out most of the sea's flora and fauna by the early 2000s, and the rate of evaporation was faster than expected. The decline of the North Aral Sea, now separated from the southern part by a desert known as the Aralkum, was partially reversed by the construction of a dam by the Kazakh government, but the South Aral continues to shrink. In Uzbekistan, the main focus is now on planting trees on over 1 million hectares of the former seabed.

Deforestation The nation's forests are slowly recovering from communist mismanagement: between 1990 and 1995 deforestation occurred at an average annual rate of 2.65%, but reforestation efforts began in the late 1990s, partly in an effort to prevent the dried-out bed of the Aral Sea from simply blowing away. By 2005, Uzbekistan's forest cover had grown by 8.2% (around 250,000ha).

Climate change Climate change is expected to increase temperatures and decrease water availability across Uzbekistan, leading to further desertification and dust storms; in addition, more intense storms will bring an increase in the number of mudslides and avalanches. Central Asia is also predicted to lose a third of its glaciers over the next 30 years; these feed the Amu Darya and Syr Darya rivers which flow through Kyrgyzstan and Tajikistan into Uzbekistan, and huge new dams are expected to reduce the amount of water reaching Uzbekistan.

ENVIRONMENTAL POLICY Uzbekistan's government recognised the country's environmental problems and adopted a 'Biodiversity Action Plan' in 1998. However, the implementation of environmental policy is poor, with numerous competing agencies and no one direction or set of objectives being followed. Inconsistency and corruption are the biggest factors holding back progress.

International donors and grass-roots groups have devised programmes and endeavoured to implement them, but as the environmental problems are largely the result of abuse and mismanagement of resources to fulfil certain economic goals, they are fighting an uphill battle. In what is naturally a desert state, cotton production is not sustainable (as exemplified in the shrinking of the Aral Sea; see box, opposite), and neither is growing watermelons. The government is now promoting a shift from cotton to less water-intensive crops, aiming to check desertification and stop the land from becoming increasingly saline and toxic

Biodiversity conservation and rural development often confront each other in Uzbekistan. Major threats to biodiversity include the destruction of flora and

NATURAL GAS

Chief among Uzbekistan's natural resources, from a strategic and commercial perspective, is natural gas. The country has 1.84 trillion cubic metres of proven reserves, largely in the west of the country, which places it 20th in the world (ahead of Kuwait). Owing to leaks and not opening up new areas for production, Uzbekistan's hydrocarbon production fell for the first 15 years of this century, but is now rising, with 63 billion cubic metres produced in 2018. The sale of natural gas accounts for 15% of GDP and a fifth of the state budget and is set to increase steadily as new gas fields and processing plans come online between now and 2025.

This hydrocarbon legacy is the result of decomposing flora and fauna deposited on the seabed millions of years ago then trapped under a layer of impermeable rock and subjected to immense pressure and heat. During the Soviet era there was some development of the hydrocarbon industries, but it was never fully exploited, in part because beyond the domestic market there was little external demand and that was met by oil from Baku and gas from Siberia. This marketplace picture has changed significantly with the economic and political growth of China to the east and the shift from coal to gas in Europe.

China became the fourth-largest natural-gas user in the world in 2010 and is set to double that demand again by 2020. The Chinese source some 15 billion cubic metres of gas from Uzbekistan each year. This is exported through a US$2.2 billion pipeline financed by the China Development Bank and China National Petroleum Corporation. The Russian hydrocarbon company Taftneft is another major investor in the sector, and the government expects to gain a significant investment of funds and technology when it floats the state oil and gas company Uzbekneftegaz. Restructuring is already underway, and the listing is expected to take place no later than 2024.

Oil and gas reform is part of a wider effort to ensure regional energy security. In winter 2012, Uzbekistan over-exported, leaving domestic users short of gas. Converting known reserves to productive gas fields and improving distribution reduces the likelihood of similar problems occurring in the future.

fauna, unsustainable natural resource use, and expansion of land occupied for agriculture at the expense of wildlife. The government of Uzbekistan has been working on research to improve the situation since 1993, and from 2001 to 2007 a Global Environment Facility project aimed to establish the Nuratau-Kyzylkum Biosphere Reserve (see box, page 216). Owing to political constraints, the reserve has yet to be fully implemented. Nevertheless, in co-operation with the German Society for Nature Protection and various local bodies, progress is being made towards the project's conservation aims, notably in community-based tourism and reforestation.

Surprisingly, Uzbekistan's first solar-generating station is only now being constructed, as the country slowly breaks away from its dependence on natural gas and hydropower; less positively, the government is keen to install a Russian-built nuclear power station on Lake Tuzkan, near Bukhara.

Since 2007, over 16,000 MacQueen's bustard have been bred in captivity and released in the Kyzylkum Desert – bizarrely, this seemingly great success has been

THE SILK ROADS OLD AND NEW

The words 'Silk Road' might bring to mind images of Marco Polo haggling in Asian bazaars, but it actually dates from as early as the 2nd century BC, and was never a road as such, rather a network of routes linking China to both India and Europe. Nor, of course, did it carry only silk, but also other precious goods, religions, philosophies and technologies.

In about 130BC Chinese envoy Zhang Qian travelled west to Fergana, Transoxiana and Bactria, and it was the desire of the Chinese emperors for the strong horses bred by the central Asian nomads (including the famed 'blood-sweating' horses of Fergana) that kickstarted trade on the eastern half of the route. Before long, the exotic Chinese silk textiles were being exchanged for horses, and then sent west into Europe. Until the 4th century AD the Scythian culture stretched from central China to Hungary, so the oasis cities of central Asia were well known, and the Sogdian language became the lingua franca of the traders travelling between them. Chinese armies tried to keep the eastern half of the route safe from nomadic bandits, and the Great Wall of China was extended to protect it.

After the devastation of Bukhara and the other cities of Maverannakhr by Genghis in 1220–21 (see box, page 15 and page 16), the trade routes shifted north into present-day Kazakhstan, then Amir Timur rampaged through the northern steppes in pursuit of the Golden Horde and trade moved back to Samarkand and Bukhara. One of the less-welcome cargoes on the camels (heading west) was the plague bacillus, and it was largely this disease that finally closed down the silk routes, although some trade did continue until about 1720.

The term Seidenstrasse, or Silk Road, was coined by German geographer Ferdinand von Richthofen in the 1860s, and you'll often come across the term 'Ipak Yuli' (or 'Buyuk Ipak Yuli'; Great Silk Road) in Uzbekistan.

A NEW SILK ROAD The programme known as TRACECA (Transport Corridor Europe–Caucasus–Asia) was set up in 1993 by the post-Soviet republics of central Asia and the Caucasus, and was soon joined by Ukraine, Bulgaria, Romania, Moldova and Mongolia. It's a sort of re-creation of the Silk Road, with substantial funding from the European Union, mainly spent on refurbishing railways and ports and introducing new train-ferries across the Caspian and Black seas. For cotton exports achieved by the Emirates Birds Breeding Centre for Conservation, which exists to breed birds for wealthy Arabs to hunt.

HISTORY

ANCIENT HISTORY Though Stone Age man carved his mark on Uzbekistan's caves as far back as 100,000 years ago, the country's better-understood history begins when Bronze Age Iranian nomads began to settle the northern grasslands around the turn of the 1st millennium BC. They lived predominantly along river valleys and made good use of the fertile land for agriculture, even building irrigation channels in the more drought-prone areas.

Their descendants, the **Scythians** (or Sakas in Persian sources), formed a loosely controlled empire stretching from Khorezm in the west to the Fergana Valley in the east. They were skilled raiders with fast, strong horses and formidable iron weapons, and their incursions struck fear into the hearts of neighbouring tribes.

from central Asia, this route is around 2,000km shorter than the one through Russia to the Baltic ports, although it is still a slower option. Similarly, there were multiple projects for pipelines to carry oil and natural gas from the Caspian and beyond, some via Russia and some explicitly avoiding it to prevent a Russian stranglehold on supplies to western Europe.

In parallel with Traceca, from 1996 Georgia, Ukraine, Azerbaijan and Moldova began to form a bloc of nations seeking to escape Russia's overpowering influence; Uzbekistan also joined, and the GUAM charter was adopted in 2001, followed by a free-trade pact (without Uzbekistan) the next year. Also in 2001, China, Kazakhstan, Kyrgyzstan, Russia, Tajikistan and Uzbekistan formed the Shanghai Cooperation Organisation, or Shanghai Pact – a Eurasian political, economic and security alliance.

In 2004, the UN's secretary-general Kofi Annan announced plans for a 'new Silk Road', a highway network that would span 32 countries and 87,000 miles 'from Tokyo to Tehran, and from Singapore to Samarkand', but since then China's need to import raw materials and export its own products has driven moves to recreate the silk routes. In 2014, China's President Xi Jinping committed US$40 billion to developing infrastructure in central Asia, then in December 2017 it was announced that former British prime minister David Cameron would head the Belt and Road Initiative, the largest infrastructure project in history, affecting two-thirds of the world's population; the UK is to invest £750 million, but this is dwarfed by the £150 billion per year that China will pay.

Oddly, 'Road' refers to the shipping routes, while the Silk Road Economic Belt refers to the overland route through central Asia, in which Uzbekistan is considered a key link. In July 2016 the Uzbek and Chinese presidents opened the 19km Kamchik tunnel, linking the Fergana Valley by rail with the rest of Uzbekistan without passing through Tajikistan for the first time; this and other rail projects will create more links from China to Iran and Europe. Sending a container by rail from China to Europe is faster than shipping it via the Suez Canal, but costs about three times more, while air freight is between five to ten times more expensive. But it's not just about through-traffic – bilateral trade between China and Uzbekistan reached US$6.4 billion in 2018 – 35% above the 2017 figure.

Cyrus the Great, the Achaemenid king of Persia, finally put down the Scythians shortly before his death in battle (against their relatives, the Massagetae) near the Aral Sea in 530BC, and his successors divided their territory into what became the Bactrian, Sogdian and Tokharian states. Silk Road trade between Persia and China began to flourish, and the populations of central Asia urbanised and fully participated in it. The Sogdians were particularly successful merchants and their capital Marakanda (today's Samarkand) became rich. The religions of Zoroastrianism and Buddhism, both of which travelled to Uzbekistan along the Silk Road with merchants and missionaries, were in the ascendency.

Alexander the Great seized Samarkand in 329BC and married Roxana, the daughter of a local Bactrian chief. He continued down the Oxus, founding the easternmost of many Alexandrias in the Fergana Valley before continuing on towards the Indian subcontinent. Though Alexander himself did not stay in central Asia, many of his troops also married local women and remained, one general establishing the Seleucid Empire. Graeco-Bactrian kingdoms would exert influence in Uzbekistan and the surrounding countries for centuries to come. Most notably, the Kushan Empire dominated central Asia, present-day Afghanistan and northern India in the early 1st century AD and played a major role in the spread of Buddhism to those areas.

In the early centuries AD, Zoroastrianism remained the dominant religion, but Manichaeism and Christianity were both on the rise. Uzbekistan was a cultural and ethnic melting pot owing to its central position on the Silk Road, and its cities were known for their intellectuals and artisans, as well as for trade.

Uzbekistan was about to enter a politically turbulent period, however. Though the Sogdian state persisted, it was ravaged in turn by the nomadic Khidarites and Khionites, and Turkish raiders from Mongolia. The Sogdians were exhausted and fatally weakened by internal divisions.

ARAB INVASION Arab forces first entered central Asia in AD649, during their conquest of Persia, but it was the crusading general **Qutaiba ibn Muslim** who entered the area of Mwarannahr, a deeply divided land with poor indigenous leadership, and finally seized Uzbekistan for Islam. The new religion spread gradually into the region, replacing the native religious identity with Persian influences. In just seven years he conquered Bukhara, Khorezm, Samarkand and Tashkent, but rather than being lauded as a hero, he was assassinated by his own troops in Fergana in 715. Although the revolts continued for a century, the Sogdians would never again control Uzbekistan, and Arab pre-eminence was guaranteed when they drove out the Chinese forces of the Tang emperor Xuanzong at the Battle of Talas (now in western Kyrgyzstan) in 751. Central Asia was now firmly established as an Islamic region; the Arab invasion totally changed its way of life. Architecture, art and science declined under the pressures of war and arose again only in the middle of the 9th century.

Though Uzbekistan's culture did continue to be influenced by its Persian past, the Arab conquest made its presence felt too. Islam replaced Zoroastrianism and other faiths; Arabic became the primary language for government, literature and commerce. The relationship was not one-way, however, as the Abbasid Caliphate, which would rule the Arab world for five centuries, defeated the ruling Umayyads in part due to central Asian support.

The 8th and 9th centuries were a **golden age** for Uzbekistan. Bukhara grew to become one of the wealthiest and most important centres in the Islamic world, a fitting rival to Baghdad, Cordoba and Cairo. The city's elite patronised some of the greatest artists and intellectuals of the day, the scientist and medic Abu ibn Sina (known as Avicenna in the West) and the Persian poet Rudaki (see box, page 34) among them.

The Samanids and Buyids grew increasingly powerful, and Ismail ibn Ahmad, ruler of Bukhara, united the independent provinces under his Samanid Empire.

The Karakhanids, Turkic nomads from the northern steppes who had adopted Islam, overran Transoxiana in 999 and, joining forces with the Turkic slave soldiers who had served in the Samanid army, formed their own state. At the same time, the Afghan Ghaznavids took control south of the Amu Darya, and slowly expanded their territories into Iran and even India.

The dominance of these groups was short-lived, however, as another Turkic group was on the rise: the Seljuks. From their capital of Merv (now in Turkmenistan) they established an empire stretching from Asia Minor to the western reaches of modern China. The Seljuks in turn fell to the Karakhitai (relatives of the Mongols), and Muhammad II of Khwarezm, a self-proclaimed second Alexander, marched on Samarkand to liberate it from these infidels in 1212, before massively miscalculating and provoking Genghis Khan to invade.

WHO WAS GENGHIS KHAN?

Genghis or, more correctly, Chingiz. It's a name that instilled fear across the medieval world from Mongolia to Moscow and Europe to the Indian subcontinent, and one that echoes to the present day, still associated with rape, pillage and brutality. But just who was this great khan, and how did a nomad from the Mongolian steppe establish an empire covering 24,000,000km² (9,300,000 square miles) in little more than a generation?

Genghis Khan (an honorific title) was born around 1162 in Deluun Boldog, not far from the modern Mongolian capital of Ulaanbaatar. The first son of a Mongol chief, he was named Temüjin, and legend has it that he was born grasping a clot of blood, a sure-fire sign that he would become a powerful leader in later life.

Temüjin's father was murdered by a rival clan while Temüjin was still a child and, too young to take over leadership of his clan, he was cast out by older, more powerful rivals. Along with his mother and younger siblings he lived in poverty, and was for a while enslaved by his father's former allies.

At the age of 16, Temüjin was married to Borte to cement an alliance between their two families. She was almost immediately kidnapped by Merkits, a rival clan, and though she was ultimately rescued, when their first child, Jochi, was born nine months later, his parentage was thus distinctly cloudy. They went on to have three other sons, Chagatai, Ögedei and Tolui, and it's among these four legitimate offspring he would ultimately divide his empire.

Temüjin rose to power through a series of careful alliances: first with Toghrul, the khan of the Kerait. Unlike other Mongol chiefs, however, he delegated authority based on merit and loyalty rather than family ties, and he motivated his followers with a share of the spoils of war. Conquered peoples were integrated into his tribe, inspiring loyalty and reducing the likelihood of future rebellion. Temüjin was a great innovator and inspired confidence in his men.

When the Keraits opposed Temüjin, he took advantage of their internal divisions to defeat them. He then turned his attentions to the Naimans, many of whom followed him voluntarily. Together they defeated the Merkits, leaving Temüjin as the sole ruler of the Mongol plains. In 1206, at a council of Mongol chiefs, he took the new title 'Genghis Khan'. All the armies of the Mongolian steppe were now willingly at his command.

GENGHIS AND THE MONGOLS The Mongol invasion was a turning point for central Asia in numerous ways: it broke Islamic hegemony, replacing it with a Turkic identity; it razed cities to the ground, destroying any pre 13th-century architecture; and it gave the region's population much of the genetic make-up it has today.

Having seized two-thirds of China, the Mongol forces marched west, and by 1218 controlled the southeastern part of what is now Kazakhstan. **Genghis Khan** (see box, page 15) initially looked towards the Khwarezmid Empire as a trading partner, but when his mercantile caravan was slaughtered and a subsequent envoy killed, battle lines were drawn. With perhaps 150,000 troops under his command, he marched across the Tian Shan Mountains in 1219 and seized Otrar (now in Kazakhstan), murdering many of its inhabitants and enslaving the rest. Inalchuq, the governor responsible for the previous envoy's demise, had molten silver poured into his eyes and ears as punishment. Marching into the heart of Uzbekistan, Mongol forces devastated Samarkand and Bukhara, leaving them as virtual ghost towns. Thousands perished – in Samarkand only 50,000 out of around a million people survived. Pyramids of severed heads were raised as a sign of victory. In Termez, the entire population was killed, and perhaps a million people were slaughtered in a similar bloodbath in Urgench.

Genghis Khan died in 1227 and his empire was divided among his four sons. From the ashes of central Asia came the Pax Mongolica, a century or so of relative peace in which merchants and travellers could journey the length of the Mongol Empire without harassment.

THE TIMURIDS As the constituent parts of the Mongol Empire began to separate in the early 14th century, various tribes competed for regional influence. Among them, **Timur** (see box, opposite) was ultimately victorious. Like Genghis Khan before him, Timur would conquer an empire stretching from Asia Minor to Delhi, even venturing up into southern Russia before his death in 1405.

The Timurids did not call themselves Timurids: contemporary chroniclers refer to them as the Gurkanis, meaning 'son-in-law', a reference to the fact that it was Timur's wife, Saray Mulk Khanum, who was the direct descendant of Genghis Khan, not Timur himself. Her title, Khanum, means the daughter of the khan, or princess.

In the earliest period of the Timurid Empire (1360–80), territorial expansion was achieved mainly through forming alliances with neighbouring tribes. Among these alliances, those with Samarkand (1366) and Balk (1369) were most significant. As an *emir* (a military commander or local chieftain) Timur was nominally subordinate to the Chagatai (Mongol) khans, but as he was able to select these khans, they were in reality no more than puppet rulers. The real power was wielded by Timur.

The Timurids' most aggressive period of military expansion began in 1380 when Timur began to seize the deteriorating Ilkhanate states, fragments of the Mongol Empire in what is now Iran, Azerbaijan and eastern Turkey. In quick succession, Timur took control of Herat, Esfahan, Shiraz and Baghdad – once the Ilkhanate heartland – and he then turned his attentions to defeating the Golden Horde in the Caucasus. By the end of the 14th century, these lands were firmly under Timurid control, and the Timurids had also made substantial territorial gains in Afghanistan, Pakistan, and in India as far east as Delhi. Timur put his own governor, Khizr Khan, on the Delhi throne, and the Delhi Sultanate became a vassal state. Before his death in 1405, Timur had made further gains in Syria, Iraq and Turkey, and was the most powerful ruler in the Islamic world.

Let he who doubts Our power and munificence look upon Our buildings.

Amir Timur, 1379

Amir Timur, Uzbekistan's national hero and one of the most accomplished warriors, rulers and patrons the world has ever seen, was born the son of a minor chief in Shakhrisabz in 1336. As with Genghis Khan, it is said he came into the world grasping a clot of blood, an omen of what was to come.

The young Timur (who you may be more familiar with as Christopher Marlowe's Tamerlane) excelled in horsemanship, sword fighting and archery, as well as raiding caravans and rustling horses. He became chief of the Barlas clan in 1360 and steadily increased his influence from the Amu Darya to the Syr Darya. In the process he incurred various injuries including one to his leg, which earned him his nickname: Timur-i Leng (Timur the lame).

In 1370 Timur conquered the last surviving Mongol khanate and made Samarkand his capital. For the next 35 years he ruthlessly expanded his territories across central Asia, Iran, Turkey and northern India. He even attempted to conquer China, but succumbed to a fever in 1405 and died with this ambition unrealised.

Historians estimate that Timur's conquests may have been responsible for the deaths of as many as 17 million people. And yet, ever the raider, he made little attempt to consolidate his conquests, smashing, grabbing and then moving on. Consequentially, the Timurid dynasty was short-lived.

Timur's personality was a dichotomy. On one side he was brutal and ruthless on the battlefield; on the other he was highly cultured: he had a thirst for knowledge and enjoyed debating history, medicine and astronomy. He was also a passionate supporter of the arts, and plundered cities such as Damascus, Baghdad, Isfahan and Delhi not only for their financial assets but also for their skilled artisans, whom he brought back to build and beautify Samarkand.

Timur made Samarkand his capital, and he rebuilt and expanded it with the finest artisans and materials his empire could offer. He patronised scientists and other scholars, and Samarkand became a centre for intellectuals and religion. Its architecture was the envy of the Islamic world.

The Timurid Empire did not survive long after Timur's death: his sons and grandsons had been appointed to governorships in different parts of the empire, but they lacked the diplomatic and military skills of Timur. The family members were also prone to infighting, so civil wars were rife and many of the territories again became independent states. Timur's grandson, Ulug Beg, clung on to Samarkand but prioritised scholarship and, in particular, his personal pursuit of astronomy (see box, page 173), over matters of state. Uzbek tribes, led by Muhammad Shaybani (see below), were therefore able to seize much of central Asia, and Uzbekistan entered into a new era: that of the khanates.

THE KHANATES AND EMIRATES The khanates were regional kingdoms controlled by a khan, self-proclaimed successors to Genghis Khan, and the most powerful of these was the Khanate of Bukhara, ruled by the **Shaybanid dynasty**. A second khanate was established at Khiva, and a third in the Fergana Valley at Kokand.

The Shaybanids were Turko-Mongols and claimed patrilineal descent from Genghis Khan through his grandson Shiban. The Shaybanid horde were the Timurids' main rivals – they believed their claim to be heirs of Genghis was far stronger than that of Timur – but it was not until the mid 15th century that they were able to start consolidating their power, first in Siberia and then in central Asia. Muhammad Shaybani (r1500–10) was able to take advantage of the disintegration of the Timurid Empire to seize Balkh, Bukhara, Herat and Samarkand, and his descendants went on to found and rule not only the Khanate of Bukhara, but also the Khanate of Khiva.

Under Shaybanid rule, Bukhara was a major centre of the arts and Islamic learning. Many of the finest surviving buildings date from this period of wealth and patronage. The city was packed with poets and calligraphers, dervishes and physicians, theologians and mathematicians. The library of Abd al-Aziz Khan was said to have no equal anywhere in the world. Public education was introduced for boys from the age of six, and the curriculum in the madrasas was expanded to include logic, jurisprudence, mathematics, music and poetry, as well as traditional classes in theology and Qu'ranic Arabic.

The Shaybanids retained control of Bukhara for a century, after which power passed to the Janids, descendants of the son-in-law of the last Shaybanid ruler, Pir Muhammed Khan.

The **Janids**, like the later Timurids, were plagued by infighting. There was no clear line of succession – any brother could inherit, regardless of age – and so fratricide and scheming were rife at court. Vali Muhammad Khan (r1605–11), for example, came to power after the death of his brother. Hearing of a coming assassination attempt, he fled to the Safavid court of Shah Abbas I to garner support, and returned home with an army, but it was not enough: Vali Muhammad Khan was killed during the insurgency.

The 17th and 18th centuries were a difficult period for Uzbekistan: Silk Road trade was in decline (see box, page 12), and the strength of the Shi'ite Safavids in Iran had isolated central Asia from other Sunni territories in the Middle East. Bandits and slave traders plagued those caravans that did brave the steppe; the Persian Nadir Shah marched through almost unopposed in 1740, medieval weaponry no match for his modern artillery; and Russian generals were starting to take a serious interest in the lands beyond their southern border.

Central Asia's khanates had become emirates: this was not out of respect for Amir Timur, however, but rather to show that their allegiances and culture lay with the Islamic world – the dominant power block at the time – rather than with their Mongol past. The **Emirate of Bukhara** (1785–20) remained the most powerful of the three and was ruled by a succession of colourful emirs. Though some of them were undoubtedly competent, others lived up to the European stereotype of the eastern despots, and tales of their excesses and cruelty spread to Russia and beyond.

When **Peter the Great** sent an expedition to Khiva in 1717, it was the first time tsarist forces had officially set foot on Uzbek soil. They were slaughtered to a man, but would be back, first invited in as allies and protectors against rival khanates, and later as invading forces. Russian forces entered Tashkent (1865), Bukhara (1867), Samarkand (1868), Khiva (1873) and finally Kokand (1875); they all became Russian protectorates.

The expansion of Russia into central Asia caused great concern for the British, who saw it as a stepping stone en route to British India, the jewel in the imperial crown. **The Great Game** (see box, opposite) ensued, each side vying for influence and territory.

THE GREAT GAME

When two mighty empires meet, there will always be blood and intrigue. As the Russian Empire spread south into the Kazakh steppe and the frontier of British India pushed across the subcontinent and up into Afghanistan, the no-man's-land in between became the jousting ground in a 19th-century 'Tournament of Shadows'. The British were keen to gain new markets here for their exported goods, and the Russians exploited the fierce rivalries of the khans of Bukhara, Khiva and Kokand, playing them off against one another to ensure protective alliances with Moscow were actively sought.

Agents, explorers and spies from both sides infiltrated courts across central Asia, Afghanistan and (what is now) Pakistan to seek information and gain influence; they sought out unmapped wildernesses, surveying and recording everything they saw. Rudyard Kipling's protagonist, Kim, and his real-life equivalents, men like George Curzon (later the Viceroy of India), Francis Younghusband, Bronislav Grombchevsky and Indian 'pundits' such as Mirza Shuja played hide-and-seek across mountains and deserts, adopting a veritable prop cupboard full of disguises in the hope that gaining a better understanding of the lie of the land (literal and metaphorical) would give their side a strategic advantage. Neither open warfare nor simply innocent exploration of the unknown, their activities were described by Arthur Conolly (see box, page 240) as 'the Great Game'. It encompassed espionage in all its intricate, innovative forms.

The central tenet of the Great Game was suspicion: lack of knowledge about what lay in this central Asian hinterland led to doubts about where the imperial frontier might lie; both sides jealously coveted the other's colonial possessions. Britain and Russia were frequently at loggerheads in Europe too, and by frightening each other into wrongly thinking that a full-scale military incursion was being planned, it tied up resources and wealth, preventing them from being deployed elsewhere.

That is not to say that actual war did not feature in the Great Game. Britain's primary strategic interest was to establish a frontier that could be securely defended against Russia. Britain invaded Afghanistan in the First and Second Afghan Wars (1838–42 and 1878–80), fearing that if they did not take control of the country first then it would almost certainly fall to the Russians. When Dost Muhammad, Emir of Afghanistan, was defeated by the British in 1839, he fled across Afghanistan's northern border to Uzbekistan and sought refuge in Bukhara at the court of Nasrullah Khan.

Though many players of the Great Game were murdered in central Asia (see box, page 240), either by each other or by the locals, or simply disappeared, those who did survive often returned to London and Moscow as national heroes. The British spoke to packed lecture halls at the Royal Geographic Society (w rgs.org) and the Royal Society for Asian Affairs (founded in 1901 as the Central Asian Society; w rsaa.org.uk), both of which exist to the present day, and accounts of daring exploits enraptured newspaper readers. Paranoia about what Imperial Russia could be up to made newspapers sell like hot cakes, much as fear of the Soviet Union did 50 or so years later, and fear of Putin's Russia does now. Indeed, the Great Game could be interpreted as a forerunner to the Cold War as there's clear continuity in the two powers' fight for influence in satellite states.

Modernity came to Uzbekistan with the arrival of the Trans-Caspian railway in the 1890s. Large numbers of Russian immigrants began to arrive, and they started to industrialise the country and introduce more intensive forms of agriculture, including irrigated cotton production. Rather than look to the Islamic or Mongol worlds for trade and influence, Uzbekistan was now looking northward to Russia.

THE SOVIET UNION The Bolshevik Revolution took place in 1917, and communism emerged as the dominant ideology from the melting pot of socialism, pan-Islamism and pan-Turkism, all of which were poised to guide the next generation of central Asia's rulers. It was not a smooth transition, however, as White Russians, the Basmachi (see box, opposite), British agents and a host of other resistance fighters opposed the Red Army.

An independent Jadist state, led by reformist Muslims, was briefly established in Kokand (page 150), but the matter was really settled in 1920 when **General Mikhail Frunze** stormed through and established the Soviet Republic of Turkestan. The People's Republic of Khorezm was set up in parallel in Khiva. These gave way to the Uzbek SSR in 1924, and with them went any real hope of political or economic autonomy in the region. Controversially, Stalin created his new states on the basis of perceived ethnicity (thus reducing the likelihood of an opposition united on the basis of shared Islamic identity), but included the Tajik-majority cities of Bukhara and Samarkand in the Uzbek state. The Uzbek-majority Khujand was given to the Tajik SSR, and a large number of Uzbeks were cut off inside the new Kyrgyz SSR, deliberately or otherwise creating long-term instability in the region.

The 1930s brought Stalinist purges to Uzbekistan. Religion, tolerated for the first few years of Soviet rule, was seen as a threat that must be eradicated. Imams were killed, going on hajj was banned, and those determined to keep their faith had to do so in the strictest secrecy. *Madrasas* (Islamic schools) and mosques were closed wholesale, many of them converted into warehouses or social clubs.

It was not all doom and gloom, however. Uzbekistan's economy modernised and grew rapidly as part of the USSR. For the first time the entire population had access to a secular education, and men and women studied and worked together. Uzbekistan's cities became increasingly cosmopolitan, with immigrants from across the Soviet Union coming to live and work. Though many of these were originally exiled to central Asia, they became well integrated, bound together by a shared Soviet identity and by the Russian language.

Under **Nikita Khrushchev** (in office 1953–64), some Russified Uzbek nationalists, formerly purged as subversive elements, were allowed to rejoin the Communist Party and rose to government positions. The most notable of these was **Sharaf Rashidov** (see box, page 181), First Secretary of the Communist Party of Uzbekistan from 1959 to 1983. Rashidov was closely aligned with Leonid Brezhnev (leader of the Soviet Union 1964–82), which gave him a certain amount of autonomy, often paying little more than lip service to Soviet policies. After Rashidov's death, however, Uzbekistan's political elite were brought sharply back into line with purges, corruption trials and the posthumous vilification of Rashidov. The backlash was a strengthening of Uzbek nationalism.

Violence flared in the Fergana Valley, on both sides of the Uzbek–Kyrgyz border, from 1989 to 1991. **Islam Karimov** (see box, page 23), a political outsider, was appointed by Moscow to the position of first secretary in a hope that it would calm the troubles.

THE BASMACHI

The roots of the Basmachi lay in the forced conscription of central Asian Muslims by the Russian Army in 1916 (not to fight, but to dig trenches and latrines). A widespread revolt was brutally suppressed: whole villages were massacred and their property burned to prevent any survivors' return. Many more families died fleeing across the mountains to China. (In World War II, 1.5 million central Asian Muslims were conscripted into the Red Army, and over half of them deserted to the Germans.)

The Basmachi developed largely as a Muslim resistance force, engaging in jihad against the 'godless' Bolsheviks. Their numbers comprised both peasants and intellectuals, and they were supported by White Russians and even British agents keen to stem Bolshevik influence in central Asia.

The Basmachi fought from 1921 under the leadership of the Turkish World War I general Enver Pasha (see box, page 196); the movement was funded by Muhammad Alim Khan, the deposed Emir of Bukhara (now styling himself Emir of Turkestan), in the hope that if they were successful then they would invite him to return.

The resistance was most successful in the Fergana Valley, where raids inflicted significant casualties among Red Army troops, but by the early 1920s the battle was already lost and many of the movement's leaders had fled to relative safety in Afghanistan.

UZBEKISTAN SINCE INDEPENDENCE The leaders of the Uzbek SSR were initially hesitant to embrace the changes leading to the break-up of the Soviet Union: the country's economy and its status on the world stage depended on being part of the USSR. Sensing which way the winds were blowing, however, they began making changes: the Communist Party of Uzbekistan (CPU) cut its ties with the central Communist Party in Moscow and changed its name to the **People's Democratic Party of Uzbekistan** (PDPU) in anticipation of forthcoming elections.

On 21 December 1991, Karimov agreed with the leaders of the other SSRs to dissolve the Soviet Union, and he declared Uzbekistan to be an independent republic and a founding member of the Commonwealth of Independent States (CIS). Karimov was elected as Uzbekistan's first president, with 86% of the vote, and the PDPU dominated the new parliament, in part because the main opposition party, Birlik, was refused electoral registration until it was too late.

Politically, there was a great deal of continuity between the 1980s and 1990s, not only in terms of key personnel. Early elections could be contested by only two parties, the PDPU and the pro-government Progress of the Fatherland Party; opposition figures were frequently arrested on fabricated charges, as were those who criticised the government in the press and there was severe repression of anyone suspected of Islamic extremism. Some 6,000 supposed members of Hizb ut-Tahrir (page 30) were incarcerated, and many were tortured and abused.

There was, quite rightly, international criticism of the government's human-rights abuses, but the invasion of Afghanistan in 2001 meant that Western governments needed allies in central Asia. Military goals took priority, as the US wanted to open an airbase on Uzbek soil. Known as the **Karshi-Khanabad Airbase**, or K2, this opened in 2001 and remained operational until 2005 when it was moved to neighbouring Kyrgyzstan. This was because, after the Andijan Massacre (see box, page 138), it became more difficult for foreign governments to turn a blind eye to Uzbekistan's flouting of international human-rights law, and they were more vocal in their criticism. In response, the Uzbek government asked the Americans to vacate the base, giving them just six months to do so. However, when NATO was withdrawing from Afghanistan in 2012, it was allowed to use Uzbek territory.

Today, relations between Uzbekistan and the West are generally good. The global economic downturn meant that many of the business deals which would have been done with European and American companies have instead been picked up by Chinese, state-backed firms, but there is a sizeable expat population in Tashkent, and foreign embassies are gently backing, and supporting, reform. Support is being given in particular to the training and modernisation of the Uzbek armed forces so that they can better control their borders and participate in regional peacekeeping missions.

GOVERNMENT AND POLITICS

The 1992 constitution of Uzbekistan describes a presidential republic in which the president is both head of state and head of government. Executive power is exercised by the government, and legislative power is divided between the government and a bicameral parliament. The president should be elected by popular vote for no more than two five-year terms. The president also appoints the prime minister, deputy prime ministers and regional governors, and together this executive holds almost all power in the country, the judiciary only being nominally independent.

The legislative branch of government is **the Supreme Assembly** or National Assembly (Oliy Majlis). There are 150 elected members in the Legislative Chamber (the lower house) and 100 members in the Senate, 16 of whom are appointed by the president (the rest are elected). The parliament can be dissolved by the president providing they have the support of the Constitutional Court, members of which are also selected by the president.

Politics in Uzbekistan is very much a one-horse race. **President Karimov** officially received more than 90% of the vote in each of the 2007 and 2015 presidential elections, and his party, now called the Uzbekistan Liberal Democratic Party, also had the largest number of seats in parliament on both occasions. After his death in September 2016, **Shavkat Mirziyoyev**, who had been prime minister since 2003, was appointed interim president by parliament and was confirmed in office in December 2016 by another sham election, winning 88.6% of the vote against token opponents.

Opposition parties in Uzbekistan are typically opposition in name only and have policies closely allied to those of the government; genuine opposition figures have been incarcerated, assaulted and generally harassed, even when outside the country, and external observers generally consider Uzbekistan's elections to be no more than political charades. Only four parties are currently allowed to contest parliamentary elections.

In June 2017, Mirziyoyev dismissed his first deputy prime minister, Rustam Asimov, who was followed in January 2018 by the long-serving security chief Rustam Inoyatov, who had not only crushed all dissent under Karimov but also effectively held a veto on government policies. It was assumed that Mirziyoyev would continue in Karimov's dictatorial footsteps, but having established himself in power, he has in fact moved fast to liberalise and open up both Uzbek society and the country's economy (without as yet allowing a real opposition to form, or promising free and fair elections). Although corruption remains endemic, there

Uzbekistan's first president, Islam Karimov, was born in Samarkand on 30 January 1938 (making him the elder statesman of the post-Soviet central Asian leaders). He survived the spartan privations of a Soviet orphanage and went on to study engineering and then economics. After spells in agricultural machinery and aircraft factories, he moved into the government apparatus, starting in the state planning office, where he learned how to handle the levers of power. He became Minister of Finance in 1983, then three years later Chairman of the State Planning Office and Deputy Chairman of the Council of Ministers. His trajectory to power was set and in 1989 he was promoted to First Secretary of the Uzbek SSR.

After initial hesitancy, Karimov embraced the break-up of the USSR and consequently benefitted considerably from it. In March 1990 he was named President of the Uzbek SSR by the republic's Soviet, and was then elected President of the Republic of Uzbekistan in December 1991, four months after independence. This garnered considerable international criticism, but though he was frequently vilified in the international press, many other heads of state found it necessary to compromise with him in order to achieve their own geopolitical aims.

Despite a constitutional restriction on presidents running for more than two terms, Karimov became president for life: he won a third term with a landslide victory in 2015 (claiming that his first term didn't count, as it was under the previous, Soviet, constitution), though the election was widely criticised by Western media and elections monitors. It seems that Tony Blair gave him (and, more famously, the Kazakh president Nazarbayev) advice on succession planning, as the power vacuum likely to follow his demise could easily destabilise the whole region. In fact, there was a smooth transition after his death in 2016, and his legacy has been honoured, with various grand statues and a mausoleum in his home city of Samarkand. Although he undoubtedly presided over a draconian police state, he modernised the country's infrastructure and rehomed many people in new houses and apartment blocks, and remains generally popular.

Karimov was married twice and had three children, his son Rustam and two daughters, Gulnara (see box, page 32) and Lola.

have been high-profile arrests, and groups such as Human Rights Watch have been allowed to operate again in Uzbekistan.

The prime driver of the reforms is job creation, given that over half the population is younger than 30 and the labour force is growing by 500,000 per year. This has also led to better relations with neighbouring states (often fraught during Karimov's period in power) – new border crossings have opened, new rail and electric power links been constructed, and the borders, never properly defined in Soviet times, are being demarcated. In fact, land mines are being removed from some border zones.

ECONOMY

Under President Karimov, statistics were a government tool, so GDP growth has declined from an optimistic 7.8% in 2016 to a more realistic 5.1% in 2018, with 6.0% projected for 2020 and 7% for 2021. Industrial production, construction and services are all growing, but there's been a decline in exports and in private consumption owing to reduced subsidies and inflation of 15.7% in 2018 (forecast to fall to 12.5% in 2020 and 10% in 2021). **GDP per capita** (PPP) was estimated at US$7,000 in 2017. Uzbekistan's consolidated budget deficit was estimated at less than 1% of GDP in 2017; public debt is also low, at about 25% of GDP.

In October 2018, the **unemployment rate** was 9.3%, but 15.9% for those under 30 and 13.4% for women; however, no fewer than 7.9 million people are estimated to be active in the informal economy, including temporary and seasonal workers and migrant labourers.

COTTON

Cotton fibre is almost pure cellulose and it grows in a boll, a protective capsule around the plant's seeds. It is native to tropical and subtropical zones, and is found growing wild in Mexico, Australia and parts of Africa. Mexican cotton (*Gossypium hirsutum*) accounts for at least 90% of commercial production worldwide.

Successful cotton cultivation requires moderate temperatures and rainfall, and plenty of sunshine. The crop is reasonably drought- and salt-tolerant, but in arid and semi-arid conditions irrigation is required to provide the requisite level of water, and much more water is needed to wash away the chemicals sprayed on it. Genetically modified cotton has been developed to reduce reliance on pesticides, but it is still not resistant to plant bugs, stink bugs and aphids.

World cotton production is around 25 million tonnes a year, and 2.5% of all arable land is given over to cotton. It is predominantly used for clothing production, but also in book binding, fishing nets and explosives (in the form of nitrocellulose). Cottonseed oil can be refined and used in cooking as if it were vegetable oil, and cottonseed meal can be fed to ruminant livestock.

Cotton was a Soviet obsession from the start of Stalin's first five-year plan in 1928, and canals were dug to irrigate vast areas of central Asia. In Uzbekistan, a notoriously corrupt republic under Brezhnev, whose power base was here and in Kazakhstan, in particular, the cotton crop was over-reported by about a million tonnes a year, with the central government's payments based on the reports, not the actual shipments. Under Gorbachev, from 1986, there was a big clean up, and by 1989, 3,600 people had been jailed for corruption, although some were simply relatives of those involved.

More recently, Uzbekistan's cotton industry has again found notoriety, this time owing to the involvement of forced labour, and particularly children, in the harvest. At one time over 2 million people were drafted into the fields, but due to international pressure substantial reforms have been introduced. In its 2019 report, the UN's International Labour Organization (ILO) stated that child labour is no longer a major concern, and 93% of those engaged in the cotton harvest were not forced to work. The workers now are mostly state employees (such as teachers, soldiers and the police) whose contracts specify that they can be moved to other work as required. Furthermore, the government is committed to eliminating forced labour by increasing mechanisation and by cutting production by 20%, especially as the world cotton price is falling – it makes more sense to grow fruit and vegetables for export to Russia and China. Human-rights activists have welcomed the progress, and the ILO has recommended the international community now support Uzbekistan's cotton sector.

In September 2017, the Uzbek som was allowed to float on the world currency markets, effectively devaluing it by 90%, but also removing the biggest obstacle to foreign trade and investment. Other continuing **reforms** include changes in the customs and foreign trade regime, fiscal and tax reform, a reduction in state-directed lending and the restructuring and privatisation of state-owned enterprises. In January 2019, a new simplified tax code introduced a flat-rate income tax (12%) as well as reductions in corporation tax and in the spring of 2019, Uzbekistan listed its first Eurobonds on the London Stock Exchange.

In addition to mining (see box, page 9), oil and gas account for 16% of GDP, and the agricultural sector employs around 26% of Uzbekistan's population and contributes 18% of GDP and 13.6% of export earnings. The most important crop is **cotton**, the so-called 'white gold', of which Uzbekistan is the world's seventh-largest producer and fifth-largest exporter. Cotton is a thirsty crop and requires significant levels of chemical fertiliser, resulting in much more water being needed to wash it. These factors have had a detrimental impact on Uzbekistan's environment. Controversially, Uzbekistan has a history of using forced labour during the cotton harvest, which has resulted in many international brands boycotting Uzbek cotton (see box, opposite).

Other major agricultural products are raw silk, fruits (notably grapes and melons) and vegetables, which are consumed domestically and exported to neighbouring countries. Some 11% of Uzbekistan is artificially irrigated, and the most fertile agricultural land is in the Fergana Valley and in the south of the country around Surkhan Darya and Qashqa Darya.

Uzbekistan also has a strong industrial base, which includes chemical industries and oil and gas refineries. Coca-Cola has bottling plants in Namangan, Samarkand and Tashkent; Texaco produces lubricants in Uzbekistan for the central Asian market; and GM-Uzbekistan, a joint venture between the government and General Motors (originally established with South Korea's Daewoo in 1996), produces Chevrolet cars at Asaka in the Fergana Valley and minibuses in Urgench. These are sold primarily in Uzbekistan, and to a lesser extent in the surrounding countries. Tourism contributed just 2.8% to GDP in 2017, with about 1.9 million arrivals per year, but is expected to rise to 6% by 2028; in 2018 the number of tourist arrivals was already double the 2017 total (although most of the growth is from neighbouring countries such as Kazakhstan).

Uzbekistan is a member of the International Monetary Fund, the World Bank, the Asian Development Bank and the European Bank for Reconstruction and Development. It has observer status at the World Trade Organization, but applied for full membership in 2017. In 2008, Russia was the dominant foreign power in the region (as it had been since the late 19th century), followed by the US. Since then, however, there has been a dramatic shift, reflecting China's growing power in the region and worldwide (see box, page 13). Nevertheless, at least 3 million Uzbeks are working (many illegally) in Russia (and in other countries such as South Korea), and their remittances are an important boost to the Uzbek economy.

PEOPLE

With a population of 32.59 million, Uzbekistan is by far the most populous country in central Asia. Although growth is now slowing owing to migration and much smaller family sizes, over half the population is under 30. The average number of children per woman is now 2.46 (2016), as opposed to 3.7 in 1996 and 2.92 in 2002.

Uzbekistan is ethnically diverse, though ethnic **Uzbeks** may make up as much as 80% of the population. The Uzbeks are a Turkic people who originated in southern Siberia and the Altai Mountains and came south with the Mongols in the early medieval period. There are also significant Uzbek populations in Afghanistan (2.7 million), Tajikistan (1.6 million) and Kyrgyzstan (800,000). The majority of Uzbeks follow the Hanafi school of Sunni Islam, though atheism is also widespread among those who grew up under the Soviet Union.

Uzbekistan has a large **Tajik** population. Although census data suggest they make up only around 5% of the population, some observers believe the real figure to be far larger as there is a tendency for some Tajiks to declare themselves as Uzbek on official paperwork in order to assimilate with the majority population. Tajiks are essentially central Asian Persians who consider themselves to be the oldest ethnic group in central Asia, tracing their ancestry right back to the Bactrians and Sogdians (page 14). The Tajiks are not a homogeneous group, however, and are deeply divided along clan-based lines with strong regional affiliations and blood ties. The cities of Bukhara and Samarkand both have large Tajik populations, and many feel, in Stalin's project to divide and rule one of the world's most complex ethnic mixtures in 1924, they should have been allocated to Tajikistan rather than Uzbekistan.

Around 2.5% of the population is **ethnic Russian**. This figure was significantly higher during the Soviet period, peaking at just under 15% in the late 1950s, but many Russians chose to leave Uzbekistan for Russia following independence, regardless of whether or not they had been born in the country. Significant numbers of Russians came to Uzbekistan from the 19th century onwards to take advantage of the economic opportunities the country offered. Others were intellectuals, petty bourgeoisie and political opponents forcibly exiled here during the purges. The Russian community tends to follow the Eastern Orthodox faith and large numbers of them still reside in Tashkent.

The Soviet policy of deporting subversive and other undesirable elements to central Asia (the alternative place of exile to Siberia), mixed with a few self-orchestrated migrations, has left Uzbekistan with notable populations of **Kazakhs**, **Tatars**, **Volga Germans**, **Poles**, **Ukrainians** and even **Koreans**. **Afghans** have also fled across the border to escape the violence and to seek work. Though these groups have frequently intermarried, and many have now re-emigrated, it is still possible to hear snatches of their languages and, more importantly for those fed up with the ubiquitous *shashlik* (page 73), to feast on their various cuisines.

Finally, there are perhaps 12,000 Tajik-speaking **Roma**, known as Lyuli or Mughat, who claim to have arrived from India with Amir Timur, perhaps as musicians and dancers.

LANGUAGE

The main languages spoken in Uzbekistan are Uzbek (74.3%), Russian (14.2%) and Tajik (officially 4.4% but potentially far higher), with other languages spoken including Kyrgyz, Kazakh, English and German. Karakalpak has official status in the Karakalpakstan Autonomous Republic. Almost all road signs and other public notices are written in Uzbek, in the Latin script.

UZBEK Worldwide, Uzbek has more than 35 million speakers, and it has been the official language of Uzbekistan since independence. Nationalists in the late 1980s campaigned strongly for Uzbek to replace Russian as the language of state in the hope it would reverse the process of Russification and in its place promote Uzbek culture.

UZBEK IN LATIN SCRIPT

Barcha odamlar erkin, qadr-qimmat va huquqlarda teng bo'lib tug'iladilar. Ular aql va vijdon sohibidirlar va bir-birlari ila birodarlarcha muomala qilishlari zarur.

UZBEK IN CYRILLIC SCRIPT

Барча одамлар эркин, қадр-қиммат ва хуқуқларда тенг бўлиб туғиладилар. Улар ақл ва виждон соҳибидирлар ва бир-бирлари ила биродарларча муомала қилишлари зарур.

UZBEK IN PERSO-ARABIC SCRIPT

و ت‌می‌ق-ردق ،نی‌کری‌ا آدملربرچ ه
حقوق‌لردده گنت گن بو‌یلی‌ب تو‌غی‌هله
دی‌د رل‌ول و لقع و وج‌دان
صاحب‌دی‌دری رل‌و ب ری‌ب-ری‌یرل‌ری ایله
ی‌رل‌شی‌ی‌لی‌ق هلم‌عامم هچ‌رل‌رداراب
رورض.

ENGLISH TRANSLATION

All human beings are born free and equal in dignity and rights. They are endowed with reason and conscience and should act towards one another in a spirit of brotherhood.

The text used here is Article 1 of the Universal Declaration of Human Rights

The Law of the Republic of Uzbekistan on State Language was passed in 1989 and amended in 1995, requiring Uzbek to be used in all public spheres and official jobs. Some have seen this as discriminating against non-Uzbek speakers in the country.

Uzbek belongs to the Karluk family of Turkic languages, from which it gets its lexicon and grammar, and it also contains many loan words from Persian, Arabic and Russian, all of which have influenced its development. It is considered to be the direct descendant of Chagatai Turkish, the language of the Timurid court, and it is from this era of linguistic development that the influence of Persian is seen most clearly.

Over its history, Uzbek has been written in all manner of **scripts**. As late as 1928, all literate Uzbeks wrote using the Perso-Arabic script, but there was then a brief period of 12 years during which the Turkic languages were typically written using the Latin alphabet. In 1940 it was all change again as Stalin decided Cyrillic was the way forward. This Russian script continued to be the primary alphabet used until 1992, when the Latin script was reintroduced. Today you may see Uzbek written in both Latin and Cyrillic scripts, often on the same billboard or page. For a comparison between Uzbek, Cyrillic and Perso-Arabic scripts, see the box above.

Grammatically, Uzbek shares many features with other Turkic languages. Words are ordered subject–object–verb, there is no grammatical gender and no definite or indefinite article. Relative clauses are replaced by various participles, gerunds and verbal nouns and the language is agglutinative (combining word elements to express compound ideas). Most word roots are monosyllabic, and suffixes are added in a fixed order.

For pronunciation and helpful phrases, see page 282.

RUSSIAN Russian remains the language of inter-ethnic communication, science, business and advertising. It is the lingua franca of central Asia (and one of the six official languages of the UN). It is the most widely spoken of the Slavic languages and has an estimated 155 million native speakers worldwide. A further 110 million people speak Russian as a second or additional language. In Uzbekistan, most people speak and understand some Russian, even if they cannot write it. It was the main language of education during the Soviet period, and so those who were schooled prior to 1991 are likely to speak the language more fluently than younger people.

TAJIK Tajik is an Indo-European language closely linked to Farsi and Dari (two varieties of Persian), hence these three languages have a shared literary heritage. Unlike most central Asian languages, it is not related to Turkish. From the 9th century, Tajik was written in a modified version of the Perso-Arabic script (it had previously been written in Sogdian), and the Arab invasions of this time account for its Arabic loan words. It was only with Stalin's division of central Asia in the 1920s that Tajik began to be seen as a linguistic entity distinct from Persian.

PROVERBS

Zabon Doni Jahon Doni (Know Language, Know The World)

Tajik proverb

Proverbs give you an important insight into a country and how its people think. What is more, learning just a few and being able to use them in conversation shows your host that you are taking an active interest in their culture, their country and their language. Here are a few of our favourites from the different communities in Uzbekistan.

UZBEK
Don't choose a house, choose neighbours.
A word said is a shot fired.
Verboseness is a load even for a donkey.
When everything you have at home is on the table, your guest will never say he has not seen anything.

RUSSIAN
It is easier for the mare when a woman gets off the cart.
The thief who stole an *altyn* (3 kopecks) is hung, and the one who stole a *poltinnik* (50 kopecks) is praised.
Your elbow is close, yet you can't bite it.
A beard doesn't make a philosopher.

TAJIK
One who is always laughing is a fool, but the one who does not laugh is unhappy.
The walls have mice, and the mice have ears.
If you sit with the moon you become the moon. If you sit in a *deg* (cooking pot) you become black.

For the first decade of being promoted as a distinct language (starting in 1929 when it was designated the official language of the Tajik SSR) it was written in a modified Latin script, but in 1939 this was replaced by Cyrillic. You will find Tajik mostly spoken in Samarkand and Bukhara, both of which are ethnically and culturally Tajik cities, even though they are within the borders of modern Uzbekistan. The majority of Uzbekistan's medieval literature, and poems in particular, is in Tajik rather than in Uzbek.

KARAKALPAK This is a Turkic language from the Kypchak family to which Kazakh and Tatar also belong. There are just over 400,000 native speakers in Uzbekistan (almost all in Karakalpakstan; page 273), and an estimated 2,000 speakers in Afghanistan. It is an agglutinative language with vowel harmony but no grammatical gender. The word order, as with Uzbek, is subject–object–verb. Although it can be written in either Latin or Cyrillic script, the latter is most common.

RELIGION

Communism was supposed to supplant religion during the Soviet period, but attempts to secularise Uzbek society were less successful than in other parts of the USSR. Many people retained their faith in private even if they publicly claimed to be atheist, and the post-independence years have seen a rise in religious practice, including mosque building, which has caused some concern among the political elite lest it provide cover for religious extremism and challenges to the state.

ISLAM Some 90% of Uzbekistan's population is nominally Muslim, though there is great breadth in both the degree of religiosity and in the form of Islam practised.

Islam arrived in Uzbekistan with Arab invaders in the 8th century. It spread through the work of missionaries, and was popularised following the conversion of the ruling elite. Bukhara, and later Samarkand, became important regional centres of Islamic learning, their mosques and madrasas heavily patronised by the likes of Timur (see box, page 17).

The mystical strain of Islam known as **Sufism** or Tasawwuf has been important in central Asia since the start of the 12th century, when the Kubrawiya order was formed in Khorezm, the Kadyriya order in Fergana and the Yassawiya order in southern Kazakhstan; in the 14th century many Sufi teachers were active in the Bukhara region, and their tombs are the objects of pilgrimages to this day.

There was a severe clampdown on all religious practice during the Soviet period, but particularly on Islam as it was feared that pan-Islamism, if allowed to develop, could challenge communism and even the USSR. The 65 registered mosques that were allowed to continue were overseen by the Muslim Board of Central Asia, and those working within them were screened for their political reliability. Other mosques were closed, many Muslims were victims of mass deportation, and the government sponsored numerous anti-religious campaigns.

Islam returned to the public sphere following independence in 1991 and though adherence is growing, particularly among the young, surveys suggest that personal understanding of what it means to be a Muslim remains limited or distorted. Self-defining as Muslim appears to be more of an attempt to align oneself with Uzbekistan's cultural heritage than a confirmation of belief in Islamic doctrine.

There has also been a rise, albeit relatively small, in militant Islam in Uzbekistan. Fomented primarily in the Fergana Valley and among politically and economically disenfranchised youth, groups such as the IMU (Islamic Movement of Uzbekistan;

see box, below) and Hizb ut-Tahrir (Party of Islamic Liberation) have found support, though this probably has more to do with poverty than ideology. The label 'Islamic extremist groups' has been used extensively by the government in recent years to describe all manner of political opponents, and fear of Islamic militancy has been used to legitimise political and religious repression. Although there are a number of Uzbeks fighting with militant groups in Syria and Iraq it is thought that they were radicalised and recruited outside Uzbekistan, not in the country itself. The three Uzbeks who killed more than 50 people in terrorist attacks in Istanbul, Stockholm and New York in 2017 were probably radicalised after leaving their homeland; even so the government continues to crack down on unauthorised Islamic schools. The marginalised Uzbek minority in the Kyrgyz

THE ISLAMIC MOVEMENT OF UZBEKISTAN

The Islamic Movement of Uzbekistan (IMU) is a banned militant organisation formed by two natives of the Fergana Valley – Tahir Yuldashev and Juma Namangani, who aimed to overthrow President Karimov and create a sharia state in the country. Originally known as Adolat (Justice), their movement briefly imposed sharia law in Namangan in 1991 but was driven out the following year. Namangani was active during the Tajik civil war as a field commander for the Islamic Renaissance Party of Tajikistan (IRPT). Yuldashev, meanwhile, spent much of the late 1990s in Peshawar in Pakistan, where he was allegedly in contact with Osama bin Laden.

After the end of the civil war in Tajikistan, Yuldashev and Namangani turned their attention back to Karimov and Uzbekistan, founding the IMU in 1998. They received funding from Pakistan's Inter Services Intelligence Agency (ISI) and became ideologically aligned with extremist groups including the Taliban. They found recruits among the Fergana Valley's impoverished and politically disaffected youth, and set to work.

February 1999 saw a series of explosions in Tashkent in failed attempts to assassinate Karimov. There is some doubt as to whether the IMU was actually responsible, but they were blamed nonetheless, and the attacks were used as a justification to crack down on Islamic groups generally. The IMU kidnapped the Mayor of Osh (Kyrgyzstan) the same year, and also abducted a group of Japanese geologists.

The IMU established training camps in Afghanistan, having offered the Taliban an alliance to help defeat the Northern Alliance, the main opposition to the Taliban during Afghanistan's civil war. The IMU was equipped with advanced weaponry (including two transport helicopters) and continued to make raids and kidnap foreigners, leading to international pressure on Karimov to fix the problem.

In the end it was the US invasion of Afghanistan that destroyed most of the IMU, as their militants were killed alongside the Taliban. Namangani was killed in an airstrike in 2001, and Yuldashev was killed by a US drone in 2009. Those IMU militants who have survived have either reintegrated into civilian society, or left central Asia and joined ISIS groups in Syria and Iraq, where they are valued for their technical skills (particularly building improvised explosive devices) and long experience of guerrilla warfare, and it is thought that the militants behind ISIS's very successful social-media network and websites are probably of Uzbek origin.

part of the Fergana Valley have proved to be far more prone to radicalisation than those in Uzbekistan itself.

CHRISTIANITY Around 5% of Uzbekistan's population are Christian, the vast majority of whom are members of the Eastern (or Russian) Orthodox Church, with small numbers of Roman Catholics, Protestants and other groups. Prior to the arrival of Islam, the country had a sizeable population of Nestorians and Jacobites, though these were largely killed or converted by Timur. Christianity returned with the arrival of the Russians in the 1860s.

There is significant concern among the international community about the persecution of those who have left their Muslim faith for Christianity, and in 2017 the government promised that it would in future observe the constitutional right of freedom of religion. So far, there has been little sign of change, although one congregation of Jehovah's Witnesses has been authorised in a Tashkent suburb.

JUDAISM Uzbekistan once had more than 90,000 Jews, most of whom lived in Bukhara; now only a fraction remain. Ancient texts imply they may have come to Uzbekistan as far back as the 10th century BC, though most trace their ancestry to Cyrus the Great's destruction of Babylon in 539BC. In any case, they have been cut off from the rest of the Jewish world for around 2,500 years. The German eccentric Joseph Wolff (see box, page 223) visited the Bukharan Jews in 1843 while searching for the lost tribes of Israel.

The 20th century saw several significant Jewish migrations. Some Bukharan Jews fled Uzbekistan for Palestine during the purges of the 1920s and 30s, but the population then swelled with Ashkenazi Jews fleeing the Holocaust. The third wave of migration took place following independence: almost all of Bukhara's Jewish community emigrated then to Israel or the USA. Daniel Metcalfe's *Out of Steppe* (page 289) contains a fascinating account of those few Jewish families who remain.

EDUCATION

Uzbekistan has nine years of free and compulsory education, starting from the age of seven. The official literacy rate in the country is 99%, a legacy of the comprehensive Soviet education system.

The vast majority of primary and secondary schools are state run and teach the national curriculum. The exceptions are a handful of international schools in Tashkent. At 1:25, the teacher:pupil ratio in primary schools is reasonably good, but teaching methods and materials tend to be outdated. The medium of instruction is Uzbek (having replaced Russian at independence) and the broad school curriculum includes languages, mathematics and science.

Uzbekistan has 65 universities and higher-education institutes, the largest of which are in Nukus, Samarkand and Tashkent. In the first decade of independence, university admissions dropped sharply from 19.4% of the college-age population to just 6.4% (2001). There are currently thought to be around 270,000 students studying for bachelors' degrees. It takes four years to obtain this, and the language of instruction here can be either Uzbek or Russian.

Although the quality of higher education in Uzbekistan is reasonable (a fine legacy of the Soviet education system), in recent years the government has encouraged foreign institutions to open campuses, bringing much-needed investment for infrastructure and also updating teaching methods and curriculums.

MUSIC Uzbekistan is widely considered to have the most diverse range of musical styles in central Asia. The classical style of *shashmaqam*, now widespread across the region, is believed to have developed in the cities of Bukhara and Samarkand in the pre-Islamic era. The term refers to the structure of music with six sections in different musical modes. This style is similar to classical Persian music and is often interspersed with devotional Sufi poetry. This lyrical, deeply spiritual music is usually accompanied by stringed instruments like the *dutor*, *tanbur*, *sato* and *ghizhzhak*. *Shashmaqam* music was placed on UNESCO's list of the world's intangible heritage in 2008, and there's a good supply of fine young musicians from the State Conservatory in Tashkent (page 103).

GOOGOOSHA

Gulnara Karimova (stage name Googoosha), the older daughter of President Karimov, released her first music video *Unutma Meni* (*Don't Forget Me*) in 2006. Cynics suggest it may have been a ploy to show the fluffier side of Uzbekistan's first family, and it certainly brought publicity, if not critical acclaim, and platinum record sales. She went on to duet with Julio Iglesias, and in 2012 released her first single, *Round Run*, and an album that was given international release.

Karimova is no star-struck show-child, however. Born in 1972, she has a fistful of academic qualifications from various Uzbek institutions, but also a master's degree in Regional Studies from Harvard. In 1998 and from 2000 to 2003 she was consul at Uzbekistan's Mission to the United Nations in New York, then minister-consul at the Uzbek embassy in Moscow. She advised the Ministry of Foreign Affairs, became the Permanent Representative of Uzbekistan to the United Nations in Geneva in 2008, and in 2010 was named Uzbek Ambassador to Spain.

However, not content with success in the worlds of music and diplomacy, she developed significant business interests in everything from retail to telecoms. These were fuelled by bribery and corruption on a massive scale, and eventually her father lost patience. In September 2012, the government stripped the country's largest mobile-phone operator, Russian-owned Uzdunrobita, of its licence and began closing down other businesses linked to Gulnara. In February 2014 she was placed under house arrest and in 2015 secretly sentenced to five years in prison. Her boyfriend, Rustam Madumarov, was jailed for ten years and about 60 others also went to prison for their involvement. The US government identified over US$300 million in accounts held in Belgium, Luxembourg and Ireland, traceable to bribes from Swedish and Dutch telecommunication companies seeking mobile-phone licences (Telia and VimpelCom ultimately paid US$965 million and US$795 million respectively in various fines). In June 2018, Uzbek prosecutors said they were in talks with their counterparts in Switzerland to repatriate some US$810 million held in accounts there, and in October the UK's Serious Fraud Office applied to recover three London properties allegedly owned by Gulnara. The Uzbek authorities have always been very reluctant to discuss her situation, but it seems that she was released to house arrest and then returned to prison in March 2019; new fraud charges followed in August 2019.

Ethnomusicologists first began recording **Uzbek folk music** in the late 19th century, and as a means of recording songs and tunes for posterity they also introduced written notation. Though banned from radio station playlists during the Soviet period, folk music continued to be enjoyed at weddings and other festivals, surviving long enough to be revived on the back of Uzbek nationalism. Uzbek television and radio stations regularly play both classical and folk music, and singers of traditional music, such as Sherali Jo'rayev, Yulduz Usmonova and Sevara Nazarkhan, have gained a wide following both in Uzbekistan and on the world music circuit. You'll probably also hear the braying of untuned long horns or *karnay* at weddings.

Pop music has flourished in Uzbekistan since the early 1990s, with Uzbek, Russian and Turkish artists dominating the charts. Several Uzbek singers, most notably Shahzoda and Sogdiana Fedorinskaya, have achieved commercial success in Russia, though Uzbek artists are not really known outside the former USSR. The exception to this rule is Googoosha (aka Gulnara Karimov; see box, opposite).

The following of other contemporary music styles is harder to judge, as much of it is underground. A few **pop–rock bands** have emerged (specifically Bolalar and Sahar), but the lifestyles stereotypically associated with heavy rock music are generally disapproved of, and Tashkent's tiny population of goths has reported being harassed by both the state and the community at large for their musical and fashion tastes. The Uzbek government has been known to censor **rap music** because it believes it is not complementary to Uzbek culture.

Uzbekistan's leading **classical musician** is actually the Australian composer and pianist Elena Kats-Chernin, who was born in Tashkent in 1957 and emigrated in 1975.

LITERATURE Uzbekistan's literary canon is a reflection of its diverse linguistic and cultural heritage. In addition to writings in Uzbek, some of the finest works of Persian/Tajik literature were written in Samarkand and Bukhara, and in the 20th century writers seeking a Soviet Union-wide audience for their work were compelled to write in Russian.

Early literature in Uzbekistan developed as an oral medium: travelling bards and local storytellers were important figures in local communities, their heroic tales an essential part of weddings, funerals and other festivals. The genre includes epic poems, known as *dastan*, in which the protagonist must protect his tribe and homeland from foreign invaders. Famous epic poems in this style include *Kyor-ogly* and *Alpamysh*, celebrations of the bravery of Uzbek warriors.

A significant proportion of Uzbekistan's classical literature dates from the medieval period. The writer and philosopher **Abu Abdullah Rudaki** (see box, page 34) is considered to be the father of Tajik literature. Along with **Ferdowsi** (934–1020), author of the epic poem *Shahnameh* (*The Book of Kings*), and the scientist **Hussayn ibn Abu Ali ibn Sina** (980–1037), known in the West as Avicenna, he is a pillar of classical Tajik literature, and rightly commemorated with street names and monuments across Uzbekistan and beyond.

The 11th century also produced didactic works based on religious norms of Islamic morality. Well-known poems include *Knowledge, Providing Happiness* (*Kutadgu Bilig*) (1069) by **Yusuf Balasaguni** and *The Gift of Truths* (*Hibat al-Haqa'iq*) by **Akhmad Yugnaki**, and especially *The Dictionary of Turkic Dialects* (*Dīwān Lughāt al-Turk*) (1072–74), composed by **Makhmud Kashgari**. The first dictionaries and grammars also date from this era.

It is sometimes said that Rudaki is to the Tajik language as Shakespeare is to English: despite the passing of centuries many know a few lines, and allusions to his work still permeate modern poetry and prose.

Abu Abdullah was born in the village of Rudak (hence his moniker) in Transoxiana (now the area surrounding Penjikent in Tajikistan), in AD857. Many of his biographers believe him to have been blind, but this seems doubtful given the vivid descriptions of colour in his poems, around 2,000 lines of which survive.

At the height of his career, Rudaki was appointed as court poet to Nasr II, the Samanid ruler of Bukhara, and it was here that he produced his greatest works. His lyrical poems were philosophical in nature and included messages of patriotism (popular with the ruler) and freedom (popular with the ordinary people but somewhat less popular with the ruler).

A refusal to stop preaching liberty to the masses ultimately ended Rudaki's life at court; he fell from favour and, without the support of a wealthy patron, died in poverty at the remarkable age of 84.

With vast sums spent on patronising the arts, and Samarkand serving as the imperial centre, it is no surprise that the Timurids presided over a golden age of literature. Both religious and secular works were produced in large numbers, the latter category encompassing everything from fiction to medical treatises and astronomical observations. The language of the court, and therefore of much of the literature, was Chagatai Turkish, and the most famous writer and cultural figure to emerge from these years is undoubtedly the epic-poet **Alisher Navoi**, though **Zakhiriddin Babur** (see box, page 142), the founder of the Mughal Empire in India, also wrote his autobiography in the Chagatai language during this period.

The 20th century gave birth to a wide number of important authors writing in Russian as well as local languages. **Khamza Khakimzade Niyazi**, **Sadriddin Aini** and **Gafur Gulyam** all rose to prominence during this period, with organisations such as the Uzbekistan Writers Union actively promoting their work. Uzbekistan's most popular novelist **Abdulla Kadiriy**, the revered poet **Chol'pon** (born Abdulhamid Sulaymon o'g'li Yunusov) and the prolific **Abdurauf Fitrat** were all shot by Stalin in 1938. Many of their homes and collected papers are preserved in house museums around the country; these are well worth visiting if you have an interest in Soviet literature.

Uzbekistan has a number of contemporary writers, though few of these are known outside the country as their works are rarely available in translation. Electronic publishing may, of course, change this. **Salomat Vafo**, a young woman from Khorezm, had some critical acclaim overseas for her 2004 novel *Tilsim saltanati* though, due to its discussion of intimate relationships, the Uzbekistan Writers Union initially tried to prevent its publication. Vafo has also published three volumes of short stories and directed a documentary film. **Hamid Ismailov**, who's lived in Britain since 1992, working for the BBC World Service, has produced many fine novels in Uzbek and Russian. His most notable work is *The Devil's Dance* (2016), a book about Kadiriy and the other writers shot by Stalin (see above), and supposedly the first novel to be translated from Uzbek into English; it won the prestigious EBRD Literature Prize in 2019.

THEATRE An appreciation of theatre and formalised performance arrived in Uzbekistan with the Russians in the late 19th century. For the first time, designated performance spaces were built, the most attractive of which is surely the Alisher Navoi Opera and Ballet Theatre in Tashkent, though several other companies have played more active roles in promoting and developing drama in Uzbekistan. The most critically acclaimed theatre company of Uzbekistan is Mark Weil's Ilkhom Theatre (see box, below).

DANCE There are two main types of dance in the Uzbek tradition: folk and classical. Some **folk dances** are reserved for special occasions, while others are impromptu expressions of joy. **Classical dance** is primarily the domain of women; lyrical upper body and hand movements, facial expressions and empathy with the music characterise performances. The three main schools developed in the Fergana Valley, Khiva, and Bukhara.

ARTS AND CRAFTS For centuries Uzbekistan has been known for its artistic output: from glazed tiles to the finest silks and finely worked jewellery set with precious and semi-precious stones to handwoven and knotted carpets.

The country is home to some of the most spectacular architecture not only in the Islamic world but worldwide, and several sites are justifiably recognised by

THE ILKHOM THEATRE   *Lainie Mullen*

The Ilkhom Theatre was founded in Tashkent in 1976 by a group of young artists and thinkers led by artistic director Mark Weil, a Tashkent-born Russian Jew. They staged bold performances about current issues and gained notoriety in the USSR by presenting material not approved by the censorship board.

Weil worked by the philosophy that theatre is a spiritual search. 'We were not a political theatre,' he wrote, 'we did not try to change anyone's thinking with our performances, we did not moralize…We just reproduced unedited life and real people on our stage.' The theatre faced ongoing opposition but survived through the country's transition to independence. It continued to present plays on contemporary and controversial themes and often pulled from Uzbek literature and traditions. The company formed many foreign partnerships and toured through Russia, Europe, Asia and North America.

Weil also developed a training programme for young actors in the 1990s that continues every several years to take in new local and foreign actors.

With the opening of the theatre's 32nd season in 2007, it suffered an irreparable blow: Mark Weil was murdered. The theatre continued to work, however. Actors collaborated with local and Russian artists to stage a stunning music-based production of Alisher Navoi's *Seven Moons* in 2010. In 2011, the theatre won the Prince Claus Award for its contribution to culture and development.

The theatre's current artistic director is Boris Gafurov, one of its leading actors. Ovlyakuli Khodjakuli, a guest director, has staged some of the most recent performances. It remains the only professional non-state-sponsored theatre in Uzbekistan. Plays are usually performed in Russian, although some are in Uzbek. A few shows per month have English surtitles; check out w ilkhom.com/en for further information.

UNESCO as being of international cultural importance. Monuments to both God and man incorporate influences from ancient Greece to the Buddhist temples of the Indian subcontinent, a riotous fusion of ideologies, tastes and techniques. A lack of stone and timber pushed forward advances in brick- and tile-making and in the design and engineering of domes (including ribbed and double domes).

Architectural decorative art holds a prominent place in the arts and crafts of Uzbekistan. The world-famous architectural monuments of Bukhara, Samarkand, Khiva and other cities testify to the mastery of medieval artists and architects, ornamental designers and calligraphers, engravers and ceramicists. Wall painting, sculptural carving and ornamental carving and painting have been practised since before the medieval period – in the 8th and 9th centuries there was a period of intensive development of ornamental, floral-vegetal polychromatic painting and relief carving. Carved wood also played a large part in architectural décor and is still used in the production of household goods and furniture.

Other crafts include engraving on copper and wood, ornamental embroidery using gold thread, decoration of tanned leather and inlaid work on musical instruments. The silk carpets of Uzbekistan, with their tight weave, smooth finish and rich colours, are made in Dzhizak, Syr Darya, Qashqa Darya, Karakalpakstan, and Samarkand. The weaving and embroidery of silks and cotton into wonderful, shimmering cloth is famously the passion and occupation of women in Samarkand, Bukhara, Shakhrisabz, Surkhan Darya, Fergana, Kokand, Margilan, and Namangan.

The most noted masters of **wall painting** in the last century were from Bukhara, and the art of master painters from Samarkand, Tashkent and Khiva is also renowned. Even today, the work of Saidmakhmud Narkuziev, an outstanding painter based in Kokand, is much admired and his sons and grandsons continue his tradition.

Natural pigments are also important for Uzbekistan's **carpet-making** industry. Though most carpets are now produced by machine, and Turkmen and Afghan carpets often labelled as Uzbek, some small workshops do still produce carpets by hand. The revival of traditional carpet making in Khiva is the subject of the fascinating and very readable *Carpet Ride to Khiva* by Chris Alexander, and you can also see carpets being made on looms in Bukhara and Samarkand.

Uzbekistan was one of the earliest producers of **silk** after the secrets of its production escaped from China, and the country's farmers and artisans continue to raise silkworms and weave high-quality silks. Some of the most attractive silk designs are dyed and woven using a method known as *ikat* (see box, below).

IKAT TEXTILES

Ikat is a word from the Javan, and thus now Indonesian, languages, referring to a dyeing technique similar to tie-dye in which either the warp or weft fibres of silk or cotton are tied in a specific pattern before being dyed. Alternating the bindings and the use of several colours produces elaborate, multi-coloured patterns. At the points where the different dyed sections meet, carefully controlled amounts of colour merge with one another randomly creating subtle, slightly blurred patterns that are unique: every dyeing will result in a slightly different appearance, even if the same colours are used. The dyed threads can then be woven. The difference between tie-dye and *ikat* is that in *ikat* the dyeing takes place before the fabric is woven.

Throughout the centuries, **artistic traditions** have been handed down from one generation to the next. The skills and knowledge imparted by the various ethnic groups that eventually came together to constitute the Uzbek nation created a true diversity, which is the distinguishing feature in works of art of all genres.

Of ever-increasing popularity are the **art galleries and workshops** that showcase Uzbek modern, classical and folk art. Tashkent, with about a dozen major galleries, hosts regular exhibitions of fine art, folk pieces and antiques. Art studios and galleries in Samarkand, Bukhara and Khiva are also enjoying success among both Uzbek and international tourists. As well as buying these products, it is also possible to attend masterclasses where the process of producing unique items is shown.

Many say Islam prohibits the depiction of living things in art, but this is scarcely evident in Uzbekistan. Though ornate calligraphy, colourful geometric patterns and nature-inspired motifs (the usual alternatives) are all in evidence, so too are tiles (see box, above) painted with animals, flowers and human faces and beautifully illustrated manuscripts depicting men, beasts and even the occasional prophet or angel.

SPORT

A diverse range of sports are practised in Uzbekistan, from traditional wrestling, tug-of-war and horse games to judo and freestyle skiing. Rugby union is on the rise, and President Karimov was a big fan of tennis.

Uzbekistan has competed as an independent nation in every Olympic and Winter Olympic Games since 1994 (prior to this Uzbek athletes competed on behalf of the Soviet Union), and has won medals in a variety of combat sports as well as gymnastics. Artur Taymazov was one of the world's most successful freestyle wrestlers, winning silver at the 2000 Olympics and gold in 2004, 2008 and 2012 – however, he has now been stripped of his 2008 and 2012 medals after retrospective drug testing; he lives in Russia where he is a deputy for Putin's party. At the 2016 Rio Olympics the Uzbek team won 13 medals, seven of these (including four golds) in boxing.

Skiing is possible near Tashkent, at Beldersay (with the longest slope of 3,000m) and Chimgan (up to 1,500m; page 129); at the time this guide went to print, the Amirsoy resort (page 129) was also under development.

FOOTBALL Nicknamed the 'White Wolves', the national football team of Uzbekistan played its first competitive match, against Tajikistan, on 17 June 1992. In 1994, FIFA and the Asian Football Confederation (AFC) officially recognised the country as an independent football-playing nation after its split from the USSR. Despite having played international matches for only two decades, the Uzbekistan Football Federation (UFF; ☐ UzbekistanFA) has actually been in charge of the national team since 1964.

The country's relatively short football history has produced surprisingly good results. They won the Asian Games Tournament in 1994 at their first attempt and reached the quarter-finals at the next competition in 1998. Since 2002, however, football at the Asian Games has been an under-23s tournament. Uzbekistan has yet to qualify for any World Cup, although the country was represented in Russia in 2018 by Ravshan Irmatov, who holds the record for refereeing most World Cup games, with 11 between 2010, 2014 and 2018.

Uzbekistan's biggest win came against Mongolia in 1998, when they won 15–0, and their biggest defeat was at the hands of Japan in 2000 when they lost 8–1. Their record goal scorer is Maksim Shatskikh, who retired in 2016. Born in 1978, Shatskikh scored an extremely impressive 34 goals in only 61 appearances for his country.

The UFF currently presides over, and organises, the Uzbekistan National League, the second tier (Uzbekistan 1-Division) and the Uzbekistan Women's Football Championship. Unlike many other Islamic countries, Uzbekistan has actively promoted the growth of women's football, with ten clubs competing annually in the national league. The two dominant women's teams are Andijanka Andijon and Sevinch Qarshi, and between them they have won every single title since the league's inauguration in 1996.

'THE TASHKENT TERROR'

Uzbekistan's most famous international sports star is Djamolidine Abdoujaparov, 'The Tashkent Terror'. He was a professional road cyclist, best known for his explosive finishes in races, and sometimes unorthodox and erratic approach towards winning them.

Born on 28 February 1964, 'Abdou' graduated from the Soviet Sports Programme just prior to Uzbek independence. After initial difficulties arising from Uzbekistan not being affiliated with the Union Cycliste Internationale (UCI), Djamolidine eventually turned professional in 1990, and raced for several European teams (including Carrera, Novell and Lotti) in his seven-year professional career. Djamolidine is perhaps best known for his tussles with fellow sprinter Laurent Jalabert for the green sprinter's jersey in the Tour de France. The two men won five consecutive green jerseys between 1991 and 1995, with Jalabert claiming two of those titles, and Abdou three.

Abdou's first victory came in 1991, despite an unbelievable crash on the Champs-Elysées (the traditional finish point of the Tour de France since 1975), which saw the Uzbek cyclist clash with a giant promotional drinks can with just 100m left in the race. Abdou was sent spiralling into the air and was seriously injured, but the rules of the competition stipulated that despite already holding enough points to win the green jersey for that year, the cyclist must cross the finish line unaided. His teammates picked him up and put him back on to his bike, and he rode gingerly to the finish line where he was greeted by paramedics and his newly claimed title.

Sadly for the sport, and despite a glittering career, the end of Abdoujaparov's career was overshadowed by his failing of an anti-doping test in the 1997 Tour de France. However, as one of only five men to have won the points competition in all three Grand Tours (the Tour de France, Giro d'Italia and Vuelta a Espana), he remains one of the greatest sprint cyclists of all time.

The men's National League consists of 14 teams and was founded in 1992. Much like the women's competition, there are three teams that dominate, all from the capital (Pakhtakor Tashkent, Bunyodkor Tashkent and Lokomotiv Tashkent). Between them they have won the trophy for 17 years in succession. Pakhtakor Tashkent are also, alas, remembered for the 1979 mid-air collision of two Tupolev jets over Ukraine, which killed all 178 passengers, including their entire team.

The professional game was reorganised at the end of the 2017 season; instead of an eastern and a western league there's now the Super League (with 12 teams) and the Pro League (with 16 teams). The bottom team of the Super League is demoted each season, the top team of the Pro League is promoted, and the next two teams meet in play-offs.

RUGBY UNION Rugby union was introduced to the Russian Empire in 1908, and the Soviet Union hosted championships in Moscow from 1936 onwards. The sport was actively promoted in Uzbekistan from the early 1960s, and regional teams were founded in addition to the national team.

Today, the sport is mainly played in Uzbekistan's universities and by the military. The fact that Kazakhstan has achieved notable success on the world stage, especially with its women's team, has led the Uzbeks to up their game (excuse the pun). The Rugby Federation in Uzbekistan (w en.rugby.uz) was established in 2001, and though an Uzbek side is yet to play in the Rugby World Cup, they do compete in the Asia Rugby Championship.

TENNIS Walk around any Uzbek city and you will quickly come across tennis courts and tennis academies. The sport was heavily promoted by President Karimov and is hugely popular. The Uzbekistan Tennis Federation (UTF; w tennis.uz) became a full member of the International Tennis Federation (ITF) in 1993, and it organises championships within Uzbekistan as well as sending the national team to major international competitions, including the Davis Cup and the Fed Cup.

Uzbekistan's number one seed is Denis Istomin (b1986), who was born in Russia to Uzbek parents and moved to Tashkent as a child. He stepped on to the international circuit in 2006 when he received the Asian wildcard to play in the Australian Open, losing gracefully to Roger Federer. The same thing happened at the 2008 and 2009 Australian Opens, where he was knocked out by Lleyton Hewitt and Richard Gasquet respectively.

He then established himself on the ATP world tour, reaching his highest singles ranking of number 33 in 2012 and winning singles titles at Nottingham in 2015 and Chengdu in 2017. In September 2018 he lost to Dan Evans when Great Britain beat Uzbekistan in a Davis Cup World Group play-off.

TRADITIONAL SPORTS Traditional sports include *ulak* or **kupkari**, a sort of prototype of polo in which teams (theoretically of six on each side, although there can be hundreds) compete to seize a headless goat's carcass and throw it into a *kazan* – a round structure of brick, concrete or truck tyres. **Kurash**, the collective name for various types of wrestling common to the Turkic peoples of central Asia, is also popular.

Both sports can be seen at the Boysun Spring festival (page 193) and the **World Nomad Games** (w worldnomadgames.com) which also features eagle hunting, dog handling, intelligence games and various cultural displays. The biennial event was first held in Kyrgyzstan in 2014; at the 2018 games Uzbekistan came fifth in the final medal table (which was topped by the home nation), taking home 33 medals comprising seven golds, eight silvers and 18 bronzes. One of these silver medals was gained in one of the games' most popular events, *kok boru* (a horseback sport similar to *kupkari*), where Uzbekistan's team was beaten by the Kyrgyz side, with a final score of 9–32. In 2020 the games are being held in Turkey (the first time that they will move out of Kyrgyzstan); they might one day be held in Uzbekistan.

2

Practical Information

WHEN TO VISIT

Uzbekistan is a year-round tourism destination, though most people choose to visit between May and October, as the winter months can be bitingly cold both in the desert and in the mountain foothills.

Spring breaks in March and April (slightly later in the mountains) and brings with it a riot of colourful flowers in the mountain pastures. The rivers are in full spate with the glacial meltwater, and the country comes swiftly back to life. If you visit in springtime, you may also be able to join in celebrations for Navruz, the Persian New Year, celebrated in Uzbekistan on 21 March. During this two-day festival, which is a national holiday, families feast, watch traditional sports including *kopkari* (horse racing) and *kurash* (wrestling), and there's plenty of musical entertainment. You'll invariably be asked to join in the fun.

The **summer** can be bakingly hot on the plains, particularly in July and August, but this is the best time to trek in the mountains and to try a night or two sleeping in a yurt. It's also the time of some interesting festivals (pages 75 and 79), including Samarkand's International Music Festival. Expect plenty of pomp and circumstance on Independence Day (1 September).

When **autumn** comes, Uzbekistan turns terracotta red and gold almost overnight. It's one of the most beautiful times to visit, with late September and early October being ideal for a visit to the big three: Samarkand, Bukhara and Khiva, as temperatures are still warm but many of the crowds have gone. By early November, the warmly dressed can have Khiva in particular almost entirely to themselves, though many restaurants and shops will be closing up at the end of their season.

In the **winter** months few tourists come to Uzbekistan, but that means you can negotiate favourable rates for hotels and tours. It's also the time for skiing: the resorts of Chimgan and Beldersay have excellent snow from January to March, and you can even risk your neck heli-skiing for descents up to 10km in length.

HIGHLIGHTS

It's clichéd but true to say that Uzbekistan offers a little something for everyone. Whether your idea of a trip of a lifetime is wandering among the medieval tombs of Samarkand, shopping in Tashkent's vast Chorsu Bazaar or trekking across the Kyzylkum Desert by camel and sleeping in a nomad's yurt, you won't be disappointed. The challenge is how to pack everything into the time available. If you're in need of a little guidance, here are our must-see sights and experiences:

CAMEL TREKKING We have sadly found that camels are invariably smelly, bad-tempered and jolly uncomfortable to ride. However, the Silk Road would never have got going without them, and so you will need to saddle up and take at least a short journey on camelback if you want the full, authentic experience. The best camel treks are around Nurata in the Kyzylkum Desert (page 217), where you can ride across the dunes well away from roads and human habitation. Make Aidarkul Lake (page 217) your destination and tie your camel on the shore while you have a swim in the slightly salty waters or try your hand at fishing. Come nightfall, you can stay with nomadic families in a traditional yurt (albeit with the added advantage of a toilet block), sit around the fire listening to stories and music, and engage in some splendid stargazing.

CHORSU BAZAAR (page 104) This bazaar is the first and only place where we have seen the boot and back seat of a Lada stacked to the gunwales with decapitated cow heads. The sight was truly gruesome. Quite what they were doing there we can only dread to think, but they didn't look a bit out of place. The modern incarnation of Silk Road trading posts now long gone, the market buzzes with energy and everything conceivable (and, like the cow heads, a few things normally inconceivable) is for sale. You can of course buy a trailer-load of watermelons and 300 plastic buckets, but the real delight comes in spending an hour or three exploring the trading domes, drinking bowls of fragrant black tea, smelling the *shashlik* grilling and engaging in an animated, good-natured haggle for a bag of salted pistachios and a fresh, pink pomegranate. Come here for some well-placed souvenirs, including a wide selection of ceramics, and the best people-watching in Tashkent.

ORIENT STAR (page 257) A single hotel wouldn't normally feature in the highlights section of a guidebook, but the Orient Star is no ordinary hotel. The Muhammad Amin Khan Madrasa, in the heart of Khiva's Ichon Qala, was sensitively converted in 2000 so that mod cons are hidden behind the elaborately tiled 19th-century façade. Each room is inside a former *hujra* (student's cell), though with slightly more creature comforts, and the hotel courtyard once housed the city's Supreme Court. When you step outside your door in the mornings, you can look up in wonder at the jewel-like Kalta Minar.

IGOR SAVITSKY MUSEUM (page 278) There would be little reason to come to Nukus at all if it weren't for the Igor Savitsky Museum, an unexpected treasure trove of Soviet avant-garde art from the 1920s and 30s. The 2010 documentary *Desert of Forbidden Art* provides an informative and moving account of Savitsky's life and work and will certainly whet your appetite and motivate you to make the trek out to what feels like the other side of the moon. In addition to the striking, and in many cases controversial, paintings Savitsky collected, you will also find galleries of folk art and archaeological finds illustrating Khorezm's rich past. The first of two new museum buildings is now open, and when the second opens (hopefully during the lifespan of this edition), an even greater part of the collection will finally be on show.

KHOREZM FORTRESSES (page 270) It is of course possible to come to Khorezm and visit only Khiva, but you would sadly be missing out. Not far away, on the edge of the Kyzylkum Desert, are a string of fortresses dating from the early centuries BC. Listed by UNESCO as the Golden Ring of Ancient Khorezm, the most impressive are the mud-brick Toprak Qala and the Koi Krylgan Qala, but there are plenty of smaller sites if you want to explore on your own. You will need your own transport to get here, but it is well worth hiring a car for a couple of days and staying in the yurt camp beside the Ayaz Qala to be able to appreciate the site at both sunset and sunrise. You can take a camel ride from the yurt camp here, too.

KHUDAYAR KHAN'S PALACE (page 143) The 19th-century palace of Khudayar Khan, ruler of Kokand, once had more than 100 rooms and was described as the most magnificent in central Asia: its nickname is the Pearl of Kokand. Though a shadow of its former self, 19 of its rooms survive today and in them are displayed an eclectic collection of jewellery, stuffed animals, fine woodcarvings and *objets d'art*. Here, you will have a sense of the exorbitant wealth and excesses of the khans, and how they were able to dazzle foreign visitors. The palace is said to have been built by 80 master builders and 16,000 conscripted labourers, the descendants of whom still live in and around Kokand today.

POI KALYON (page 237) The entirety of Bukhara probably deserves mentioning as a highlight, but it is the Poi Kalyon that particularly caught our eyes. This simple square is framed by some of the most spectacular buildings on earth: the Mir-i Arab Madrasa, the Kalyon Juma Mosque and the majestic 11th-century Kalyon Minar, one of the few buildings in the city to pre-date Genghis Khan's invasion: he saw its elegant silhouette from a great distance away as he rode across the steppe and found it so beautiful that when he arrived in Bukhara he could not bear to see it destroyed. Everything else, however, was razed to the ground and the population of Bukhara was butchered (page 221).

SHAH-I ZINDA (page 170) Most people come to Samarkand for the Registan but, though it is undoubtedly impressive, the city's real gem is the collection of medieval tiled tombs known as the Shah-i Zinda (the Living King). Arriving at dusk, the experience is magical. The tour groups have retreated to their hotels for dinner, as have the schoolchildren; if you're lucky you'll have the place to yourself. You can expect to see every variety of turquoise- and lapis lazuli-coloured glazed tiles attached to the façades of the tombs of female members of the Timurid dynasty, as well as generals, advisors and holy figures.

SUGGESTED ITINERARIES

How much you can see in Uzbekistan is very much dictated by the length of your stay and your modes of transport. Travelling by camel may sound romantic, but it's still rather faster to go by plane. These itineraries give an idea of what you can hope to accomplish in different amounts of time, and which sites you should endeavour to squeeze into your trip.

With just a **weekend** at your disposal, you have two options: focus on Tashkent (page 87) and see most of what the city has to offer, or take the incredibly convenient high-speed train to Samarkand (page 157) and write-off the 4 hours' drive in each direction as the price you have to pay to see one of central Asia's most remarkable cities.

If you choose to stay in Tashkent, start in the Old City with the Hazrat Imam Square (page 107), the world's oldest Qu'ran in the Muyie Muborak Library (page 107), and the 15th-century tombs of the Sheikhantaur Mausoleum (page 109). Have a late lunch at one of the *plov* stalls in Chorsu Bazaar (page 104) and explore the stalls in the afternoon before taking in a performance at either the Alisher Navoi Opera and Ballet Theatre (page 102) or the Ilkhom Theatre (see box, page 35) in the evening. The following morning you should visit Amir Timur Square (page 110) for a view of post-independence Uzbekistan before going to the State Fine Arts Museum (page 114), the core of whose collection was confiscated from Grand Duke Romanov, who in turn had stolen many of the items from the Hermitage in St Petersburg. We also like the Tamara Khanum House Museum (page 123) with its collection of theatrical and dance costumes, photos and posters, and the Railway Museum (page 124) where you're still allowed to climb on and inside many of the exhibits.

In a **week** you can comfortably expect to see Tashkent, Samarkand and Bukhara (page 220). The roads between these three locations are well maintained and relatively fast, and you can also take the train. In Samarkand, book into the Antica B&B a stone's throw away from the Gur-i Amir, Timur's gilded mausoleum (page 176), and explore the heart of the city on foot. The Registan (page 168), Shah-i Zinda (page 170) and Ulug Beg's astronomical observatory (page 174) should not be missed, and neither should the ancient ruins of Afrosiab (page 172).

Travelling on to Bukhara, you should stay in a hotel close to Lyabi Hauz or the Kalyon Minar and pace yourself as you explore the bewildering selection of beautifully decorated mosques, madrasas and tombs. The Ark (page 233), Bolo Hauz Mosque (page 243) and the Chor Minor (page 242) are all best seen from the outside, while the Lyabi Hauz (page 239) should be appreciated while relaxing with a bowl of tea by the water.

With **two weeks** to spare, you can do all this and take in the highlights of Khorezm (page 249). Visiting Khiva's Ichon Qala (page 260) goes without saying, but don't miss the Khorezm fortresses in the Kyzylkum Desert (page 270), or the chance to sleep in a nomad's yurt beneath the endless sky. Make sure you go to Nukus for the Igor Savitsky Museum (page 278) and then continue through Karakalpakstan as far as Moynaq for the graveyard of ships left behind by the retreating Aral Sea (page 280).

A **month** is ample time to take in everything Uzbekistan has to offer. Consider taking the train at least part of the way (page 49) for a taste of travel in a bygone age, and allow at least a week to explore the little-visited Fergana Valley. Kokand (page 150) is famous for its ornate 18th- and 19th-century architecture and also its craft workshops, Margilan (page 147) has fascinating silk factories, and the base camp at Nanay is an ideal point from which to explore Kapchugai Gorge and the Chatkal Mountains (page 128).

TOUR OPERATORS

Though it is possible, and indeed relatively straightforward, to travel independently within Uzbekistan, many first-time visitors choose to go with a recognised tour operator as it generally reduces the hassles of registration, arranging internal transport and the language barrier. The companies below, all of which offer specialist, small-group tours, also provide knowledgeable guides, helping you to get the most out of the country. Generally, we have featured their Uzbekistan-only tours, but they also often offer trips combining Uzbekistan with a neighbouring country or all the Stans.

UK
Audley Travel Witney OX29 9SX; ℳ 01993 838450; w audleytravel.com. High-end, tailor-made trips to Uzbekistan, taking in the key sights of Tashkent, Samarkand, Bukhara & Khiva. Trips are arranged on a private basis, with a professional, English-speaking guide & driver throughout. Prices for the 11-day 'Uzbekistan Discovered' tour start from £2,790.
Cox & Kings London SW1P 4EE; ℳ 020 3918 3562; w coxandkings.co.uk. Excellent small-group guided tours, including the 12-day 'Uzbekistan: Heart of Central Asia' (£1,745).

Dragoman Debenham IP14 6LA; ✆01728 861133; w dragoman.com. Overland tours in thoroughly converted trucks, starting from £1,070 for a 16-day trip from Tashkent to Bishkek (Kyrgyzstan), all the way up to £8,365 for the 120-day haul from Istanbul (Turkey) to Ulaanbaatar (Mongolia). In Uzbekistan, the tours visit the main Silk Road cities. Prices exclude flights & kitty.

Exodus Travels London SW12 0NE; ✆020 8131 6034; w exodus.co.uk. Their 'Uzbekistan Uncovered' trip (£1,869) is a 12-day excursion to the main cities & also includes camel trekking & visits to the desert castles of Toprak Qala, Qavat Qala & Ayaz Qala.

Explore Farnborough GU14 7PA; ✆01252 884218; w explore.co.uk. Explore's 'Golden Road to Samarkand' trip is a small-group adventure (£1,965) that takes in Uzbekistan's highlights over 12 days, including a yurt stay. The tour runs on fixed departure dates from Mar to Oct.

Golden Eagle Luxury Trains Altrincham WA14 4QF; ✆0161 928 9410; w goldeneagleluxurytrains.com. Luxury journeys by private train. The 'Silk Road', 'Taste of the Silk Road', 'Caspian Odyssey' & 'Persia Odyssey' trips (from 13 days, US$22,995 to 21 days, US$26,295; the company lists their prices in USD) all make stops in Uzbekistan.

Into Russia London W11 4TR; ✆0207 603 5045; w into-russia.co.uk. A variety of Silk Road rail tours, which can be booked either on their own (from £720 for 6 days, plus flights) or with a 3-day extension in Moscow.

Intrepid Travel London SW9 8DJ; ✆0808 274 5111; w intrepidtravel.com/uk. Intrepid offers a number of scheduled group tours to Uzbekistan, including the 9-day 'Uzbekistan Adventure' (£945), which includes the big Silk Road cities & a night in a yurt camp; longer trips include neighbouring countries.

Lupine Travel ✆01942 497209; e info@lupinetravel.co.uk; w lupinetravel.co.uk. Operating budget tours to an eclectic mix of unusual destinations since 2008. Runs a popular 5 Stans Tour. See ad, inside-back cover.

Martin Randall Travel London W4 4GF; ✆020 8742 3355; w martinrandall.com. Expert-led 11-day tours (£3,090 plus flights) between Apr & Sep. Itineraries include all the main cultural sites & in-country travel is by coach. 'Samarkand & the Silk Road Cities' is escorted by an expert lecturer.

Regent Holidays Bristol BS1 4XE; ✆0117 3215657; w regentholidays.co.uk. A range of imaginative, top-end itineraries from the 9-day 'Essential Uzbekistan' tour (£1,860) to the 18-day 'Explore Uzbekistan' trip (£2,515) as well as rail journeys & tours combined with neighbouring countries. See ad, inside-front cover.

Steppes Travel Cirencester GL7 1QD; ✆01285 601638; w steppestravel.co.uk. Specialises in private holidays based on personal specifications & wants, ranging from a couple of days to a couple of months. Steppes currently has 3 expert-led group tours in Uzbekistan, ranging from a 9-day trip for £1,860 to an 18-day trip for £2,515, as well as a special 'Carpet Ride to Khiva' trip (11 days from £2,795), plus rail tours & other trips combined with neighbouring countries.

Sunbird Potton SG19 2NP; ✆01767 262522; w sunbirdtours.co.uk. Specialists in birding tours, with expert guides. 'Central Asia: Birding the Silk Road' combines Uzbekistan & Kazakhstan & is the foremost birding tour in the region (15 days for £4,180 plus flights).

Sundowners Overland ✆020 8877 7660; w sundownersoverland.com. Eurasia specialist with a wide selection of fully escorted & independent tours, as well as tailor-made experiences. Luxury train travel is a speciality. Check out in particular the 12-day 'Tamerlane's Empire' (£1,430), the 30-day 'Silk Road Railway' (£5,625) & the 41-day 'Grand Asia Caravan' (£8,000) trips. See ad, 3rd colour section.

Travel Local w travellocal.com. A UK-based website where you can book direct with selected local travel companies, allowing you to communicate with an expert ground operator without having to go through a third-party travel operator or agent. Your booking with the local company has full financial protection, but note that travel to the destination is not included. Member of ABTA, ASTA.

Travel the Unknown ✆020 7183 6371; w traveltheunknown.com. Offering tours such as Silk Road Through the Stans & 5 Stan Odyssey. See ad, 1st colour section.

Voyages Jules Vernes London SE1 0BE; ✆020 3131 5658; w vjv.com. The 'Golden Road to Samarkand' is an 11-day upmarket tour of Tashkent, Khiva, Bukhara & Samarkand (£1,895).

Wild Frontiers London SW13 9JJ; ✆020 8741 7390; w wildfrontiers.co.uk. Wild Frontiers has numerous tailor-made & group itineraries including Uzbekistan, some of which are quite extraordinary. For the trip of a lifetime, pick the 48-day 'Great Silk Road Adventure' (from £10,595).

SWITZERLAND

Kalpak Travel 5415 Nussbaumen; \+41 78 657 27 01; w kalpak-travel.com. Run by a Swiss-Kyrgyz couple, Kalpak only do tours to the Stans – both group & individual options, including the 8-day 'Classic Uzbekistan' tour to Tashkent, Samarkand, Khiva & Bukhara (€1,390 plus flights).

USA AND CANADA

Bestway Tours and Safaris Burnaby, BC V5J 3M6, Canada; \+1 800 663 0844; w bestway. com. Regular group tours visiting Uzbekistan in combination with the other Stans, Pakistan or China, starting from US$3,095 for 12 days in Uzbekistan & Tajikistan. Programmes often have a specific focus, such as sacred architecture, caravan routes or train travel.

MIR Corporation Seattle, WA 98102, USA; \+1 800 424 7289; w mircorp.com. The USA's Russia & central Asia experts (with an office in Tashkent [113 H4]), they offer exceptional tours of Uzbekistan, including not only multi-country Silk Road tours, but also one-off art, dance & cultural tours, starting from US$4,895 for 15 days in Uzbekistan. Uzbekistan can be combined with neighbouring republics & also with Iran. Highly recommended.

AUSTRALIA AND NEW ZEALAND

Odyssey Traveller Edgecliff, NSW 2027, Australia; \+61 1300 888 225; w odysseytraveller.com. Small-group tours for mature travellers including a 27-day Silk Road tour (from AUD13,370).

Peregrine Adventures Melbourne, Victoria 3000, Australia; \+61 1300 655 433; w peregrineadventures.com. Small-group adventures, including the 'Jewels of Uzbekistan' tour (11 days, from AUD2,570).

Silk Road Adventures 415 Main South Rd, Greymouth 7805, New Zealand; \+64 3 762 6673; w silkroad.co.nz. Small-group tours to Uzbekistan. The 'Persian Trilogy' tour combines Uzbekistan, Turkmenistan & Iran (22 days, US$6,400; the company lists their prices in USD), while the 'Uzbekistan Silk Roads' trip is a comprehensive tour of the country, including Nukus, Asraf & the Fergana Valley (14 days, US$3,900).

Sundowners Overland Melbourne 3000, Australia; \+61 1300 559 860; w sundownersoverland.com. See page 45.

Uzbek Journeys Leura NSW 2780, Australia; \+61 404 172 961/0404 172 961 (within Australia); w uzbekjourneys.com. Small operator specialising in art & crafts tours (16 nights from US$3,100; the company list their prices in USD).

UZBEKISTAN

In addition to full programmes of tours, these local companies are also useful for day trips & guides, & there's lots of handy information on their websites.

Advantour [112 D6] 47A Mirobod-1, Tashkent 100015; \71 150 3020; w advantour.com. With offices in Tashkent, Bishkek (Kyrgyzstan) & Tbilisi (Georgia), this company covers the region. They have a wide range of tours & are also useful for booking trains.

Asia Special Tourism [113 E7] 18 Mironshoh, Tashkent 100100; m 90 370 7009; w ast.uz. This local operator is recommended for active breaks from Tashkent, including cycling & hiking in the Chimgan area, although they run cultural tours as well.

DOCA Tours (Discover Oriental Central Asia) [160 A1] 34A Rustaveli, Samarkand 140117; m 93 350 2020; e info@doca-tours.com. Very capable & knowledgeable company, with a wide range of tours; fluent German & English. See ad, 3rd colour section.

Marco Polo Central Asia Travel [112 C6] 20 Shota Rustaveli, Tashkent 100070; \71 252 7641; w marcopolo.uz. The owners of the Asia Hotels chain offer horseriding & golf tours.

MIR Corporation [113 H4] 1/121 Mirzo Ulug Beg, Tashkent 100001; e centralasia@mir-dmc. com. See left.

Sitara International Travel [112 C7] Office 42, 45 Shota Rustaveli, Tashkent 100100; \71 281 4148; w sitara.com. A range of tours in Uzbekistan, including an 11-night trip to the Aral Sea, & also separate trips to Afghanistan & Pakistan.

Steppe Journeys [113 F2] 1 Niyazbek Yuli, Tashkent 100035; \71 235 7906; m 90 998 1723; w steppejourneys.com. Widely recommended for local knowledge & add ons, such as ceramics classes or day trips from Samarkand into Tajikistan.

Uzbek Travel [112 A3] 26 Furkat, Tashkent 100021; \71 227 0293; m 90 350 2214; w uzbek-travel. com. A good range of general & specialist tours.

Veres Vert [162 C2] 31 Hussein Baykaro, Samarkand 140100; \66 233 4594/66 233 1010; m 93 330 0131; w veres-vert.com. Specialist tours, for instance to sacred sites of the 3 Abrahamic religions.

For a long time a bureaucrat's dream, Uzbekistan is opening up fast and dispensing with Soviet-era red tape. There's no need now for a Letter of Invitation to get a tourist visa – increasingly, there's no need for a visa at all (if you do need one, in many cases this can be done online).

VISAS In February 2018 the first seven countries (Israel, Indonesia, South Korea, Malaysia, Singapore, Turkey and Japan) were dispensed from requiring a visa for a 30-day visit, and in July 2018 procedures were further simplified and an e-visa system introduced, plus a five-day visa-free stay for air passengers in transit from 101 countries.

From February 2019 visas are no longer required for single-entry visits of up to 30 days for citizens of another 45 countries, including most of Europe (the UK and Switzerland included; though after the UK leaves the European Union, documentation requirements for UK citizens may change – check before travelling) plus Canada and New Zealand (although they are still necessary for residents of Australia and the USA). In all, 76 countries are now eligible for e-visas, which also allow multiple entries. There's also talk of a common central Asian visa (a 'Stangen' visa?) being introduced.

Unless your country is on the visa-free list, you will need a visa (paper or electronic) before you fly. The easiest option is an **e-visa** (apply at w e-visa.gov. uz), which costs US$20 and is valid for 90 days from the date of issue for a single entry and a stay of up to 30 days in Uzbekistan (but not beyond the expiry date of the e-visa).

Even if your country is on the visa-free list, a standard visa is required if you wish to visit other countries and return to Uzbekistan, or if you wish to stay in the country for more than 30 days. To get one, fill out the online application form at w evisa. mfa.uz and print it. Be sure to sign it in black ink as this box is easily overlooked. Submit the form with two passport photos, a photocopy of your passport and the passport itself to the embassy.

The cost of this visa is dictated by your nationality, where you are applying, the length of your stay and whether it is for single, double or multiple entry. At the time of going to print, a UK national applying in London will pay £67 for a single-entry, 30-day visa (an additional entry costs £9 more, a 90-day visa costs £84, and an urgent application costs £92). Visas typically take five working days to process.

If Uzbekistan does not have diplomatic representation in your country of residence, it is sometimes possible to arrange in advance for a visa to be issued on arrival in Tashkent. You should contact a travel agent to arrange this, and you will need both your Letter of Invitation (if required; see below) and approval letter (a form you will be issued to present on arrival) to check in for your flight.

It is theoretically possible to extend your visa for up to seven days once you are in Uzbekistan, but in practice people often prefer to leave for a neighbouring country and apply for a new Uzbek visa there. If you are feeling optimistic (or have run out of options), you can obtain a seven-day extension from the Office of Visa and Registration (OVIR) at Tashkent Airport or at 22 Chekhov [112 D6] (\71 256 9586/71 256 9614) for US$40, a big smile and a lot of persistence.

No exit visa or stamp is required for Uzbekistan: just make sure your visa is in date and you have the requisite registration slips (page 48).

Letter of Invitation You may need a Letter of Invitation (LOI) in order to be issued a **business visa** or if your country of residence is different from your country of citizenship, in which case you will need to budget around US$40 and contact a travel company such as Stantours (w stantours.com) or a visa specialist such as Travcour (w travcour.com). You will need the LOI prior to making your visa application and should allow at least ten days for the LOI to be processed. If you do require a LOI, your inviting partner will have to gain written authorisation from the Ministry of Foreign Affairs (MFA) in Tashkent before you apply for the visa. The visa costs are the same.

For nationals who do not require a LOI, the process for obtaining a business visa is the same as for a tourist visa.

REGISTRATION The requirement for foreigners to register within three days of arriving in any given place is an irritating overhang from the Soviet period which should soon be abolished (visit w bradtupdates.com/uzbekistan for more information). Hotels now use an online-registration system, but you will still collect a passport-full of slips which will be ignored when you leave the country. If you take an overnight train journey, keep the ticket stub or booking confirmation as proof of your whereabouts. If you are camping, staying with friends or at a homestay for more than three nights, you should register at the local OVIR to ensure you (and your hosts) are in the clear. There is no cost associated with this.

ADDITIONAL PERMITS Uzbekistan requires foreigners visiting sensitive border areas and some areas of military or special scientific interest to have a travel permit in addition to their visa. If you intend to mountaineer in Uzbekistan, or to visit either the Ugam-Chatkal or Zaamin national parks, then you may be affected. Check with a Tashkent-based travel agent (page 96) for the latest information. They will also be able to apply for a permit on your behalf, often prior to your arrival in Uzbekistan. If arranging guides with the company, the cost of this may be included, otherwise there will be a charge.

EMBASSIES For a full list of embassies both overseas and in Tashkent, visit w embassypages.com/uzbekistan. The below-listed embassies can all be found in the capital.

🄔 **Afghanistan** [89 E2] 1 Batumskaya; ✆71 140 4132
🄔 **Kazakhstan** [113 E6] 23 Chekhov; ✆71 152 1654; w mfa.gov.kz/en/tashkent
🄔 **Kyrgyzstan** [113 G2] 30 Niyozbek Yuli; ✆71 237 4794
🄔 **Tajikistan** [88 D7] 61 Kakhkhara; ✆71 254 9966; w tajembuz.tj
🄔 **Turkmenistan** [112 D5] 19 Afrosiab; ✆71 256 9402; w http://uzbekistan.tmembassy.gov.tm
🄔 **UK** [113 F4] 67 Gulyamov; ✆71 120 1500; w gov.uk/government/world/uzbekistan
🄔 **USA** [88 D1] 3 Moyqorghon; ✆71 120 5450; w uz.usembassy.gov

GETTING THERE AND AWAY

For somewhere so centrally located geographically, Uzbekistan can be surprisingly challenging to reach. There is a shortage of direct flights from Europe and the US, land borders open and close on a whim, and arriving by train requires a passport full of transit visas and the patience of a saint.

BY AIR The vast majority of visitors arrive in Uzbekistan on a flight to Tashkent and this is, on balance, the easiest way to travel.

With the exception of Uzbekistan Airways (see below), direct flights to Uzbekistan tend to come only from the Middle East, Russia and the other CIS countries. Otherwise, you'll probably have to get a connection in one of the regional hubs (Almaty, Istanbul or Moscow).

At the time of going to print, all of the below-listed airlines had regular scheduled flights to Tashkent, unless otherwise specified.

✈ **Aeroflot** ☎71 120 0555; w aeroflot.ru. Daily flights to & from Moscow (4½hrs). Useful for onward connections to Europe & the US.

✈ **Air Astana** m 90 936 2533; w airastana.com. Kazakh national carrier. Daily flights from Almaty with connections from Europe, the Middle East & domestic destinations within Kazakhstan. Efficient. See ad, 2nd colour section.

✈ **Air Baltic** ☎71 120 9012; w airbaltic.com. Latvian national carrier. Budget airline providing European connections via Riga 2–4 times a week, depending on the season.

✈ **Air Manas** ☎71 147 0740; w airmanas.com. 2 flights a week from Bishkek.

✈ **Asiana Airlines** ☎71 140 0900; w flyasiana.com. 5 flights a week from Seoul.

✈ **China Southern Airlines** ☎71 231 8880; w csair.com. Daily flights from Beijing with connections from the Far East, Australia & domestic destinations within China.

✈ **Iran Air** ☎71 233 5082; w iranair.com. Flights once a week from Tehran.

✈ **Korean Air** ☎71 254 2001; w koreanair.com. 3 flights a week from Seoul with connections across the Far East.

✈ **Malaysia Airlines** ☎78 140 4623; w malaysiaairlines.com. 2 flights a week between Tashkent & Kuala Lumpur with connections across southeast Asia & Australia.

✈ **Nordwind** ☎+7 (495) 730 5080/8 (800) 222 4844; w nordwindairlines.ru. Flights from Moscow to Karshi, Fergana, Namangan, Samarkand & Tashkent, & from Kazan to Tashkent (all twice a week).

✈ **Rossiya** ☎71 255 5815; w rossiya-airlines.com. 4 flights a week from St Petersburg with connections across Europe & Russia.

✈ **S7 Airlines** ☎71 252 7871; w s7.ru/en. S7 (originally Siberian Airlines) has flights from

Moscow to Tashkent, Namangan, Samarkand & Urgench.

✈ **Turkish Airlines** ☎71 147 0849; w thy.com. Daily flights from Istanbul to Tashkent (also 2 per week to Samarkand) with connections from Europe & the US.

✈ **Ural Airlines** ☎8 (800) 200 0262; w uralairlines.com. Direct flights from Ekaterinburg (Mon) & Krasnodar (Thu) to Tashkent with connections across Russia & the CIS, plus 1 from Moscow to Navoi (Mon).

✈ **UTair** w utair.ru/en. 6 flights a week from Moscow.

✈ **Uzbekistan Airways** [113 E5] 41 Amir Timur, Tashkent 100060; ☎78 140 4623 & 9 Usman Nosir; ☎71 256 3837; w uzairways.com. From Tashkent, Uzbekistan's national carrier serves Almaty (Kazakhstan; 4/week), Nur-Sultan (Kazakhstan; 8 flights, 4 days/week), Baku (Azerbaijan; 2/week), Bangkok (Thailand; 3/week), Beijing (China; 2/ week), Bishkek (Kyrgyzstan; 4/week), New Delhi (India; 9/week), Dubai (UAE; 3/week), Dushanbe (Tajikistan; 2/week), Frankfurt (Germany; 2/week), Istanbul (Turkey; 9/week), London (UK; 2/week), Milan (Italy; 1/week), Moscow Vnukovo (Russia; 2/day), New York (USA; 2/week), Paris (France; 2/ week), Rome (Italy; 1/week), Seoul (South Korea; 6/week), St Petersburg (Russia; 5/week) & others. Flights also operate from Bukhara, Samarkand, Fergana, Navoi & Termez to Istanbul, Kazan, Moscow & St Petersburg, & there are seasonal flights from Urgench to Paris, Milan, Rome & Frankfurt. Domestic routes connect Tashkent to Andijan, Bukhara, Fergana, Karshi, Namangan, Navoi, Nukus, Samarkand, Termez & Urgench. The airline has an all-Boeing fleet (including 3 new Dreamliners) & is entirely safe & competent. You can now book on their website & pay with Visa or Mastercard. See ad, 3rd colour section.

BY RAIL There is a certain romance attached to train travel, and if you have the time to sit and watch the world pass by at a leisurely pace (very leisurely in the case of the old Soviet rail network), it is still a viable way to reach Uzbekistan. Depending on your nationality, you may need transit visas for the countries en route.

Ticket classes are categorised in the Russian style. First-class accommodation (*Spalny Vagon; SV or es-veh; also known as deluxe*) buys you an upholstered seat in a two-berth cabin. The seat turns into a bed at night. Second class (*Kupé*) is slightly less plush, and there are four passengers to a compartment. Third class (*Platskartny*) has open bunks (ie: not in a compartment) and lots of interaction with fellow passengers. Bring plenty of food for the journey, and keep an eye on your luggage, particularly at night, as theft is sadly commonplace.

There are three trains a week between both Moscow and Tashkent and Almaty (Kazakhstan) and Tashkent. The **Moscow service** (train numbers five or six depending on the direction of travel) takes 62 hours (US$166/340/352 third/second/first class one-way). The **Almaty service** is a modern Talgo train which takes 16½ hours (US$14/31/37 third/second/first class). There's also a weekly train **from Bishkek** (Kyrgyzstan) to Tashkent, passing through Kazakhstan (20hrs 40min; US$55/83/160 third/second/first class one-way); it actually starts from Balykchy (formerly Rybachye), a resort on Lake Issyk-Kul. From Tashkent, weekly trains also run to Ekaterinburg, Novosibirsk and Ufa in Russia.

The train timetable for the whole Russian rail network (including central Asia) is online at **w** poezda.net. The Uzbek Railways site, parts of which are in English, is **w** uzrailpass.uz. *The Man in Seat 61* (**w** seat61.com/silkroute.htm) also has detailed information, including personal reports, about train travel in the former USSR.

If you are coming to Uzbekistan **from China**, it is possible to take the train line from Urumqi to Almaty, and change there for Tashkent. We have not personally taken this route, but the intel from *Caravanistan* (**w** caravanistan.com) and *The Man in Seat 61* is that the Urumqi–Almaty train goes twice a week, and costs US$130. It is, however, pretty slow, taking 33 hours; the bus is 10 hours faster. At the far western end of Uzbekistan, you can cross from Kazakhstan with the daily train between Kungrad and Beyneu that takes 12 hours.

If you love the romance of train travel but the thought of having to deal with all the bureaucracy and then slumming it onboard fills you with dread, there is another option. Voyages Jules Verne (page 45) and Cox & Kings (page 44) among others can book you on to the Orient Silk Road Express, a private train with creature comforts to rival those of the Orient Express, which does Silk Road tours. An 11-night journey with Cox & Kings, stopping at Tashkent, Shakhrisabz, Bukhara, Khiva and Samarkand, starts at £3,445.

BY ROAD Personally, we prefer to reach Uzbekistan overland, not because customs and immigration make it a particularly easy or pleasant experience, but because of the freedom having your own transport gives you once you finally make it inside. For information on road safety in Uzbekistan, see page 59.

If you are bringing your own vehicle into Uzbekistan (regardless of the entry point) you will have to declare it on the usual customs form, plus fill in additional paperwork to be entered on to the computer system. If you're entering in a vehicle with a Tajik registration plate, see the box on page 53. Theoretically at least, you will not be allowed to leave the country unless you take the vehicle with you. You may be told that right-hand-drive vehicles cannot enter Uzbekistan; this is not true so hold your ground. Expect to have the vehicle thoroughly inspected, sluiced with disinfectant, and to have all of its contents (sometimes right down to the jack and spare wheel) passed through the X-ray machine.

The information given here was correct at the time of going to print, and more detailed information about each border, including its times of operation, is given in *Part 2* of the guide. Be aware that border crossings open and close regularly, often with little warning, and some crossings are open only to locals and not to foreigners. The most up-to-date and accurate source of information about border crossings is available from *Caravanistan* (**w** caravanistan.com). Embassies and local tour operators (page 96) may also be able to help.

From Afghanistan
Reaching Uzbekistan from **Afghanistan** tends to be fairly straightforward as diplomatic relations between the two countries are generally good. The main border crossing is at **Hairatan** between Mazar-i Sharif and Termez. Theoretically, the border is open 24/7, but you may have to wait if the relevant official is at dinner or sleeping. You'll have to walk over the Friendship Bridge (about 1km) then, once through Afghan immigration, shared taxis to Mazar take an hour and cost US$4 per person.

From Kazakhstan
There are several crossing points between **Kazakhstan** and Uzbekistan. The main crossing at **Chernayevka and Jibel Joly** (between Shymkent and Tashkent) is open 24/7, but there are often long queues. Cash can be exchanged on either side of the border. For some years you could not cross this border in your own, foreign vehicle, but it is now possible. There are quieter, alternative crossings (⊕ daylight hrs) nearby, between Kaplanbek and Saryagash and Serke and Turkistan.

We have also used the **Konysbayeva** (also known as Yalama) crossing (⊕ 24/7) north of Chinaz, which is considerably faster but only usable if you have your own transport in Uzbekistan. There are shared taxis on the Kazakh side only.

At the far western end of Uzbekistan, you can cross from Kazakhstan at **Tajen** on the (fairly poor) Beyneu–Kungrad road (⊕ daylight hrs); shared taxis wait on both sides.

Unusually, the Tashkent–Shymkent route is one where **public transport** works well – there's an hourly bus (⊕ 07.00–20.00; US$5) between Shymkent's old bus station on Volodarskogo (☏ +7 707 475 8660) and the Tashkent bus station, which is fast-tracked through the border crossing and takes 4 to 5 hours. There are taxis too (US$20 for the entire taxi, or US$5 per seat), and you can also take shared taxis or minibuses to the border and cross on foot, avoiding the vehicle queues. On the Uzbek side you have to walk about 400m to find taxis and *marshrutkas* (which run to and from the Univermag supermarket on Amir Timur in Yunusobod, in northern Tashkent).

From Kyrgyzstan
Diplomatic relations with **Kyrgyzstan** are now stable and border crossings are straightforward. The main border post (⊕ 24/7) is at **Dostyk** on the road between Osh and Andijan. There can be long queues, but Westerners generally get fast-tracked. You can change money on the Kyrgyz side, and public transport and shared taxis are available on both sides, including *marshrutka* 107 to the bazaar in Osh.

Potentially more useful due to being closer to both Tashkent and Bishkek is the **Uch-Kurgan** crossing (⊕ 08.00–20.00 daily), east of Namangan. This has reopened to foreigners, though there's a 10-minute walk between the two border posts. On the Uzbek side there are minibuses to Uch-Kurgan Town and taxi drivers who will change dollars and take you to Uch-Kurgan or Namangan; on the Kyrgyz side there's plenty of public transport heading to either Bishkek or Osh.

Note that minibuses and trains (see opposite) between Bishkek and Tashkent all pass through Kazakhstan, for which you may need a transit visa.

From Tajikistan Relations with Tajikistan have been a little erratic, but are now stable. The most useful crossing (although it was closed until 2018) is at **Penjikent**, between Samarkand and Dushanbe, which also gives access to the Fann Mountains for trekking. From the Kaftarkhona bus station on the east side of Samarkand you can get a *marshrutka* (1hr; US$0.60) or shared taxi (US$2.50 pp) to the border, or more often about 1km before it; on the Tajik side there are shared taxis to Penjikent and Dushanbe. You can change cash on the Uzbek side of the border, or in the town of Penjikent.

Heading south from Tashkent, the main crossing (⏰ 24/7) is at **Oybek**, between Chanak (on the road to Bekobod) and Bo'ston, from where you should continue to Khojand, make a sharp turn westwards to pass just south of Bekobod and then head south to Dushanbe; there's a crossing point at Bekobod which seems to be closed but would be far more direct if you found it open. There's a daily bus from the Olmazar bus station [88 A7] in Tashkent to Khojand (⏰ about 08.00; 5hrs; US$6), or you can go to Kuyluk Bazar and then to the border at Oybek by bus (2hrs; US$0.70) or shared taxi (US$2 pp). On the Tajik side, take a shared taxi to Bo'ston then a taxi or minibus to Khojand. Uzbek customs used to be utterly paranoid, wanting to X-ray every last sock (we saw one elderly gentleman even having to remove his car bumper and mud flaps to put them through the machine) and allowing their (admittedly very cute) sniffer dog (a spaniel) to jump over everything (it got overly excited and peed on our picnic). It should be calmer now.

Continuing east from Khojand, there's a crossing back into Uzbekistan, **between Konibodom and Beshariq** – this provides a low-level route between Tashkent and the Fergana Valley that's useful when the Kamchik Pass is closed by snow. From Khojand's bus station *marshrutkas* take an hour to Konibodom, where *marshrutka* 114 continues to the border post; on the Uzbek side there may or may not be taxis (try to arrange one in advance – the *marshrutka* driver may be able to call ahead) for Beshariq, from where buses and shared taxis go to Kokand.

The **Tursunzoda–Denau** crossing (⏰ 24/7) is the closest to Dushanbe. It is well served by minibuses and taxis running in both directions, and providing you're not stuck behind a busload of returning migrant workers carrying all their worldly possessions, processing is fairly quick, although it seems the Uzbek border guards can be obsessive about checking for illegal medications. It takes about an hour by shared taxi from Dushanbe to Tursunzoda (US$15) and another 10 minutes to the border from where it's 40km to Denau (45min; US$2 by shared taxi). A taxi directly to or from Samarkand will cost US$50–80 (7–8hrs).

By the Amu Darya at the southern end of the Uzbek–Tajik border, the **Gulbahor** crossing is closest to Termez. From Shahrtuz, shared taxis take an hour to the border, where you'll need to take a shuttle between the posts; on the Uzbek side minibuses to Termez should charge US$1.25.

From Turkmenistan Crossing to or from **Turkmenistan** takes around 2 hours; if you're leaving Uzbekistan you must pay a US$14 entry tax (payable in US dollars only) when you arrive in Turkmenistan. Most foreigners use the Farap–Alat crossing between Turkmenabat and Bukhara, though the Shavat–Dashoguz border near Khiva and the Hojali–Konya-Urgench crossing near Nukus are also well used. **Farap–Alat** is open from 08.30 to 20.00, with a break from 12.30 to 13.30. A taxi ride from Farap–Alat to Bukhara takes around 3 hours and should cost you no more than US$25. Shared taxis and minibuses are, of course, much cheaper. An overnight train from Tashkent runs as far as the town of Alat, a short drive north. You need to take a shuttle (US$0.15) for the last kilometre to the Uzbek post, then walk 1.5km

A NOTE ON TAJIK VEHICLES

That vehicles with Tajik registration plates cannot enter Uzbekistan, and those with Uzbek plates must pay import duty if they enter Tajikistan. This applies to taxis as well as private vehicles, so if you are travelling by taxi you should get dropped off at the border and pick up a second vehicle on the other side.

to the Turkmen post, then take another shuttle (US$1) to the end of the border zone, where taxis await, charging no more than US$5 to Turkmenabat. Entering Uzbekistan, you can buy vehicle insurance, and change money at very bad rates.

The **Shavat–Dashoguz** crossing (🕘 09.00–12.30 & 13.30–18.00), around 50km west of Urgench, can only be reached by taxi (around US$15 from Khiva) and requires a shuttle (US$1) between the border posts; on the Turkmen side, there are shared taxis to Dashoguz (US$1).

The **Hojayli to Konya-Urgench** crossing (🕘 09.00–12.30 & 13.30–18.00), just southwest of Nukus, has been rebuilt and no longer requires a shuttle across no-man's-land; shared taxis wait on both sides (US$10 to Nukus; US$1 to Konya-Urgench).

HEALTH *With Dr Felicity Nicholson*

BEFORE YOU GO Comprehensive **travel insurance** should be high on your list when you contemplate travelling to Uzbekistan. Choose a policy that includes medical evacuation (medevac) and make sure you fully understand any restrictions: it is not uncommon for insurance companies to exclude certain activities (including mountaineering and skiing) from cover. Leave a copy of the policy documents at home with someone you trust and keep a copy of it, along with the emergency-contact number on you at all times.

Your GP or a specialised travel clinic (page 54) will be able to check your immunisation status and advise you on any additional **inoculations** you might need. It is wise to be up to date on **tetanus**, **polio** and **diphtheria** (now given as an all-in-one vaccine, Revaxis, that lasts for ten years), and **hepatitis A**.

Hepatitis A vaccine (Havrix Monodose or Avaxim) comprises two injections given about a year apart, though you will have cover from the time of the first injection. The course typically costs £100 and, once completed, gives you protection for 25 years. The vaccine is sometimes available on the NHS. **Hepatitis B vaccination** should be considered for longer trips (one month or more) and by those working in a medical setting or with children for any length of time. The vaccine schedule comprises three doses taken over a six-month period, but for those aged 16 or over it can be given over a period of 21 days if time is short. The rapid course needs to be boosted after a year. A combined hepatitis A and B vaccine, 'Twinrix', is available, though at least three doses are needed for it to be fully effective. For those under 16, the minimum time is over eight weeks.

The newer injectable **typhoid vaccines** (eg: Typhim Vi) last for three years and are about 75% effective. Oral capsules (such as Vivotif) may also be available for those aged six and over. Three capsules taken over five days last for approximately three years but may be less effective than the injectable version if they are not taken correctly owing to poor absorption. Typhoid vaccines are particularly advised for those travelling in rural areas and when there may be difficulty in ensuring safe water supplies and food.

Rabies is prevalent throughout Uzbekistan and vaccination is highly recommended for those travelling more than 24 hours from medical help or for those who will be coming into contact with animals as there is unlikely to be treatment available within the country.

Crimean Congo haemorrhagic fever is a viral illness spread by ticks. The animal reservoirs are cattle, sheep and goats or through contact with infected animal blood. The peak season is during the summer months and mortality can be high. That said, the risk for most travellers is low, although it is higher for those in contact with animals or for those at increased risk of tick bites.

Precautions against **tick bites** should be taken by inspecting the skin daily for ticks. Ticks should ideally be removed complete, and as soon as possible, to reduce the chance of infection. You can use special tick tweezers, which can be bought in good travel shops, or failing this with your finger nails, grasping the tick as close to your body as possible, and pulling it away steadily and firmly at right angles to your skin without jerking or twisting. Irritants (eg: Olbas oil) or lit cigarettes are to be discouraged since they can cause the ticks to regurgitate and therefore increase the risk of disease. Once the tick is removed, if possible douse the wound with alcohol (any spirit will do), soap and water, or iodine. If you are travelling with small children, remember to check their heads, and particularly behind the ears, for ticks. Spreading redness around the bite and/or fever and/or aching joints after a tick bite imply that you have an infection that requires antibiotic treatment. In this case seek medical advice.

The risk of **malaria** is low in Uzbekistan, so there is no need to take antimalarials.

TRAVEL CLINICS AND HEALTH INFORMATION A full list of current travel clinic websites worldwide is available on w istm.org. For other journey preparation information, consult w travelhealthpro.org.uk (UK) or w wwwnc.cdc.gov/travel (US). Information about various medications may be found on w netdoctor.co.uk/travel. All advice found online should be used in conjunction with expert advice received prior to or during travel.

PERSONAL FIRST-AID KIT

While pharmacies in Uzbekistan are numerous, especially in the main cities, and some are well equipped, you should still pack a **first-aid kit** (a comprehensive kit is essential for trekkers and others visiting remote areas) and any prescription medicines you require. A minimal kit should contain:

- A good drying antiseptic, eg: iodine or potassium permanganate
- A few small dressings (plasters)
- Suncream
- Insect repellent, ideally containing around 50% DEET
- Aspirin or paracetamol
- Imodium and rehydration salts
- Ciprofloxacin or norfloxacin (for severe diarrhoea)
- A pair of fine-pointed tweezers (to remove thorns, splinters, ticks, etc)
- Alcohol-based hand sanitiser or bar of soap in plastic box
- Clingfilm or condoms for covering burns (for anyone with a camping stove)
- A small needle and syringe kit

Dr Felicity Nicholson

Any prolonged immobility, including travel by land or air, can result in deep-vein thrombosis (DVT) with the risk of embolus to the lungs. Certain factors can increase the risk, these include:

- History of DVT or pulmonary embolism
- Recent surgery to pelvic region or legs
- Cancer
- Stroke
- Heart disease
- Inherited tendency to clot (thrombophilia)
- Obesity
- Pregnancy
- Hormone therapy
- Older age
- Being over 1.83m (6ft) or under 1.52m (5ft)

A DVT causes painful swelling and redness of the calf or sometimes the thigh. It is only dangerous if a clot travels to the lungs (pulmonary embolus). Symptoms of a pulmonary embolus – which commonly start three to ten days after a long flight – include chest pain, shortness of breath, and sometimes coughing up small amounts of blood. Anyone who thinks that they might have a DVT needs to see a doctor immediately.

PREVENTION OF DVT
- Wear loose, comfortable clothing
- Do anti-DVT exercises and move around when possible
- Drink plenty of fluids during the flight
- Avoid taking sleeping pills unless you are able to lie flat
- Avoid excessive tea, coffee and alcohol
- Consider wearing flight socks or support stockings, widely available from pharmacies

If you think you are at increased risk of a clot, ask your doctor if it is safe to travel.

IN UZBEKISTAN The medical system in Uzbekistan is seriously overstretched. The quality of medical training has fallen since the end of the USSR era: many doctors have left to find work abroad, hospitals are rundown and equipment is out of date. Outside the major cities there is also a shortage of drugs and other medical supplies. If you are ill or have an accident, you will be able to receive emergency treatment at one of the good private **hospitals** in Tashkent or at a more basic regional hospital, but will then require medevac to a country with more developed medical infrastructure for ongoing care, either in Europe or India. British citizens should be aware that the reciprocal health-care agreement between the UK and Uzbekistan ended in 2016.

Every town in Uzbekistan has countless **pharmacies** (marked 'Apteka' or 'Darikhana'), selling a range of generic drugs. You do not need a prescription to purchase medication but should read the instructions carefully (or get someone to explain them to you).

It's illegal to bring codeine, Valium, Xanax and Temazepam into Uzbekistan – nowadays customs officers are unlikely to look too hard, but it's best to bring the prescriptions for your medicines and to keep them in their original packaging.

A quarter of the adult population **smokes** tobacco, with limited restrictions on smoking in public places introduced in 2016 (some designated spaces are now smoke-free) and tobacco taxes rising sharply. Restaurants and bars can still be unpleasant for non-smokers.

POTENTIAL MEDICAL PROBLEMS

Altitude sickness Acute mountain sickness can affect everyone – even really fit people – during a rapid ascent, and staying above 2,500m (8,203ft) for more than 12 hours. In the mountainous east of Uzbekistan and, in particular, in the upper reaches of the Pskem and Gissar mountain ranges, where there are a number of peaks over 4,000m, it is important for climbers to be aware of the possibility of altitude sickness. It is caused by acute exposure to low partial pressure of oxygen: in layman's terms this means that the amount of available oxygen decreases as you ascend, to the point that the body has insufficient oxygen in the blood to continue functioning normally. Symptoms of mild altitude sickness include headaches, nausea, anorexia, insomnia and confusion and can be minimised by taking time to acclimatise to the altitude. Many people recommend taking acetazolamide (Diamox) prophylactically to assist in acclimatising. Discuss this with your doctor or other health-care professional before you go. Even if you are taking Diamox, developing any symptoms which might be AMS means that you should descend at least 500m as soon as possible.

More serious forms of mountain sickness include **pulmonary oedema**, also known as HAPE (fluid on the lungs) and **cerebral oedema**, also known as HACE (swelling of the brain). The first is characterised by a shortness of breath, dry cough and fever and the latter by a persistent headache, unsteady gait, confusion, delirium and loss of consciousness. These are both serious medical emergencies and need immediate evacuation and treatment by qualified professionals.

A useful free download on altitude sickness can be found at w medex.org.uk.

Travellers' diarrhoea Diarrhoeal diseases and other gastrointestinal infections are fairly common, and perhaps half of all visitors will suffer in this way. Travellers' diarrhoea, as well as more serious conditions such as typhoid, comes from getting bacteria in your mouth. To avoid getting ill you should ensure that you observe good hygiene practices, such as regular hand washing, using bottled or purified water (including for cleaning teeth), and avoiding foods of doubtful provenance. Many travellers use the following maxim to remind them what is safe:

PEEL IT, BOIL IT, COOK IT OR FORGET IT

This means that fruit you have washed and peeled yourself and hot foods should be safe, but raw foods, cold cooked foods, salads, ice cream and ice are all risky, and foods kept lukewarm in hotel buffets often harbour numerous bugs. That said, plenty of travellers and expatriates enjoy fruit and vegetables, so do keep a sense of perspective: food served in a fairly decent hotel in a large town or a place regularly frequented by expatriates is likely to be safe.

If you are struck down with diarrhoea in spite of your precautions, remember that dehydration is your greatest concern. Drink lots of clear fluids. Sachets of oral rehydration salts give the perfect biochemical mix to replace all fluids you are losing. If you don't have rehydration salts, or can't stand the taste, any dilute

Although Uzbekistan is not an area with a high risk of malaria, mosquitoes can carry other diseases and their bites are, in any case, uncomfortable. As the sun is going down, don long clothes and apply repellent on any exposed flesh. Pack a DEET-based insect repellent (roll-ons or stick are the least messy preparations for travelling). Repellents should contain between 50% and 55% DEET and can be used by children and pregnant women. Insect coils and fans reduce rather than eliminate bites. Travel clinics usually sell a good range of nets, treatment kits and repellents.

Mosquitoes and many other insects are attracted to light. If you are camping, never put a lamp near the opening of your tent, or you will have a swarm of biters waiting to join you when you retire. In hotel rooms, be aware that the longer your light is on, the greater the number of insects will be sharing your accommodation.

mixture of sugar and salt in water will do you good: try Coke or orange squash with a three-finger pinch of salt added to each glass (if you are salt-depleted you won't taste it). Or add eight level teaspoons of sugar (18g) and one level teaspoon of salt (3g) to one litre (five cups) of safe water. A squeeze of lemon or orange juice improves the taste and adds potassium, which is also lost in diarrhoea. Drink two large glasses after every bowel action, and more if you are thirsty. These solutions are still absorbed well if you are vomiting, but you will need to take sips at a time. If you are not eating, you need to drink three litres a day plus whatever is pouring into the toilet. If you feel like eating, take a bland, high-carbohydrate diet. Plain rice, dry bread or digestive biscuits are ideal.

If the diarrhoea is bad, you are passing blood or slime or you have a fever, you will probably need antibiotics in addition to fluid replacement. Consult a doctor as soon as possible. A dose of norfloxacin or ciprofloxacin repeated twice a day until better may be appropriate (if you are planning to take an antibiotic with you, note that both norfloxacin and ciprofloxacin are available only on prescription in the UK).

Prickly heat Uzbekistan can become exceptionally hot in summer: temperatures above 45°C are common. A fine pimply rash on the chest or forearms is likely to be heat rash; it is caused by sweat becoming trapped beneath the skin and causing a histamine reaction. Cool showers, dabbing dry, and talc will help. Treat the problem by wearing only loose, 100%-cotton clothes and sleeping naked under a fan. An antihistamine tablet may help reduce the itching, as will hydrocortisone cream or Sudocrem.

Sunstroke and dehydration The sun in Uzbekistan can be very harsh, even in the mountains where the lower temperatures may suggest otherwise. Sunstroke and dehydration are serious risks.

Wearing a hat, long loose sleeves and sunscreen helps to avoid sunburn. Prolonged unprotected exposure can result in heatstroke, which is potentially fatal. Stay out of the sun between noon and 15.00.

In the heat you sweat more, so dehydration is likely. Don't rely on feeling thirsty to tell you to drink – if your urine is anything other than colourless then you aren't drinking enough. Carry bottled water with you at all times and make sure you stop to drink it.

Practical Information   HEALTH

2

Rabies Rabies can be carried by all warm-blooded mammals and the disease is transmitted to humans through contact with an infected animal's saliva. If you are bitten, scratched or simply licked, you must assume that the animal has rabies. Scrub the area with soap under a running tap for around 10 to 15 minutes or while pouring water from a bottle, then pour on antiseptic (or alcohol if none is available). This helps stop the rabies virus entering the body and will guard against wound infections, including tetanus.

Uzbekistan is classified as a high-risk rabies country. Vaccination before travel is strongly recommended as there is almost certainly going to be a shortage of the specific post-exposure treatment in the country itself. If you have not had a course of pre-exposure vaccine, then you are likely to require a blood product Rabies Immunoglobulin (RIG) and definitely four doses of vaccine, given over 21 days. The RIG and first dose of vaccine should be given as soon as possible and ideally within the first 24 hours. RIG is not usually available at the time of writing in Uzbekistan and there have been some problems with sourcing rabies vaccine, too. If neither of those products is available, evacuation would be the only recourse. Having three doses of the vaccine before travel over a minimum of 21 days (it can be compressed over seven days if time is short, but requires an extra booster after a year) simplifies the post-exposure treatment by removing the need for RIG and reducing the post-exposure treatment to two doses of vaccine given three days apart. While evacuation may still be necessary, it is less of an emergency. Three doses of vaccine cost around £180 in the UK and last for at least five years, unless you are planning to work as a vet abroad when boosters are recommended annually. Without the correct treatment for rabies following exposure the mortality is almost 100%.

Tetanus Tetanus is caused by the *Clostridium tetani* bacterium and though it can accumulate on a variety of surfaces, it is most commonly associated with rusty objects such as nails. Cutting yourself or otherwise puncturing the skin brings the bacteria inside the body, where it will thrive. Clean any cuts thoroughly with a strong antiseptic.

Immunisation against tetanus gives good protection for ten years, and it is common practice to give a booster injection to any patient with a puncture wound. Symptoms of tetanus may include lockjaw, spasms in any part of the body, excessive sweating, drooling and incontinence and the disease results in death if left untreated. Mild cases of tetanus will be treated with the antibiotic metronidazole and tetanus immunoglobulin while more severe cases will require admission to intensive care, tetanus immunoglobulin injected into the spinal cord, a tracheotomy and mechanical ventilation, intravenous magnesium and diazepam.

SAFETY

The UK's Foreign and Commonwealth Office (FCO) generally considers Uzbekistan to be a safe place for foreigners to travel. They regularly update their travel guidance, and the latest advice for Uzbekistan is available online at w fco.gov.uk.

The FCO advises caution when **travelling to border areas**, in particular the border between Uzbekistan and Afghanistan, as there is a threat of land mines. These regions can also be flashpoints for inter-ethnic violence, as was seen in the Fergana Valley in 2010. Such violence is not typically targeted at tourists, but there is a risk of being caught up in the upheaval.

There is also an underlying threat from **terrorism**. Attacks could be indiscriminate, including in places visited by tourists. Security was increased at airports and railway and metro stations as a result of the bombing at Moscow Airport in January 2011, with an increased police presence and the introduction of X-ray machines in the country's main railway stations. It is, however, now legal to take photos of the Tashkent metro.

Some visitors have been victims of **petty crime**, particularly mugging and pickpocketing, and many also used to experience low-level **corruption** from traffic police and other officials. This has pretty much ended, but if someone tries it on, ask for a receipt and don't hand over documents or cash on the street. Ask to be taken to the police station instead. In fact, there are many **police** visible across the country, including the Tourist Police who are helpful and may speak some English. Their job title is in English on their uniforms, making them easily identifiable.

Uzbekistan is seismically active, and there is therefore a risk of **earthquakes**. On 20 July 2011 an earthquake measuring 6.2 on the Richter scale hit Batken, just across the Uzbek border with Kyrgyzstan, and tremors were felt in Tashkent. A number of deaths and injuries were reported. This was the country's most recent serious quake, although there have, of course, been tremors.

ROAD SAFETY Driving standards in Uzbekistan are generally poor, and the motorists in Tashkent can be remarkably boorish. The wide variety of vehicles on the roads, from decrepit Soviet-era makes to large modern 4x4s, makes for traffic travelling at different speeds. Overtaking on the inside and illegal U-turns are among many common infringements in the cities. The poor state of repair of many roads, with pot-holes and often inadequate or non-existent street lighting, adds to the difficulties. In rural areas, animals and pedestrians wandering into the road present a considerable risk.

If you are **driving** in Uzbekistan you will need to be careful and cautious, always wear a seat belt and never drink and drive. Try to avoid driving outside cities after dark as roads are poorly lit and other vehicles may not have working lights. Bad driving also creates a risk to pedestrians.

When **on foot**, you should avoid the local practice of crossing busy roads by walking out to the centre and waiting for a gap in the oncoming traffic, even if this means taking a detour to cross at the next set of traffic lights. Do not expect cars to stop for you, even if you are on a zebra crossing.

WOMEN TRAVELLERS Uzbekistan is generally a safe country for women to travel in, and there are no specific legal or cultural restrictions imposed on women (either locals or foreigners). The social conditions of women improved significantly during the Soviet period, and the enrolment of women in education and in the workplace remains high. Gender roles remain traditional but relaxed.

Women should, however, exercise the usual **personal safety precautions**. Particular caution should be taken when hailing taxis: in Tashkent phoning for a cab, or getting the establishment you are in to do this for you is probably a safer option. Unaccompanied women may receive unwanted attention in bars and clubs, but this is usually deflected with a few terse words. If the harassment continues, alert the management or leave the premises and find a more pleasant alternative. Try to avoid physical confrontation, as alcohol-fuelled violence and being tailed home are not uncommon. Domestic violence is high in Uzbekistan, as it is across central Asia. There have been suspected cases where 'date rape' drugs have been used; keep a close eye on your drink, and do not accept drinks from strangers.

You should dress modestly, especially in conservative rural areas and in the Fergana Valley, where religious sentiments often run high.

Practical Information SAFETY

2

59

LGBT TRAVELLERS Homosexuality is illegal in Uzbekistan and Article 120 of the country's penal code punishes voluntary sexual intercourse between two men with up to three years in prison. Sexual intercourse between two women is not mentioned in the code.

Many people in Uzbekistan are deeply conservative, especially when it comes to the issue of sexuality, and homosexuality is still often seen as a mental illness (a hangover from the Soviet period). Muhammad Salih, leader of the People's Movement of Uzbekistan, said publicly in 2012: 'I support a civilised way of isolating gays and other sick members of society so that they could not infect healthy people with their disease.' Sadly, his views are widely shared. Homosexuals in Uzbekistan regularly experience harassment, including from the police, who heavily monitor gay-friendly establishments, often forcing them to close. Police detention and the threat of prosecution are regularly reported.

If you are travelling with a same-sex partner you should refrain from public displays of affection and be exceptionally cautious when discussing your relationship with others: it is often simplest to allow others to assume you are simply travelling with a friend. Double rooms frequently have twin beds, so asking for one room is unlikely to raise eyebrows in any case.

TRAVELLING WITH A DISABILITY Travellers with disabilities will experience difficulty travelling in Uzbekistan. Public transport is rarely able to carry wheelchairs, few buildings have disabled access, and streets are littered with trip hazards such as broken paving, uncovered manholes and utility pipes. Hotel rooms are often spread over multiple floors without lifts and assistance from staff is not guaranteed. If you have a disability and are travelling to Uzbekistan, you would be advised to travel with a companion who can help you when the country's infrastructure and customer service fall short.

TRAVELLING WITH CHILDREN This is relatively easy given Uzbeks' focus on family life. Children are welcomed in restaurants and shops, but you may have difficulty manoeuvring pushchairs in and out of buildings and along broken pavements. Nappies, baby food and other similar items are available in supermarkets and larger stores, but you are unlikely to find European brands. In 2008, adulterated baby-milk powder, produced in China, killed six infants there and led many parents in Uzbekistan to choose Russian- or European-made brands instead; this is still seen as a safer choice.

INFORMATION ON TRAVELLING WITH A DISABILITY

The UK's **gov.uk** website (w gov.uk/guidance/foreign-travel-for-disabled-people) provides general advice and practical information for travellers with disabilities preparing for overseas travel. **Accessible Journeys** (w disabilitytravel.com) is a comprehensive US site written by wheelchair users who have been researching wheelchair-accessible travel full-time since 1985. There are many tips and useful contacts (including lists of travel agents on request) for slow walkers, wheelchair travellers and their families, plus informative articles, including pieces on disabled travelling worldwide. The company also organises group tours. **Global Access News** (w globalaccessnews.com/index.htm) provides general travel information, reviews and tips for travelling with a disability. The **Society for Accessible Travel and Hospitality** (w sath.org) also provides some general information.

Journeys by car and public transport are often long and uncomfortable, and food supplies erratic, which may deter families with younger children travelling beyond Tashkent and the main tourist sites. Ensure you stock up with plenty of snacks before leaving a town, and take plenty of entertainment options along for the ride.

WHAT TO TAKE

You may wish to consider the following, in addition to the usual holiday packing.

- **Plug adaptors** Sockets in Uzbekistan are the twin round pin, continental European type. The voltage is 220V.
- **A torch** Many parts of Uzbekistan, including city streets, are unlit at night, and pavements may conceal dangers such as uncovered manholes. Power cuts are not uncommon. If you are planning to camp, or use homestays in rural areas, you'll need a torch to navigate to the latrine at night.
- **Water purification tablets** Unless you want to be constantly buying water in plastic bottles, bring a litre bottle and chlorine or iodine tablets.
- **Mosquito repellent** Uzbekistan may not be a malarial country, but the swarms of mosquitoes you may encounter in summer among its lakes and forests can still damage your enjoyment of your holiday. Make sure you also pack **long-sleeved shirts** (you'll also need these for visiting conservative areas and religious places). For more information on avoiding insect bites, see the box on page 57.
- **Warm clothing** If you are planning a trip to Uzbekistan in the winter months (which in the north of the country means November to April), or plan to head up into the mountains or spend a night in the desert, you need to treat its cold temperatures with respect, with good warm clothing minimising areas of exposed skin. The locals often wrap themselves in fox or wolf furs; if you do not want to wear fur clothing, outdoor adventure shops are probably the best source of suitably warm garments. Dress in several layers, with particularly warm (and preferably wind- and waterproof) outer garments.
- **Good footwear** In winter, wear strong, rubber-soled boots, preferably lined with fleece. If you are trekking, good hiking boots are essential.
- **Flip-flops** You'll need these inside homestay accommodation (shoes are left at the front door in Uzbek homes). They also come in useful in less-than-savoury bathrooms.
- **Sheet sleeping bag** If you will be staying in bottom-range accommodation, a sleeping bag, of the kind used by youth hostellers, can help save you from unsavoury bedding.
- A **universal sink plug** is also worth packing.
- **Sun protection** Including good suncream, a lip salve and sunglasses (spare sets of any **prescription glasses** are also useful).
- **Toilet paper, wet wipes** and **hand sanitiser gel** are highly advisable and will make staying clean infinitely easier.
- **Dental floss** and a **needle**, a roll of **gaffer tape** and a packet of **cable ties** will enable you to fix almost anything while you're on the go.
- **Small gift items** related to your home country make ideal presents for hosts. Chocolates often melt, but photographs and souvenir items (think snow globes with castles or tea towels featuring cathedrals) go down a treat. Pictures of your home, family and friends are also popular.

2

Exactly what you need to pack for your trip to Uzbekistan will depend on the time of year that you are travelling, the duration of your trip, where you are going, and the types of activities you intend to undertake. On the assumption that you are travelling in high season (page 41) and will be moderately active, perhaps taking a day trek or spending a night in a yurt in addition to city sightseeing, the following items would stand you in good stead.

- Sturdy **walking boots** or shoes with a closed toe and a good grip on the sole
- **Natural fibre socks** that allow your feet to breathe
- Light-weight **trekking sandals**, again with a good rubber grip
- Crease-free, easy-dry **travel trousers** or capri pants (not shorts)
- Light, **long-sleeved cotton shirts**
- **Light sweater or jacket** for cooler evenings
- **Sun hat** with a brim that protects your neck as well as your face
- **Cotton scarf** or wrap
- **UV sunglasses** to protect your eyes from the intense sunlight

Although most hotels in Uzbekistan do offer a laundry service, there will be occasions when it is faster, easier and cheaper to hand wash a few things in the sink. You can get both dry and liquid travel wash, the former being lighter and less likely to spill.

MONEY AND BUDGETING

MONEY The unit of currency in Uzbekistan is the Uzbek som (UZS). It was first issued in 1993, and the current version in 1994. Notes are printed in denominations of 50, 100, 200, 500, 1,000, 5,000, 10,000, 50,000 and 100,000 som, though you are unlikely to see the smaller denominations owing to their virtual worthlessness. Change, in fact, may be given in small sweets or packets of matches, and any coins you receive are good only as souvenirs. Prices are commonly given in US dollars even though the som is fairly stable at the moment; shopkeepers will often accept dollars at a fair exchange rate (clean, uncreased bills of US$20 upwards are best). We have quoted prices in US dollars throughout this guide.

What to carry The standard advice for travellers in the developing world used to be to carry most of their money in travellers' cheques. With the worldwide spread of ATMs, that is no longer the case, and in Uzbekistan it is almost impossible to change travellers' cheques outside the largest banks in Tashkent. Even there you'll get an unfavourable rate.

You will need to carry most of your money in **cash**. It is wise to divide your money between multiple locations about your person and carry a dummy wallet with just a few dollars and some old supermarket loyalty cards as a decoy for pickpockets and anyone attempting to extract a bribe.

Uzbekistan is very much a cash economy and there are few **ATMs**, and fewer outside Tashkent, probably due to the logistical challenge of restocking them after every other transaction. Those that do exist are often inside banks or in the lobbies of larger hotels. Asaka Bank ATMs work with Mastercard and Maestro cards (on the Cirrus network) and dispense US dollars. Most others (especially Kapitalbank, the most common) work with Visa (the Plus network) and dispense Uzbek soms. Sometimes the machines run out of cash, and they may also stop working for a few minutes each day when the connection to the issuing bank's network is down.

If you run out of cash in a smaller town, banks will often advance you cash on a Visa or Mastercard, or you can receive Western Union, MoneyGram and other money transfers. If you are stuck, look for a branch of the National Bank of Uzbekistan as they most often perform this service.

Changing money Banks are now more or less everywhere in Uzbekistan and, providing they have sufficient cash behind the counter, all of them will change dollars, euros and roubles. If you need to change less-common currencies (including sterling and the Swiss franc), you will need to take them to a branch of the National Bank of Uzbekistan. You're unlikely to have the time or inclination to count every note, but you'll swiftly become adept at calculating how many inches of som there are to US$100; fast, automatic money-counters are widespread and reliable.

Uzbekistan's banks are less fussy than others in the region, but you should keep your foreign notes clean, unfolded and uncreased. If there are any marks on the notes, including ink stamps from being counted in a bank, they may be rejected. High-denomination bills are preferred, as are US dollars printed since 2006.

For up-to-date exchange rates, visit w xe.com.

BUDGETING Uzbekistan is, on the whole, a cheap country in which to travel. Yes, it is possible in Tashkent to spend upwards of US$500 a night in a hotel, eat in expensive restaurants, and hire a car and driver to escort you to every last lamppost, but fortunately this is a lifestyle choice only, and in many parts of the country it would be an impossibility in any case as top-end facilities with top-end prices are simply not there.

In Tashkent it is possible to get a dormitory bed for US$10–15, a clean budget double room for US$40 and a mid-range room with breakfast included will set you back US$60–80. Upwards of US$200 a night is not uncommon for the top-end hotels. The price of meals is similarly varied: café snacks start at around US$1.50, while a meal in a hotel restaurant costs about US$10, or double that with good wine.

Outside Tashkent your money will go noticeably further. This is particularly true out of the tourist season when room rates fall significantly. Other than accommodation, transport and meals will be your greatest expenditures. If you are travelling on a tight budget, you will survive on US$25 a day but this will restrict your sleeping options and require you to travel solely by public transport. A budget of US$50 would give you far greater flexibility.

Prices start rising dramatically when you make special arrangements. Car-and-driver hire is particularly expensive if you only plan to travel in one direction as you may end up paying for the driver's return journey, too. Guides, trekking guides and pack animals are reasonably cheap by international standards, but the costs quickly add up if you are trekking for a protracted period or are part of a very small group.

Museum and theatre tickets are an absolute steal in Uzbekistan, so even

WHAT DOES IT COST?	
1 litre petrol	US$0.53
½ litre beer	US$0.90–2
Postcard	US$1
Postcard stamp (international)	US$3
Loaf of bread	US$0.15
Mars bar	US$1

2

budget travellers should be able to enjoy plenty of culture and entertainment. You will rarely pay more than US$2 to visit a museum or cultural site, and seats at theatrical performances, including the opera and ballet, are typically between US$2 and US$10.

GETTING AROUND

Uzbekistan is a large country and, though road infrastructure between the main cities is steadily improving, travelling from A to B by road can still take up a significant proportion of your time. This is particularly true if you plan to travel from Tashkent to Khiva, Nukus or other sites in Karakalpakstan. If you are short on time, consider a domestic flight or overnight train journey. However you choose to travel, look out of the window and try to enjoy the views. It's all part of the big adventure.

BY AIR Uzbekistan Airways (w uzairways.com; page 49) has domestic flights connecting Tashkent with other major cities in Uzbekistan; Samarkand, Bukhara, Nukus and Urgench are served on a daily basis, while Andijan, Fergana, Namangan,

---

THE OPEN ROAD: MOTORCYCLING IN UZBEKISTAN   *Bryn Kewley*

You wake up in a tent, under a bridge or in a bush and think, 'Where shall I go today?' Mounting your steed, bags loaded behind you and only a map in front, all you have to do is choose. Overland travel by motorbike is quite possibly the most liberating form of travel: there's something about being able to reach out and touch what's around you.

Uzbekistan is, by regional standards, a relatively sedate place to bike, but head into the mountains or desert and it's definitely a more serious undertaking. What appear to be major roads on the map can still have large stretches of broken rock or dirt track. The seasons should also be taken into account as high passes are likely to be snowy (not much fun on four wheels, let alone on two) and riding conditions are often quite literally freezing. That said, the views along these routes are unsurpassed, with a rugged, harsh beauty and that tingling feeling of being on roads a stone's throw from Afghanistan should bring some warmth back to your toes.

If you think you are ready for the challenge, source a suitable bike and fly it (or, even better, ride it) to Uzbekistan. Look for something with long suspension, a front disc brake, a big front wheel and a rack or other way of carrying your kit, as keeping it on your back is far from advisable. Before you leave make sure you check the lights and horn (the louder the better), the front and back brakes (it's a long way down those precipices), the suspension (you're going to need it) and that the chain is in good condition with plenty of oil. Make sure the wheels are round (seriously) and the tyres have a good amount of tread left in them. If the bike looks too old, is making particularly odd noises or rattles on tarmac, find something better. Traffic is rare and mechanics are only to be found in big towns. There are more fulfilling things than finishing an epic journey with your bike in the back of a truck.

Before you leave ask yourself lots of questions. What's my fuel range? Do I know how to repair a puncture? How will I navigate? Do people know where I'm going and what time I'll check in with them? Do I have enough clothes to be warm and dry? Will I need a sleeping bag?

Tashkent to Nukus is only around 1,250km but can easily take a motorcyclist two, or even three, days to travel safely. En route you can be struck by anything from dust storms to a herd of camels. If that sort of thing excites you, get to it.

Navoi and Termez see between two and four flights weekly. All these flights take around an hour (1½hrs to Nukus or Urgench). Poor Karshi has just one return flight a week, as does the Samarkand–Nukus route. Fares are not high – from Tashkent it costs US$10 to fly one-way to Samarkand, or US$49 to Nukus.

BY RAIL High-speed trains make it very easy to travel from Tashkent to Samarkand, Bukhara and Khiva. Slower (but still perfectly decent) trains also run on the same routes, although buses, minibuses and shared taxis cost much the same and may be faster. For longer-distance journeys (from Tashkent to Nukus, Termez, Urgench and various other cities), flying is the fastest option (see opposite), but travelling by train is cheaper, more spacious and allows you to save on overnight accommodation. Journeys are listed here, with details covered in the cities' respective chapters and also on the Uzbekistan Railways' website (w uzrailpass.uz), where you will find an up-to-date **schedule** for the entire network and ticket prices, which are updated on a regular basis.

Uzbekistan's railway network has seen a lot of recent investment, especially on the main tourist axis from Tashkent to Samarkand, Bukhara and Khiva.

ESSENTIAL EQUIPMENT
Spare key
Puncture repair kit
Engine oil
Covers for baggage rack
Basic tools (spanners, pliers, screwdrivers)
Emergency food and water
Reliable map and compass (1:500,000 or less)

EXCEPTIONALLY USEFUL EQUIPMENT

Wire	Spare throttle and clutch cables
Duct tape	Spark plugs
WD40 and grease	Spare bulbs

CLOTHING

Helmet with visor, goggles or sunglasses (for dust)	Jeans (or similar) with over-trousers
Thick bike gloves	Sturdy walking boots or biker boots
Hardwearing jacket	Thermal layer
	Fleece jacket

The kit listed here is the absolute minimum for a short ride. Anyone wishing to go a long distance should read *The Adventure Motorcycling Handbook* by Chris Scott for practical information on bikes, preparation and maintenance as well as known trips and overland adventure stories. The website w horizonsunlimited.com is an unparalleled resource for up-to-date overland information, and w advrider.com gives plenty of inspiration.

Don't drive after dark, and keep it rubber-side down.

Bryn Kewley travelled with Sophie on her first trip across Uzbekistan, caught the overland bug, then started motorcycling all the way from the UK to Singapore.

The most useful train is the high-speed **Afrosiyob** service, which links Tashkent, Samarkand, Shakhrisabz, Bukhara and Khiva and is targeted at tourists, though locals make use of it as well. It is more expensive than the slower trains operating the same route (at the time of writing it was almost twice the price, although this keeps increasing), but makes a day trip to Samarkand possible. Train 762 leaves Tashkent daily at 07.30 for Samarkand and Bukhara; train 760 leaves at 08.00 for Samarkand, Karshi and Shakhrisabz and train 766 leaves at 18.50 for Samarkand and Bukhara. It takes just over 2 hours to reach Samarkand, just over 3 hours to reach Bukhara and 4½ hours to reach Shakhrisabz. Returns are at 04.55 and 15.48 from Bukhara; 06.37, 17.00 and 17.30 from Samarkand and 15.43 from Shakhrisabz. They are modern Spanish-built Talgo trains, clean and well maintained, and running at up to 250km/h.

Also useful (and cheaper) is the **Sharq service** (⊕ not Tue), with train 10 leaving Tashkent at 09.13 for Samarkand and Bukhara, returning (as train 9) at 15.50 from Bukhara and 17.20 from Samarkand, and various night trains from Tashkent via Samarkand to Termez, Bukhara, Urgench, Khiva and Nukus.

In 2016 a new line, incorporating a 19km tunnel beneath the Kamchik Pass, linked Tashkent directly with the Fergana Valley (rather than having to pass through Tajikistan) and allowed daily services to Andijan (rather than one a week), as well as overnight trains from western Uzbekistan. In 2018, a direct line opened between Bukhara and Urgench, and in December of that year a new branch opened from Urgench to Khiva – at present it's served only by an overnight train from Tashkent (via Samarkand and Bukhara; 16hrs in total) and a day train from Bukhara, but a high-speed Afrosiyob service from Tashkent should start within the lifetime of this edition.

Uzbekistan's trains generally have three **ticket classes**, known as Economy, Business and VIP on the Afrosiyob trains and Platskartny, Kupé and SV on the older, Soviet-style Sharq and overnight trains – these are hardly glamorous or fast but tend to keep more or less to the timetable. For more information on these ticket classes, see page 50.

Tickets are purchased from a Kassa outside the railway station, though local travel agents are usually able to assist if you lack the requisite language skills, time or patience. *Caravanistan* (w caravanistan.com) can also book tickets on certain routes and deliver them to your hotel. Online bookings for all trains (w eticket. uzrailway.uz) are possible from a couple of weeks ahead of travel, although you may get a 'server overloaded' message or some other bug. After payment a 14-digit electronic ticket is issued, which you have to take to a Kassa to be printed out. If you are going to travel long distance, pay the extra for a berth (first class) and be sure to take plenty of food and drink onboard with you as the options available on the train and at stations will be decidedly limited.

You should arrive at stations at least 20 minutes ahead of departure – there will be passport and ticket checks outside the station, X-ray and metal detector checks to enter the building, and then your ticket has to be stamped. Note that the main Tashkent station was being rebuilt at the time this guide went to print and all trains except the Afrosiyobs and international services were using Tashkent Yuzhniy (south) station. The Afrosiyobs were likely to move as well (see above).

BY ROAD Wherever you want to go in Uzbekistan, getting there is half the fun. Hitchhiking (see box, opposite) and riding around in the back of a truck are still distinct possibilities in remoter areas, but in general things are getting easier: the new multi-lane highway under construction between Bukhara and Khiva should be completed during the lifespan of this edition, greatly reducing driving times to

With thanks to our hitchhiking guru, Steve Dew-Jones (author of The Rule of Thumb*)*

It is never possible to recommend hitchhiking without a word of caution, due to the inherent risks involved, but I know from experience that it is both possible and a lot of fun, wherever you are in the world.

Uzbekistan is no exception, although – as with much of central Asia – the Western concept of hitchhiking does not exist, as the bulk of vehicles double up as taxis. As such, it is important to proceed with caution, both in terms of choosing which driver and vehicle you trust to brave the winding (and in some cases nausea-inducing) mountain roads, and clarifying whether you are willing to pay a small sum for the privilege.

Beyond this, the same rules and advice apply to Uzbekistan as to anywhere else in the world. Top tips include standing in a visible position (but not the middle of the road), making sure there is space for drivers to pull in on either side of where you are standing, and having a few words of the native language under your belt (20 words can get you a surprisingly long way; page 282) to ease with negotiations over direction and any monetary contribution you do (or do not) wish to make.

Patience, as ever, is a virtue when hitchhiking, and this is not helped by the noticeably decreased volume of traffic in remote areas. Try to make sure your driver takes you to a helpful spot, although this may be hard to communicate. Where possible, aim for petrol stations or main roads leading out of town (in the direction you wish to travel), and make sure you have a map.

the west of the country. It is, however, a big project and progress is slow. There's a distance marker every kilometre along the main highways, along with a reasonable number of road signs in Latin script.

However close your destination, you should allow plenty of time to get there. **Taxi** and **minibus** drivers may appear to be in a rush, but they're also the most likely to get flat tyres or to break down entirely. Snowfall and avalanches stop even the most determined of drivers in mountainous areas, and it's not uncommon for vehicles to run out of fuel. The journey may take a while, but you will get there eventually, *inshallah* (God willing). Bad roads and cramped buses can be physically very wearing, so make sure you factor in as much time as you can between long trips for recharging your batteries.

One thing to bear in mind when travelling by road is dust. Even on predominantly paved roads there is plenty of sand and grit. Keep a scarf or bandana handy to protect your nose and mouth and keep anything that might get damaged (specifically electronics) inside the vehicle with you, as any bags on the roof will look like they've been through a dust storm.

By bus, minibus and shared taxi For long-distance road journeys you have the choice of these modes of transport. Uzbekistan's buses fall into two categories: the relatively modern, usually Chinese-made **buses** that serve set, inner-city routes and take approximately as many passengers as they have seats, and the *marshrutka*: mostly overcrowded Damas minibuses built in Urgench. These minibuses, sadly, are by far the more common, and if you are travelling between smaller cities they'll be the most

Practical Information GETTING AROUND

2

Prices and durations of bus journeys are given first, followed by those for minibus journeys.

Bukhara–Urgench	US$9/US$10	9hrs/6hrs
Samarkand–Bukhara	US$5/US$5	8hrs/5hrs
Samarkand–Termez	US$8/US$8	10hrs/7hrs
Tashkent–Samarkand	US$5/US$5	7hrs/5½hrs
Tashkent–Bukhara	US$9/US$10	14hrs/10hrs
Tashkent–Urgench		
(for Khiva)	US$18/US$20	25hrs/18hrs
Urgench–Nukus	US$3/US$4	3hrs/2½hrs
Urgench–Khiva	US$0.30/US$0.50	1½hrs/1hr

frequent form of transport. You are not guaranteed a seat, and will likely spend much of your journey with someone else's shopping on your lap and their elbow in your face.

Buses and minibuses operate between all of the major cities and towns in Uzbekistan. As a rule of thumb, you will pay around US$0.50 per hour of bus travel, and US$0.70 per hour of minibus travel. The minibuses drive much faster, so the cost of a ticket to any destination tends to be roughly the same.

On intercity routes the most common solution is to **share a taxi** with strangers. Shared taxis normally complete a journey in half the time that it would take a bus, but fares are correspondingly higher. They usually wait close to markets and bus stations and will leave when all the seats are full. If you want to leave earlier, you can pay for the remaining seats. Try to get the front seat as you'll have the most leg room and avoid any sharp elbows.

Each city or town has a **bus station** or stand where the buses, minibuses and shared taxis congregate, often near the central market. In the case of larger cities, there may be more than one stand, with vehicles to different destinations departing from different places. Be sure to check the name of the correct bus station in the *Getting there and away* section of the relevant chapter.

By taxi Most towns have taxis. Drivers instantly mark up their fares for a foreigner, so be prepared to haggle. There are two types of taxi: professional taxis, which may even have a sign on the roof and can sometimes be summoned by calling a central taxi-dispatch office (around US$1 for 2km), and general motorists who are happy to pick up passengers and drop them at their destination for a few thousand som. In both cases you will need to agree a fare at the start of your journey and be prepared to stop and ask directions en route. Having a map and the name of any landmarks close to your destination will certainly help, as will writing down the address in Uzbek.

For longer drives it is often possible to hire a **car and driver** (who will not, as a rule, speak English). Again, you will need to confirm the price in advance, though remember the final price may depend on the distance driven. To give a rough indication, you can expect to pay US$60–70 a day for a week or US$70–80 a day for a few days. Ordinary taxi drivers may consent to being hired for several days, otherwise approach a local tour company (pages 46 and 96) or hotel.

Self-drive Having your own vehicle gives you the ultimate freedom to travel where you want, and we would thoroughly recommend it. The key to safe driving in Uzbekistan is to constantly look out for cars stopping suddenly to the right (as every car is potentially a taxi) and to the left, as they try to make a swift U-turn through a gap in the central barrier. Surprisingly perhaps, drivers also stop on the flashing green phase that precedes the amber and red lights and give way to traffic entering roundabouts (ie: there is priority to the right). They pass breathtakingly close to other vehicles, and you can assume they're all on their phones.

Officially, it is not permitted to bring a right-hand-drive vehicle into Uzbekistan, or to drive it on Uzbek roads, but we have done so on a number of occasions and had no problems. There is no fee for bringing in a foreign-registered vehicle temporarily (so stand your ground if you are asked for a bribe) and the third-party motor insurance which you may be offered is optional. If you're planning on bringing a Tajik vehicle into the country, see the box on page 53.

The only international **car-hire company** present in Uzbekistan is Sixt (from US$22/day; page 93), from whom you can hire ordinary vehicles and 4x4s.

Road surfaces vary greatly. Throughout this guide we have attempted to give a guide to the general quality, but local conditions can vary significantly, with a gravel surface suddenly giving way to a kilometre of deeply rutted tracks. A **4x4** is not essential for overlanding, but it certainly makes for a more comfortable ride on bad roads. In more remote areas, particularly in the mountains mud and landslips can be a challenge, especially in spring, while rocks, pot-holes and random obstacles can blow a tyre at any time of year. You will need the extra power to keep yourself from getting stuck. The Land Rover is still the vehicle of choice for most overlanders, but getting parts in Uzbekistan is nigh on impossible: you'll need to bring your own spares, or compromise and get a Toyota Hilux, which local mechanics will be more familiar with. If you do need spares, the best bet is to contact Sanar Motors in Tashkent [88 B7] (6 Borovsky; ⍀71 132 0353).

SELF-DRIVE CHECKS

- Drive a locally made Chevrolet if possible (commonly available to hire with Sixt; page 93): you won't stand out and if you break down, the parts and expertise to repair it are more likely to be available.
- If you have the option, get central-locking, electric windows and air conditioning: they give you greater control over what (and, indeed, who) comes into the vehicle with you.
- Make sure you know the rules of the road and have a good idea about where you are going. Tell someone you trust your route and your expected time of arrival.
- Carry your driving licence and any vehicle documentation with you at all times. Photocopies are useful for handing to police and other interested parties.
- Ensure there is a first-aid kit (see box, page 54), food and plenty of drinking water in the boot in case of emergencies.
- A mobile phone (or a satellite phone in remote locations) is essential in the event of an accident or a breakdown you can't fix by the side of the road.
- Check you have a spare tyre, jack, handle and wheel wrench. Spare oil and water, a tow rope, a jerry can of fuel and a shovel are also highly advisable.

Petrol (*benzin*) is sold by the litre and is usually available as 91 or 92 octane – 95 octane is much rarer. Diesel (80 octane) is significantly cheaper and has the added advantage that you can always siphon some off a truck (with the driver's permission) if you run low in the middle of nowhere. Along with fuel, carry as much water as possible, both for yourself and to cool your engine in case of overheating. Most local vehicles use gas (methane or propane), far cheaper than petrol or diesel but it doesn't last long – every journey over a couple of hours requires a fill up (when all passengers have to get out and wait at the petrol station's exit). There are now no shortages of fuel for cars (although lack of fuel for heating houses leads many to move from villages to city apartments for the winter), and petrol stations are fairly easy to come by.

You need to be well prepared and do your research beforehand (the encyclopaedic *Vehicle-dependent Expedition Guide* by Tom Sheppard and *The Adventure Motorcycling Handbook* by Chris Scott stand out) but Uzbekistan has some spectacular drives and some out-of-the-way destinations it would be a pity to miss out on just because of lack of your own transport.

Other essentials to carry are a comprehensive toolkit and manual for your vehicle, key spare parts and tyres (the locals often carry two) and a first-aid kit (see box, page 54). If you plan on doing any off-road driving either in the mountains or in the desert, sand mats or tracks and a tow rope are strongly recommended.

Last but not least, the **speed limits**. Uzbekistan has two basic speed limits: in built-up areas it is 50km/h and elsewhere it is 100km/h. There may not be signs to this effect, so use your own judgement and be aware that police often carry out speed checks with radar.

By bike

An increasing number of cyclists pass through Uzbekistan, some using the country as a warm-up exercise before pitting themselves against the challenges of the Pamir Highway in neighbouring Tajikistan. It is not unusual to see Lycra-clad foreigners sweating their way up long and lonely hills, and they inspire both curiosity and confusion in the local population. Cycling is rare in Tashkent, despite the high profile of the Tashkent Terror (see box, page 38), but people do use cheap bikes for short trips elsewhere in the country, so there are some limited repair possibilities, just ask locally. That said, replacement parts are not readily available and Uzbekistan's roads are hard on both cyclists and their bikes: if you require spares you'll likely have to wait for DHL to deliver whatever is needed from home.

MAPS

Uzbekistan has been fairly well mapped, first by the Soviets for military and geological purposes, and more recently thanks to the influx of information-hungry tourists, and online mapping and GPS are now available. If you are buying maps before you go, then Stanfords in London or Bristol has the most comprehensive selection; they also sell maps online at w stanfords.co.uk.

Our most-used country map is the 1:1,500,000 *Uzbekistan* published by the Russian company Roskartografia. It includes the country's road and rail networks (without the latest additions), and has larger-scale coverage of the Fergana Valley (1:750,000) and Tashkent (1:22,000). The map comes with a separate index of place names and notes on history and geography. Its only downside is that place names are written in Cyrillic. Another reasonable option, this time in English, is the slightly newer (2008) 1:1,700,000 *Uzbekistan Tourist Map* produced by the state-run Cartographiya. It's in full colour, illustrated around the edges with a few good photographs, and the reverse side has street plans of Tashkent (1:33,000) and Samarkand (1:14,000). You may also like ITMB's (International Travel Maps and Books) *Uzbekistan* (1:1,580,000), which is the most up to date of the three options listed here (2010); ITMB also publish *Uzbekistan, Kyrgyzstan and Tajikistan* (1:1,600,000).

City maps of the main tourist sites are easy to come by and are often given away for free at the larger hotels. The locally produced *Tashkent Pocket Guide* has a fold-out map useful for getting your bearings, and also a metro map.

The best **digital mapping** is by Yandex (**w** yandex.com/maps), the Russian equivalent of Google, although Google Maps (**w** maps.google.com) and OpenStreetMap (**w** openstreetmap.org) are also available. Serious hikers may also be interested in the old Soviet military maps of the area (at 1:200,000, 1:100,000 and 1:50,000), which can be downloaded for free at **w** loadmap.net.

ACCOMMODATION

Uzbekistan has hotels for all budgets, and types of accommodation range from large, Western-style hotels to converted madrasas (religious schools), and family-run guesthouses to desert yurt stays.

At the **top end** of the market (luxury and upmarket), Tashkent has hotels with marble bathrooms, quality restaurants and hot- and cold-running 'flunkies'. They typically fall into the four-star bracket, though the prices they charge might suggest otherwise.

Mid-range hotels are a mixed bag, with some charging excessive sums for fairly basic facilities. The Soviet-era hotels often fall into this bracket, and are generally to be given a wide berth, but there are also an increasing number of pleasant, affordable choices. The best options are in Bukhara, Khiva and Samarkand, where competition has led to an improvement in quality but kept prices low. The mid-range bracket also includes a small number of boutique or heritage hotels, where historic buildings have been restored and converted into atmospheric places to stay. In addition to an attractive exterior, you can expect your room and public spaces to have ornately plastered or hand-painted ceilings, antique or hand-crafted furniture, and colourful, locally produced textiles.

Uzbekistan has plenty of **budget** rooms. Family-run guesthouses (some now calling themselves hostels) are frequently the best option (and ideal for meeting other travellers); many of them offer beds in shared dorms as well as simple doubles. The room rate typically includes breakfast, and hosts may be able to arrange evening meals as well. Uzbekistan has a small number of homestays, all of which fall into the budget bracket, though in the accommodation listings we have typically not differentiated between these and guesthouses, as in the latter the family still tends to live on site and frequently will share meals with visitors. The purest homestays

ACCOMMODATION PRICE CODES

The price codes used in this guide indicate the approximate price of a standard double room, per night, excluding the cost of any booking fee.

Luxury	$$$$$	US$200+
Upmarket	$$$$	US$100–200
Mid-range	$$$	US$50–100
Budget	$$	US$20–50
Shoestring	$	<US$20

are the yurt stays around Aidarkul (page 217) where you will stay with a family in their traditional tent and see how they really live: tourists bring additional (and much-needed) income but host families do not lay on facilities over and above what the family already requires.

Shoestring options typically provide accommodation in dormitories; you may have a basic single bed or, more likely, a mattress and blankets on the floor. The bathrooms, as you might expect at this end of the market, are a little bit hit and miss, so prepare yourself for the occasional squat toilet and cold water in a jug.

Campsites are relatively uncommon in Uzbekistan and those informal sites that do exist are frequented almost entirely by foreigners. While it is permitted to camp in the national parks and in the deserts (for example at the camel camps), setting up a tent in other public places is generally frowned upon. If you wish to put up a tent on private land, you will need to ask the owner and will usually be expected to pay a few dollars for the privilege.

Note that many hotels in Uzbekistan, especially older, Soviet-built accommodation, offer a wide variety of room permutations and rates, so the rates given can only serve as a rough guide. The number of rooms has been listed where possible, though there are some instances where an establishment either could not or would not confirm the number of rooms on offer.

As a rule of thumb, you'll be expected to take your shoes off to enter guesthouses, homestays and hostels, but not hotels. Wi-Fi is generally available in the hotels and hostels listed throughout this guide, unless otherwise stated.

EATING AND DRINKING

Uzbek food is typically Turkic, dominated by mutton, noodles and bread, but with many Persian flavours added, such as saffron, pomegranate, pistachio, almond and dried fruit. It tastes wonderful, but it's worth mentioning that Uzbekistan suffers the world's highest rate of diet-linked death (892 per 100,000 people a year), due above all to high salt levels.

Uzbekistan's national dish is *plov* (also known as *osh*), an oily rice-based dish with pieces of meat, grated carrots, onions and, if you are particularly fortunate, roasted garlic and hard-boiled egg. It is typically only available at lunchtime, and is popular at weddings and other large celebrations when male chefs (*oshpaz*) cook huge quantities outdoors in giant dishes known as *kazans*. Local variations are proudly maintained: in Bukhara *plov* is cooked in three separate cauldrons and mixed only when it is served, in Fergana two specific types of *dezvira* rice are used, with hot pepper and a pinch of cumin, and in Khiva it was originally made in a

RESTAURANT PRICE CODES

The price codes used in this guide indicate the average price of a meat-based main dish, excluding vegetables and service charge. The price of a full meal is likely to be several times higher.

Expensive	$$$$$	US$4+
Above average	$$$$	US$2–4
Mid-range	$$$	US$1–2
Cheap & cheerful	$$	US$0.70–1
Rock bottom	$	<US$0.70

cauldron of hot sand. *Plov* is invariably washed down with green tea, its astringency helping to cut through the mutton fat. If you'd like to try your hand at making *plov*, see the box on page 74.

Other notable national dishes include **shurpa**, a soup with fatty mutton and vegetables; **norin** and **lagman**, two mutton-broth soups with noodles that may also be topped with a piece of horse meat; **dimlama**, meat and vegetables stewed slowly in a tightly sealed pot; and the ubiquitous **shashlik**, grilled kebabs with cubes of mutton or beef and fat, which is considered to add to the flavour. Contrary to what you might expect, pork can be found, especially in Karakalpakstan or any Armenian quarter. For a quick snack, consider either **manti** (also called *qasqoni* and found across the Turkic lands), a steamed dumpling containing minced mutton, the similar **chuchvara**, or **somsa**, a fried or baked pastry parcel (not quite a samosa) that contains either mutton or, occasionally, mashed potato. You could also try **kurt**, dry cheese balls that are hard work without a drink.

Every meal is accompanied by the flat, round loaves of bread known as **non**. The most common form, **obi non**, is cooked in a clay tandoor oven. The bread's rim rises; the centre is flattened with a pattern or dots imprinted in the dough. Non is generally torn into chunks rather than sliced, and you should show respect by not placing it upside down on the table.

Vegetarians are in for a tough time: the concept is little understood, and even less frequently catered for. Meat-free versions of the classic Uzbek dishes tend to be pretty dull, but you should at least be able to get a Greek or *achichuk* salad, consisting of tomato, onion, cucumber and dill. Better restaurants may have a pasta dish, and pizza is a staple of the fast-food joints. Luckily, Uzbek **breakfasts** are excellent, with plenty of eggs, cheese, bread and fruit, and will set you up for the day.

If you are in Uzbekistan in summer and early autumn, the country is bursting with **fresh fruits**. Stalls in bazaars and by the roadside sell an amazing variety at knockdown prices. The season starts with strawberries in April, then various kinds of cherries in May, peaches and apricots in June, watermelons (the size of beach balls) in July, plums in August and grapes, pomegranates, pears, and persimmons in September and October, as well as apples (which originated in central Asia) which are available all year.

An Uzbek's veins run with **tea** as much as blood, and the *chaikhana* (tea house) is central to any community: people go to do business as much as to gossip and relax. Green tea (*zilloniy chai*) is most common in the provinces, but black tea (*chorniy chai*) is preferred in Tashkent. Both are available wherever you go, but expect a funny look if you want your tea with milk (tea with sugar is fine). In summer you may also be offered **ayran** or **kefir** (chilled yoghurt drinks).

Alcohol is consumed in Uzbekistan, though less so than in the other central Asian republics, and both beer and spirits are widely available in shops and larger restaurants. Uzbek beer is horrid, supposedly in the Czech style, but in reality fizzy and tasteless. The country has a number of vineyards, mainly around Samarkand. Some are quite well established, and if you're offered the opportunity to try a glass or two of wine (or indeed cognac), you should take it. The most drinkable brands are Bagizagan (a good Chardonnay) and Sultan (a very decent Cabernet); the Hovrenko Wine Factory in Samarkand produces good reds, but they can be hard to find. Tashkentvino produces sweet wines (red Pinot Noir and white Rkatsiteli) for the Russian market.

EATING OUT Uzbekistan does not have a long tradition of eating in **restaurants**: finding one was nigh on impossible during the Soviet period owing to food shortages and the fact that people were encouraged to eat collectively in the work canteen.

It sometimes seems that Uzbekistan runs on *plov*, the heavy, calorie-laden dish that is the nation's undisputed favourite.

Serves 8

INGREDIENTS
1kg of lamb shoulder, separated from the bone and cubed
1kg paella rice
250ml sunflower oil
1kg peeled carrots cut into 1cm lengths
3 whole garlic bulbs
3 medium-sized onions, sliced thinly
1 tbsp cumin
pinch of salt
2 chillies (optional)

You will also need a 5-litre cooking pot.

METHOD
1. Wash and soak the rice in cold tap water.
2. Heat the oil in the cooking pot over a high flame and deep fry the meat until it is golden brown. Take the meat out and put to one side.
3. Fry the onions until they are golden and then add the meat again, as well as the carrots. Heat for 20 minutes (stirring frequently) or until the carrots are soft and slightly caramelised. Add the cumin.
4. Reduce heat and add water to cover the carrots and meat. Leave it to gently simmer for 1 hour, or until most of the water has evaporated.
5. Place the whole bulbs of garlic and the chillies (if using) on the top of the meat and carrots.
6. Add the rice that has been soaking on top of the meat and carrot layer in the cooking pot, and then cover contents with 2cm depth of boiling water. Boil it gently until the rice has completely absorbed the water. Be careful it doesn't burn on the bottom.
7. Reduce the heat and cover the pot with a lid. Allow the *plov* to steam for 20 minutes. If you think it might be catching, remove it from the heat entirely.
8. Remove the garlic bulbs and chillies and put them to one side. Don't stir too much – the *plov* should be served upside down, ie: with the rice on the bottom, vegetables in the middle and meat on top, on a large communal dish, and decorated with the garlic bulbs and perhaps quail eggs, herbs and spring onions.

Enjoy with a tomato and onion salad, flat bread and a pot of freshly brewed tea.

This is slowly changing in urban centres, particularly those with a significant tourist footfall, though you will not find the density or quality of restaurants typical in some other parts of Asia. Hotels have restaurants, of course, but don't assume they will be available in the evening, as they're often taken over for weddings, especially at weekends.

The restaurants that do exist (other than in Tashkent and the main tourist cities) tend to cater primarily to wedding parties, and this is where they make their money. If the restaurant is not fully booked for a celebration you won't need a reservation, nor to wait for a table. Expect a fairly limited menu of Russian and Uzbek dishes and beware that it's unlikely that everything listed will be available. If you have any doubt about what to order, look around at what the other diners are eating and physically point a dish out to the waitress. Service may be chaotic (you may wait a long time for your starters then the mains will arrive a couple of minutes later), but it is generally good-natured. You'll be expected to leave a **tip**: 10% is standard. If you're lucky you may be invited to join a bride and groom at their dinner table and will spend the next few hours drinking the requisite toasts!

Tea houses (which are authentically central Asian) and **cafés** (which are more Western) are found in most town centres and serve drinks and lighter meals. More common (and cheaper) than restaurants and cafés are **street-side food stalls**: from American fast-food stands with burgers and fries, to smoking grills and the vinegary smell of *shashlik* and onions wafting down the road, making your stomach rumble. Women with trays piled high with savoury pastries saunter through markets and the lobbies of office buildings; trestle tables nearly buckle beneath the weight of freshly baked bread.

NIGHTLIFE

Nightclubs, in their Western sense, are illegal in Uzbekistan, but entrepreneurs get around this by opening bars and hosting DJs or live music. There are, however, very few such establishments, other than in Tashkent and a few larger cities. These tend to be frequented predominantly by businessmen (both local and foreign); it's unusual to see unaccompanied women in bars unless they're working. Single women should therefore not go to a bar alone unless they want to be hassled.

Champagne and expensive vodka brands such as Beluga are the status drinks of choice, and cocktails are increasingly popular. Drinking to excess is common, as is drink-driving home. Face control is normal, so dress up smartly and don't wear trainers or jeans.

PUBLIC HOLIDAYS AND FESTIVALS

1–2 January	Yangi Yil Bayrami	New Year
14 January	Vatan himoyachilari kuni	Day of Defenders of the Motherland
8 March	Xalqaro Xotin-Qizlar Kuni	International Women's Day
21 March	Navro'z Bayrami	Navruz (Persian New Year)
9 May	Xotira va Qadirlash Kuni	Remembrance Day
1 September	Mustakillik Kuni	Independence Day
1 October	O'qituvchi va Murabbiylar Kuni	Teachers' Day
8 December	Konstitutsiya Kuni	Constitution Day

The **Islamic festivals** of Eid ul-Fitr and Eid al-Adha are also celebrated, but as they are based on the lunar calendar their dates change from one year to the next. For the lifespan of this edition, the likely dates are as follows: 24 May/31 July 2020; 13 May/20 July 2021; 3 May/10 July 2022; 22 April/29 June 2023.

2

SHOPPING

Shopping in Uzbekistan encompasses a complete range of experiences, from rummaging in workshops and warehouses akin to Aladdin's caves of carpets, silks and antique jewellery, to standing befuddled in a neon-lit supermarket attempting to work out quite which of the 101 different dairy products labelled in Russian might actually be milk. These experiences can be exhilarating and they can be infuriating, and sometimes both at once.

Souvenirs in Uzbekistan fall loosely into two categories: the mass-produced items (often manufactured in China) that the Uzbeks think foreign tourists want to buy and that are on sale outside every museum, mosque and madrasa, and the handmade, vintage or otherwise more individual pieces that you'll actually treasure once you get them home. Finding the last can be slightly harder, but they're often competitively priced, particularly if they've originally been produced for the domestic market. You are expected to haggle quite hard and should aim to pay no more than 70% of the original asking price. If you buy old craft pieces, ask the seller for a certificate stating that it's less than 50 years old to ensure you can take it out of the country. Uzbekistan has always been known for its **textiles**, and though during the Soviet period mass production rather than quality was the focus, in recent years smaller, independent workshops have once again sprung up. Many of them produce carpets, silks and embroideries in traditional styles and using long-established techniques and buying directly from them supports the artisans and their families.

There are also some beautiful **ceramics** thrown, painted and fired in Uzbekistan. Gijduvan is particularly famous for its painted plates, as you can see from the

UZBEK CARPETS

Every house in Uzbekistan is decorated with carpets and *suzanis* (see box, page 78). Though these days they will often be factory-made synthetic rugs from China, traditionally they would have been handwoven locally. Each community would have produced carpets in a distinctive style, and they were valued as much for their artistic qualities as for their functional properties. The largest single collection of carpets is thought to have belonged to the Emir of Bukhara: he had over 10,000 examples in his palace.

There are three main types of carpet produced in Uzbekistan: felt mats, flat-woven carpets and pile or tufted carpets. The first of these is the most ancient form, and would have first been produced by nomadic herders with surplus wool from their sheep. When wool is kneaded with soap and water, it becomes a thick, heavy felt that is not only warm but, as local saying has it, cannot be walked upon by a spider, nor crawled upon by a snake. It is either left in its natural colour (usually a cream or grey) or dyed with natural pigments such as indigo (for blue), moraine (red) and pomegranate bark (yellow). In desert areas, women also made similar rugs with camel hair.

It's not known exactly how long carpets have been woven in Uzbekistan, but archaeologists have found spindles in Stone Age sites that are similar to the wooden spindles still used in some rural areas of the country today. On the spindles you can spin a thick, coarse yarn that is required for *julhirs*, the loosely woven carpets still produced around Dzhizak and Nurata. Such carpets are often woven with a pattern of longitudinal stripes, edged with a chain of rhombuses and triangles. Modern flat-weave carpets can be woven from either woollen or numerous ornate façades, though the manufacture of tiles and other ceramics was once a major industry nationwide. We're particularly pleased with our giant teapot and handle-less tea bowls (drinking from them is an art, but one that you quickly get used to), and the small tiles, often painted with replica designs from the Registan and other major tourist sites, work well as coasters, heatproof mats or, as their predecessors were intended, simply to decorate your wall.

If you visit Uzbekistan on a package tour, or have the budget to eat predominantly in restaurants, **food shopping** in the country will be of little concern. You might decide to pick up the odd half kilo of pistachios or pomegranates in the bazaar (highly recommended when the latter are in season), but this is a charming novelty rather than the hard-fought prelude to every budget meal.

If your budget requires regular picnics or cooking for yourself, however, life becomes rather harder. The bazaars, found in every town, are a reliable source of bread and fresh produce, but there's often little on sale beyond this, even in the small convenience stores that brand themselves, misleadingly, as supermarkets. The market for pre-prepared and processed foods is still in its relative infancy in Uzbekistan; as you survey row upon row of tinned fish and jars of pickled vegetables, the merest thought of a deli counter or ready meal may well cause feelings of longing.

ARTS AND ENTERTAINMENT

Uzbekistan does not have a long tradition of going out in the evening: entertainment typically came to you. At weddings and other festivities, such as Navruz (the Persian New Year, celebrated in Uzbekistan on 21 March), families and friends would come

cotton threads. The smooth surface is created by interlocking the warp (vertical) and weft (horizontal) threads. They are produced on a simple loom made from narrow, wooden beams. The width of the carpet strip is dictated by the width of the loom, but typically does not exceed 50cm. To make a wider carpet, therefore, several strips must be stitched together. The flat-weave carpets produced in Bukhara are considered to be the finest in the country; those from Surkhan Darya are unique in that the base threads are in two colours.

The most valuable carpets, however, are the tufted carpets. The finest fleece is used to produce their thread, and a thread count of 100 or more knots per centimetre is not uncommon. This makes the production process exceptionally time-intensive, and it requires an extremely high level of attention to detail; a single knot of the wrong colour in the wrong place will result in months of work being ruined.

Though men do sometimes produce knotted carpets, it is generally considered a job for women as it helps to have small, deft hands. Women pass carpet-making techniques from mother to daughter, and it is still commonplace to see young girls working away at a loom. The warp threads are stretched on the loom, and on to these the weaver knots individual threads, hitting each one down with a metal hook so that it sits tightly alongside the previous knot.

Historically, a small number of carpets were woven with golden thread and silk. Produced in Bukhara, Samarkand and Khiva for their respective courts, they became famous well beyond Uzbekistan and were prized as diplomatic gifts. Without royal patronage, such carpets are increasingly rare.

THE *SUZANI*

The *suzani* is an Uzbek embroidery; the word is derived from the Persian for needle. Though *suzanis* can be sewn on to a single piece of fabric (usually cotton), it is not uncommon for several pieces to be stitched together into an elaborate patchwork.

The three main stitches used in embroidering *suzanis* are chain (*yurma*), cross (*iroqi*) and satin (*bosma*) stitches. The most popular motifs are flowers, leaves and fruits, though the designs often also take on symbolic properties: suns represent life, pomegranates indicate fertility and peppers give protection from the evil eye. Representations of living things such as fish and birds do sometimes appear, though they are less common owing to the widely held belief among Muslims that they should not be depicted in art.

The earliest *suzanis* seen today, either in shops or in museums, date from the 18th and 19th centuries. Then, as now, they were made by young women for inclusion in their wedding dowries. *Suzanis* for use as bedspreads, wall hangings and throws were therefore particularly common. They were undoubtedly being produced before this, however, as Ruy Gonzales de Clavijo, the Castillan ambassador to the Timurid court, described the fine embroidery work he saw in the 15th century, and there are definite similarities between 18th-century *suzanis* and the embroideries produced in Mughal India two centuries earlier. The Mughals, of course, were Timurids, their founder Babur (see box, page 142) a native of the Fergana Valley.

together at home, and poets, musicians and singers would come to the house to perform. If the entertainment was particularly good, the guests would be inspired to dance and sing themselves.

This slowly began to change during the Soviet period, when theatres and concert halls were built across the country, and a professional class of entertainer emerged, some of them performing traditional Uzbek works, but the majority spreading high culture from Russia such as academic works of drama, ballet and opera. Tickets were cheap (and remain so) in order to democratise access to the arts, and new works were commissioned that praised the worker and explored his/her life and experience, rather than focusing on kings, queens and fairytales as was popular before. Every town, however small, had its own performance space, and the populace was actively encouraged to attend.

Today, Uzbekistan's **theatres** are a mixed bag. Often housed in striking Neoclassical buildings, they have suffered since independence due to funding cuts and the cessation of movement of companies, directors and artists from other parts of the Soviet Union. Whereas once an Uzbek ballerina could have hoped to travel to Moscow or St Petersburg to train, and would have enjoyed an illustrious and peripatetic career, now such opportunities are few and far between. That said, there are companies that are thriving: the Ilkhom Theatre in Tashkent (see box, page 35) continues to put on challenging, world-class productions, including many new plays, and a night at the ballet at Tashkent's Alisher Navoi Opera is a highlight of any trip to Uzbekistan, particularly if you dress up and enjoy the sweet Georgian *champanska* during the interval.

Uzbekistan's larger cities all have **cinemas** showing the latest Russian and Hollywood blockbusters and in 2019 a government programme was building 50 small cinemas in smaller cities across the country. English-language films are almost always dubbed or subtitled in Russian, though you can usually follow the plot of action films and thrillers. Art-house films are a little more challenging, even if you understand the language. Cinema tickets tend to be slightly more expensive than theatre tickets, though still rarely more than a few dollars a head.

In recent years, Uzbekistan has started to host several annual **festivals,** designed to showcase the country's artistic heritage to the world. The Silk and Spice Festival takes place for a week each year in Bukhara (page 231), and singers and storytellers perform at Chimgan's Echo Festival of Bards during the first week of June. In Samarkand, the Sharq Taronalari International Museum Festival (w n.sharqtaronalari.uz) happens in the main Registan Square (⊕ Aug of odd years), and is very impressive indeed.

OPENING TIMES

Companies in Uzbekistan do not typically keep to set opening times: restaurants, shops and other businesses will open in the morning when they are ready, will frequently close early if things are quiet, or they may not open at all. As a general guide, however, the working week runs from Monday to Friday; although it is the Muslim holy day, businesses still work on Friday as they did during the Soviet period. Shops will typically be open on Saturday as well, though offices will be closed. Museums tend to be open six days a week, taking their day off either on Sunday or Monday; check individual entries for which day they are closed.

Banks, shops and museums tend to keep standard office hours: they open around 09.00 and close at 17.00, often with an hour's lunch break between 13.00 and 14.00. Unless they are serving breakfast, cafés and restaurants open late morning and keep serving until the last customer has left; in larger places this may not be until 23.00, though *shashlik* stands and other local cafés will usually be finished around 19.00.

MEDIA AND COMMUNICATIONS

MEDIA A government decree officially ended state censorship of the media in 2002. In reality, however, all forms of media in the country remained strictly controlled under Karimov, and the situation has only slowly begun to improve under President Mirziyoyev. In the 2018 World Press Freedom Index, Uzbekistan inched upwards to 165th of 180 countries. Some detained journalists have been freed, but at least seven other journalists and bloggers were arrested in 2017 and 2018 and, at the time of writing, remained in detention. A number of foreign news agencies, including the BBC, were banned from operating in the country. As of 2019, there has been some relaxation of rules regarding foreign press, and the BBC was finally given full accreditation and now has a correspondent in Tashkent. Although visiting journalists are expected to request media accreditation from the government before travelling, this is increasingly a formality. The government broadcaster operates the main TV and radio networks and the government also keeps a tight grip on the internet. Websites such as Radio Free Europe-Radio Liberty (w rferl.org) and w change.org are blocked; even Facebook seems not to work half the time.

NEWS The readership of newspapers in Uzbekistan is low, with figures estimated to be not more than 50,000 people countrywide. The state controls newspaper distribution and materials supply, hence the market is dominated by the three state-owned papers *Halq Sozi*, *Narodnoye Slovo* and *Pravda Vostoka*. Popular privately owned papers include *Novosti Uzbekistan* and *Noviy Vek*, though even they cannot be considered independent. Apart from *Halq Sozi* they're all Russian-language papers.

Uzbekistan's national news agency, the imaginatively named Uzbekistan News Agency, is state-controlled. Reuters and the Associated Press (AP) both have offices in the country, though they are only able to work within strictly enforced confines.

The four state-owned television channels dominate the television market, though there are a large number of small, private channels in existence. The State Press Committee and the Inter-Agency Coordination Committee issue broadcast licences to such channels, and withdraw licences swiftly from those organisations pursuing too independent a line. There's also strong censorship of 'indecency', eg: short skirts on TV. Live broadcasts are prohibited.

The most balanced news sources are to be found online from agencies based outside Uzbekistan, such as the *Times of Central Asia* (w timesca.com), *Eurasianet* (w eurasianet.org), the *Tashkent Times* (w tashkenttimes.uz) and *Novastan* (w novastan.org/fr/ouzbekistan).

PHONE The country code for Uzbekistan is +998. To call abroad from inside Uzbekistan, dial 810 and then the country code. In 2018, all phone numbers became nine digits long; in other words the former local codes (eg: 71 for Tashkent) need to be added at all times. **Mobile numbers** begin with 09 (drop the 0 when calling from abroad) and do not need to be prefixed with an area code. **Emergency numbers** are 101 for fire, 102 for police and 103 for ambulance.

Like so many other developing countries, Uzbekistan has jumped from having almost no communications infrastructure to having around 60% of the population connected by mobile phone. With fewer than 2 million landlines, and most of those used by businesses, they're simply not a consideration for individuals wanting to keep in touch.

Uzbekistan's most popular **mobile-service providers** are UMS, UCell, Beeline and UzMobile. Regulations have changed to enable foreigners to buy SIM cards. To get a SIM card you will need to take your passport to one of the providers' offices or branded stores. They can also be obtained in the arrivals hall at Tashkent Airport. Filling out the various forms and processing them takes about 15 minutes. Depending on the network, you'll either pay around US$3, or the SIM will be free when you top up by a certain amount.

Topping up your phone is easy. You can do it in any store that shows your network's logo and at any Paynet machine, found in or outside convenience stores or other places with high foot traffic. These allow you to type in your phone number, feed in bank notes and *voilà*! You've topped up.

Though the coverage of phone networks is improving, it is still by no means universal and large sections of the country (particularly remote and mountainous areas) are black holes for reception.

INTERNET Uzbeks have taken to the internet like ducks to water, and half the population now has access (mostly on mobile phones). Local SIM cards now include data packages, and it is also possible to buy an internet dongle for your laptop, enabling you to get online wherever there is 3G. Wi-Fi is standard in hotels and hostels, and internet cafés are increasingly common in the larger cities; however, connections are, generally speaking, very weak. WhatsApp messages may take a week to reach you and it is often impossible to check in for flights online. Faster connections are promised with new Korean hardware.

When you're surfing the web, you may find sites you normally looked at are blocked. VPN access is required for most foreign media sites, and even the BBC Uzbek service is only accessibly via VPN or a proxy server. You'll also find that many Uzbek websites have vanished due to incompetence and lack of payment.

POST Uzbekistan does have a domestic postal service with a central post office (marked O'zbekiston Pochtasi) in most large towns, but you are likely to arrive home before your postcards (US$3), if indeed they arrive at all. Letters and parcels are generally transported internally by hand (you may be asked to carry a gift to your next destination for so and so's relative) and couriers and diplomatic bags are the preferred method to send and receive anything overseas. DHL and UPS both have offices in Tashkent (page 105), as do the state-owned EMS [113 F6] (w ems. post) and a number of smaller courier firms.

BUSINESS

Uzbekistan is a tough place to do business, for both locals and foreign investors. The country ranked 76th out of 185 countries for ease of doing business in 2018 (w doingbusiness.org/rankings), a significant improvement from 2013 when the country was in 154th position, with the biggest causes for concern being cross-border trade, taxes and dealing with permits. That said, the government is seeking foreign investment and has recently taken steps to simplify business procedures. Credit is much more readily available than it was a few years ago.

Any legal entity, be it an individual or an organisation, may invest in Uzbekistan. Foreigners can both establish companies and buy shares in existing companies. A company will be considered a foreign investment if its fund capital exceeds US$150,000 and 30% of the share value is held by foreign entities. Investments can be made into all economic sectors. Investment into some preferred sectors is tax exempt (see below).

Under Uzbek law foreign investors have the right to make contracts, acquire, own and dispose of their investments at will, freely dispose of revenue and attract credit or loans; inventions and designs can be patented abroad as well as in Uzbekistan. They are entitled to receive compensation in case of the requisition of assets and also to receive indemnification for damages caused as a result of the illegal actions (or inaction) and decisions taken by state bodies. Foreign investments and other assets of foreign investors in Uzbekistan are protected by law from nationalisation. Enforcing such regulation may, however, be difficult.

Any individual who resides in Uzbekistan for 183 days or more during a financial year is considered as a tax resident of the Republic of Uzbekistan. Legal entities (specifically companies) are considered tax resident if they are registered in Uzbekistan or registered abroad but have their headquarters in Uzbekistan. Non-residents and foreign legal entities doing business in Uzbekistan are only taxed on their income from activities performed in the country. Reciprocal tax arrangements are in place with some foreign governments.

Tax exemptions of up to seven years are available for companies investing in the manufacturing of electronic components, light industry, silk production, construction materials, food production (in particular poultry, meat and dairy products), chemicals and pharmaceuticals. To qualify for these tax breaks enterprises must be located in regions with a labour surplus, have at least 50% foreign ownership, and the investments must be made in hard cash and/or modern equipment. Foreigners are able to participate in the privatisation of state assets and industries. Depending on the investment proposal, it's sometimes possible to acquire unplaced state assets at zero cost.

Investment in Uzbekistan is promoted through the 'UzInfoInvest' Informational Support and Foreign Investments Promotion Agency. The agency is responsible for providing potential and existing foreign investors with information on prospective projects and investment legislation, including on guarantees and incentives.

Doing business in Uzbekistan is strongly dependent on personal relationships. You will be expected to spend significant time getting to know potential business partners or clients and how they work, and this may include socialising and spending time with their family as well as more formal business meetings. If you are pitching for a contract, your bid will be considered not solely in terms of cost or quality; how the client feels about you and your colleagues will often be a contributing factor too.

The overlap between personal relationships and business often wrong-foots foreign business people working in Uzbekistan, and indeed across central Asia. Whereas Westerners may consider getting drunk on vodka and even sharing a naked *banya* (sauna) session with prospective business partners to be unprofessional, in Uzbekistan it is completely normal and you may be commercially disadvantaged if you are unwilling to participate since such activities are considered part of the process of building up trust. That said, there are Uzbeks who do not drink heavily on health or religious grounds, and if you decline offers politely and with a good reason, your hosts are unlikely to push you. Consider offering an alternative leisure activity that you can do together and that you are more comfortable with.

Problems also occur from mismatched expectations; though Uzbekistan is now nominally capitalist, central planning and state ownership still dominate many people's thinking, and intricacies of concepts that Western companies take for granted, such as investment and shares, may have to be carefully explained. Understanding of what does and does not constitute corruption are often wildly different, as is the extent to which fast-tracking, the payment of fees, goodwill gestures and even all-out extortion are acceptable. You will need to maintain good lines of communication, explain everything clearly (even if you think it is obvious) and ask plenty of questions.

BUYING PROPERTY

Uzbekistan's 1998 Land Code and Law on Land is ambiguous about the legality of both private ownership and foreign ownership, leaving the door open for the government to potentially seize assets in the future. In practice, foreigners do buy property in Uzbekistan and are permitted to do so providing they have residency in the country. The government is attempting to make it easier for foreigners to invest, though you will still need a reputable local lawyer to help you navigate the extensive red tape. The process is relatively straightforward, but often frustratingly slow.

Before signing a purchase agreement you need to check the land registry (ideally several times) to ensure that the property being bought is legally owned by the seller. You pay a deposit to secure the property, then the purchase agreement and all supporting documents are sent to the local registry for the title to be signed over to the buyer. You then settle the balance of the purchase price, along with applicable taxes and notary costs.

There are no restrictions on foreigners leasing property in Uzbekistan. Rents are typically inflated by three to five times for expats, though you can always bargain with the owner for a fairer deal.

Residents of Uzbekistan are taxed on their worldwide income, from 9% to 22%. Rental income earned by non-residents is taxed at a flat rate of 20% and capital gains are taxed at a standard rate of 20% for non-residents.

CULTURAL ETIQUETTE

Hospitality towards guests is an important part of Uzbek culture. If you are invited to an Uzbek home, you should take a small gift for your hosts. A souvenir item, such as a picture book, from your home country is ideal, but if you have brought nothing suitable with you a gift such as a bouquet of flowers (get an odd number) or box of chocolates or *halva* is fine. Note that an invitation to go to someone's house for 'a cup of tea' invariably means something more substantial: often a full meal. If you bring biscuits, dried fruit and nuts or chocolates, they might well be added to the spread.

On entering a home or guesthouse in Uzbekistan (regardless of whether it is a flat or a house in the country) you should remove your shoes at the door. There is usually a mixture of assorted slippers and flip-flops available to wear around the house.

In more **traditional households** you may find that men and women are entertained separately, often in different rooms. Although there is little concern about women being seen by non-family members, they often feel more comfortable sitting and talking with their own gender. The general assumption is that women will be happier talking to other women in the kitchen or dining room, and that men will do their own thing outside, or elsewhere in the house.

At the end of the meal, thanks are given by the act of bringing the hands together in front of the face, then moving them down in an action symbolising a washing gesture. This is the signal for everyone to get up from the table. You shouldn't continue to pick at food after this point.

Mosques, **shrines** and **other holy places** often have their own sets of rules and you should endeavour to observe these. If in doubt, ask the guardian or someone else who appears to work or worship there, as it is better to appear naïve than disrespectful. Requirements are likely to include removing your shoes, covering your head (women only) and wearing long trousers or a skirt which covers the knees. Clothing which is revealing is unacceptable. You may be expected to wash your hands and face to enter active mosques, and occasionally only men, or practising Muslims, are permitted to enter. Whatever your personal opinion about this, you should respect the local community's wishes.

In general, men do not wear shorts except for sport, but foreigners are generally excused. Some women also cover their legs and hair; again, foreigners are free to dress as they wish.

And finally, **toilets** – you'll usually find Western-style WCs in hotels and restaurants, but some 'Turkish' squats are still to be found. In either case you should always put used paper in the bin provided. Public toilets are marked *khojathana*.

PHOTOGRAPHY As in any country, it is always polite to ask before taking someone's photo. If you are using a long lens this may not be necessary because they may not notice you taking the picture from a distance. But if you can, it's still wise to ask permission first, then take a few shots quickly to be sure of capturing a good expression, and giving yourself options later. Do not worry excessively about photographing children in Uzbekistan, as they are usually happy to pose and there is absolutely no risk to them or you in your doing so.

2

Again, as in most countries of the world, pointing any sort of camera in the direction of anything military, border crossings or governmental buildings is to be avoided. It is not worth having your camera kit seized just for the sake of an otherwise useless picture of a typical border post or concrete bridge across the Amu Darya. Attitudes are now more relaxed, however, and it's certainly permitted to take photos in the Tashkent metro.

TRAVELLING POSITIVELY

Uzbekistan needs foreign investment, foreign recognition and foreign scrutiny. Responsible tourists can contribute in all these areas by becoming both observers and ambassadors. Think about where and how you spend your money, remembering that family-run guesthouses, local restaurants and co-operative craft workshops are the best way to put your money into the local community.

If you want to **volunteer** in Uzbekistan, an internet search will reveal a small number of NGOs working within the country, most of which are in the environmental and social sector. Most Western NGOs were expelled from the country in 2005–06 following international criticism of the Andijan Massacre (see box, page 138). The work of the remaining NGOs is strictly controlled, and their workers are often viewed with suspicion by the authorities. It is not uncommon for NGO workers to have their visas terminated suddenly.

One charity worth mentioning is **SOS Children's Village**, which has an office in Tashkent [112 D7] (79A Nukus; ✆ 71 120 3783; e sos-na@sos-kd. uz; w soschildrensvillages.org.uk) and works with orphans throughout the country. It is always in need of extra hands and donations of spare cash, toys and children's clothing.

SEND US YOUR SNAPS!

We'd love to follow your adventures using our *Uzbekistan* guide – why not tag us in your photos and stories via Twitter (🐦 @BradtGuides) and Instagram (📷 @bradtguides)? Alternatively, you can upload your photos directly to the gallery on the Uzbekistan destination page via our website (w bradtguides. com/uzbek).

Part Two

THE GUIDE

3

Tashkent

Too frequently passed over in favour of the Silk Road's UNESCO stars, Tashkent is a vibrant crucible of historic architecture and Islam, Soviet town planning and propaganda and 21st-century nation building. The varying, often seemingly incompatible strands of modern Uzbek identity are all entwined here, and to understand both where Uzbekistan has come from and where it is going, you need to visit. A stone's throw from the capital in Tashkent and Syr Darya *viloyati* (provinces), the Syr Darya River carves up the steppe and cultivated lands. To the northeast of the city, the Ugam-Chatkal National Park, with its alpine meadows and mountain forests, is a welcome natural haven among the mines, factories and infrastructure projects that are driving the Uzbek economy forwards.

Tashkent morphs and expands with every new generation. With an official population of 2.5 million (although some estimates place it as high as 4.45 million), it is far and away the largest city in central Asia: only Kabul comes anywhere close. A stroll through any bazaar reveals the ethnic diversity of its people, with not only Uzbeks, Tajiks and Russians but also Crimean Tatars, Koreans, Bukharan Jews and other unexpected minorities each contributing to the city's cultural *smorgasbord*. Though first impressions may be of chaos, concrete and cars, a stroll through the backstreets of the Old City (page 105) or a rummage through Chorsu Bazaar (page 104) reveal an older, slower way of life that continues to underpin modernity.

HISTORY

An oasis on the Chirchik River (460m above sea level), Tashkent began its life as a staging post for Silk Road merchants, missionaries and mercenaries en route between the Tian Shan Mountains in the east and the Kyzylkum Desert to the west. The archaeological site of Kanka (page 125), 80km southwest of the modern city, was already thriving in the 4th century BC, so much so that it can be identified even in ancient-Greek sources (recorded there as Antihiey Zayaksartskoy). The capital of the principality of Chach, it flourished for a thousand years at the heart of a network of more than 30 towns, 50 irrigation canals and numerous *caravanserais*. The Battle of Talas in AD751 ushered in a new era: the Arab Abbasid Caliphate conclusively defeated the forces of Tang emperor Xuanzong, halting Chinese expansion in central Asia and instead putting the whole Syr Darya region firmly under Arab (and therefore Islamic) control. The Samanids (819–999) called their new capital Binkath; the name Tashkent (meaning stone city) did not come into use until the time of the Karakhanid Khanate in the 10th century.

Tashkent became a wealthy and cosmopolitan city on the back of Silk Road trade between Kashgar (China), Samarkand and Bukhara. Its wealth made it an inevitable target for looters, however: the city was sacked in 1214 by the Khwarazmian ruler Ala ad-Din Muhammad, and then again just five years later by Genghis Khan

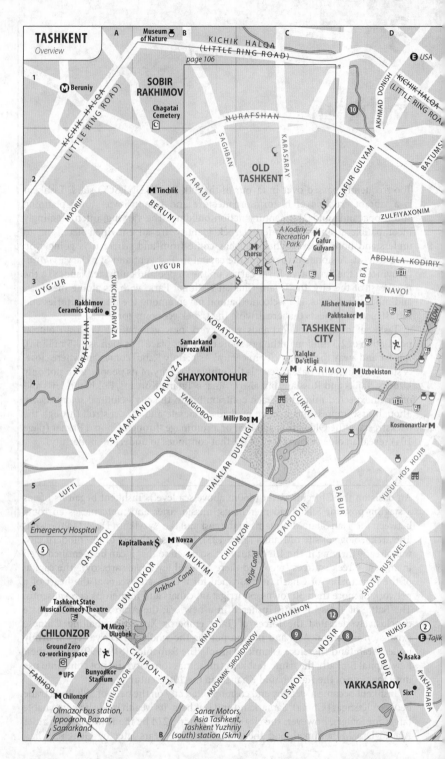

TASHKENT
Overview

A   Museum of Nature **B**   KICHIK HALQA (LITTLE RING ROAD) **C**   **D**

E USA

page 106

Ⓜ Beruniy

KICHIK HALQA (LITTLE RING ROAD)

SOBIR RAKHIMOV

Chagatai Cemetery Ⓒ

NURAFSHAN

AKHMAD DONISH

KICHIK HALQA (LITTLE RING ROAD)

⑩

BATUMS

SAGHBAN

FARABI

KARASARAY

OLD TASHKENT

GAFUR GULYAM

ZULFIYAXONIM

Ⓜ Tinchlik

BERUNI

A Kodiriy Recreation Park

Ⓜ Gafur Gulyam

Ⓜ Chorsu

$

ABDULLA KODIRIY

UYG'UR

NAVOI

UYG'UR

NURAFSHAN

KUKCHA-DARVAZA

Rakhimov Ceramics Studio

KORATOSH

Samarkand Darvoza Mall

SHAYXONTOHUR

SAMARKAND DARVOZA

YANGIOBOD

Milliy Bog Ⓜ

HALKLAR DUSTLIGI

FURKAT

ABAI

Alisher Navoi Ⓜ
Pakhtakor Ⓜ

TASHKENT CITY

Xalqlar Do'stligi

KARIMOV Ⓜ Uzbekiston

Kosmonavtlar Ⓜ

BAHODIR

BABUR

YUSUF HOS HOJIB

FLOW

LUFTI

Emergency Hospital

⑤

QATORTOL

BUNYODKOR

Kapitalbank $ Ⓜ Novza

MUKIMI

Ankhor Canal

CHILONZOR

Bojsu Canal

SHOTA RUSTAVELI

Tashkent State Musical Comedy Theatre

CHILONZOR

Ⓜ Mirzo Ulugbek

ARNASOY

AKADEMIK SIROJIDDINOV

SHOHJAHON

⑫

⑨

NOSIR

⑧

Ground Zero co-working space

Ⓔ

• UPS

Bunyodkor Stadium

CHUPON-ATA

USMON

NUKUS

②

Ⓔ Tajik

$ Asaka

BOBUR

YAKKASAROY

Sixt

KAKHHARA

FARHOD

Ⓜ Chilonzor

CHILONZOR

Olmazor bus station, Ippodrom Bazaar, Samarkand

Sanar Motors, Asia Tashkent, Tashkent Yuzhniy (south) station (5km)

A   **B**   **C**   **D**

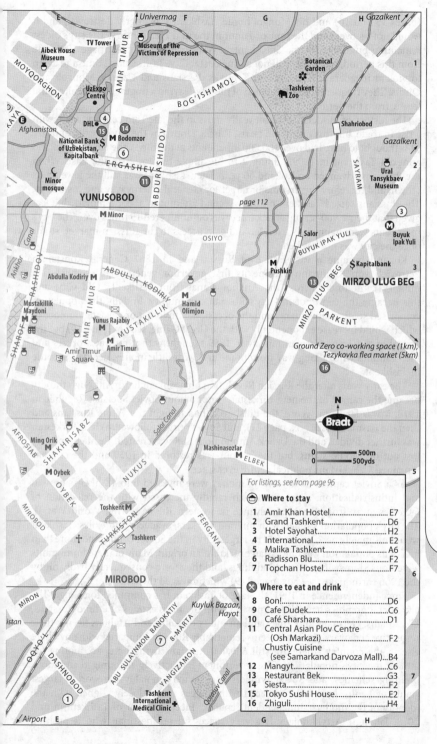

Univermag ↑   **Gazalkent** ↗

TV TOWER

Aibek House Museum

MOYQORGHON

Museum of the Victims of Repression

UzExpo Centre

AMIR TIMUR

BOG'ISHAMOL

Botanical Garden

Tashkent Zoo

Afghanistan

DHL ● ④

⑮ ⑭ **Bodomzor**

National Bank of Uzbekistan, Kapitalbank

Shahriobod

ERGASHEV

⑥

Gazalkent ↗

Minor mosque

ABDURASHIDOV

⑪

YUNUSOBOD

SAYRAM

Ural Tansykbaev Museum

page 112

Minor

OSIYO

Salor

BUYUK IPAK YULI

③

Buyuk Ipak Yuli

Ankhor Canal

RASHIDOV

Abdulla Kodiriy

ABDULLA KODIRIY

Pushkin

MIRZO ULUG BEG

Kapitalbank

MIRZO ULUG BEG

SHARQF

Mustakillik Maydoni

AMIR TIMUR

Yunus Rajabiy

MUSTAKILLIK

Hamid Olimjon

⑬

PARKENT

Amir Timur Square

Amir Timur

Ground Zero co-working space (1km),
Tezykovka flea market (5km)

AFROSIAB

SHAKHRISABZ

Salor Canal

Ming Orik

⑯

N

Mashinasozlar

ELBEK

Bradt

OYBEK

Oybek

0   **500m**
0   **500yds**

MIROBOD

NUKUS

Toshkent

FERGANA

TURKISTON

Tashkent

MIROBOD

MIRON

Kuyluk Bazaar,
Hayot

istan

TO'RKO

DASHNOBOD

ABU SULAYMMON BANOKATIY

8-MARTA

⑦

YANGIZAMON

Tashkent International Medical Clinic

Qorasuv Canal

①

Airport ↙

For listings, see from page 96

🛏 **Where to stay**

1	Amir Khan Hostel	E7
2	Grand Tashkent	D6
3	Hotel Sayohat	H2
4	International	E2
5	Malika Tashkent	A6
6	Radisson Blu	F2
7	Topchan Hostel	F7

✕ **Where to eat and drink**

8	Bon!	D6
9	Cafe Dudek	C6
10	Café Sharshara	D1
11	Central Asian Plov Centre (Osh Markazi)	F2
	Chustiy Cuisine (see Samarkand Darvoza Mall)	B4
12	Mangyt	C6
13	Restaurant Bek	G3
14	Siesta	F2
15	Tokyo Sushi House	E2
16	Zhiguli	H4

(pages 15 and 16) and his Mongol horde. Tashkent was utterly destroyed, and it would not recover until the time of Timur in the mid 15th century. The city's oldest remaining buildings (in the Sheikhantaur Mausoleum Complex, page 109) date from this period, but it was still not a time of stability: Tashkent fell time and again to violent invaders – Kazakhs and Kalmyks, Persians and Uzbeks, Mongols and Oirots. They frequently levelled much of the city, leaving a fragmented architectural legacy from the period.

The history of modern Tashkent really starts in the late 18th century, again with a rise in trade, but this time from tsarist Russia. Drawn by the city's wealth and size (it is thought to have had over 100,000 inhabitants at the time), the Khan of Kokand annexed Tashkent in 1809, adding it to his ample territories in the East. When the Russians advanced on Kokand 60 years later, Tashkent was still the jewel in its crown, and therefore the first major target for General Chernyayev and his troops. The Russians seized Tashkent on their second attempt in 1865, a remarkable feat given that their 1,900-strong attack force was outnumbered 15 times over. The city's merchants were happy to surrender and gain access to the Russian market, so for once the city was not levelled.

Kokand became a vassal state of Russia, and in 1867 General Konstantin Petrovich von Kaufmann became its first governor general. He established a military cantonment across the Ankhor Canal from Tashkent's Old City, and this became the centre of the city's Russian community. Initially the population comprised soldiers, merchants and the occasional diplomat or spy (the number of which would increase exponentially with the Great Game; see box, page 19) but the arrival of the Trans-Caspian railway in 1889 brought with it railway workers and their families who, a long way from home and with little money, decided to settle in Tashkent.

The early years after the Russian Revolution hit Tashkent hard. Although the city became the capital of the new Turkestan Autonomous Soviet Socialist Republic in 1918, it was far from secure: the Bolsheviks had to fight the White Russians and then the Basmachi (see box, page 21), and Soviet purges followed. When Turkestan was further divided and the Uzbek Autonomous SSR was created, Tashkent initially lost out on capital status, but the honour was restored in 1930 and the city has remained Uzbekistan's political centre ever since.

As a Soviet capital, huge sums of money were invested into Tashkent's growth and industrialisation, a process which rapidly increased with the relocation of factories away from the Nazi advance in western Russia during World War II. The city's population swelled with migrant workers, evacuees and exiles: Tashkent would ultimately become the fourth-largest city in the Soviet Union, and more than half of its population was of Russian or Ukrainian origin. Many of these immigrants were housed in swiftly erected buildings, and they were consequently badly hit by the 1966 earthquake (see box, page 119) which ravaged the city.

Since independence in 1991, the face of Tashkent has continued to change. The city's demographics have shifted notably with the mass exodus of ethnic Russians, Ukrainians, Germans and Poles, and an influx of Tajiks and Afghans fleeing their respective civil wars, yet it still seems remarkably Russian compared with anywhere else in the country (there are still 600,000 Russians living here, accounting for 20% of the city's population). The government has actively encouraged ambitious building schemes, and Soviet symbols and statuary, notably the world's largest statue of Lenin, have been replaced with images more closely aligned with the identity of the modern, independent republic. Elected Mayor of Tashkent in mid 2018, Jahongir Artykkhojaev is a very successful businessman who is pushing ahead with modernising the city, which reportedly involves evicting residents with next-to-no notice when a decision is made to demolish their homes. Tashkent City [112 B3], a glitzy high-rise development of offices and hotels, is now rising on the former Olmazor area of the Old City; up to 10,000 people have been relocated while, bizarrely, the boxer Mike Tyson appears on their TVs promoting the new apartments on offer.

GETTING THERE AND AWAY

BY AIR Tashkent's **Islam Karimov International Airport** [map, page 125] (TAS; ✆71 140 2801), Uzbekistan's main aviation hub, is in Tashkent's southern suburbs, around 6km from Amir Timur Square. It has three terminals, two next to each other for international arrivals and departures, plus the domestic Terminal 3 across the runway. If you have a transit connection, an airside transfer will be provided to the domestic terminal, otherwise you'll need to take a taxi (US$4–10) or bus 11 or 77 from the city to reach it. Facilities are somewhat dated – there's no ATM and the only exchange counter is before the immigration booths (to the right); staff then urge tourists to use the new green channel, avoiding baggage X-rays and questions about how much cash you're carrying. For a list of **airlines** serving Tashkent, see page 49.

As you would expect, you'll be met by the usual selection of aggressive **taxi** drivers demanding upwards of US$10 for the 20-minute drive to the city centre. If you have not pre-arranged a hotel taxi to collect you, simply walking out of the airport to the main road will reduce your taxi fare to US$4. Be prepared in any case to haggle hard.

From the far side of the departures car park, **buses** 11 and 76 go from the airport to Chorsu Bazaar, bus 40 heads for the north and south stations (check which way it's going before boarding), bus 67 travels along Shota Rustaveli and Shakhrisabz to Amir Timur, and bus 77 passes the Novza metro station. Pay the conductor on the bus.

BY RAIL Tashkent's **main railway station** [113 F6] (zheleznodorozhny vokzal; ✆71 299 1873) is south of the city centre on Turkiston, served by the Toshkent metro station [113 F6]. While it is possible to arrive in Uzbekistan by rail from Russia, Kazakhstan, Tajikistan or Turkmenistan (page 50), it is not a journey for the faint hearted or time-poor. Far more useful are Uzbekistan's domestic rail links, the latest fares and timetables for which are detailed at w uzrailpass.uz.

The main station was being rebuilt at the time of writing, and many domestic services were only using the new **Tashkent Yuzhniy (south) station** [88 C7], about 5km southwest; be sure to check your ticket carefully! Buses 40 and 62 link the main (north) station and the south station in about 15 minutes (heading south, you'll need to take the underpasses to or from the far side of the ring road); a taxi will cost about US$1. International trains still arrive at the main station, where you'll find an ATM and a scrum of taxi drivers wanting to take you to the airport, the Fergana Valley or to the city centre; you'll find city buses to the south, but you're best off taking the metro, to the north through the underpass.

Tashkent's south station also has an ATM but no metro – buses 8 and 131 will get you to the Chilonzor metro station, buses 40 and 62 to the airport and the north station, bus 80 will eventually get you to Nukus and S Azimova streets just southeast of the city centre, and bus 84 runs via Chorsu Bazaar.

Attempting to buy the **ticket** is likely to be the most stressful part of your rail journey. You will need your passport to buy one and it is helpful if you write down

3

both your destination and the six-digit date you wish to travel so as to avoid confusion. The Kassas (⏲ 08.00–20.00 daily), to the right (southwest) of the two main station buildings are your best bet if you want to buy a ticket on the day of travel, or one or two days beforehand. If you know your travel plans further in advance and want to be relieved of the hassle for a small fee, *Caravanistan* (w caravanistan.com) offer a reliable reservations service, and the tickets will be delivered to your hotel.

The following **services** are likely to be the most useful on your travels. We have listed the fastest and most popular options first. Fares and journey times are given for all stops, return time refers to the final destination. For more information on rail travel in Uzbekistan, see page 65.

762/761 (Afrosiyob service) Tashkent–Samarkand–Bukhara; departs 07.30 daily, returns 15.48; 2hrs 18min/3hrs 49min; tickets start at US$11/19. High-speed service with restaurant car & AC.

760/763 (Afrosiyob service) Tashkent–Samarkand–Shakhrisabz; departs 08.00 daily, returns 15.43; 2hrs 16min/4hrs 25min; tickets start at US$11/20. High-speed service with restaurant car & AC.

766/765 (Afrosiyob service) Tashkent–Samarkand–Bukhara; departs 18.50 daily, returns 04.55; 2hrs 8min/3hrs 48min; tickets start from US$11/19. High-speed service with restaurant car & AC.

10/9 (Sharq service) Tashkent–Samarkand–Bukhara; departs 09.13 (not Tue), returns 16.03; 3hrs 16min/5hrs 56min; tickets start from US$4.70/7. Comfortable, reasonably fast AC train.

662/661 Tashkent–Samarkand–Bukhara; departs 22.12 daily, returns 22.43; 3hrs 48min/8hrs 25min; beds in 2- & 4-berth cabins cost US$8/11 & US$16.50/22.50 respectively.

56/58 Tashkent–Samarkand–Bukhara–Urgench; departs 20.27 Tue, Wed, Fri & Sun, returns 15.50 Mon, Wed, Thu & Sat; 3hrs 46min/7hrs 15min/14hrs 35min; seats start from US$6/8/12, cabin bunks from US$8.50/12/17.

60/61 Tashkent–Andijan; departs 08.07 (not Mon), returns 06.18; 5hrs 44min; from US$5.50.

BY ROAD Tashkent is well connected to all of Uzbekistan's main road transport arteries, and within easy reach of the borders with both Kazakhstan and Tajikistan. The roads around the capital are generally well maintained and, unusually for Uzbekistan, well signposted, making navigation relatively straightforward. If you are approaching the city from the opposite side to your destination, taking the ring road is preferable to driving through the centre, even if the route is a little longer. This especially applies at rush hour.

If you are driving your **own vehicle** and approaching or leaving Tashkent via the M39 (the main road southwest from the capital towards Samarkand), note that it passes briefly through Kazakhstan. If you do not have visa-free access to Kazakhstan, or a transit visa, you will need to travel instead on the M34 via Gulistan; take the A376 east from the Dzhizak bypass as far as the village of Hovos (or Khavast), then the M34 north to Gulistan and Tashkent. It is a reasonably good road and well marked. However, owing to the increased distance and travel time, we prefer to take the smaller and rougher but more direct A373 via Sardoba and Yangiaul to Alkaltyn, west of Gulistan. Signposts along this route are few and far between; if you don't have GPS, expect to stop and ask for guidance and to rely heavily on your own sense of direction. At some point, a Tashkent–Samarkand toll road will open, also keeping south of the Kazakh border.

Tashkent has a number of bus stations, and the one you require will depend on your destination and choice of transport. For long-distance services it is advisable to book a day in advance as the scheduled buses fill up quickly. To do so, and for timetable information, just turn up at the station. The public bus station [88 A7] (Tashkent Avtovokzal; ✆ 71 279 3929) is just north of the Olmazor metro station on Bunyodkor, and it's from here that most **scheduled long-distance bus services** leave, while minibuses wait just outside. From here you can take a bus or minibus to Samarkand (7/5½hrs; US$5/5), Bukhara (14/10hrs; US$9/10) or Urgench (25/18hrs; US$18/20). Shared taxis also wait outside the bus station and will complete the same journeys in half the time but at approximately twice the price. If you are in a hurry or want to stretch out, you can always pay for the additional seats in the car rather than waiting for it to fill up. **For Karshi, Denau and Termez**, use the private bus station at Ippodrom Bazaar, 2km further southwest along Bunyodkor, which also has minibuses and shared taxis for these cities. The bus to Termez takes about 16 hours (US$17) and the minibus 12 hours (US$18).

There are currently no buses east to the Fergana Valley from Tashkent, but shared taxis **to Kokand, Namangan and Andijan** leave from Kuyluk Bazaar on the Fergana Highway (5hrs; US$10–12). You can get here with bus 12 from the main station, bus 68 through the centre from Chorsu Bazaar, or *marshrutka* 18 from the Do'stlik metro station.

Finally, *marshrutkas* and shared taxis **to Chimgan, Beldersay and Lake Charvak** (1hr 20min; US$2.30) leave from the north side of Buyuk Ipak Yuli metro station – if there's no direct service running when you arrive, take one of the frequent minibuses on route 550 to Gazalkent and change there.

GETTING AROUND

BY CAR Soviet planners may have laid out much of Tashkent on a grid, but they didn't anticipate the boom in car ownership and resultant gridlock. Navigating Tashkent in your **own vehicle** is a challenging affair owing to the lack of street signs, and drivers in the capital can be pretty pushy. You'll require a fairly detailed map (page 70) or GPS and plenty of patience.

The only international **car-hire** firm currently in Tashkent is Sixt (see ad, 3rd colour section), who has two branches in the city, one at 104A Kichik Beshagach [88 D7] (❜ 71 120 9010; e reservations@sixt.co.uz; w sixt.co.uz; ⊕ 09.00–18.00 Mon–Fri) and one at the Wyndham hotel (page 97). You can also try local firms Rentcar.uz, located across the road from the Wyndham in the City Palace (page 97) (m 97 155 0555; e info@rentcar.uz; w rentcar.uz) Autoprokat (99A Amir Timur; m 93 574 4545; w autoprokat.uz/en). Alternatively, you can rent a vehicle with a driver from Advantour (from US$28/day; page 96).

Parking in the city is a perpetual hassle; there are few planned parking areas and drivers typically park two or even three cars deep along the edge of the road, causing chaos. Outside popular restaurants and other premises where there is competition for space, you may be asked for a semi-official parking charge by an attendant. Although you can usually get out of paying this, it is easier to hand over 1,000 som or thereabouts. Do not, however, part with your keys, even if they claim valet parking is available; there's a real chance you'll never see your car again.

Cycling on the roads is virtually unknown in Tashkent, but people do cycle in parks so there is potential, and in 2018 the city authorities started to paint in some cycle lanes. A potential north–south route already exists along the Ankhor Canal, with a link west past the Pakhtakor Stadium [112 C3]. Bikes can be hired in the Broadway park [112 D3], immediately west of Amir Timur Square (around US$1/hr), though mainly at weekends, and you're not expected to go far.

BY PUBLIC TRANSPORT Most cars serve as impromptu **taxis**, so if you need a ride simply stand by the kerb and put your hand out. Fares are typically US$3–4 depending on the length of the trip, but make sure you agree a price in advance. If you prefer a pre-booked taxi, O'zbegim Taxis (℡ 71 220 0300), Allo Taxi (℡ 71 120 1010), Express Taxi (℡ 71 239 9999/71 239 9930) and Millennium Taxi (℡ 71 129 5555) are all reputable firms. Services such as Uber and Lyft are not allowed here.

Tashkent has a large number of buses and minibuses. **Minibuses** are bigger than the tiny Damas vehicles elsewhere in the country; they tend to be more frequent than buses and cost a little more (typically US$0.16 per ride), but are still at the mercy of the traffic jams. The destination and route number (if applicable) are written on the front of the minibus or on a card in the window; they run from around 07.00 to 20.00. In terms of helpful **bus** routes, Bus 67 starts at the airport and has stops on Shota Rustaveli, Afrosiab, Sharof Rashidov, Uzbekiston and Amir Timur, terminating at Yunusabad. Bus 94 also has the airport as its terminus and runs to Karavanbazar, and buses 11 and 76 run from the airport to Chorsu Bazaar. Buses generally run from around 05.00 until around 22.30, at approximately 15-minute intervals; tickets cost US$0.14. Timetables can be found at a few of the stops, and information is also available on w wikiroutes. info/en/tashkent and the MyBus Tashkent app.

There are also now double-decker **hop-on-hop-off tour buses** run by Tashkent City Tour (℡ 71 232 3090; w tashkentcitytour.uz; US$8.50); they leave every hour from the Hotel Uzbekistan (page 97) and make 10-minute stops at key sites.

The best way to get across Tashkent, particularly during rush hour, is undoubtedly by **metro** [map, below]. Opened in 1977 with one line and 12 stations, the system has since been expanded to take in all parts of the city you're likely to want to visit. Tokens cost US$0.14 (one token is needed per journey), the trains run every 5–10 minutes from 05.00 to midnight and, as well as being theoretically earthquake-

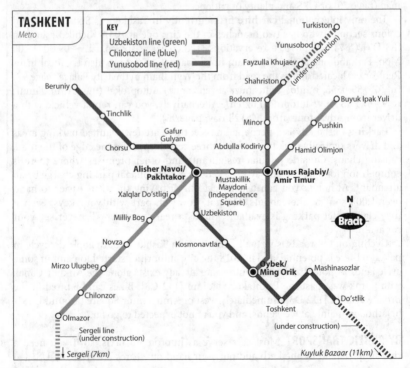

THE TASHKENT METRO

Sometimes great adversity can present the opportunity to implement great solutions, and so the Tashkent metro, the city's most important transport artery, was born out of the destruction caused by the earthquake that levelled much of the Old City in April 1966. Planners, architects and workers came from across the USSR to build a new model Soviet city, installing sewerage systems, wide boulevards and parks and, as a centrepiece, a metro system whose design and architectural beauty drew considerable inspiration from the jewel-like Moscow metro.

The Tashkent metro, opened in 1977, has 29 stations on three lines (Uzbekiston, Chilonzor and Yunusobod), covering 36km in total. As the city sprawls out ever further (building wider, not higher, is a logical plan for a conurbation in a seismically active area), so will the metro. Extensions to the first two lines opened in stages in 1991, and the first 6km phase of the third line (Yunusobod) opened in 2001. More extensions, due in 2020, will, in theory, see the Yunusobod line continuing 3km north, a fourth line (Sergeli) (7km, above ground) heading south from Olmazor (the current terminal of the Chilonzor line), and the first stage of a new ring line running south from Do'stlik to Kuyluk Bazaar (for transport to the Fergana Valley).

The system is exceptionally clean, safe and runs reliably until late at night. A typical travel experience might begin with consulting the metro map (posted at the entrance to each metro station; see also opposite), a relatively courteous inquiry by a policeman to check your bag, the purchase of a small, translucent blue plastic token (US$0.14) and then descending into the station to join some of the 400,000 commuters who use the metro each day. Station signs are in both Cyrillic and Latin scripts, a boon to foreign travellers. On the train, the first word of the arrival announcement is the name of the station, and the last word of the departure announcement is the name of the next station.

What you first notice is the space: it's not something normally associated with the economics of creating a subterranean complex. The platforms are wide and the ceilings are high. Each station is unique in its décor, which is generally themed on some aspect of Uzbek life or culture. For instance, in the Mustakillik Maydoni station, Ulug Beg, grandson of Timur (see box, page 173) and historical astronomer of note, is acknowledged with the star patterns in the marble floor of the platform. The beautiful mosaics of cotton found on the walls of Pakhtakor station acknowledge the impact this crop has had on life in Uzbekistan. And at Kosmonavtlar, where Valentina Tereshkova, the first woman in space, is immortalised, the ceramic wall panels fade from blue to black in imitation of Earth's atmosphere. You are now able to photograph these beautiful stations.

proof, many of the stations are elaborately decorated with golden domes, chandeliers, mosaics and other delightful frippery. Photography, once banned here, is now allowed.

TOURIST INFORMATION AND TOUR OPERATORS

There is no official tourist information centre in Tashkent. Hotel staff, fellow travellers and the tour operators listed here are typically the best sources of tourist information in the city. Every other street corner seems to have an Aviakassa selling airline tickets, largely because credit-card sales and online booking are still limited here. The following companies can sell you tickets and are sometimes able to accept card payment for their services. If not, dollars are preferred. In addition to making bookings, their English-speaking staff can also advise you on things to see and do, whether or not you require a personal guide.

Abda Travel [112 D4] Lotte City Hotel Tashkent Palace, 56 Buyuk Turon; `71 236 2653; e abdatravel@yahoo.com; w abdatravel.uz. A joint Malaysian–Uzbek venture, Abda specialises in all-inclusive package tours within Uzbekistan. Prices are determined by the duration of your itinerary & number of people in your party. When planning your trip, ask for the English-speaking Robert Shin.

Advantour [112 D6] 47A Mirobod; `71 150 3020; e tashkent@advantour.com; w advantour. com. In addition to their country-wide tours (page 46), the helpful staff here can arrange city tours, guides, hotels, flights & car rental.

Asia Adventures [112 D6] 27/10 Mirobod; `71 254 4100; e info@centralasia-adventures. com; w centralasia-adventures.com. Tour specialist with a range of programmes from horse trekking & mountaineering to escorting VIP business trips around Tashkent's cultural sites. Also make hotel bookings.

Dolores Travel [88 D6] 104A Kichik Beshagach; `71 120 8883; e info@dolores.uz;

w dolorestravel.com. Offers car & minivan rental (with or without driver), hotel reservations &, in addition to the standard sightseeing packages, also has more unusual options such as camel trekking, long-distance cycle rides & railway tours. See ad, 3rd colour setion.

Marco Polo Central Asia Travel [112 C6] 20 Shota Rustaveli; `71 252 7641; e info@ marcopolo.uz; w marcopolo.uz. Specialist cultural tours with knowledgeable, multilingual guides. Translation services also available.

Novo Tours 14/49 Center-5, Tashkent City; `71 235 4548; e info@novotours.uz; w novotours.uz. Tour operator with English-, French- & Russian-speaking guides. Also visa support, airline ticketing & hotel reservations.

✴ **Sitara Travel** [112 C7] Office 42, 45 Shota Rustaveli; `71 281 4148; e tashkent@sitara. com; w sitara.com. Exceptionally helpful & professionally run tour operator with some of the best English-speaking guides in Uzbekistan; their prices are very competitive. Highly recommended.

🏠 WHERE TO STAY

Like any large post-Soviet city, Tashkent has a vast number of places you could stay, but relatively few where you'd actually want to. Star ratings seem to be decidedly creative (certainly not comparable to international standards), and price is no guarantee of quality. Check out a number of rooms in your chosen establishment before parting with your cash, and always haggle hard on price.

Contrary to what the staff may tell you, Tashkent is not overrun with tourists, meaning you're well placed to get a discount if you ask. Expect to pay cash (either US dollars, the currency in which hotel prices tend to be quoted, or som): outside of the top-end hotels, few businesses have the capacity to take credit or debit card payments. You may also find a city tax of around US$2 per night added to the bill. The majority of accommodation options are centrally located within the city, and few are more than 10 minutes' walk from a metro station. Most top-end hotels are predictably clustered around Amir Timur Square or the UzExpo Centre; cheaper options are typically found south of the city centre around Shota Rustaveli, and also near Chorsu Bazaar.

TOP END

🏠 **Grand Mir Hotel** [112 D6] (126 rooms) 2 Mirobod; `71 140 2000; e info@grandmirhotel. com; w grandmirtashkent.com. Modern,

comfortable hotel designed to appeal to the Russian market. Rooms are large & clean. The Harem restaurant on the rooftop has great views over Tashkent & is open between 19.00 & 02.00

($$$$$). There is also a beauty salon & fitness centre. $$$$$

🏠 **International Hotel** [89 E2] (233 rooms) 107A Amir Timur; 🞂 71 120 7000; e reservation@ihthotel.uz; w ihthotel.uz. When InterContinental dropped this huge hotel from their chain in 2012, there were a few halcyon days when staff would announce proudly to guests that this was now the Incontinental Hotel. Disappointingly for those of us with a puerile sense of humour, some spoilsport alerted them to the shortcomings of this as a brand, & the hotel is now boringly the International. Thoroughly renovated in 2010, public areas are immaculate & bedrooms are understated but equipped with all mod cons. The lake-facing rooms have one of the best views in Tashkent, particularly in the winter when it freezes. $$$$$

✳️🏠 **Lotte City Hotel Tashkent Palace** [112 D4] (232 rooms) 56 Buyuk Turon; 🞂 78 120 5800; e lotte_tashkent@mail.uz; w lottecityhoteltashkent.com. Opened in 1958 as the Tashkent Hotel, this historic property has now been taken over by the South Korean chain Lotte. Facing the Navoi Opera Hse, it is probably the city's best-located hotel, & numerous foreign statespeople have stayed here in the past, including Indira Gandhi. The architecture is charming & the rooms well maintained & clean. The outdoor swimming pool is a real asset in summer. The b/fast buffet (US$20) is somewhat on the pricey side but tasty, & there is a well-stocked bar with local & foreign liquors & courtyard & rooftop bars in summer. $$$$$

🏠 **Hotel Bek Tashkent** [112 B6] (24 rooms) 64A Yusuf Hos Hojib; 🞂 71 215 5888; e info@bek-hotel.uz; w bek-hotel.uz. A plush new hotel with large, comfortable rooms; b/fast is very good (from about 07.30, at any rate), but the restaurant is overpriced otherwise ($$$$). $$$$

🏠 **Hyatt Regency** [113 E3] (300 rooms) 1A Navoi; 🞂 71 207 1234; e tashkent.regency@hyatt.com; w hyatt.com/en-US/hotel/uzbekistan/hyatt-regency-tashkent/tasrt. Opened in 2016, this luxury hotel is easily the best in the country. It's centrally located, has good restaurants (notably the rooftop Sette, for Italian food ($$$$), swimming pool, gym & conference & wedding facilities. The large rooms have work areas & big bathrooms with a shower & bath tub. $$$$

🏠 **Radisson Blu** [89 F2] (110 rooms) 88 Amir Timur; 🞂 71 120 4900; e reservation.tashkent@radissonblu.com; w radissonblu.com/hotel-tashkent. Clean, professionally run hotel targeted at businesspeople. Rooms are well equipped & comfortable, if a little unimaginative. The 24hr exchange counter is useful, as are the free fitness centre & the free Wi-Fi in the foyer. The outdoor pool comes into its own in summer. $$$$

🏠 **Wyndham** [113 E2] (206 rooms) 7/8 Amir Timur; 🞂 71 120 3700; w wyndhamtashkent.com. Solid, unglitzy & centrally located, this is one of the city's better business hotels, with indoor & outdoor pools, sauna & gym all included in the room rate; there's also a 24hr café & a good restaurant ($$$$). $$$$

MID-RANGE

🏠 **Ramada Tashkent** [112 C1] (120 rooms) 1 Abdulla Kodiriy; 🞂 71 140 6000; w ramadatashkent.com. Formerly the Park Turon, this hotel has been massively improved, especially in the area of service. Beds are apparently a bit hard, but otherwise it's very comfortable. There's also an Irish pub as well as an indoor swimming pool & sauna. $$$$

🏠 **City Palace** [113 E3] (251 rooms) 15 Amir Timur; 🞂 71 238 3000; w citypalace.uz/en/. A glitzy tower that opened as a Sheraton in 1998 & is now refurbished. It has indoor & outdoor pools, a gym, jacuzzi & saunas. $$$–$$$$

🏠 **Hotel Uzbekistan** [113 E3] (223 rooms) 45 Musakhanov; 🞂 71 113 1111. Right on Amir Timur Sq, the huge Hotel Uzbekistan is a Tashkent icon & architectural marmite: you'll either love it or hate it. Soviet concrete is in abundance, barely broken up by the colourful flags & fountain outside, & the service is also typically Soviet. It was put up for sale by the government in mid 2018, & has improved somewhat. The hotel's redeeming feature is that, while it claims to be one of the city's best hotels, huge discounts are available (turn up & ask about them); it also has Visa & Mastercard ATMs & a 24hr restaurant ($$$– $$$$). $$$–$$$$

🏠 **Hotel Sayohat** [89 H2] (81 rooms) 115 Buyuk Ipak Yuli; 🞂 71 268 1630/71 268 6815; e sayohathotel@mail.ru; w sayohathotel.uz. Rather disorganised & with little English spoken, the Sayohat is partially redeemed by its unexpectedly splendid rose garden & the ludicrous Neoclassical wedding banqueting hall. $$$

🏠 **Malika Tashkent** [88 A6] (27 rooms) 53A Chupon-ata; 🞂 71 150 3020/71 273 0203;

w malika-tashkent.com. Tricky to find but worth the effort. Heading west on Lufti, Chupon-ata is the last road on the left before you reach the ring road. The 2 carriageways on Chupon-ata are separated so you will need to drive past the hotel to the junction with Katartal before you can double back to the Malika. Look for the large cream plaster & stone façade with green blinds in the ground-floor windows. The Malika has comfortable rooms with twin beds & reasonable bathrooms. Meals are fairly basic, but the small garden at the rear is a pleasant place to drink tea & relax. We were accosted by an overly enthusiastic, German-speaking *babushka* trying to sell paintings in the lobby, but managed to escape unscathed. $$$

🏠 **Mirzo Hotel** [106 C5] (15 rooms) 4 Zarqaynar; e turkturizm@mail.ru. No expense has been spared on this brand-new hotel opposite the Circus (replacing the Mirzo Guesthouse), from the Timurid-style portal & the waterfall just inside, to the recycled tiles in the rose garden & the sculpted ceramic scenes of the Silk Road cities. There are comfortable AC rooms & 2 yurts (with solid walls & underfloor heating). Bikes & tennis & conference facilities available. $$$

🏠 **Retro Palace Hotel** [112 C6] (55 rooms) 65 Vohidov; \71 256 3106; w retropalace.uz. Large, clean rooms with plenty of light. The staff are pleasant & the outdoor pool area has lots of sun loungers on which to relax. The gaudy pink bar is a good place to meet other travellers. Accepts payment by Visa & Mastercard. $$$

🏠 **Rovshan Hotel** [112 D7] (87 rooms) 118 Katta Mirobod; \71 120 7747; e stay@ rovshanhotel.com; w rovshan-tashkent.com. In a quiet residential neighbourhood (on a side street west of the better-known Mirobod), the Rovshan has reasonable rooms that are generally clean. A few of the staff speak English & they're relatively helpful by Tashkent standards. $$$

🏠 **Shodlik Palace** [112 C2] (107 rooms) 5 Pakhtakor; \78 120 9977; e reservation@ shodlikpalace.com; w shodlikpalace.com. Totally refurbished in 1997, the Shodlik briefly claimed to be the city's second-best hotel (after the International; page 97) & remains a clean & pleasant business establishment. The website is only in Russian, but staff do speak English & are generally helpful. $$$

BUDGET

🏠 **Anvar's Guests** [112 C5] (12 rooms) 26/2 Vohidov; \71 256 7162; e anvarsguests@gmail. com; f anvarsguests. Pleasantly furnished rooms & apts in a quiet area; Anvar & his staff are immensely friendly & helpful, & he speaks excellent English. There's a swimming pool & sauna & guests can use the kitchen. $$

🏠 **Grand Tashkent** [88 D6] (27 rooms) 57 Kakhkhara Ln VI; \71 255 0599; e hotel@grand-tashkent.com/hotel_grand_tashkent@yahoo.com; w grand-tashkent.com. Unremarkable option with rock-hard beds & the finest synthetic furnishings China produces. The in-house travel agency is useful. $$

✳ 🏠 **Gulnara Guesthouse** [106 A5] (8 rooms) 40 Ozod; \71 240 6336; m 98 360 0774; e gulnarahotel@gmail.com. A budget favourite since 1999, this friendly, family-run guesthouse offers comfortable rooms & b/fast in the courtyard garden. Recommended for those travelling with children or who have had their fill of post-Soviet service & want a human touch. Guests can use the kitchen & there's a book swap; transfers available. Some twin rooms have en-suite bathrooms. Dorm beds US$15. $$

🏠 **Sam-Buh Elite Hotel** [112 C7] (36 rooms) 10 Tsekhovaya; \71 120 8826; w sambuh-hotel. com. The décor at Sam-Buh is a rather nasty flashback to the 70s, but if brown & orange are your thing, rooms are a reasonable size & come with a b/fast buffet. $$

HOSTELS

🏠 **Amir Khan Hostel** [89 E7] (30 beds) 16 Dashnobod; m 97 414 4010; e amirkhanhostel@ gmail.com; w amirkhanhostel.uz. A friendly small hostel (run by Uzbeks, not Russians, for a change) & the nearest to the airport (a 20min walk along Tolipov, or take bus 106 from the airport & get off immediately after the railway crossing). 2 small mixed dorms & 1 male & 1 female (all with curtained bunks with a reading light & power socket) & a kitchen; there are good food options a block to the east. $

🏠 **Art Hostel** [112 C5] 3 Zanjirbeg; \71 252 6134; m 91 133 1015; e info.arthostel@mail. ru; w arthostel.uz. Tashkent's first hostel is a 5min walk from Kosmonavtlar or Oybek metro stations. Mixed & female-only dorms & sgl, dbl & tpl rooms, some en suite & all AC; excellent

English-speaking staff, a good kitchen (with free tea & b/fast), swimming pool & lots of useful info on noticeboards. **$**

🏠 **Topchan Hostel** [89 F7] 108 8-Marta; m 90 319 9998; e knock-knock@topchan-hostel.com; w topchan-hostel.com; 🇫 @topchanhostel.

A real backpackers' place – cheap, with English-speaking staff & a graffiti visitor book on the walls. No b/fast until 08.30. It's also spacious & quite comfortable, with a kitchen & laundry service. Mixed dorms (1 female-only) & private rooms. **$**

✖ WHERE TO EAT AND DRINK

Forced migrations within the Soviet Union had one remarkable benefit for central Asia's capitals: the diversity of food now available. Whereas in the provinces you'd better get familiar with mutton, Tashkent has a pleasantly surprising array of restaurants, with options ranging in price from the economic to the exorbitant. **Vegetarians** may still go hungry (though some possibilities are included in the listings below), but everyone else should be well fed.

Perhaps predictably, Tashkent's most expensive restaurants are predominantly in upmarket hotels and the streets around Amir Timur. This is also where you'll find the greatest range of international cuisine. Central Asian restaurants tend to be cheaper and scattered more widely across the city; they cater predominantly to local diners and are therefore found in more residential areas as well as commercial districts. Chorsu Bazaar (page 104) is the best location for cheap eats, both in terms of fresh produce but also *shashlik* and other hot snacks cooked right under your nose. Unless otherwise stated, restaurants are open for both lunch and dinner.

Most of Tashkent's larger hotels are equipped with **cafés** that are open around the clock, but it's cheaper and more interesting to head out into the city. Traditional Uzbek **tea houses** can be found in many of Tashkent's parks and are open late into the evening, particularly in summer. They're great for people watching as locals come to gossip, read the paper and do business. In Chorsu Bazaar, taking tea is a rather more frantic affair as shoppers and stallholders tend to be in a hurry, but a cup will set you back a fraction of what it would elsewhere and it is fun to be part of the hustle and bustle. If you prefer more Western surroundings (and/or want to drink coffee and eat cake), the places on page 101 are recommended. They typically open late morning for coffee and pastries, are busy around lunchtime, and stay open until 21.00 or so, often serving light dinners and alcoholic drinks as well as snacks.

CENTRAL ASIAN CUISINE

✖ **Caravan** [112 C7] 22 Kakhkhara; 📞 78 150 6606/78 150 7555; w caravan.uz; ⏰ 11.00–midnight daily. Upmarket Uzbek-themed restaurant overrun with tourists & children. Food is delicious & the atmosphere lively, but prices are many times higher than for similar dishes elsewhere. **$$$$–$$$$$**

✖ **Afsona** [113 E5] 30 Shevchenko; 📞 71 252 5681; e afsona@afsonamakon.uz; 🇫 afsonatashkent; ⏰ 11.30–23.00 daily. An upmarket place offering a contemporary spin on Uzbek cuisine, including genuine vegetarian versions of the standard dishes plus salads & desserts. **$$$$**

✖ **La Piola** [113 E7] 50 Avliye Ota; m 99 878 8888; 🇫 lapiolauz; ⏰ 09.00–23.00 Mon–Sat,

09.00–22.00 Sun. This spacious Mauresque-style restaurant near the Orthodox cathedral (page 124) is the best option on this side of town. Fine Uzbek food. **$$$$**

✖ **Sato** [112 C7] 18 Kakhkhara; 📞 78 150 0660; w sato.caravangroup.uz; ⏰ 11.00–03.00 Sun–Thu, 11.00–06.00 Sat. An unusual menu fusing Uzbek & Middle Eastern cuisines, upstairs from Izumi (page 100) & almost next door to Caravan (see left) – they're all owned by the same group. **$$$$**

✖ **Café Sharshara** [88 D1] 10 Bobojonava; 📞 71 144 5835; ⏰ 10.00–midnight daily. Lively restaurant with great location (including a manmade waterfall) & freshly baked bread. Menu helpfully has pictures so just choose & point. **$$$**

✕ Mangyt [88 C6] 12 Usmon Nosir; ✆ 71 252 3811. 2 yurts erected in a residential courtyard is a surprising place for a restaurant, but the crowded interiors give an authentic feel for nomadic life in Kyrgyzstan. Dishes include roasted horse meat, *shashlik* & *beshbarmak* (noodles & mutton); good Georgian wines. $$$

✕ Chustiy Cuisine [88 B4] Samarkand Darvoza Mall, 5A Koratosh; m 95 193 1515; ◷ 11.00–23.00 daily. Bahriddin Chustiy (who's from the Fergana Valley) has been called the Uzbek Jamie Oliver, producing refined fine-dining versions of traditional Uzbek dishes (& being active on TV & social media). Try the tasting platter. $$–$$$

✕ Central Asian Plov Centre (Osh Markazi) [89 F2] Cnr Ergashev & Abdurashidov; ✆ 71 234 2902; ◷ 10.30–16.00. The best *plov* in central Asia is indeed served up here. A passionate team cooks vast *kazon* (cauldrons) of the stuff in a street-front kitchen for customers to watch before tucking in to *plov*, salad & tea at a plastic patio table. You can even add a horse sausage on top. Highly recommended for both the experience & the food. It's busiest on Thu as the special *plov* is believed to have aphrodisiac properties! $$

✕ Milliy Taom [106 D5] Sebzor, Gafur Gulyam; ✆ 71 244 7703; ◷ 10.00–14.00 daily. Traditional, meat-heavy, Uzbek food including *shorpa* (soup) served in clay pots, *hasip* (sausage), *halim* (porridge) & *chuchvara* (ravioli). There's no menu, just order at the counter. This lunch-only restaurant is unmarked, but it's opposite the circus. Exceptionally popular with locals. $$

✕ Restaurant Bek [89 G3] 13 Mirzo Ulug Beg; m 90 953 7901; ◷ 09.00–22.00 daily. Always busy with local families, Bek offers a range of fairly tasty dishes, mostly Uzbek or Russian. One of a row of big lively places, you can eat on the terrace or in a side room when the music gets going. $$

✕ Sunduk [113 F4] 63 S Azimova; ✆ 71 232 1146; ◷ 10.00–23.00 Mon–Sat. Charming eatery with cosy rooms, contemporary art & just a few tables, plus a terrace in summer. Service is fast & polite, the food is Russian/Armenian/Uzbek & there are even vegetarian dishes on the menu, plus excellent coffee. $$

INTERNATIONAL CUISINE

✕ Affresco [112 B6] 14 Babur; ✆ 78 129 9090; w affresco.caravangroup.uz; ◷ 11.00–00.30 daily. Excellent pizza & homemade pasta, with a variety of more unusual authentic Italian dishes, too. A number of the staff are Italian & the menu is available in both English & Italian. $$$$$

✕ Gruzinski Dvorik [112 C7] 25 Kakhkhara; ✆ 78 129 0770; w gruzdv.caravangroup. uz; ◷ 11.00–23.00 daily. The best Georgian restaurant in Tashkent. Quality of both food & wine is high, but so are the prices. There's often live music in the evenings. $$$$$

✕ Izumi [112 C7] 18 Kakhkhara; ✆ 78 150 9949; w izumi.caravangroup.uz; ◷ noon–midnight daily. Eye-wateringly expensive restaurant, serving Chinese, Korean & Thai dishes as well as sushi, but a great choice for a blowout meal. Seating is on traditional Japanese tatami mats, & the adjoining karaoke rooms are ready & waiting when you finish your meal. Discounts often available on Tue. $$$$$

✕ Tokyo Sushi House [89 E2] 95A Amir Timur; m 90 961 8888; f tokyo.uz; ◷ noon–23.00 daily. Tashkent's smartest sushi restaurant is a stone's throw from the national bank & attracts a smart, wealthy crowd. $$$$$

✕ City Grill [113 E4] 23 Shakhrisabz; m 90 977 7116; ◷ noon–23.00 daily. Top-end steak house with high-quality food & imported wines, but predictably a price tag to match. English menus. $$$$–$$$$$

✕ Amaretto [112 C6] 28 Shota Rustaveli; ✆ 71 215 5557; f amaretto.uz; ◷ noon–23.00 daily. Popular Italian restaurant with take-away option for pizzas. Refurbished in 2018, but the best tables are still on the terrace. $$$$

✕ Jumanji [112 B6] 62/2 Yusuf Hos Hojib; ✆ 71 255 4200; m 90 188 6159; ◷ noon–23.00 Mon–Sat, 17.00–23.00 Sun. Pub-like restaurant full of young people (shame about the TV screens), serving big portions of good European/Asian fusion food, including various vegetarian options. $$$$

✕ Manna [113 E6] 29 Nukus; ✆ 71 254 1796; ◷ 10.30–22.00 Mon–Sat. Near the station, this is the best Korean restaurant in Tashkent (the Ambassador of South Korea definitely approves), with a charming garden behind a plain wall. $$$$

✕ Sema de Roma [112 D6] 40 Chekhov; ✆ 71 150 1835; ◷ 10.30–23.00 daily. Excellent Italian restaurant with a large terrace, serving classic dishes with vegetarian variations & wines from Italy & Georgia. $$$$

✕ Siesta [89 F2] 98 Amir Timur; m 91 190 9939; ◷ 11.00–23.00 daily. A Western-style pub-restaurant opposite the International Hotel (page 97), serving steak, pasta, pizza & salads, as well as fresh juices. English is spoken, & there's an English menu. **$$$$**

✕ **Raaj Kapur** [113 F3] 2 Uzbekiston Ovozi; ✆ 71 120 0603; ⏱ noon–15.00 & 19.00–23.00 daily. Inside the Tata-owned Le Grande Plaza Hotel (**$$$**), this is the closest Tashkent gets to an authentic Indian restaurant. Not cheap (a meat thali costs US$14), but the paratha & naan breads are particularly good. **$$$**

✕ **B & B Coffee House** [112 C6] 30A Shota Rustaveli; ✆ 71 281 6060; f bnb.uz; ⏱ 08.00–23.00. This stylish café-restaurant is popular with expats, especially for Sun brunch; great coffee, juices & pastries, plus sharing plates & sandwiches. **$$**

✕ **Efendi** [113 F5] 79A S Azimova; ✆ 71 233 1502; ⏱ 09.00–midnight daily. Atmospheric Turkish restaurant with a wide menu of kebabs, salads & surprisingly good desserts – a rarity in Tashkent. Popular dishes do sell out, so arrive early for max choice & the chance of a table on the terrace. **$$**

✕ **Yolki-Palki** [113 F3] 5 Shakhrisabz; m 97 233 2259; ⏱ 11.00–23.00 daily. Part of a Russian café chain serving Russian & Ukrainian dishes – expect everything to come with dill. Service is slow but the food is cheap. **$$**

FAST FOOD
✕ **Toronto Restaurant/Golden Wing** [113 F3] 30A Shakhrisabz; ✆ 71 232 2035; f toronto. restourant; ⏱ 09.00–midnight Mon–Sat. Turkish kebabs, burgers, salads, French fries & the best selection of ice creams in Tashkent. Free Wi-Fi. **$$$–$$$$**

✕ **New World Pizza-Bakery** [112 D4] 26A Bukhoro; ✆ 71 256 0445; m 90 187 9950; ⏱ 09.00–22.00 daily. Decent American-style pizza at semi-American prices in a central site. **$$$**

✕ **Broccoli** [113 E6] 7 Chekhov; m 95 195 1144; ⏱ 07.00–23.00 daily. A self-service health food eatery near Oybek/Ming Orik metro station, serving baked goods, salads, soups, chicken & steamed-vegetable dishes. **$$**

CAFÉS AND TEA HOUSES
☕ **Al-Aziz** [112 D2] Abdulla Kodiriy; m 90 926 2913; ⏱ 10.00–23.00 daily. It's the lovely stream-side setting (despite being under a ring-

road flyover) on the edge of the park that makes it worth stopping on a hot day for a drink or snack in this creeper-clad pavilion. The restaurant food & service are less good. **$$**

☕ **Reggae Bean** [113 E7] 40 Oybek; m 95 145 3145; f reggaebean; ⏱ 09.00–23.00 Mon–Fri, 10.00–23.00 Sat. Great coffee, lemonades & mocktails, plus Jamaican-, Indonesian- & Uzbek-inspired food. In addition to the chilled reggae-themed interior there's a garden lounge. Excellent English spoken. **$$**

☕ **Studio Café** [113 F4] 1 Toytepa; ✆ 71 233 0601; ⏱ 08.00–23.00 daily. Garish, Hollywood-themed café blaring Russian pop. You can order anything from a coffee to a steak. **$$**

☕ **Angel's Café** [112 D5] 16 Afrosiab; ✆ 71 252 6565/71 140 0404; w angels.uz; ⏱ 09.00–23.30 daily. At the Oybek metro station. Modern café selling coffee, juices, pastries, cakes, light lunches & snacks. **$**

☕ **Bon!** 22 Navoi [112 B2] (✆ 71 241 2067); 63 Usmon Nosir [88 D6] (✆ 71 280 5116); 40 Chekhov [112 D6] (✆ 71 150 1833); 21 Chimkent [112 D4] (✆ 71 256 3404); 14A Ak-Kurgan [113 H1] (✆ 71 268 9302); 44A S Azimova [113 F4] (✆ 71 232 0008); f boncafe; ⏱ 08.00–22.00 daily. Small chain of classy cafés, serving good coffee & tea (by the cup or the pot), ice cream, sandwiches & mouth-watering patisserie such as strudel, sachertorte or macarons (very on trend). **$**

☕ **Bookcafé** [113 E4] 8 Istiqbol; ✆ 71 200 8008/71 233 7263; f bookcafetashkent; ⏱ 09.00–23.00 daily. Popular with students because of its central location, adequate Wi-Fi & booklined ambiance, this has great coffee & pastries. **$**

☕ **Café Jum** [112 B5] 3 Babur; m 91 192 1561; ⏱ 09.00–18.00 Mon–Sat. Café serving real Italian roasted coffee & patisserie. Coffee machines, beans & other assorted coffee paraphernalia are also on sale. There's also a 24hr branch at the airport. **$**

PUBS
🍺 **Cafe Dudek** [88 C6] 42 Mukimi; m 90 940 5955; f dudekuz; ⏱ noon–23.00 Mon–Sat, 14.00–23.00 Sun. To the southwest near the ring road, this is a Czech pub that not only brews its own beer (Pilsner, wheat beer & dark beer), but also makes its own bread & sausages. There's a sunny terrace, & occasional live music. **$$$$**

🍺 **Irish Pub** [113 E5] 30 Shevchenko; ✆ 71 252 7842; ⏱ 11.00–23.00 daily. A taste of the Emerald

Isle in Tashkent: naff, but entertainingly so. Major football matches are screened on the big-screen TV, bands play nightly & it draws a large (& loud) expat crowd; upstairs is a restaurant featuring 7 types of Irish sausage. $$$$

⊖ **Ye Olde Chelsea Arms** [112 C7] 25 Kakhkhara; m 98 309 3434; w chelsea. caravangroup.uz; ⊕ 15.00–05.00 daily. Chelsea claims to be an English pub, though the interior

will leave most Brits bemused. Major sporting events are shown on the big screen, but it lacks the atmosphere of the Irish Pub (page 101). Sandwiches, salads, burgers & grilled meats. $$

⊖ **Zhiguli** [89 H4] 74 Sultanali Mashkhadi; m 99 817 1003; ⊕ 11.00–02.00 daily. Opened in 2016 to the rear of the station, this is a sort of Russian pub, with car-themed décor, home-brewed beer & filling food. $$

ENTERTAINMENT AND NIGHTLIFE

BARS AND CLUBS

Tashkent has no shortage of bars & clubs, particularly if vodka is your thing. The 'in' places to be seen are constantly changing, but they're generally more or less in the same locations. The Russian-language website w afisha.uz has the most up-to-date listings.

Although generally fairly safe, visitors should note that many of the attentive single women in bars & clubs are working girls. Men simply interested in a quiet drink (or a genuine date) need to be clear about what they are & aren't paying for, & women should be prepared to fend off unwanted advances.

♀ **The Bar** [112 D4] 56 Karimov; m 90 185 3003; ⊕ 18.00–05.00 daily. An unmarked door on the side of the Lotte City Hotel Tashkent Palace (page 97) gives access to this speakeasy-style bar where a serious mixologist will make genuine cocktails to your taste.

♀ **One More Bar** [113 F1] 60 Amir Timur; m 99 890 9998; f bar.onemore; ⊕ 18.00–06.00 daily. A trendy bar/lounge just north of the city centre (one of a group of bars & clubs actually on Niyozbek, just east of the main drag), with a small dance floor (playing a mix of house, rap & R&B) & strict entry controls – dress smart.

♀ **Steam** [113 E1] 2 Niyozbek; ☎71 235 0522; f steam.tashkent; ⊕ 11.00–midnight daily. A lively but easy-going student bar with a steampunk theme & live bands playing covers of international hits. They serve food & draught beer & staff are friendly & speak English.

☆ **CMI after party Bar** [113 G2] 68 Niyazov; m 99 835 8500; f cmibar; ⊕ 20.00–late. A well-established DJ club with a good choice of cocktails that gets busy around 01.00. Entry (including 1 drink) US$6–15 depending on which night you visit.

THEATRES AND MUSIC VENUES

The theatre season in Tashkent runs roughly from Oct to Jun. Performances start early, sometimes at 17.00.

🎭 **Alisher Navoi Opera & Ballet Theatre** [112 D4] 28 Otaturk; ☎71 233 9081; w gabt.uz; ⊕ 13.00–19.00 (ticket office), 18.00 Mon–Fri, 17.00 Sat & Sun (performances), matinées sometimes available at w/ends. A trip to the ballet or opera at the Navoi is a highlight of any trip to Tashkent. The building, set in an attractive square with musical foundations, was designed by the same architect responsible for Lenin's mausoleum in Red Sq & completed by Japanese POWs in the 40s. A plaque in Japanese on the outside of the building commemorates their contribution. The standard of performance is high & a live orchestra comes as standard. You can see the national opera & ballet companies & foreign troupes often visit on tour. Closed for renovation in 2014–16, the theatre is now resplendent inside & out. The lobbies are covered with scenes from Uzbek folk tales. Guided tours start from the box office.

🎭 **Bakhor Concert Hall** [112 C3] 5 Independence Sq; ☎71 139 0136. Built in 1931 as Government Hse, the Bakhor Concert Hall is now home to an Uzbek dance troupe & hosts occasional musical recitals.

🎭 **Ilkhom Theatre** [112 C2] 5 Pakhtakor; ☎71 241 2241; w ilkhom.com; ⊕ performances 18.30 Tue–Sat (check website for season). Founded in 1976, Ilkhom was the 1st independent theatre in the USSR (see box, page 35 for its history). Productions are typically in Russian (occasionally with English surtitles) & are highly innovative. The company tours internationally & is well regarded both at home & overseas.

📷 **Istiqlol Palace** [112 A4] Halklar Dustligi Sq; ☎71 244 5607/71 245 9251. Built as the International People's Friendship Hall to commemorate the efforts to rebuild Tashkent after the 1966 earthquake, this is Uzbekistan's largest cinema/concert hall, with space for 6,000 people.

📷 **National Academic Drama Theatre** [106 D6] 34 Navoi; ☎71 244 1751. Founded in 1914 (but now in a modern building), this company offers both classical & contemporary works by Uzbek playwrights. Performances are in Uzbek.

📷 **Republican Puppet Theatre** [112 C4] 1 Afrosiab; ☎71 256 7395; ⏲ performances 11.00 (Russian) & 13.00 (Uzbek) Sat & Sun. 2 theatre companies (Uzbek & Russian language) perform a repertoire of more than 20 fairytales with everything from marionettes to sock puppets. The elaborate building is almost as much of an attraction as the plays; designed in 1979 to recall a fairytale castle, there's a gallery upstairs where kids can try out various puppets. Highly recommended.

📷 **Russian Drama Theatre** [112 E3] 24 Ataturk; ☎71 233 8165; ⏲ performances 18.30 Wed–Fri, 19.00 Sat & Sun; tickets start at US$2. Professional theatre companies perform both Russian classics & contemporary pieces in this modern theatre.

📷 **State Conservatory** [112 B3] 1; ☎71 241 2991; **w** konservatoriya.uz. Chamber concerts in Western & Uzbek styles.

📷 **Tashkent State Circus** [106 C6] Khadra Sq; ☎71 244 3223; ⏲ performances 11.00 & 15.00 Sat & Sun. Purpose-built spaceship-style building hosting regular sell-out performances. The acrobats on camels are a Tashkent speciality.

📷 **Tashkent State Musical Comedy Theatre** [88 A6] Chupon-ata, Block Ts; ☎71 273 8591; **w** operetta.uz. Known as the Operetta, this was founded in 1972 by Alexander Ginsburg, a well-known dissident who was expelled from the Soviet Union in 1979. It puts on song & dance shows mainly in Uzbek. Located near the Mirzo Ulugbeg metro station.

📷 **Turkistan Concert Hall** [112 D2] 2 Navoi; ☎71 235 4440. Another huge concert hall, built in 1993, with a popular open-air summer theatre behind.

CINEMAS

📷 **Alisher Navoi Kino Saray** [112 C2] 15 Navoi; ☎71 200 0050; **w** myticket.uz; ⏲ showings 11.00–19.30 daily; adults US$1.50. The circular Panorama building, a masterpiece of Soviet Brutalism built in 1961, has been divided into separate screens with a new wing added to the south; architectural purists were outraged, but at least it's still in use, showing mainly Uzbek films.

📷 **NEXT Mall Cinema** [112 B5/6] NEXT Mall, 6 Babur; ☎71 231 8282; **w** nextmall.uz/en. A modern multiplex including a 5D cylindrical screen.

📷 **Premier Cinema** [112 D6] 25 Mirobod; ☎71 252 3787/71 252 1625; **w** premier-hall.uz. Watch the latest blockbusters dubbed into Russian on the big screen or hire the intimate 12-seat hall to watch a film of your choice for US$10.

📷 **Royal Cinema** [88 B4] 4th fl, Samarkand Darvoza Mall, 5A Koratosh; **m** 95 143 3535; ⏲ 11.00–21.30. A modern multiplex, showing American (in English) & Russian blockbusters.

SPORT ARENAS

Bunyodkor Stadium [88 A7] 47 Bunyodkor. Built in 2012 & also known as the Milliy (National) Stadium, this modernist football stadium, seating 34,000, is home to the Bunyodkor club & the Uzbek national team. It's in the southwest of the city at the Mirzo Ulugbeg metro station.

Pakhtakor Stadium [112 C3] Home to FC Pakhtakor Tashkent, this wide-open stadium, right in the city centre, was built in 1956 & modernised in 1996, with seating for 35,000.

SHOPPING

Tashkent is yet to mark itself out as a shoppers' paradise, but new money is spurring the opening of Western chain stores and, if you're happy to haggle, almost anything can be purchased in the city's bazaars.

The **souvenirs** on sale in Tashkent don't really compete with those in Uzbekistan's tourist hubs, either in variety or quality, as there's little market for them: the appeal of shopping here instead comes from barging elbows with locals and snatching a glimpse of everyday life. From the mounds of melons to the wafting smell of freshly baked *non* bread, the street-side butchers, the chinking and sparking of metal workshops, and a gay array of rainbow-coloured plastic goods from China, an hour or two spent shopping here is a multi-sensory feast.

MARKETS

Chorsu Bazaar [106 B5] Beruni; ⏱ 09.00–18.00 daily (partly closed Mon). Meaning 'the crossroads', Chorsu is the commercial heart of Tashkent & has been for hundreds of years. Originally open-air (as parts of it still are today), the maze of covered stalls was largely cleared away in the mid 20th century. Soviet architects replaced them with vast mosaic-covered domes: blue & turquoise space bubbles that still protect merchants & their goods from the elements & give the bazaar's skyline its distinctive shape. Each dome or area of the market houses a different type of merchandise: take a stroll around the dried fruit & nut stands if you want to try plenty of free samples but beware of the dried cheese balls: they're something of an acquired taste. If you have the time to hunt, almost everything is for sale here: plastic Chinese household goods battle for attention with hand-painted ceramics & fox-fur hats, almost-antique knick-knacks, dried fruits & imported car parts in varying states of decay. The market is liveliest first thing in the morning when the wholesale deliveries are made, & the cheap chai & kebab stalls provide sustenance while you watch the world go by. Come here to get a feel for 'real' Tashkent & an echo of Silk Road trade in centuries past. The easiest way to reach the market is to take the metro to Chorsu station, which is just a minute's walk from the first stalls (although this is still a bizarre area of arbitrary fences).

Mirobod Dehoon Bazaar [112 D7] Cnr Mirobod & Nukus. In addition to the great Chorsu Bazaar (see above), if you're wanting to buy food the Mirobod Dehoon Bazaar is a good alternative south of the centre.

Tezykovka flea market [89 H4] Yangiobod (about 6km southeast of the main railway station);

⏱ Sun mornings. Here you can find anything from books & clothing to car parts & animals. Watch your belongings, & you'll need a Russian speaker if you want to shop.

BOOKS

Sharq Ziyokori [112 D4] 26 Bukhara; ☏ 71 233 3590; ⏱ 09.00–18.00 Mon–Sat. Best option for buying maps, including the Uzbek equivalent of Ordnance Survey (Ozbekiston Viloyatlari). Mostly in Uzbek or Russian, but they do have some language-learning materials & guidebooks.

SOUVENIRS

Abdul Khasim Madrasa [112 A4] Alisher Navoi Park; ⏱ 10.00–16.00 daily. Take the opportunity to watch Tashkent's artisans at work & buy directly from them. The stringed instruments make particularly tasteful mementos, & you can also buy miniature paintings, wood- & metalwork & lacquer.

Human House [112 D7] 43 Ivliev; ☏ 71 255 4411; m 90 937 8373; w humanhuman.net; ⏱ 10.00–19.00 Mon–Sat. One of Tashkent's coolest boutiques, Human Hse sells Uzbek textiles, ceramics, homeware & toys. Prices are high but the quality is good & the choice is wide.

Sharq-Guli [112 C1] 78 Abdulla Kodiriy; ☏ 71 412 056. Once a Soviet women's collective, this embroidery company continues to use traditional designs to decorate *suzanis* (see box, page 78), bags, skull caps & other textiles. More than 3,000 women still work here, doing embroidery by machine & by hand. This is a great option for gift shopping, particularly if you won't have the opportunity to travel beyond Tashkent, & if you call in advance you can usually see the women at work.

OTHER PRACTICALITIES

EMERGENCIES

In an emergency, you can call the following free numbers for assistance. It is unlikely, however, that the operator will speak any English, & help is not guaranteed to arrive. In the case of medical emergencies, you are usually better off hailing a taxi or using a private vehicle to get to hospital (see opposite).

Ambulance ☏ 103
Fire ☏ 101
Police ☏ 102

INTERNET

Getting online in Tashkent is becoming easier, though connections are often rather slow. Wi-Fi is normal in hotels & hostels & increasingly common in cafés. Internet dongles are also widely available (page 80). The following internet cafés were open at the time of going to print.

ⓔ Ground Zero co-working spaces
w groundzero.uz; ⏰ 09.00–22.00 daily. 3 locations: 146 Timur Malik [89 H4] (m 90 938 7877), 6 Mustakillik Av [112 E3] (m 90 955 9969) & 50 Bunyodkor [88 A7] (m 90 901 2001).
ⓔ Internet Center [112 D6] 13A Shota Rustaveli; ☎ 71 215 5525
ⓔ Internet Markazi [113 E3] 7 Shakhrisabz. Inside the main post office (see right).
ⓔ Prime Time [112 D6] 27/9 Mirobod; ☎ 71 252 2401

MEDICAL

Tashkent's medical facilities are a mixed bag, & the quality is usually dictated by whether or not you can pay (cash only, as a rule). In an emergency you should contact your embassy (page 48) for assistance & to arrange medical evacuation, but the following options (all offering 24/7 emergency care) should be able to patch you up if the worst comes to the worst.

✚ Emergency Hospital [88 A5] 2 Farkhad; ☎ 71 277 9740/71 150 4600; w med.uz/emergency. Large, state-run hospital with proficient staff.
✚ Safo Tibbiyot [112 D7] 21 Ivliev; ☎ 71 255 9550; m 98 127 9470; e info@safouz.com; ⏰ 09.00–18.00 Mon–Fri, 09.00–13.00 Sat. Large private clinic offering a full range of services.
✚ Tashkent International Medical Clinic [89 F7] 38 Sarikul; ☎ 71 291 0142; w tashclinic.org. Privately run medical clinic catering to the expat community in Tashkent. Dental clinic also available. Consultations cost US$120–150.

MONEY

There is still a severe shortage of cash machines in Tashkent, & those that exist may not always have cash in them.

$ Kapitalbank 6 branches: [88 B6], [89 E2], [89 H3], [113 E6], [113 E2], [113 H5]. All have Visa (Plus) ATMs.
$ Kishlok Kurilish Bank [113 E5]
$ Mastercard ATMs 6 options: 1 Istiqlol, 73 A Qakhar & in these hotels: Grand Mir (page 96), Ramada Tashkent (page 97), Hyatt Regency (page 97), Hotel Uzbekistan (page 97) & Radisson Blu (page 97).
$ National Bank of Uzbekistan [106 D4] NBU; ⏰ 09.00–18.00 Mon–Fri, 09.00–16.00 Sat. It is possible to change money, cash travellers' cheques & get a cash advance here. If you need to change Swiss francs (CHF) or other less-common currencies, the NBU is the only place to do so.
$ Visa (Plus) ATMs In 10 hotels: the Asia Tashkent, Grand Mir Hotel (page 96), Wyndham (page 97), International (page 97), Le Grande Plaza (page 101), Lotte City Tashkent Palace Hotel (page 97), Ramada Tashkent (page 97), Radisson Blu (page 97), Hotel Uzbekistan (page 97) & Hayot [89 G6].

POST

✉ DHL If you want to increase the likelihood of your post actually arriving at its destination, DHL has several offices [112 D7] (32 Oybek; ☎ 71 120 5525; ⏰ 08.00–19.00 Mon–Fri, 09.00–14.00 Sat), [113 F6] (4 Turkistan; ⏰ 09.00–18.00 Mon–Fri, 09.00–14.00 Sat) & [89 E2] (107B Amir Timur; ⏰ 08.30–17.30 Mon–Fri).
✉ Express Mail Service [113 F6] EMS; 4 Turkiston; ☎ 081; w ems.post. This state-owned venture operates both domestic & international services, tends to be slightly cheaper than its foreign competitors, & will collect mail from you for dispatch.
✉ Post office [113 E3] 7 Shakhrisabz. The main post office is centrally located but tends to be busy & the staff are unhelpful. There are other branches by the station [113 F7] (4 Turkiston) & in most neighbourhoods.
✉ UPS [88 A7] 52 Bunyodkor; ☎ 71 120 3838; ⏰ 09.00–18.00 Mon–Fri

WHAT TO SEE AND DO

Points of interest covered in this chapter are alphabetised under their geographical heading.

IN AND AROUND THE OLD CITY Tashkent's historic heart is jam-packed with museums, mausoleums and mosques, many of which are within walking distance of one another. They are the sole survivors of the 1966 earthquake (see box, page 119) and so it is here that you will get a sense of Tashkent in times gone by – the pace of life is a little slower, the people watching richer, and the ghosts of the past are veritably trampling over one another to be seen. The popular Chorsu Bazaar (page 104) can also be found in this area.

Alisher Navoi Literary Museum [112 B2] (69 Navoi; ✆71 241 0275; ⊕ 09.00–17.00 Mon–Fri, 09.00–14.00 Sat; US$1) Although he was born in Afghanistan, the Uzbeks have taken Alisher Navoi very much to heart and declared him the father of

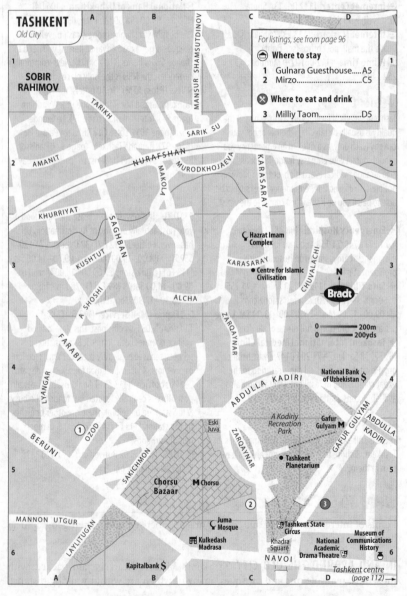

TASHKENT Old City

For listings, see from page 96

⬡ **Where to stay**
1 Gulnara Guesthouse..... A5
2 Mirzo...................................C5

✖ **Where to eat and drink**
3 Milliy Taom.....................D5

SOBIR RAHIMOV

MANSUR SHAMSUTDINOV

TARIKH

SARIK SU

NURAFSHAN

AMANIT

MAKOLA

MURODKHOJAEVA

KARASARAY

KHURRIYAT

SAGHBAN

KUSHTUT

Hazrat Imam Complex

KARASARAY

CHUVALACHI

A SHOSHI

ALCHA

Centre for Islamic Civilisation

N

Bradt

FARABI

ZARQAYNAR

LYANGAR

0 ——— 200m
0 ——— 200yds

National Bank of Uzbekistan $

ABDULLA KADIRI

BERUNI

OZOD

Eski Juva

A Kodiriy Recreation Park

Gafur Gulyam M

GAFUR GULYAM

ABDULLA KADIRI

SAKICHMON

ZARQAYNAR

Tashkent Planetarium

Chorsu Bazaar

M Chorsu

Juma Mosque

Tashkent State Circus

MANNON UTGUR

LAYLITUGAN

Kulkedash Madrasa

Khadra Square

National Academic Drama Theatre

Museum of Communications History

Kapitalbank $

NAVOI

Tashkent centre (page 112) →

Uzbek literature (see box, page 116). Housed in an attractive Neoclassical building built in 1941 to mark the 500th anniversary of Navoi's birth, the museum contains manuscripts, photographs and archive documents as well as a small number of paintings, some of them replicas. The interior of the museum building is itself decorated with large-scale murals depicting garden and palace scenes inspired by Navoi's *Khamsa*.

Chagatai Cemetery [88 B1] (319 Farabi; ☉ daylight hrs) Little-visited by tourists but offering a fascinating insight into both Muslim and Soviet funereal habits, this large cemetery is stuffed with mausolea to the great and the good of Tashkent society. Lack of space has historically necessitated the burying of bodies on top of one another, but the numerous plaques commemorate those hidden below. Look out for the surprisingly un-Islamic busts and engraved depictions of the deceased, and particularly the leading figures of the Uzbek SSR (to the right of the entry). The poet Aibek (see box, page 108) is buried here, as is former president Rashidov, and you'll also find memorials to lesser-known Uzbek heroes, such as Hero of Labour Turson Akhunova, the first woman to drive a cotton-picking machine. Shockingly, she died aged 46 from cancer caused by the unregulated chemical fertilisers sprayed on the cotton fields.

Hazrat Imam Complex [106 C3] (Karasaray; ☉ 09.00–13.00 & 14.00–16.00 Mon–Fri, 09.00–noon Sat) Northeast of Chorsu Bazaar is the historical spiritual heart of Tashkent, a glimpse of what much of the city must have been like before it was levelled by the 1966 earthquake or replaced with Soviet concrete. At its heart is **Hazrat Imam Square** (sometimes also written as Khast Imom Square). Between here and the main road is the **Hazrat Imam Mosque**, constructed in just four months in 2007 on the instruction of President Karimov. Then the largest mosque in the city, it was an expensive undertaking: the sandalwood columns came from India, the dark-green marble is Turkish, and the interior of the blue-tiled domes is decorated with genuine gold leaf.

Of the numerous sites surrounding the square, the most important is undoubtedly the **Muyi Muborak Library** (☉ 09.00–noon & 14.00–17.00 Mon–Fri, 10.00–15.00 Sat; US$1.25). 'Muyi Muborak' means 'the sacred hair', a reference to a holy relic held here: a hair said to have belonged to the Prophet Muhammad. Pride of place is given, however, to the world's oldest Qu'ran, supposedly produced just 19 years after the death of Muhammad, and one of four copies ordered by the third Caliph, Othman. It is said to be stained with the blood of the Caliph, who was reading it at the time of his assassination in Medina in AD656, but in fact modern scientific analysis has shown that it was produced between AD765 and AD855, and that the blood you see is of animal origin. This huge Qu'ran was brought to Uzbekistan by Amir Timur. It would have been displayed on special occasions on the vast stone Qu'ran stand in the centre of the Bibi Khanym Mosque in Samarkand (page 170), which is still *in situ*. Today, it is displayed in a glass-fronted case, and although the text appears to be written on parchment, it is in fact on deerskin. Other highlights of the library's manuscript collection include Qu'rans from the 8th century onwards, illuminated pages, and modern Qu'rans in numerous foreign languages.

Next to the library is the **Tillya Sheikh Mosque**, formerly Tashkent's main place of worship. Founded by Mirza Akhmed Kushbegi in 1856 (but mostly dating from 1902), the mosque is a peaceful place with some attractive carved pillars and painted ceilings (though it is notably less ornate than the Hazrat Imam Mosque

'Aibek' (or 'Oybek') was the pen name of Musa Tashmukhamedov (1905–68), a polymath born into a family of weavers in Tashkent. He took full advantage of the Soviet higher-education system, graduating in turn from the Tashkent Teacher Training Course, Leningrad Economics Institute and then the Central Asian State University in Tashkent.

Aibek's literary career began in 1926 when he published *Emotions*, a collection of poetry about life in Soviet Uzbekistan. His subsequent poetic works included *Torch* (1932) and *Vendetta* (also 1932), both of which discuss the abandonment of the vestiges of traditional life. In the late 1930s, having completed his education, Aibek really began to establish himself as a writer. He published the remarkable *Sacred Blood* in 1943. It is recognised as one of the most outstanding works of social realism in Uzbek literature, and it describes the contribution of Uzbeks in World War I and their role in the 1916 uprisings. Also of note are Aibek's novels *Navoi* (1945) and *Khamsa* (1948) in which he gives fictionalised accounts of the inner feelings of the poets Alisher Navoi and Khamza Khakimzada Niyazi. Not only was Aibek a central figure in 20th-century Uzbek literature, but he was also a scientist, translator and publicist. He became a member of the Uzbek SSR's Academy of Scientists, and his translations of important Russian literary works, including writings by Pushkin, Gorky and Lermontov, are still widely read in Uzbekistan.

that has effectively replaced it; page 107). On the west side of the plaza, facing the library, is the 16th-century **Barak-Khan Madrasa**. Built by Barak-Khan from 1502 in honour of Mirzo Ulug Beg's grandson and another unknown Timurid, its dome was destroyed in an earthquake in 1868 and it was rebuilt and then over-restored by the Soviets. Unusually, this madrasa only ever had a single storey: it was built to educate local students from Tashkent and so there was no need to construct the accommodation cells that would have been situated on the first floor. The ground-floor cells now house craft shops. Until 2007, this was home to the Muslim Board of Uzbekistan, now in a plain building to the north by the car park.

At the northwest corner of the complex is the 19th-century **Al-Bukhari Institute** (once the Namozgoh Mosque), one of the few Islamic centres allowed to operate during the Soviet period. For much of the 20th century it was restricted in the scope of its work and limited to just 25 imams; now there are more than 130 people studying here. Last but not least, also in the northwest corner of the complex, the **Tomb of Kaffal Shashi**, built in 1541–42, marks the final resting place of the local poet-philosopher Abu Bakr Muhammad Kaffal Shashi (903–976). You can see his sarcophagus, and also the tombs of numerous later muftis. Pilgrims, in particular women hoping to conceive a child, still pray, donate alms and help with the cleaning and maintenance of the shrine in the hope that the saint will give them help.

The new **Centre for Islamic Civilisation** [106 C3] (47 Karasaray; w cisc.uz/en) will rise from the building site immediately to the south of the Hazrat Imam Complex; the Othman Qu'ran will be moved to its museum, which will display over 40,000 other historical items.

Kulkedash Madrasa [106 B6] (46 Navoi; ⊕ 10.00–18.00 daily; US$1.25) Tashkent's own Registan centres on the Kulkedash Madrasa, an Islamic school built between 1551 and 1575 of mud bricks decorated with majolica and painted ceramic tiles. In the 18th century it was converted first into a *caravanserai* for merchants trading at the nearby bazaar, then into a fortress. Finally, it was used as the setting for public executions: unfaithful wives in particular were stoned to death with rocks hurled from the parapet of the central portal. Earthquakes in 1866 significantly damaged the structure, and it lay in ruins until it was restored in the mid 20th century.

The towering archway that marks the entrance to the madrasa is decorated externally with stars; the lancet niche above the doors serves to emphasise its height. The cells around the central courtyard once housed the madrasa's students; their modern counterparts study in more comfortable, though less picturesque, surroundings. Next door is the **Juma Mosque**, built in the 15th century, although only fragments of the original structure survive – it's now rather Russian in style.

Museum of Communications History [106 D6] (28A Navoi; \ 71 244 9909; w aloqamuzeyi.uz; ⊕ 10.00–13.00 & 14.00–18.00 daily)

A fairly new, free museum, this was built by the Uzbek Agency for Communication and Information to explain the history of communication from the Middle Ages to the present day. The exhibition includes a historic mail wagon, models of the Timurid fortresses and their fire-signalling techniques, and you can make short-range phone calls on the antique telephones. Soviet-era technology – computers, televisions, record players, etc, is inevitably particularly well represented, and is a really fascinating way to look back at the past. Few exhibits are labelled, but they have a new interactive tablet guide and there's a virtual tour on the museum's website.

Sheikhantaur Mausoleum Complex [112 C2] (State Islamic University, Navoi)

Just three mausoleums remain here in what was once a necropolis of 16 tombs – the others fell prey to earthquakes and short-sighted Soviet planning. You now have to approach down a side alley which branches off a larger alley between Navoi and Abdulla Kodiriy on the east side of the International Islamic Academy of Uzbekistan.

Sheikhantaur's Mausoleum is the small, brick-built structure with dark-blue majolica tiles and twin domes. Sheikhantaur (or, to use his real name, Sheikh Khovandi Tahur) was a local Sufi saint, born in the late 13th century and believed to be a descendant of the Rashidun Caliph Umar. As a child he was initiated into the Yasaviyya order of Khodja Ahmed Yassaui and he was known in Tashkent as a spiritual guide. He died in the city in around 1360; his tomb is contemporary, though heavily restored. There are comfy sofas, a tree trunk in the first chamber (for some reason), and two smaller tombs in the second.

Just north of **Sheikhantaur's Mausoleum** is the **Kaldirach Bey Mausoleum**. A 15th-century ruler of Moghulistan, his tomb is unusual because its turquoise roof is dodecahedral on the outside but domed on the inside. The *gurkhan* (burial room) has beautiful carved wooden exterior doors and deep alcoves decorated with stalactite-like carving.

The largest of the tombs, dating from the end of the 15th century, is that of **Yunus Khan**, descendant of Genghis Khan, grandfather of Babur, and one-time ruler of Tashkent, found in the west of the complex. Although you cannot go inside (it's inside the Academy and almost always locked), it's still possible to appreciate the fine lancet arch of the portal, the turquoise dome and the Arabic calligraphy that decorates the façades. The tile work was restored in the 1970s.

Tashkent Planetarium [106 C5] (6 Zarqaynar; \ 71 244 7720; ⊕ 09.00–17.00 daily; US$2)

Close to Chorsu Bazaar, the planetarium combines exhibition halls with a 60-seat auditorium, with projectors showing the movement of the planets, meteors, comets, black holes and other fabulous things. You can ask for an English showing.

Founded relatively late (only in 2003), the planetarium has an admirable dual remit of entertainment and the promotion of astronomy, and so on weekdays you will most likely be surrounded by groups of schoolchildren. The building's design – a cube overlapped with a dome – is supposed to represent the earth beneath the heavens, and the exhibits are regularly updated to reflect the latest astronomic discoveries. Of course, the discovery here of a new, minor planet named Samarkand in 2008, caused particular excitement for Uzbekistan's astronomers.

AROUND AMIR TIMUR AND INDEPENDENCE SQUARES The heart of the modern city, **Amir Timur Square** is a lush, green space with plenty of flowers and fountains, laid out in the 1870s. Roads radiate from here to the north, east and south of Tashkent, and the city's most important buildings, both political and cultural, are concentrated on the square and in the immediate vicinity. The only remaining original building, on the west side, is the University of Law, built by von Kaufmann as a girls' high school. A large statue of Timur himself (see box, page 17), sitting astride his horse and proclaiming 'strength is in justice', is the square's current centrepiece, but he is simply the latest in a long line of former residents: General von Kaufmann, Lenin, Stalin and Karl Marx all occupied this spot before him. This particular statue, a 7m-high bronze by sculptor Ilhom Jabarov weighs in at 30 tonnes and is one of three erected in Uzbekistan to commemorate the 660th anniversary of Timur's birth. To the right of the huge and very distinctive Hotel Uzbekistan (page 97) is the Forum Palace, built for President Karimov's daughter Gulnara (see box, page 32) and disused since her downfall; in 2009, dozens of 135-year-old plane trees were controversially cut down on the president's orders to give a clear view of the white-marble monstrosity.

Independence Square (Mustakillik Maydoni) covers 7ha, making it the largest square in Tashkent. It is packed with monuments and fountains, including a particularly impressive one with 500 water jets. First the site of a fortress in the mid 19th century, it later became a parade ground for the military and for workers' processions on national holidays. The most important monument here is the golden globe on a pedestal, showing Uzbekistan's place in the world, and beneath it a mother with a child in her arms. Erected in 1992 to replace the world's largest Lenin statue, the monument marks Uzbek independence. Unfortunately, the square is regularly closed to the public.

Alisher Navoi Library [112 D2] (1 Independence Sq; w natlib.uz; ⊕ 08.00–20.00 Mon–Fri, 08.00–17.00 Sat & Sun) The National Library of Uzbekistan, named in honour of the 15th-century polymath Alisher Navoi (see box, page 116), is a sprawling modern building that opened at the end of 2011. Dating back to 1870, the core of the collection includes books and manuscripts originally owned by General von Kaufmann. The rare books department has a vast number of pre-revolutionary Turkic-language newspapers, and separate catalogues list materials in Uzbek, Russian, Kyrgyz and Kazakh plus Soviet-era journals relating to Uzbekistan. Though not of such great interest to general visitors due to the language barriers involved, it is nonetheless an invaluable resource for research, and many of the items are visually appealing, whether you can read them or not.

Art Gallery of Uzbekistan [112 D3] (2 Buyuk Turon; ☏ 71 233 5674; ⊕ 11.00–17.00 Tue–Sat; US$0.50) Uzbekistan's most modern exhibition hall, this was opened by President Karimov in 2004 to display the collection of 20th-century Uzbek art acquired by the National Bank of Uzbekistan. It's a pretty decent collection, spanning landscapes, portraits, still lifes and abstract art, both pre and post independence, as well as a substantial coin collection and space for temporary exhibits, often of foreign art, and other cultural events, plus a café and gift shop.

Geology Museum [113 E5] (11A Shevchenko; \71 256 1192; w muzeygeologii. uz; ⏰ 10.00–16.00 Mon–Fri; US$2) Geology may not be the most fashionable of subjects, but we wouldn't be here without it. This unsophisticated museum explains the formation of the earth and our place in the solar system, and has a few tatty dinosaur displays. More importantly, however, it also has a large collection of precious stones and minerals from central Asia, and a set of the excellent Soviet geological survey maps produced to show the extent of the USSR's natural resources. It's popular with school groups.

House of Photography [113 E4] (4 Istikbol; \71 233 5168; ⏰ 10.00–17.00 Tue–Sun; US$0.50) This striking, unexpectedly light display space, built for the Academy of Arts in 1934, showcases exhibitions from internationally known photographers. Though many are Uzbek or have links with Uzbekistan, this is not always the case. The museum also arranges photography competitions, conferences and workshops, and there's also a contemporary art gallery here. It is a good place to get in touch with Tashkent's artistic community. From here, you can walk a couple of blocks east to the **Art + Fact Gallery** [113 G4] at 20 S Azimova 1st Lane (\71 232 0360; **f** bunkeruz; ⏰ 10.00–18.00 Mon–Fri), another space dedicated to photography, with exhibition areas on the ground floor and in a former nuclear bunker.

Memory Square [112 D2] (Independence Sq; ⏰ 09.00–18.00 daily) Inside a quiet garden, this memorial remembers the 40,000 Uzbek soldiers who died in World War II and the mothers they left behind. The names of the deceased are inscribed on granite walls of the Alley of Memory, at the centre of which is the Eternal Flame and the Lamenting Mother statue (by Ilhom Jabarov). The monument is flanked by busts of two war heroes, Viktor Malyasov and Jurakhon Usmanov.

Mukarram Turgunbaeva Museum [112 D3] (5 Independence Sq; \71 239 1296; ⏰ 09.30–17.00 Mon–Sat) One of the best-presented small museums in Uzbekistan, this collection showcases the life of Mukarram Turgunbaeva, one of the country's most famous dancers and the founder and director of the Bahor folk dance ensemble. Focused on dance in the late 1920s and 1930s, exhibits include elaborate and beautifully displayed costumes, performance posters and memorabilia. There is also an extensive archive of Uzbek folk song and music recordings. Fascinating and highly recommended; look for the side door of the Bakhor Concert Hall.

Romanov Residence [112 D3] (Sayilgokh, between Sharof Rashidov & Buyuk Turon) Built for Grand Duke Nikolai Konstantinovich Romanov (see box, page 114) in 1891, this private residence has gone through a number of incarnations, being used in turn to accommodate the Museum of Art, National Palace of Young Pioneers (a Boy Scout-type organisation established by Lenin) and the Museum of Uzbek Jewellery. The palace is currently used by the Ministry of Foreign Affairs for official receptions. Though it is not currently possible for the public to go inside, the building, designed by Wilhelm Heinzelmann and Al Benoit, is an attractive structure with rose windows, turrets and life-sized sculptures of guard dogs. It is surprisingly small, but set among pleasant gardens just back from the pedestrianised street.

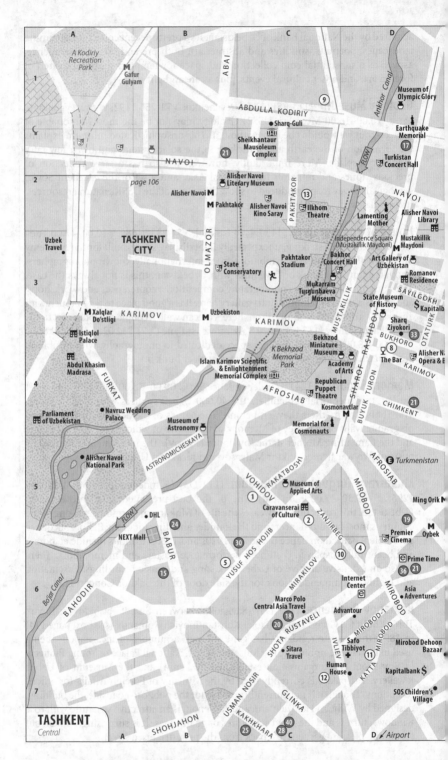

TASHKENT
Central

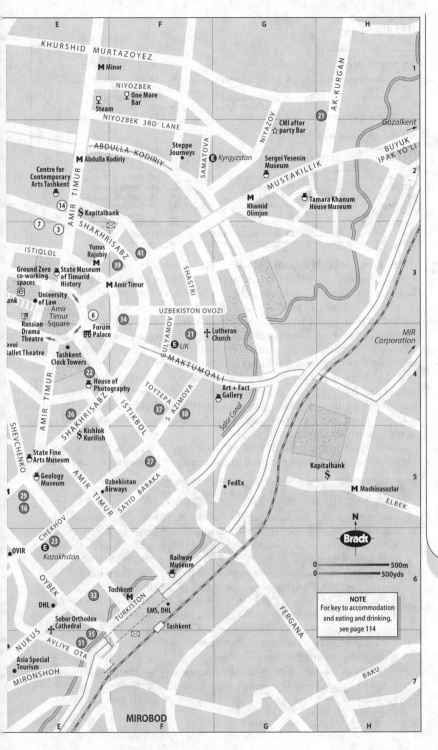

KHURSHID MURTAZOYEZ

M Minor

NIYOZBEK
Steam One More Bar

NIYOZBEK 3rd LANE

ABDULLA KODIRIY Steppe Journeys

M Abdulla Kodiriy E Kyrgyzstan Sergei Yesenin Museum

CMI after party Bar 21

Gazalkent

BUYUK IPAK YO'LI

Centre for Contemporary Arts Tashkent

14

7 3

S Kapitalbank

SHAKHRISABZ

Yunus Rajabiy 41

ISTIQLOL

Ground Zero co-working spaces M State Museum of Timurid History

39

M Amir Timur

ank University of Law

Amir Timur Square

Russian Drama Theatre

avoi allet Theatre

6 Forum Palace 34

Tashkent Clock Towers

22 House of Photography

AMIR TIMUR

SHAKHRISABZ

26 S Kishlok Kurilish

State Fine Arts Museum

Geology Museum

29

16

AMIR TIMUR

Uzbekistan Airways

27

SHEVCHENKO

CHEKHOV

23 E Kazakhstan

OVIR

OYBEK

DHL

32 Toshkent M

TURKISTON

Sobor Orthodox Cathedral

NUKUS

31 35

AVLIYE OTA

Asia Special Tourism

MIRONSHOH

MIROBOD

ISTIKBOL

TOYTEPA S AZIMOVA

37 38

SAYID BARAKA

MUSTAKILLIK

M Khamid Olimjon

Tamara Khanum House Museum

SHASTRI

UZBEKISTON OVOZI

G MAKTUMQALI

E UK 21 Lutheran Church

Art + Fact Gallery

Salor Canal

FedEx

NIYAZOV

AK-KURGAN

MIR Corporation

Kapitalbank S

M Mashinasozlar

ELBEK

N

Bradt

0 500m
0 500yds

NOTE
For key to accommodation and eating and drinking, see page 114

EMS, DHL

Tashkent

FERGANA

BAKU

SAMATOVA

G ULYAMOV

113

TASHKENT *Central*
For listings, see from page 96

⊖ **Where to stay**

1	Anvar's Guests..............C5	6	Hotel Uzbekistan...................E3	10	Retro Palace.......................C6
2	Art Hostel.......................C5	7	Hyatt Regency.......................E3	11	Rovshan............................D7
3	City Palace....................E3	8	Lotte City Hotel	12	Sam-Buh Elite...................C7
4	Grand Mir.....................D6		Tashkent Palace.................D4	13	Shodlik Palace..................C2
5	Hotel Bek Tashkent.....B6	9	Ramada Tashkent................C1	14	Wyndham.........................E2

⊗ **Where to eat and drink**

15	Affresco.........................B6	25	Caravan............................C7	34	Raaj Kapur.........................F3
16	Afsona............................E5	26	City Grill............................E4	35	Reggae Bean.....................E7
17	Al-Aziz...........................D2	27	Efendi..............................F5		Sato............................(see 25)
18	Amaretto.......................C6	28	Gruzinski Dvorik...............C7	36	Sema de Roma..................D6
19	Angel's Café...................D5	29	Irish Pub.......................... E5	37	Studio Café........................F4
20	B & B Coffee House......C6		Izumi.........................(see 25)	38	Sunduk..............................F4
21	Bon!.....B2, D4, D6, F4, H1	30	Jumanji............................B6	39	Torento Restaurant/
22	Bookcafé........................E4	31	La Piola.............................E7		Golden Wing...................F3
23	Broccoli..........................E6	32	Manna..............................E6	40	Ye Olde Chelsea Arms.....C7
24	Café Jum........................B5	33	New World Pizza-Bakery.....D4	41	Yolki-Palki..........................F3

State Fine Arts Museum [113 E5] (16 Amir Timur; ✆ 71 236 7436; w stateartmuseum.uz; ⊕ 10.00–17.00 Tue–Sun, 10.00–14.00 Mon; US$1.25) One of the largest museums in central Asia, the current buildings opened in 1974 to house an extensive collection of paintings, ceramics and other artefacts, most of which were confiscated from Grand Duke Nikolai Romanov (see box, below) in 1918 and once displayed in his former home (page 111), then functioning as the Museum of Art.

Some 50,000 paintings and artefacts are now held at the museum, originating not only from Uzbekistan and Russia, but also from Europe. Uzbek art dominates the ground and first floors: the earliest pieces, which include sculptures, ceramics and murals, date back to the 1st century BC and are remarkably well preserved. Look here for 9th-century ceramics, tiles from Samarkand, Bukhara and Shakhrisabz, Bukharan court robes weighed down with decadent gold embroidery and finely carved wooden shutters and doors.

European art works are displayed on the second floor, including pieces from Romanov's original collection as well as some remarkable medieval Russian icons

---

THE EXILE OF GRAND DUKE NIKOLAI ROMANOV

Cousin of Tsar Nicholas II and grandson of Nicholas I, Nikolai Konstantinovich Romanov was born in St Petersburg in February 1850, the first son of Grand Duke Konstantin and Grand Duchess Alexandra. He had a successful military career but was an infamous womaniser and allegedly stole three of his mother's diamonds to give to his American lover, Fanny Lear. When the theft was discovered, Nikolai was declared insane and banished in perpetuity to Turkestan.

Nikolai put his time in Tashkent to good use, building two large canals (the Bukhar-aryk and the Khiva-aryk) to irrigate lands between Tashkent and Dzhizak. He ordered the construction of his own palace in 1890 in part to showcase his vast art collection, which now forms the core of the collection at the State Fine Arts Museum (see above).

Nikolai died in 1917, though sources disagree as to whether pneumonia or Bolshevik bullets caused his demise. He was buried in St George's Cathedral (now demolished) and was survived by his wife, two sons, and at least six illegitimate children.

from Novgorod. Though they are not necessarily to everyone's taste, nor are the 20th-century Russian landscapes chosen for their lack of controversy, the standard of exhibits is generally high and whether you have a preference for Russian portraits in oil, Chinese scrolls or Uzbek art from the early Soviet period, there will undoubtedly be something that catches your eye. If you don't have the opportunity to visit the Igor Savitsky Museum in Nukus (page 278), this museum also has a good Russian and Uzbek avant-garde collection.

If you have time, take a look at **Zulfiya Park**, directly behind the museum. Initially laid out in the 1880s, it became the burial place (and de facto memorial to) Bolshevik fighters who died in street fighting in Tashkent in 1917 and the 14 Turkestan Commissars betrayed by Ossipov in 1919. Yuldush Akhunbabaev and Sabir Rakhimov, respectively the first chairman and first secretary-general of the Uzbek SSR, are also buried here. These have now been sidelined in favour of an Alley of Writers; oddly, the central statue of the Uzbek poet Zulfiya was replaced in 2018 by one of the Belarusian poet Konstantin Mickiewicz (known as Yakub Kolas), who lived in Tashkent in 1941–43 and formed strong links with local writers.

State Museum of History [112 D3] (3 Sharof Rashidov; ☏ 71 239 1083; w history-museum.uz; ⊕ 10.00–17.00 Tue–Sun; US$1.25) The State Museum of History has had two lives. The quintessential example of Soviet orientalism, the building opened in 1970, the centenary of Lenin's birth, as a memorial to the Soviet Union's first leader and a means of expounding the Lenin cult beyond Russia's borders.

Independent Uzbekistan has done away with Lenin and, to some extent, his memory. The 250,000-plus exhibits now housed were relocated from the Aibek Museum (now closed). The collection, which began as Uzbekistan's first public museum in 1876, includes some 60,000 archaeological finds, 80,000 coins and 35,000 remarkable negatives, black-and-white photos and reports from early archaeological digs. It is the largest repository of historical artefacts in central Asia.

Heading upstairs past a 3D map of the country and turning left, the main floor displays ancient history, from skeletal hominid remains uncovered in the Selangor Cave in Fergana, thought to be 1.5 million years old, to a 4th-century BC bronze cauldron carved with writhing animals. There's also Uzbekistan's only complete Buddha figure (1st–2nd centuries AD), from Surkhan Darya in eastern Uzbekistan where ancient Silk Road monasteries flourished. The exhibits are arranged more or less in chronological order, with plenty of information boards, maps, models and graphics to help you understand what you are looking at; however, there's not enough text in English, and you have to ignore the silly speculative statues of ancient Uzbeks.

Don't miss the ibex petroglyphs found in the Fergana Valley (dating from around 5000BC) in the first room you enter and the Saramysh rock carvings, dating from the 3rd millennium BC. There are models of key items from the Oxus (or Amu Darya) Treasure (the originals of which are in the British Museum), and there is an excellent display on Khorezm (6th–4th centuries BC), which includes statuary, fresco fragments, cooking vessels, ossuaries and architects' models of the fortresses. On the upper floor is a new and very dull exhibit on independent Uzbekistan, showcasing achievements of the post-communist government.

A small gift shop on the ground floor sells the usual selection of souvenirs as well as a few books in English. **Guided tours** (US$3) are available in English and are the best way to understand the collection and ensure you don't miss the highlights. If you want to take photos in the museum, you will need to buy a photo permit (US$3) with your entrance ticket.

Tashkent **WHAT TO SEE AND DO**

3

State Museum of Timurid History [113 E3] (1 Amir Timur; ☎ 71 232 0212; ⊕ 10.00–17.00 Tue–Sun; US$2) One of Tashkent's more iconic buildings, the Amir Timur Museum with its turquoise dome and crenulated roofline is undoubtedly an attractive, if slightly out-of-place, addition to the city's skyline. Inside is a succession of beautifully painted displays about the history of central Asia, in particular the Timurid period (page 16). Exhibits include copies of historical documents and illustrated manuscripts, weapons, gold-embroidered gowns, jewellery and astronomical instruments, some purportedly linked to Timur himself and some linked to Babur, the Andijan-born first emperor of Mughal India. There are also fine architectural models of Timurid buildings in Samarkand and Bukhara.

Tashkent Clock Towers [113 E4] (Amir Timur Sq; ⊕ 09.00–16.00 daily) Built more than 50 years apart, these twin clock towers on Amir Timur Square have fast become Tashkent icons. The first tower was constructed in 1947 to house the clock mechanism from the City Hall in Allenstein in East Prussia (now Olsztyn in Poland), a war trophy brought home by a Tashkent watchmaker named Eisenstein.

ALISHER NAVOI

Mir 'Alī Shīr Navā'ī (russified as Alisher Navoi) was born in Herat (now in Afghanistan) on 9 February 1441. He was a politician, mystic, linguist, painter and poet, and is considered by many to be the founder of Uzbek literature.

Herat was an important city in the Timurid Empire, and a cultural and intellectual centre. Navoi was born into the city's political elite, and so he had access both to education and to patronage. His father was one-time governor of Sabzawar, and when he died the ruler of Khorasan became the guardian of the young Navoi. Navoi studied in Herat, Mashhad (now in Iran) and Samarkand, returning to Herat to work at the court when his childhood friend Husayn Bayqarah seized power there in 1468.

Navoi was a fearsome administrator and keen builder, endowing and constructing 370 mosques, madrasas, libraries and *caravanserais* in Khorasan and managing the running of 40 *caravanserais*, 20 pools, 17 mosques, ten mansions, nine bathhouses and nine bridges in Herat. When time allowed, he was patron of scholarship and the arts, a composer, calligrapher, painter and sculptor, and wrote such impressive literature that the English historian Bernard Lewis declared him to be 'the Chaucer of the Turks'.

In the course of 30 years, Navoi produced 30 literary works. Most of these were in Chagatai Turkic, though he also wrote in Persian (under the pen name Fāni), Arabic and Hindi. Navoi produced four collections of poetry amounting to some 50,000 verses, each collection corresponding to a different phase in a man's life: *Ghara'ib al-Sighar* (Wonders of Childhood), *Navadir al-Shabab* (Rarities or Witticisms of Youth), *Bada'i' al-Wasat* (Marvels of Middle Age), and *Fawa'id al-Kibar* (Advantages of Old Age). His other important works include *Khamsa*, a collection of five epic poems that includes the famous love story of Layla and Majnun, a comparison of the Turkic and Persian languages, and an exploration of his views on religion and Sufism.

Navoi never married or had children, and he remained in the service of Husayn Bayqarah until his death in 1501. He was buried in Herat but is commemorated across Uzbekistan with statues and street names. The Alisher Navoi Opera and Ballet Theatre in Tashkent is also named in his honour.

The architectural design was chosen from competition entries and the 30m tower now displays an ethnographic collection of traditional Uzbek textiles (including embroidery), woodcarving and ceramics. The external decoration was done by Usto Shirin Muradov, a famous Uzbek ganch carver.

The second tower, completed in 2009, contains a showroom exhibiting antique and modern jewellery by Uzbekistan's master craftsmen.

WEST TASHKENT The Ankhor Canal leads southwest to an area of fairly sterile parkland, in which stand some grand public edifices.

Alisher Navoi National Park [112 A5] This celebrated and rather attractive park, west of the city centre, is a much-needed green space in the over-crowded capital city. Manmade lakes, canals and fountains, cafés and ornamental gardens seem to cool the air in the sweaty summer months, and they make it a pleasant place to relax or picnic if you have an hour or two to spare. With the **Navruz Wedding Palace** [112 A4], the Istiqlol Palace and the Parliament of Uzbekistan all within the park, there are plenty of opportunities for people watching.

Abdul Khasim Madrasa [112 A4] (✆ 10.00–16.00 daily) Although medieval in style, this madrasa in fact dates from the mid 19th century. It was famously the location of the signing of the peace treaty following the capture of Tashkent by the Russian general Chernyayev in 1865, and from 1919 to 1974 it was home to more than 70 Russian families who had fled from famine in Samara.

The madrasa was restored in 1987 and its cells now house workshops for Tashkent's artists and craftsmen. More than 30 artisans work here, producing fine jewellery, paintings, ceramics and prints. It is possible (and recommended) to buy souvenirs straight from these producers.

Istiqlol Palace [112 A4] Built as the People's Friendship Palace in the 1970s, Istiqlol Palace is a massive event and concert hall in a sort of techno-oriental style. In front stands a monument to Shoahmad and Bahri Shomahmudov, who adopted 15 war orphans of Russian, Kazakh, Belarusian, Moldovan, Latvian, Jewish and Tatar origin from the western Soviet Union in the 1940s. Erected in 1982, it was removed from the city centre in 2008 but returned in 2018 owing to popular demand.

Parliament of Uzbekistan [112 A4] (1 Halklar Dustligi) Constructed with Bukharan granite and marble from Samarkand, capped with a turquoise dome, and decorated with a 10m-high, 4.5-tonne chandelier of crystal and gold in the central hall, Uzbekistan's parliament building is designed to impress. Uzbek nationals can gain access to the ground floors of the building; foreigners must be content viewing the ostentatious structure from outside.

Bekhzod Miniature Museum [112 C4] (K Bekhzod Memorial Park; ✆ 10.00–18.00 Tue–Sat; US$2) The Bekhzod Miniature Museum and accompanying Memorial Park were opened in 2002 to commemorate Kamoliddin Bekhzod (1455–1536) and to popularise the art of miniature painting. More commonly known as Bihzad, this Herati-born artist is to Persian miniatures what Constable is to English landscapes or Da Vinci is to anatomical drawing. He is, quite simply, the master, and his original paintings (or at least those attributed to him, as it was rare for miniaturists to sign their work) are prized pieces in national collections from New York and London to Tehran.

Unlike neighbouring Kazakhstan, with its Baikonur Space Launch Station, Uzbekistan is not immediately associated with the space race. One man has, however, helped to put the country on the map: Vladimir Dzhanibekov.

Born Vladimir Krysin in 1942, Dzhanibekov's family moved to Tashkent from Iskandar when he was a child. He briefly studied physics at Leningrad University before deciding his real passion was for flying, after which he enrolled at the V M Komarov Higher Military Flying School in Yeisk. On graduation, having also taken a course in radio engineering at Taganrog State University, Dzhanibekov became a flying instructor in the Soviet Air Force and joined the Communist Party. It was to do his career no harm.

Dzhanibekov was selected for cosmonaut training in 1970. Over the next 15 years he was to make five space flights, spending a total of 145 days in space. His missions were to the Salyut 6 and Salyut 7 space stations, and included two space walks.

Dzhanibekov became a Soviet celebrity: he was twice Hero of the Soviet Union, five times recipient of the Order of Lenin, and received both the Order of the Red Star and an additional Medal for Merit in Space Exploration. Foreign recognition included becoming a Commander of the Legion of Honour in France, and receiving honorary citizenship of Russia, Kazakhstan and Houston, Texas.

On retiring from space travel, Dzhanibekov entered politics in Uzbekistan and became interested in hot-air ballooning. Sadly, his ballooning exploits were about as successful as Richard Branson's, and his round-the-world attempt in 1993 lasted just 30 minutes. He survived the ordeal and now occupies himself making paintings about space, keeping his feet firmly on the ground.

The museum holds nearly 100,000 illustrated manuscripts, though sadly few are the work of the master himself. Around 500 items are on show at any one time, and they include printed books and lithographs as well as miniatures and manuscripts. Displays change frequently.

Alongside this plain museum is the lavishly decorated modernist **Academy of Arts** (⊕ 10.00–18.00 Tue–Sun), which exhibits new work from local artists.

Islam Karimov Scientific and Enlightenment Memorial Complex [112 C4] (Afrosiab; w islamkarimov.uz/en; ⊕ 08.30–21.00 Tue–Sun) The grandiose **Oksaroy Palace**, built by Uzbekistan's first president (see box, page 23), has been transformed into a memorial complex with a museum, exhibition hall and library, all glorifying Islam Karimov. Portraits are mostly kitschy, although some are in a more sober socialist realist style. There are family photos featuring his wife Tatiana, but not their daughters Gulnara and Lola (see box, page 32).

Memorial for Cosmonauts [112 C4] (Cnr Afrosiab & Sharof Rashidov) A space-themed monument raised in 1984 to commemorate the scientists and cosmonauts of Uzbekistan, from the royal astronomer Mirzo Ulug Beg to five-time cosmonaut Vladimir Dzhanibekov (see box, above).

Museum of Astronomy [112 B4] (33 Astronomicheskaya; ⊕ 10.00–18.00 Tue–Sun; US$2) The year 2009 was the UN's International Year of Astronomy and also

the 615th anniversary of the astronomer and emperor Ulug Beg's birth (see box, page 173). Tashkent marked the event with the opening of this new museum, supported by UNESCO. Exhibitions chart the development of astronomy from ancient times through medieval discoveries to the present. The most interesting artefacts are the huge number of telescopes and quadrants, and, for those unable to make it to Samarkand, a scale model of the meridian quadrant once used in Ulug Beg's Observatory. Though not on the standard tourist itinerary, the museum is well worth a visit.

The Rakhimov Ceramics Studio [88 A3] (15 Kukcha-Darvaza (1st side st); ☏71 249 0435; m 90 987 2063; e alisherceramic@gmail.com) Created by a celebrated potter and scholar of traditional Uzbek ceramic technique, this lovely studio and teaching centre is now run by his son and grandson. You can see (and buy) a superb range of both traditional and contemporary pieces here. You may want to call ahead to double check, but it should be open during normal working hours.

NORTH TASHKENT Hidden in parks and suburbs to the north of the city centre are a few sites that may be of interest to those with a little more time to spend in the capital.

Aibek House Museum [89 E1] (26 Tazetdinov; ☏71 248 0900; ⏱ 10.00–17.00 Mon–Sat; US$1) In the home of the author Aibek (or Oybek; see box, page 108), designed by his wife Z N Said-Nasirova, this museum reveals much of everyday life for Uzbekistan's literary elite in the 1940s. The six rooms are stuffed with photos, magazines, press cuttings and, of course, Aibek's books. Canvases by Aibek's artistic contemporaries line the walls, and the extensive archives are actively used by modern academics.

Botanical Garden [89 G1] (232 Bog'ishamol; ☏ 71 289 1060; w academy. uz; ⏱ 09.00–20.00 daily; US$0.50) Belonging to the Academy of Sciences, the Botanical Garden was founded in 1920 and now covers 66ha in the northeastern part of the city. The extensive arboretum has more than 3,000 species of plant, divided into five geographical zones: central Asia, Europe, the Americas, south Asia

---

THE 1966 EARTHQUAKE

At 05.23 on 26 April 1966, Tashkent's skyline changed forever. An earthquake, measuring 7.5 on the Richter scale, ripped through the city as residents slept. Remarkably, only ten people were killed, but the quake damaged an estimated 70% of the city's buildings. Over 28,000 were flattened completely, and 100,000 people were left homeless. The Old City was worst hit owing to the number of traditional, adobe brick-built structures and their close proximity to one another.

In the aftermath of the earthquake, Tashkent became a blank canvas for the Soviet Union's leading urban planners: they envisaged a model Soviet city with wide boulevards lined with trees and fountains, a metro, public squares for parades, and hundreds of apartment blocks with workshops, canteens and nurseries where the city's populace could live, work and play together. By 1970, an estimated 100,000 new homes had already been constructed, and further areas of the city continued to be cleared to implement the planners' grand new designs. This era of building contributed the heart of today's city.

and the Far East. Medicinal tropical plants are housed in a number of hot houses and specialist nurseries. In 2018, a new mini garden was introduced, showing endangered varieties of herbaceous perennials. At the time this book went to print, an exhibition hall in the world's sixth largest herbarium was set to open.

Though attractive year-round, the garden really comes into its own in autumn when the heat of summer days has subsided and the trees are sliding from green into every shade of red, orange and gold. Inquisitive squirrels, some nearly tame, raid picnics and dart back and forth across the gravel paths while the garden's guides introduce visitors to the more important specimens in the botanical collection.

Tashkent Zoo (⊕ 08.00–20.00 Tue–Sun; US$1.25), the oldest scientific zoo in central Asia (founded in 1924), covers 22ha in the west of the garden. There are more than 300 species of animal, including bears, gorilla and giraffe, and an aquarium houses freshwater and marine creatures. Children will enjoy feeding time, which takes places in different enclosures throughout the day.

Centre for Contemporary Arts Tashkent [113 E2] (Building B, 6 Amir Timur; ☏ 71 207 4080; w ccat.uz; ⊕ 10.00–20.00 daily) Uzbekistan's first contemporary art gallery will open fully in 2020 and a pre-opening programme was already underway at the time of writing. It's housed in a former generating station for the city's first tram line, built in 1912 by Wilhelm Heinzelmann, who designed other buildings such as Grand Duke Nikolai Romanov's residence (page 111).

Earthquake Memorial [112 D1] (Sharof Rashidov) This dramatic memorial, also known as the Monument to Courage, was erected in 1976 to mark the tenth anniversary of the 1966 earthquake (see box, page 119). It is in several parts: the broken labradorite cube bears the date on one side and a clock face showing the time of the earthquake (05.23) on the other. The zigzag crack through the cube directs the eye to the bronze sculpture alongside: a father protecting his wife and child from danger. The unusual shape of the statue's plinth is supposed to symbolise the quake's destruction, and the surrounding stelae remember those who rebuilt the city in the following months and years: the military, architects, builders and, of course, the ordinary people of Tashkent.

Minor Mosque [89 E2] (Kichik Halqa Yuli (Little Ring Rd); ☏ 71 235 1733) Uzbekistan's largest mosque (not minor at all), opened in 2014, sits amid broad promenades by the embankment of the Ankhor Canal, a few hundred metres west of the Minor metro station, making it a popular spot for evening strolls and people watching. It's in traditional style but with far more white marble; the main hall with its gold-plated *mihrab* sits beneath a turquoise dome and the open front section brings its total capacity to over 2,400 people.

Museum of Nature [88 B1] (1 Kichik Halqa; ☏ 71 246 9531; ⊕ 10.00–17.00 Tue–Sun; US$2) Tashkent's own dead zoo is home to more than 400,000 exhibits, among which are numerous stuffed birds and animals and their skeletons. The oldest museum in Uzbekistan, it was founded in 1876 and includes what is probably the world's largest collection of central Asian flora and fauna, albeit in a poor state of preservation.

The museum is of interest to two types of people: serious naturalists who can look beyond the dust and fake blood-dripping plastic dinosaurs and appreciate the diversity of the region's wildlife, including many species now extinct; and those intrigued by the Soviet Union at large and its admirable attempts to educate the masses. The vast dioramas, including scenes of dinosaurs, mammoths and early man, provide an easy (if not always chronologically or anatomically accurate) introduction to pre-history for children.

Museum of Olympic Glory [112 D1] (4A Sharof Rashidov; ✎ 71 244 7602; ◷ 09.00–13.00 & 14.00–17.30 Mon–Sat) Opened in 1996 by President Karimov and the then president of the International Olympic Committee, Juan Antonio Samaranch, the museum holds a predictable collection of photographs, medals and trophies from international competitions.

Museum of the Victims of Repression [89 F1] (Martyrs Memorial Sq; ◷ 10.00–17.00 Tue–Sun; US$1) This harrowing museum, opened in 2002, focuses on the violent repression of the Uzbek people, starting with the Tsarist clampdowns in the late 19th century and the elimination of the Basmachi uprising after the 1917 Revolution (see box, page 21), through Stalin's purges to ethnic cleansing and the gulags. Exhibits include *moquettes* of the gulags and prisons, a prison van, photos, documents and personal belongings of those who were imprisoned or killed. The cotton trials of the 1980s are covered but not, of course, the repression of the museum's founder, President Karimov. Though the curators are inevitably espousing a very specific message, and there's not enough information in English, the displays do flesh out an understanding of what was, until very recently, a particularly secretive aspect of Uzbekistan's history. The archives are widely used by academics, and the building in which the collection is housed is an attractive affair that incorporates various aspects of traditional Uzbek design.

TV Tower [89 F1] (109 Amir Timur; ◷ 10.00–17.00 daily; US$4.70) Rising 375m above the city, Tashkent's TV Tower was built in 1979–85 and was, until 1991, the third-highest tower in the world; it is still the second-tallest structure in central Asia (after a power-station chimney in Kazakhstan). The architects, D Semashko and N Terziev-Tzarukova, were tasked with coming up with a design capable of withstanding earthquakes up to 9.0 on the Richter scale, and their solution was the latticed trunk supported by a gigantic tripod.

Entering the lobby, you'll see the slightly incongruous Romanesque mosaic of semi-precious stones, metals and marble by artist A Buharbaev. Three high-speed elevators will take you to the top of the tower at a rate of 4m per second; you can step off at one of the revolving restaurants (Blue for Uzbek food or Red for European, though neither is very good; $$$) or at the observation deck. Situated 97m up, it has predictably impressive views in all directions. On occasions it is also possible to visit the meteorological station in the upper reaches of the tower; ask in the lobby if you're interested.

If heights aren't your thing and you prefer to keep your feet on the ground, the TV Tower is floodlit at night, making for memorable photographs.

UzExpo Centre [113 E1] (107 Amir Timur; w uzexpocentre.uz) Uzbekistan's main exhibition centre hosts a revolving schedule of trade fairs, most of them linked to the energy and chemical sectors. Forthcoming fairs are listed on the centre's website.

Aqua Park (✎ 71 238 5625; ◷ May–Sep 10.00–20.00; adult/child US$2.50/1.25) Inevitably popular with Tashkent's youth, this large water park has numerous flumes, wave pools and other watery attractions, ideal for cooling down during the heat of the summer. Tickets are valid for 3 hours and adults can either get wet

with the kids or chill out in the cafés (**$$**) and jacuzzi. There's also a short cable-car (US$1) parallel to the main road.

Japanese Garden (🕐 09.00–21.00 Mon–Sat; US$2.35) A small but tranquil space that is popularly used as the backdrop for wedding photos. Though not authentically Japanese in its design, it is charming nevertheless, with a wooden bridge across the water, a tea house (**$$**) lotus flowers in the pond and carved granite lanterns along the walkways. Storks, ducks and peacocks roam freely. Cultural events are occasionally hosted in the garden; the events calendar is listed on the UzExpo website (page 121).

Tashkentland (🕐 10.00–21.00 daily, last entry 19.00; US$2.50/4 under/over 12s) This amusement park has a rollercoaster, swings, Ferris wheel, an 'African jungle' boat trip and a castle of horrors.

EAST TASHKENT Between the ring road and the railway are a few museums of fairly specialised interest, as well as a couple of amusement parks.

Lutheran Church [113 F4] (37 S Azimova) Tashkent's German *kirche* is the city's only Lutheran church. Built in 1899, it was the work of architect A L Benoit, who also designed Prince Nikolai Romanov's residence (page 111). An attractive Neogothic building, its yellow-brick structure was sufficiently strong to survive the 1966 earthquake intact.

The original worshippers at the church belonged to Tashkent's ethnic German community, many of them officers in the Imperial Russian Army. Services then, as now, were delivered in both Russian and German, and hymns are still sung to the accompaniment of the organ. During the Soviet period, the church was first used as a warehouse and then, thankfully, given to the Tashkent Conservatoire, who used it as an opera studio and concert venue. Renovations took place in the 1990s when the church was returned to the Lutheran community which, though small, continues to take pride in its place of worship.

Sergei Yesenin Museum [113 G2] (Just off Mustakillik; ☎ 71 237 1179; e esenin@mail.tps.uz; 🕐 10.00–17.00 Mon–Sat) On a road just off Mustakillik you'll find the house museum of Russian poet Sergei Yesenin (1895–1925) who visited Tashkent for a month in May 1921. The museum, opened in 1999, contains 3,000 manuscripts, photographs and autographs, along with furniture typical of a Tashkent home in the 1920s. It often hosts poetry recitals. Free guided tours are available in Russian – just turn up and request one.

Yesenin was a fascinating character. Born to a peasant family in Konstantinovo, he began writing poetry at the age of nine. Having studied first in Moscow, he moved to St Petersburg and became well known in Russian literary circles. He published *Ritual for the Dead* in 1916 before being drafted to fight in World War I. Initially a supporter of the Bolshevik Revolution, he quickly became disillusioned, and some of his subsequent poems, including *The Stern October Has Deceived Me*, were openly critical of the new regime. Although initially celebrated, his works were later banned by the Kremlin. Only in 1966 were his poems republished.

Yesenin was a hit with the ladies, and married four times during his short life (including a brief marriage to the American dancer Isadora Duncan). He was a tormented soul, however, and though he continued to write, he suffered from alcoholism and mental illness. Following a month's hospitalisation, he cut his wrist, wrote a farewell suicide poem in his own blood, and hung himself from the heating pipes in his hotel room. He was just 30 years old.

Tamara Khanum House Museum [113 G2] (1/41 Tamara Khanum; ☏ 71 267 8690; ⏲ 10.00–16.00 Mon–Sat) Just off Mustakillik is the house museum of actress and dancer Tamara Khanum (1906–91), credited with creating modern Uzbek dance. An ethnic Armenian, born Tamara Petrosian in the Fergana Valley, she was the first woman in Uzbekistan to perform publicly with her face uncovered. Awarded the title of People's Artist of the USSR, she toured internationally in the 1940s and 50s, winning fans as far away as Norway and China. Small but lovingly curated, the museum contains 70 or so ballet and folk-dance costumes, around 30 of which are on display at any time, as well as photographs, letters and gifts received by Khanum herself.

Ural Tansykbaev Museum [89 H2] (5 Cherdantsev; ☏ 71 162 6230; ⏲ 10.00–18.00 Tue–Sun) Central to this house museum is the easel of the USSR's People's Artist Ural Tansykbaev, with his final, unfinished work still stretched across it. The museum includes his studio, living quarters and small garden, as well as a purpose-built gallery displaying the work of contemporary Uzbek artists. Tansykbaev's own paintings, dating from the 1920s until his death in 1974, are also on view, notably his moody blue landscapes, such as a depiction of men hauling in their nets on the shore of the then fish-filled Aral Sea.

SOUTH TASHKENT South of the city centre, a little removed from the political and commercial heartland, are a variety of attractions for culture vultures and, appropriately situated next to the train station, the Railway Museum.

Caravanserai of Culture [112 C5] (37A Yusuf Hos Hojib; ☏ 71 233 5674; w caravanserai.uz; ⏲ 09.00–18.00 daily; US$2) Dedicated to the cultures of the Silk Road, this modern *caravanserai* (decorated, somewhat incongruously, with a miniature pagoda) and the surrounding Garden of Friendship host a succession of exhibitions, a permanent collection of archaeological artefacts and a large library of books on the history, architecture and ethnography of the Silk Road. It was founded by Ikuo Hirayama (1930–2009), a very successful Japanese painter of Silk Road scenes.

Museum of Applied Arts [112 C5] (15 Rakatboshi; ☏ 71 256 4042; w artmuseum. uz; ⏲ 09.00–18.00 daily; US$3) Possibly the best-looking museum in Tashkent, the Museum of Applied Arts occupies the former home of Imperial Russian diplomat Alexander Polovtsev. Polovtsev was an avid collector of handicrafts and his personal possessions still form the heart of the museum's superb collection of decorative arts. The first public exhibition was held here in 1927, and it was classified as a national collection a decade later.

As photographs on display inside show, the façade of the building has changed surprisingly little since its construction in the early 20th century: the gardens have matured, but the delicate columns and the pale-blue colour scheme are original. In the mosque-like central hall, it is the building itself that is the attraction: it is a stunning space with an ornately carved and vividly painted ceiling. The wooden doors and their frames are particularly elaborate, as are the decorative pillars supporting the roof. The walls are painted and tiled with so many contrasting designs that in any other context they'd make your eyes go funny. Here, however, they look exquisite.

Other galleries are arranged by the type of item on display, and their exhibits include fine ceramics, crystal and glass, clothes and embroidered textiles, musical instruments, jewellery and carpets. The costume and textile displays are particularly good. Though there are items of considerable note in each of the galleries, our particular favourites are the musical instrument and the textile rooms, where you can see not only the finished garments and accessories but also the different types of *ikat* fabric, each with their own distinctive designs. Although these aren't labelled, your guide will be able to explain them to you.

Two workshops at the museum restore antique pieces and give classes in various crafts, while three shops sell a refreshing selection of handmade items, prints and vintage clothing. There is a small café in the central courtyard where you can have a tea or coffee. Guided tours are available in various languages (US$4) – just turn up and ask about them. If you want to take photos, you will need to buy a camera permit (US$2) from the ticket desk.

Railway Museum [113 F6] (6 Turkiston; ☏ 71 299 7040; ⏰ 09.00–13.00 & 14.00–21.00 daily; US$1.30) Appropriately located beside Tashkent's main station, the open-air Railway Museum may not be top on everyone's sightseeing list, but it offers a charming insight into the early development of the railway in central Asia. Here, you will find 13 well-preserved steam engines, as well as diesel and electric locomotives, train carriages and communication systems. The collection of coaches reveals the different uses of the railways, both for passengers and cargo, and there are numerous accessories (semaphore and radio systems, etc), too. The exhibits are generally impressive in scale and in good condition, and you are welcome to climb inside.

Uspensky Sobor Orthodox Cathedral [113 E6] (Cnr 91 Avliy Ota & Nukus; ⏰ 09.00–18.00 daily) The Assumption Cathedral (Uspensky Sobor) is one of four Russian Orthodox churches in Tashkent. It began life as a chapel at Tashkent's military cemetery in the 1870s. Wanting something more impressive, General von Kaufmann allotted 3,000 roubles for the construction of a larger church, and the city's mercantile guilds also contributed. Consecrated in 1879, the new building was dedicated to St Panteleimon the Healer. After the Bolshevik Revolution, the church was used as a sanitary depot for the military and it wasn't returned to religious use until after World War II, when it was given its current name and upgraded to the status of a cathedral. Best visited on a Sunday morning when a service is in full flow, this small but attractive building, replete with solemn icons, onion domes and lots of gilt, was largely rebuilt in 1958–60 and restored in 1996 for the visit of His Holiness Patriarch Alexy II. In 2009, 13 new bells were added to the bell tower, and an additional tower was completed the following year. The cathedral's ark is said to contain relics of the Holy Cross.

AROUND TASHKENT

Easy **day trips** from Tashkent, the following sites provide interest for both long-term expats and visitors keen to get away from the usual tourist sites. The Zangiota Complex and Kanka can be combined in a single day trip, as can Lake Charvak and Chimgan. They're listed in order of distance from the city centre.

ZANGIOTA COMPLEX Some 15km southwest of the city along the M34 brings you to Zangiota village, which has grown up around the Timurid-era mausoleum

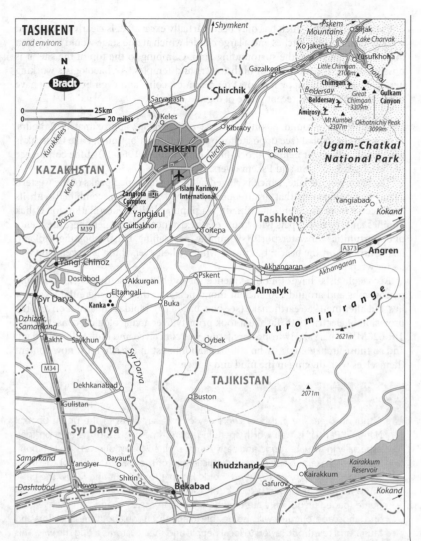

of Zangiota, a 13th-century Sufi saint and shepherd who is still believed to have healing powers. People come here to pray and seek his blessings. Surrounded by a well-maintained garden, this is a tranquil spot and far less visited than Uzbekistan's other Timurid sites, despite its similarly beautiful (if over-restored) portal, dome and tile work. Zangiota's inscribed marble tombstone is particularly fine. The neighbouring cemetery, still in use, contains the tomb of Zangiota's wife, Anbar Bibi, where women hoping to conceive pray for children.

KANKA On the southern outskirts of Eltamgali village, 80km southwest of Tashkent, are the archaeological remains of Kanka, the earliest incarnation of Tashkent. To visit, you will need your own transport: take the M34 from Tashkent towards Yangi-Chinoz, turn left just before you reach the town and head to Dostobod (formerly known as Soldatskiy). Eltamgali and Kanka are reached along an unmade road heading southeast from here. The journey should take around an hour in total.

The vast Kanka site, which has only been partially excavated, is clearly demarcated with defensive walls, ditches and a large citadel which at one stage would have risen more than 35m above the surrounding land. Climbing to the top of the site, it is possible to see the footprint of both towers and temples. Archaeologists working here are more than happy to show you ceramics, coins and even bones they have unearthed in the most recent phase of digs.

LAKE CHARVAK Around 60km northeast of Tashkent, approximately 2 hours' drive from the capital (see opposite for public-transport options), Lake Charvak is a manmade reservoir behind a rock-filled dam, built in 1964–70 at the confluence of the Chatkal, Kok-Su and Pskem rivers.

The beauty of the lake, which is ringed by the green-sloped peaks of the western Tian Shan Mountains that are frequently topped with snow, combined with its easy access from Tashkent, have made it a popular holiday destination for Uzbek families and the few expats who know of its existence. In summer, there are plenty of opportunities for watersports (swimming, parasailing, banana boating, etc) and lazing around on the beach; but in the winter when everything is frozen, you had better wrap up warm.

Archaeologists have found evidence of prehistoric settlements, including petroglyphs and around 150 ancient monuments, in the area where the lake now lies, but after the 1966 earthquake (see box, page 119), rapid reconstruction and the provision of electricity to Tashkent took priority over archaeological conservation. The 620MW Charvak Hydropower Station was conceived and built below the dam, and so those archaeologists who still have an interest in the site must now content themselves with digging in the mud and sludge.

FIVE-DAY CHIMGAN TREK

Although there are plenty of short day or half-day hikes in the Ugam-Chatkal National Park, it is well worth spending more time exploring the area on foot, especially in the late spring and early summer when the wildflowers are in bloom. If you purchase a detailed topographical map of the area from one of the book shop in Tashkent (page 104), you should be able to pick out and follow the basic route we have described below, but it is generally recommended to hire a local guide (page 96): not only are they better able to assess changes in the weather and landscape, but they will also be able to enlighten you about the local flora and fauna, and to introduce you to local people and their customs along the way. This trek is suitable for someone of moderate fitness, wearing proper walking boots or walking shoes. Campsites are unofficial but are used regularly for pitching tents.

Day 1: Starting at **Beldersay** (1,600m; page 129), follow the **Marble River**, with its sparkling waterfalls and lush scenery, up and over the **Urta Kumbel Pass** (1,820m). It is then an easy descent to the **Beldersay River**, where you can pitch a tent for the night. The camp has superb views of **Great Chimgan Mountain** (3,309m), a magnet for skiers and snowboarders in winter but a photogenic peak at any time of the year.

Day 2: Start early on the second day as there is plenty of distance to cover. A short climb to the top of the **Chet-Kumbel Pass** (1,850m) grants you panoramic views of the **Beldersay River** and the western slopes of Great Chimgan Mountain. Having caught your breath, continue along the **Beldersay Gorge**, climbing steadily to its highest point (2,450m). Look out for the ancient rock paintings along the way,

Getting there and around Buses (route 550), *marshrutkas* and shared taxis run from the north side of Buyuk Ipak Yuli metro station to Gazalkent, 50km northeast of Tashkent; from here you can take shared taxis to villages on the south side of the lake (see below). If you want to get to the north shore you'll really need your own car. Shared taxis also run from Buyuk Ipak Yuli metro station to the Chimgan and Beldersay ski resorts (around 1hr 20min; US$2).

Where to stay, eat and drink The vast majority of visitors come to the lake solely for recreational purposes. The shoreline is 100km in length, and hotels and campsites have popped up in many villages.

About 25km east of Gazalkent in **Yusufkhona** (a centre for paragliding, and the junction to the Charvak ski resort), there are some affordable hotels (with swimming pools, great views, and accommodation in rooms and cottages).

Many houses display 'Dacha' signs, often coupled with 'Bassein' (swimming pool). These are generally modern apartments, suitable for multi-day family stays rather than overnighting lone hikers; you'll usually need to call their mobile number in advance rather than just turning up.

In **Slijak**, at the northern end of the lake, there's a project to create low-impact guesthouses in family homes – just turn up and ask for Mashkhura Sametova, Zafar Mirzayev or Sardor Tursunbayev.

Avenue Park Yusufkhona; m 98 311 1919; w avenuepark.uz/en. A comfortable modern resort hotel, with a swimming pool, spa & a decent restaurant ($$$). **$$$**

Charvak Oromgokhi (208 rooms) Bokachul village; \ 71 232 2282; w chorvoq.uz. The lake's most developed hotel is just a stone's throw from the sandy beach on the south shore of the lake.

then cross over the **Kumbel Pass** (2,550m) and into another small gorge. Arrive sufficiently early to sit, beer in hand, and watch the sunset and then one of the most incredible night skies you'll ever see. You can pitch your tent by the river at the bottom of the gorge.

Day 3: There is a straight track up to the **Tahta Pass** (2,620m), which overlooks the distant Pulatkhan Plateau, where you'll often see patches of snow even in the height of summer. The route continues along the slopes of the plateau, which is a natural fortress surrounded by a ring of peaks, and then to the bank of the Kara-Archa River where you can camp for the night.

Day 4: This is the hardest day of trekking, with a descent of 1,000m in altitude. The day begins with a short climb up the southeastern slope of Great Chimgan Mountain, then a very long descent into the Gulkam Gorge, during which you will have a clear view of **Okhotnichiy Peak** (3,099m) and, in the distance, **Lake Charvak** (see opposite). The lower you descend, the lusher the flora, and amid the grassy meadows and groves of juniper trees you are likely to meet shepherds with their flocks of sheep and goats. The final campsite is on the bank of the **Gulkamsay Stream** (1,650m).

Day 5: Start the morning with a short diversion into the **Gulkam Canyon**, a haven for climbers. If you want to climb here, you will need to bring your own helmet and ropes. Complete your trek with one last climb over the **Pesochniy Pass** (1,820m) which overlooks Chimgan village, an hour's walk further along the track. Arrange your onward transport from here.

Also known as the Pyramid Hotel, it consists of 3 gigantic pyramid-shaped buildings. Standard rooms have queen-sized beds, central heating & AC, & there's 24hr room service. The hotel is popular with conference organisers, so rooms may well be booked up by groups in advance, but individual travellers can still make use of the restaurant ($$) & other facilities. $$$

🏠 **Krokus Park** Yusufkhona; m 90 356 1807; w krokus.uz. This resort offers accommodation in comfortable split-level wooden cottages, & activities such as cycling, fishing, badminton & table tennis, as well as a swimming pool & sauna. $$$

UGAM-CHATKAL NATIONAL PARK The Chatkal Mountains rise up from the steppe 80km northeast of Tashkent, creating one of the most picturesque landscapes in Uzbekistan. Whether walking and picnicking, windsurfing and climbing, or heli-skiing at rock-bottom rates is your thing, in little over an hour's drive from central Tashkent you can be making the best of the great outdoors.

🏠 **Where to stay, eat and drink** Camping is common and encouraged. Make sure you take your rubbish away with you (in spite of the poor example set by the locals). However, if you prefer a proper bed there are various options. Alternatively, you could stay at one of the places at nearby Lake Charvak, listed on page 127.

🏠 **Beldersay Oromgohi** (38 rooms, 16 cottages) m 90 176 3826. This swish hotel has a stunning position, with 4-star rooms, cottages, tennis, indoor & outdoor swimming pools & restaurants ($$$). $$$$

🏠 **Nebesa Guest House** 7 Rublevka; 🌂 71 200 8887; w nebesa.uz. In Chimgan village, 3km north of the slopes, this comfortable hotel has log cottages, a terrace & bar & rather variable service. $$$$

🏠 **Archazor** 🌂 71 252 0026; m 90 322 2200; w en.archazor.uz. A comfortable mountain resort hotel in the trees below Chimgan village, with decent restaurant ($$), 3 cottages, a swimming pool & sauna. $$$

🏠 **Rake Nur Hotel** 2km north of the Chimgan ski area, just before the village. This renovated Soviet block is perhaps the best budget option here, with small, clean rooms with balconies. $$$

🏠 **Layner's Mountain Resort** 🌂 71 207 7676; w layner.uz. About 1.5km down the washed-out old road north of Chimgan village, this is something of a luxury mountain resort, although it has a strangely nautical style, with a ship's mast & anchor. There's a good restaurant ($$), outdoor pool & tennis court. $$

🏠 **Sky Village Resort Hotel** 🌂 71 286 1217; m 90 187 5904. A relatively economical option, 1.5km from the Chimgan ski area, with a restaurant ($$) & 2 rooms in the main building plus 5 cottages, an outdoor pool, sauna, gym & billiards. $$

DAY HIKE IN GULKAM CANYON

Just 2 hours' drive from Tashkent, inside the Ugam-Chatkal National Park, the Gulkam Canyon offers a number of different trekking routes. The route below is suitable for trekkers of all abilities, and can be completed in 4–5 hours, including picnic time.

Starting from the road through the **Chimgan resort**, it is an hour's pleasant walk to the **Pesochniy Pass** (1,900m). Those with stamina can climb a little further to the top of **Little Chimgan** (2,100m), with its panoramic views across the Chatkal, Pskem and Ugam ranges, as well as the Charvak Reservoir. From the pass a path winds down through birch groves into the **Gulkam Canyon**: stop by the river for lunch, and perhaps even a swim, before retracing your steps to Chimgan.

What to see and do From December to March, the **Chimgan Ski Resort**, which can be reached in a shared taxi (page 127) is packed each weekend with Tashkent's beautiful people and a host of foreign adrenalin junkies. Though not comparable to European resorts (there are only half a dozen or so slopes, none more than 1,500m in length), it's a popular excursion nonetheless and a cheap place for beginners to develop a taste for the powder. The majority of skiers take the chairlift (US$1.50 for a single journey), taking them to an altitude of 1,975m, but it is also possible to fly up to 3,000m and be deposited on virgin snow. Asia Adventures (page 96) has heli-skiing packages from US$500 per day but, if your budget won't stretch quite that far, a day's lift pass is a snip at US$10. Ski and snowboard gear is available to hire.

A few kilometres to the southwest, the **Beldersay resort** (c1,600m) is for slightly more advanced skiers. It has two chairlifts, the longer of which starts from a height of 2,200m, near the summit of Mount Kumbel. On the west side of Beldersay, the new **Amirsoy resort** (w amirsoy.com) will have 13 slopes by 2022, totalling 21km, with two Doppelmayr gondolas, lighting and modern snowmaking equipment.

Once the snow has melted, the national park becomes an ideal **trekking** ground. There are numerous routes suitable for all degrees of fitness: serious trekkers should take a guide (page 96), who should organise a border permit to reach the spectacular 'jade' lakes and the glaciers of the Pskem Mountains, squeezed between Kazakhstan and Kyrgyzstan in the northeastern corner of Uzbekistan. This part of the national park is included in the transnational western Tien Shan biosphere reserve, listed by UNESCO as a World Heritage Site in 2016.

There are also ample opportunities for more casual trekkers with a day or two to spare. The chairlifts at the ski resorts can help, at least at weekends, and helicopters are also an option – Ulysse Tour (w ulyssetour.com) offer tours in Soviet-built Mi-8s to the lakes, the Chimgan weather station and elsewhere.

A stroll along the park's juniper-covered slopes can reveal not only ancient petroglyphs, but also 280 species of fauna and more than 2,000 species of plants, including many varieties of tulips (*Tulipa kaufmanniana*, *T. tschimganica*, *T. greigii*, *T. bifloriformis* and *T. dubia* can all be found here).

There's a wealth of **birding** in the Chimgan/Beldersay area, with the white-winged woodpecker, rufous-naped tit, yellow-breasted tit and white-crowned penduline tit among the most sought-after species; others of interest include the Indian golden oriole, white-throated dipper, Asian paradise flycatcher, Turkestan tit, sulphur-bellied warbler, Eastern rock nuthatch, blue-capped redstart, red-fronted serin, white-capped bunting, rock bunting and Hume's warbler. Soaring above, you may see Himalayan and Eurasian griffons, lammergeier, cinereous vulture, booted eagle, oriental and European honey-buzzards, as well as alpine swifts.

RAFTING ON THE CHATKAL RIVER The Chatkal River is 3 hours' drive northeast from Tashkent, beyond the ski resorts and further up into the Tian Shan Mountains. It offers some of the best white water in central Asia, and 183km of its 223km length is suitable for rafting. It is known colloquially as the Five Canyons River. Waterfalls, cascades of rapids, whirlpools and rocky gorges all offer physical challenges, but the landscape is diverse, and the route is filled with excitement. Rafting on the Chatkal is particularly delightful in the spring, when the waters are at a safe level and the spring flowers are a riot of colour in the surrounding meadows; autumn can also be delightful.

For guided rafting tours and equipment hire, the Tashkent-based **Asia Raft Tour Company** ✳ (77 M Riezey; ☏ 71 267 0918; e asiaraft@fromru.com; w asiaraft.uz) is highly recommended. Booking on to their ten-day trip gets you all meals, transfers and camping equipment as well as raft, medical kit, life jacket and safety helmet. You should satisfy yourself as to the condition of any equipment you use, particularly if it is hired locally, and should wear a life jacket and helmet at all times. Comprehensive medical insurance is essential. The **first canyon** contains a perilous waterfall, with two steps, each of around 4m. It is followed by a 100m stretch of rapids, and the confluence of the Chatkal and Ters rivers. The rapids here are considered one of the most difficult parts of the route.

In the **second canyon**, the stone walls tower high above the river on either side.

The **third canyon** is narrow; the river winds through a corridor 200–300m high, the rocks pitted with grottoes and caves. Cornices overhang the water, in places blocking out the sky. The riverbed narrows to just 6m wide, but then opens out again to floodplains of forest and meadow. Chatkal Peak (4,503m) rises majestically in the distance.

Traversing the **fourth canyon** is relatively straightforward, but you quickly enter the most dangerous rapids of the trip, situated in the **fifth canyon**. The rocks narrow into a corridor known as 'the diaphragm', after which the river calms and widens. There are sandbanks and pebble beaches either side of the water. The final stretch of rapids is after the fifth canyon at Aurahmat. They occur only when dams upstream are opened for irrigation.

4

Fergana Valley and the East

The Fergana Valley is a depression between the Tian Shan Mountains in the north and the Gissar-Alai range in the south. Some 300km long, up to 70km wide and watered by the Kara Darya and the Naryn rivers, which join to form the Syr Darya, it is the most fertile part of Uzbekistan and hence the country's agricultural heartland. Agricultural wealth historically gave rise to Silk Road trading towns, fortresses and, most importantly, the Khanate of Kokand, between 1709 and 1876.

For much of the past 100 years it has also been an area that is deeply troubled. Stalin's border policies divided the valley between Uzbekistan, Kyrgyzstan and Tajikistan; not only are there main international borders here, but also a bewildering number of enclaves and exclaves that are nigh on impossible to administer but are fiercely defended at great financial and human cost. Communal violence has regularly reared its ugly head, for instance between Kyrgyz and Uzbeks in the summer of 2010, often spurred on by governments and other regional players when it suits their political objectives to do so.

The direct route from the Fergana to Tashkent (the A373 road) crosses the Catkalski range (a spur of the Tian Shan Mountains) via the Kamchik Pass (2,268m). This is often closed by snow and fog in winter, and sometimes by mudslides at other times. Buses are not allowed to cross the pass, and when it is closed all traffic has to transit via Tajikistan – hence the significance of the railway tunnel that opened beneath the pass in 2016 (page 66).

NAMANGAN

Some 300km east of Tashkent in the northern part of the Fergana Valley, not far from the border with Kyrgyzstan, is Namangan. The confluence of the Kara Darya and Naryn rivers, two tributaries of the Syr Darya (or Jaxartes), lies just outside the city's confines, and the local area has been populated since at least Sogdian times, as is attested to by the remarkable remains of Aksikent, Namangan's biggest draw.

HISTORY Namangan City, which takes its name from a local salt mine (*namak* meaning 'salt'), developed as the Fergana Valley's religious centre in the 17th century after Akiskent was finally abandoned. At its height, there were more than 600 mosques in the district, and a population of a third of a million people.

The religiosity of the local population, never fully suppressed during the Soviet period, has been a cause of concern since independence. Wahhabism, an extreme Islamic sect from Saudi Arabia, took root in the area, and in the mid 1990s it was the heartland of the now-banned Islamic Movement of Uzbekistan (see box, page 30).

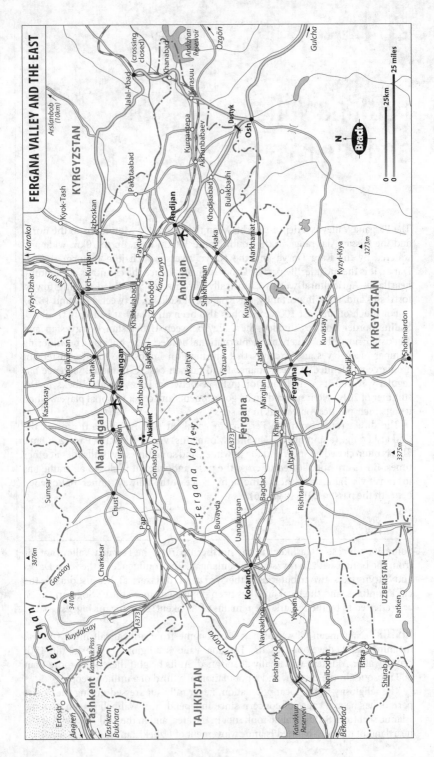

FERGANA VALLEY AND THE EAST

GETTING THERE AND AROUND Namangan is in the northern central part of the Fergana Valley, roughly equidistant between Kokand and Andijan. There are currently no passenger trains to Namangan.

By air Namangan's **airport** (✆ 69 232 2890/69 228 6890; e ap.nma@uzairways.com) is on the western edge of the city (12km from the centre), and **Uzbekistan Airways** (page 49; see ad, 3rd colour section) flies to Tashkent three times a week (Tue, Thu & Sun) for around US$25. Flights take 55 minutes and tickets can be purchased either from the ticket desk at the airport, or from their ticket office in the city (41 Mashrab; ✆69 226 2483).

Travelling **to or from Russia**, there are also scheduled departures between Namangan and Moscow (Uzbekistan Airways, Ural Airlines; page 49), Krasnodar (Ural Airlines), Novosibirsk (S7 Airlines; page 49), Yekaterinburg (Uzbekistan Airways, Ural Airlines) and St Petersburg (Uzbekistan Airways, Ural Airlines).

By road Namangan has two bus stands: the **long-distance bus stand** is about 2km west of the city centre, and from here you can get buses to Andijan (65km; 1hr 20min) and Fergana (85km; 2hrs), turn up at the station to find out what is departing when. There are no direct minibuses to Tashkent, so you'll need to find a **shared taxi**, waiting on Galaba, in the valley between the Old Town and the Irvadan quarter. The 290km journey to the capital along the A373 takes under 4 hours and a seat should not cost more than US$8.

If you are travelling to or from Kyrgyzstan (see box, page 140), the **Uch-Kurgan border post** between Namangan and Karakol (not the famous Karakol on Lake Issyk-Kul) is now open to foreigners (page 51). It's considerably closer to Tashkent than the crossing between Andijan and Osh (see box, page 140), which is beneficial if you're simply passing through the valley to get to northern Kyrgyzstan and Bishkek.

For getting around the city, **the local bus stand** is by the bazaar and the spaghetti junction at the eastern end of Navoi and a succession of minibuses (numbers 13, 17, 21, 22 and 33A) also run from the bazaar and along the length of Navoi to Do'stlik. The most useful minibus is number 4, which runs between the local and long-distance bus stands. If you are travelling beyond the city limits, Namangan Travel (see below) can arrange a car and driver; otherwise, the best place to find a taxi is at the Chorsu Bazaar (page 104).

TRAVEL AGENTS The following travel agents can arrange onward transport (including general flight ticketing) and accommodation bookings.

Adelaida Travel 32 Mashrab; ✆69 227 8833/69 227 7788; e adelaida_trevel@inbox.ru
Akram Trans Servis 16A Nodira; ✆69 226 5453; e umarov.79@mail.ru
Namangan Travel 1 Nodira; ✆69 226 1733. Guided tours, transport & trekking options.

Turism Namangan 2 Mashrab; ✆69 227 2300; m 91 181 0550; e sputnik@mail.ru; w turizm.namangan.uz

WHERE TO STAY *Map, opposite*
Namangan has a number of places to stay, though sadly none of them is particularly exciting. In addition to the Turkiston (page 135), there are a few other modern hotels nearby, on the main road towards the airport and Tashkent.

NAMANGAN

For listings, see from page 133

Where to stay
1 Orzu Grand Tour
2 Sayhun

Off map
Turkiston

Where to eat and drink
3 Kafe Kosmos
4 Sharshara
5 Super Gold Swits
6 Visol

Off map
Do'stlik Tennis Centre
La Calcio
Rubin Saz

N

Brandt

0 400m
0 400yds

KHODJAMNI

Local bus stand

Mullah Kyrgyz Madrasa

Khodjamni Kabri Mausoleum

Khodja Amin Mosque

Ota Valikhon Tur Mosque (1km), Uch-Kurgan border post

Chorsu Bazaar

Stadium

Navoi Theatre

Cinema Mashrab

NOSIR

Turism Namangan

Babur Park

Kinoteatr O'zbekiston

Asaka $

MARGILAN

BABUR

NAVOI

Andijan

M-A-SHR-A-B

Uzbekistan Airways

Adelaida Travel

Saydana Hospital

Namangan Travel

NODIRA

Infin $

Akram Trans Servis

Polyclinic #1

NAMAGONI

AKUNBABA

MANGUBERDI

GALABA

Long-distance bus stand

AMIR TIMUR / SOVIETSKAYA

Namangan Aqua Park

NAVOI

NAVOI

TORAKORGAN

Ipoteka $

Aloka $

Railway station (no commercial trains)

DO-S-T-L-I-K

Do'stlik Bazaar

Republican Scientific Centre for Emergency Medicine (500m), Microcredit, Do'stlik Tennis Centre, Turkiston, La Calcio (6km), airport (12km), Akiskent (22km), Chust (30km), Tashkent (284km)

Shared taxis to Tashkent, Ipak Yuli Bank, Rubin Saz, Turakurgan

🏠 **Sayhun** (20 rooms) 12 Namagoni; 📞78 223 0505; e hotel.sayhun@mail.ru. A modern, friendly hotel, linked to the Tibbiy Diagnostika 24hr diagnostic clinic & Kafe Evro-Asia (**$**) next door; there's a gym & a Mastercard ATM. **$$$**

🏠 **Orzu Grand Tour** (43 rooms) 1 Nodira; 📞69 223 0017; e orzuturgrand@gmail.com. The most acceptable of Namangan's budget options is in the Saydana private hospital (it uses its own entrance, with wheelchair access). Rooms are basic but have a balcony, TV & adequate Wi-Fi. **$$**

🏠 **Turkiston** (30 rooms) 32B Do'stlik; 📞69 232 0505; e buyuk.turkiston@mail.ru. Located opposite the Do'stlik Tennis Centre, a long way west of the city centre & one of Namangan's newer hotels, the Turkiston is comfortable with pleasant staff. There are 2 saunas & a swimming pool, as well as an attached restaurant (**$$**). **$$**

✕ WHERE TO EAT AND DRINK *Map, opposite*

Namangan is well equipped with places to eat. All are open for lunch and dinner unless otherwise stated. During summer, outdoor cafés pop up in parks, and Babur Park is stuffed with *chaikhanas*. Our favourites are **Sharshara**, **Super Gold Swits** [*sic*] and **Visol**, all of which fall into the **$$** bracket. They're at their liveliest on summer evenings.

✕ **Do'stlik Tennis Centre** 32B Do'stlik; ⏰ 09.00–02.00 daily. All those tennis players must provide good business, as the restaurant here is always buzzing (as is that of the Turkiston hotel across the road; see above). The menu offers the usual selection of grilled meats & salads, & it's an ideal place to spend a few hours, especially when there is a live band playing. **$$$**

✕ **La Calcio** Do'stlik; 📞69 232 8080; m 93 927 6008; f LaCalcio; ⏰ noon–midnight daily. An Italian restaurant serving real pizza, as well as steak & other dishes. Around 6km from the city centre. **$$$**

✕ **Rubin Saz** 7A Galaba; 📞69 681 3131. Popular spot for a quick bite, but nothing remarkable & rather out of the way (around 4km from the city centre). **$$**

🍽 **Kafe Kosmos** 8 Navoi; 📞69 212 6606. Cheap & cheerful café for tea & snacks. **$$**

ENTERTAINMENT AND NIGHTLIFE

🎬 **Cinema Mashrab** Navoi; 📞69 226 4039. Regular showings of the latest Russian blockbusters.

🎬 **Kinoteatr O'zbekiston** Navoi. On the south edge of Babur Park, this shows current blockbusters.

🎬 **Navoi Theatre** 2 Nosir; 📞69 226 2432. Occasional productions of Russian & Uzbek dramas with tickets starting from US$2–3. Call in at the theatre to get the current programme.

Namangan Aqua Park Amir Timur. A huge draw for local families, particularly at w/ends. On Fri & Sat evenings in summer it attracts a slightly older crowd for the popular (& very loud) open-air disco. It's one of the few places in the Fergana Valley where you can have a beer & let your hair down without the censure of more conservative types.

SHOPPING
For foodstuffs and general household goods, **Chorsu Bazaar** at the northeastern end of Navoi and **Do'stlik Bazaar** on Do'stlik are well stocked and easily accessible. Though less lively than some of Uzbekistan's other bazaars, they're still worth a casual forage if you're passing by.

OTHER PRACTICALITIES
Communications
✉ **Main post office** 54 Amir Timur; ⏰ 09.00–18.00 Mon–Fri. By the roundabout next to the train station.

Medical
Namangan sadly hit the news in 2010 when it was revealed that nearly 150 children had been infected with HIV while in hospital. Though this problem has now been solved, you should still bring your own needles & sterile kit (purchased from a local pharmacy if there isn't already one in your first-aid kit; see box, page 54) to ensure peace of mind. There are plenty of pharmacies in town.

✚ **Polyclinic #1** 37 Navoi; ☎69 227 9064. For general health problems.
✚ **Republican Scientific Centre for Emergency Medicine** 2 Go'zal; ☎69 226 2815. For an emergency.
✚ **Saydana Hospital** 1 Nodira; ☎69 223 1010. For general health problems; accommodation is also available here (page 135).

Money

Namangan has no shortage of **banks** for currency exchange & money transfer, though the only **ATMs** are at the Sayhun hotel (Mastercard; page 135) & Ipak Yuli Bank (Visa; see right).

$ **Aloka Bank** ☎69 233 2946; ⏱ 09.00–18.00 Mon–Fri
$ **Asaka Bank** ☎69 227 2145; ⏱ 09.00–17.00 Mon–Fri
$ **Infin Bank** ☎69 227 8032; ⏱ 09.00–18.00 Mon–Fri
$ **Ipak Yuli Bank** ☎69 232 4881; ⏱ 09.00–17.00 Mon–Fri
$ **Ipoteka Bank** ☎69 223 0300; ⏱ 09.00–17.00 Mon–Fri
$ **Microcredit Bank** ☎69 223 0620; ⏱ 09.00–17.00 Mon–Fri

WHAT TO SEE AND DO In the centre of town, **Babur Park** is a pleasant spot to spend an hour or two. It began life in the late 19th century as the garden of the Russian governor, but it is now open to the public. If you arrive in the late afternoon, you'll see Namangan's elders gathering in the dappled shade beneath the chinor (plane) trees to drink steaming bowls of tea and play games of chess or *nards* (a Persian board game similar to backgammon); it's an unexpectedly civilised haven of calm. At weekends, however, its amusement park becomes much livelier, as do its cafés and restaurants (page 135).

Namangan is also home to a number of attractive religious sites, one of which is closely linked to the controversial Wahhabi sect. The **Mullah Kyrgyz Madrasa** (built 1910), just east of the bazaar, on Uychi, is named after its talented local architect, Usto Kyrgyz. It is said that one day the architect sat in the middle of the madrasa building site drinking tea and watched a particularly useless apprentice trying (and failing) to build a wall. Exasperated, Usto Kyrgyz hurled a brick at the young man from across the courtyard which, unsurprisingly given the distance, missed him but landed in exactly the right place on top of the wall, just as if Usto Kyrgyz had carefully placed it there by hand.

The madrasa, which is an irregular pentahedron in shape due to the local topography, is surrounded by evenly placed *hujras*. It was closed by the Soviets and spent much of the 20th century as a literary museum, but was restored by local residents following independence and briefly served as a madrasa again before being closed by the Uzbek government. It is now a museum-monument, not in active use but currently being restored, and named in honour of the craftsman responsible for its construction.

There is some attractively carved woodwork, both ceilings and columns, and the main portal is decorated with a fine mosaic depicting flowers in blue, green, yellow and white; above the interior courtyard you'll see some interesting calligraphy outlined in brick.

A 5-minute walk south along a lane (Khodjamni) that rings and sparks with the striking of metal sheets and bars in tiny workshops brings you to the **Khodjamni Kabri Mausoleum** and neighbouring **Khodja Amin Mosque,** which has recently been renovated. Both of these buildings date from the 1720s and are the work of architect Usto Muhammad Ibrahim. The portal-domed mosque, open on all four sides, is typical of local mosque architecture of this period. The intricate terracotta tilework on the front of the mausoleum is particularly interesting as the tiles were produced using a method revived from the 12th century that had more or less disappeared in Fergana. You should note that only men are permitted inside these particular buildings.

About 1km east of the bazaar along Uychi is the **Ota Valikhon Tur Mosque** (built 1915) with its large ribbed dome featuring unusual stripes of blue mosaic, Arabic calligraphy in brick on the exterior and star-shaped carvings inside the entrance way. It is better known as a centre for the extreme Islamic Wahhabi sect during the 1990s; they spent large sums of money (mostly gifts from Saudi Arabia) developing the site as a modern madrasa, only for it to be closed by the government. It is now the gallery of the Namangan Artists' Union, usually showing the work of local artists.

AROUND NAMANGAN

Aksikent Namangan's most interesting site is outside the actual city. Some 22km to the southwest are the ruins of Aksikent, a fortified city on the Syr Darya River. It's possible to drive here yourself, or look for a shared taxi to Jomasho'y.

Aksikent (also known as Akhsi) was already well established by the 3rd century BC. The Chinese commander Li Guanli besieged the city with 60,000 soldiers for 40 days in 103BC in an attempt to gain control of the surrounding territory and, in particular, its famed blood-sweating horses.

Early in the 1st millennium AD, the city was conquered first by the Kushans and then by the Turks. It was a caravan stop en route from Kashgar to Byzantium, and locally made goods were traded all along the route: the strong but flexible steel produced in kaolin-lined smelting furnaces here was famous as far away as Baghdad and Damascus. By the early medieval period the town had become the capital of the Fergana Valley and had grown to such an extent that the perimeter wall was 18km long, and the central citadel contained a palace, mosque and bathhouse. Soldiers kept an eye on the trading domes and hostels from watchtowers along the walls.

In the early 13th century, Aksikent was sacked first by the Karakhitai and then in 1219 by Jebe Noyan, one of Genghis Khan's commanders. The city fell into decay and though attempts were made to rebuild it several kilometres down the river, it never really recovered. What little remained collapsed during an earthquake in 1620.

Aksikent is not a popular site for tourists, despite its historical significance, so you're likely to have the ruins to yourself. Start by climbing new metal steps to the top of the site where power lines lead to a new museum, now under construction. This was once the centre of the fort and, as the Emperor Babur recorded in his memoirs, the *Baburnama*, the suburbs of Aksikent stretched out from here for 3km in each direction. Looking down the steep drop to the row of plane trees alongside the river, you can clearly see the strategic value of this site: it's a spot that is easy to defend, and you could see enemies advancing from any direction.

Although initially the earthen mounds around you look just like arid humps, if you look closely, you'll be able to differentiate between the underlying earthworks and the stocky mud-brick walls. Millions of bricks, each one made by hand, comprised walls more than 2m thick: it's little surprise that it took Li Guanli's forces so long to break inside.

Chust The town of Chust, some 30km west of Namangan, is famed for its production of knives and skull caps, and a visit here will enable you to see the workshops and purchase fine examples of Uzbek craftsmanship. From the Chorsu Bazaar, midi-bus 245 runs frequently along Navoi and Do'stlik to Chust (45min; US$0.30).

In the **National Knife Factory** (46 Chusti; \ 69 423 6942), which is open to the public, metalworkers smash and grind their knives from short lengths of steel or iron, honing each blade into the desired shape with a meticulous attention to detail. The tip of each knife should curl, a trademark of the Chust design. The neighbouring rooms owe more to artists' ateliers than the blacksmith's shop next door. While some knife makers carve the haft, or handle, of the knife from animal horn, others painstakingly slice slivers of mother of pearl and arrange them in elaborate patterns of flowers and geometric designs.

The *tubeteika*, the black, tetrahedral skull cap worn throughout the Fergana Valley, is also made in Chust but unlike the knives, these are the handicraft of the town's womenfolk. Each black cap is lovingly embroidered in white: the four arches represent impenetrable gates that will keep all enemies at bay; the burning peppers protect against the evil eye; and the almonds (*bodom*), symbolise life and fertility.

ANDIJAN

Uzbekistan's fourth-largest city, Andijan has a rich past and vibrant Uzbek culture but a troubled recent history, and consequently few foreign tourists come here unless they're passing quickly through en route to Kyrgyzstan.

HISTORY Andijan was founded by the 9th century and was just getting on its feet when Genghis Khan rode through and razed it back to the ground. Fortunately for Andijan, his grandson Kaydu Khan saw potential in the ashes, rebuilt the town and made it his capital. This was a shrewd move, as the city became the lucrative gateway between Samarkand and Bukhara in the west, and Kashgar and Chinese Turkestan in the east.

The Andijan you see today is mostly of 20th-century construction, with wide boulevards. An earthquake in 1902 more or less levelled the Old Town, with the

ANDIJAN MASSACRE

There's no doubt that 13 May 2005 ranks among the blackest days in Uzbekistan's recent history. One of the few things about this event that is certain is that National Security forces opened fire into a crowd of protesters gathered in Babur Square; the identity of the protesters, the purpose of their protest and the number of fatalities are facts that are hotly contested.

According to Human Rights Watch (w hrw.org) and the BBC, on the morning of 13 May gunmen broke into a prison in Andijan to release 23 local businessmen on trial for alleged religious extremism, a particularly sensitive issue in the country since the end of the civil war in Tajikistan in the late 1990s and the invasion of Afghanistan in 2001. There had been several days of peaceful protest in the city beforehand, and following the men's release the number of protesters swelled to several thousand, their grievances ranging from the government's heavy-handedness and corruption to economic woes.

Around 18.00, security forces were given orders to break up the protests and regain control of the government buildings that they were occupying. Using snipers and troops in armoured personnel carriers, they shot repeatedly into the crowd. The government maintains only 187 were killed, all 'terrorists', but the total may have been 500 or more. President Karimov refused to allow an independent inquiry into the massacre and denied responsibility for the killings of unarmed protesters; the United Nations concluded that lethal force was used excessively, and subsequent investigations support that view.

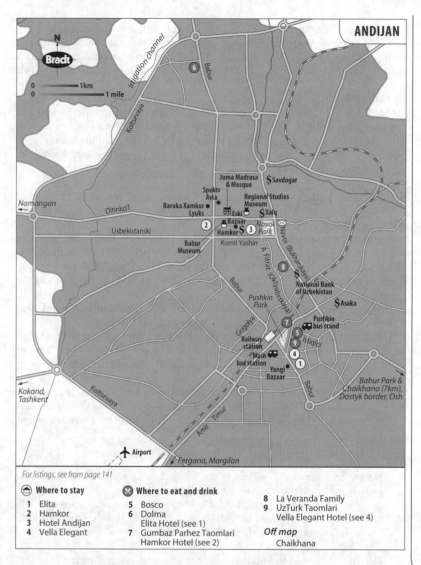

For listings, see from page 141

🛏 Where to stay	🍴 Where to eat and drink	8 La Veranda Family
1 Elita	5 Bosco	9 UzTurk Taomlari
2 Hamkor	6 Dolma	Vella Elegant Hotel (see 4)
3 Hotel Andijan	Elita Hotel (see 1)	
4 Vella Elegant	7 Gumbaz Parhez Taomlari	*Off map*
	Hamkor Hotel (see 2)	Chaikhana

exception of the Juma Madrasa (page 143), taking with it 4,500 lives. In the Soviet period, Andijan industrialised and grew wealthy on the profits of black and white gold: oil and cotton. They're still the mainstays of the local economy, along with the Chevrolet car factory in nearby Asaka, which opened in 1996. After the massacre of 2005 (see box, opposite), the city's people were cowed until the death of President Karimov; since then, the situation has relaxed and the city feels busy and positive.

GETTING THERE AND AROUND

By air Andijan's airport is 5km southwest of the city centre, immediately outside the ring road. **Uzbekistan Airways** operates two flights a week between Andijan and Tashkent (Thu & Sat, returning Wed & Fri; 1hr 5mins; US$75); there are less-regular services to Bukhara and Urgench, and also to Moscow, Krasnoyarsk and Novosibirsk.

Tickets can be bought from the airline at the airport, at 1 Koltsevaya (✆ 74 224 4864) or, more conveniently, from one of the many Aviakassas on Babur Square, such as **Baraka Xamkor Lyuks** (38 Babur; ✆ 74 263 4311; e baraka_xamkor@mail. ru) or **Spektr Avia** (43 Babur; ✆ 74 224 5937; m 90 624 9926; e spektr-avia@bk.ru).

By rail Daily trains run from Andijan's station south of the centre on Amir Timur via Margilan and Kokand **to Tashkent**, taking 6 hours or less, and overnight trains run once a week to Bukhara (Sun; via Tashkent & Samarkand) and twice a week to Moscow (Tue & Sun; via Tashkent). **Tickets** can be bought from the Kassa on the west side of the train station or, more easily, if you don't speak Russian, through an air-ticket agent (see above).

By road Most visitors arrive in Andijan by road as it is well connected to the other cities in the Fergana Valley, and it is usually faster to drive to/from Tashkent than it is to go by train.

The **main bus station** is on Amir Timur, close to the train station, and from here you can pick up both minibuses and shared taxis to destinations within the valley. The ride to Namangan takes 1 hour and the shared taxi costs US$3 per seat. The minibus to Fergana takes 1¼ hours and costs US$3, or US$4 per seat by slightly faster shared taxi.

If you're going **to Tashkent** by bus, you need the **Pushkin bus stand** near Pushkin Park. Shared taxis take around 5 hours and cost US$10 per seat.

Heading to **Kyrgyzstan**, you need to go to the Yangi Bazaar, south of the station on Babur, where minibus and shared taxi drivers all cry out 'Osh! Osh! Osh!' In reality, they only go to the border, although there's talk of reintroducing direct buses to Osh. There are two border posts close to Andijan, but at the time this guide went to print, only one of these was actually open for foreigners to cross into Kyrgyzstan. This is at Dostyk, an hour from Andijan on the road to Osh, and public transport is plentiful on both sides (page 51). It costs US$1.25 for a seat in a shared

CONTINUING TO KYRGYZSTAN

A significant number of visitors to the Fergana Valley will be continuing their journey by crossing the border into Kyrgyzstan. Since the overthrowing of the government in 2010, the country has become more open and prosperous and it boasts some of the most beautiful and unspoilt mountain scenery on earth. Within easy striking distance of the border are several sites of interest.

OSH Just 5km from the border is Osh, the second city of Kyrgyzstan, which celebrated (accurately or otherwise) its 3,000th birthday in 2000. Though there is little to see of the original citadel, a bastion of Islam against the marauding, infidel nomads, the Tacht-i Suleiman (Throne of Solomon), the looming hill that dominates the city's skyline, is one of the holiest sites in central Asia and an important pilgrimage site. Osh is also home to a sprawling bazaar, a vast statue of Lenin that was supposedly brought here from Bishkek, and the Silk Road Museum at the base of the holy Sulaiman Too Mountain, which has a number of reasonable ethnographic displays. There's the usual range of hotel and hostel options, and the Community Based Tourism programme (CBT; e cbtgulcho@ mail.ru; w cbtkyrgyzstan.kg) is able to make homestay bookings and arrange tours and transport.

taxi to reach here. The crossing at Khanabad, on the road between Andijan and Jalal-Abad, is shut.

To get around Andijan, set minibus routes radiate from the Eski Bazaar to cover most of the city. Minibus 8 links the city centre and the airport via the rail and bus stations, 14 goes to Babur Park, and 33 goes from the Old Town along Babur.

For more information on continuing into Kyrgyzstan, see the box below.

🏠 WHERE TO STAY Map, page 139

There are several options, some quite reasonable and others rather grim. The same contrast sometimes applies to rooms within a single hotel, so if in doubt you might want to ask to see a couple of options before committing to checking in.

🏠 **Hamkor Hotel** (26 rooms) 53 Babur; ✆74 298 0808; **w** hamkorbc.uz. Over-the-top new business hotel set over 2 floors, in the centre of Andijan (5km from the station). Staff are professional & polite. It can feel like a conference & business centre & has a large restaurant (**$$**) & bar. **$$$**

🏠 **Elita** (48 rooms) 19B Babur; ✆74 228 1692. Relatively modern (2005), this mid-size hotel has large, comfortable rooms, good bathrooms & a restaurant (**$$**). Sgl, dbl & quad rooms available. **$$**

🏠 **Hotel Andijan** 241 A Fitrat; ✆74 223 7040. Despite its ornate windows, beautiful foyer & central location, this is now something of a shoestring option. Some rooms have been renovated; opt for one with a private bathroom. **$$**

🏠 **Vella Elegant** (120 rooms) 40 Babur; **m** 95 200 6336/95 202 8588; **e** vellaelegant@ mail.ru; **w** vellaelegant.uz. Split between 2 buildings on either side of the road, Vella Elegant has large rooms, clean bathrooms, a decent restaurant (**$$**) & a pleasant, grassy courtyard with an outdoor pool. The new building (to the east) is better; the old building is used as an overflow. **$$**

✘ WHERE TO EAT AND DRINK Map, page 139

Andijan is famous for its *plov*, so even if you haven't eaten it anywhere else in Uzbekistan, you should probably try it here. It's served up to a hungry local crowd

ÖZGÖN An hour's drive northeast of Osh on the banks of the Kara Darya River is Özgön, the erstwhile capital of the Karakhanid dynasty. A stone's throw from the town's bus station are three mausoleums and a minaret, important by virtue of the fact they are among the few surviving examples of pre-Mongol architecture. Each of the sites is finely decorated, and it is an intriguing sight to watch women touching the walls of the tombs with reverence. You can reach Özgön by bus from Osh (60 Kyrgyz som).

ARSLANBOB Three hours' drive northeast through the mountains from Andijan (along paved roads) is Arslanbob, a Shangri-la scene with snow-capped peaks, waterfalls and alpine lakes. The area is famous for its ancient walnut forests, which support a diverse range of wildlife, and for the nomads who drive their flocks here to fatten them in the lush, green pastures. Arslanbob is cloaked in snow in the winter months, but an ideal place for horse trekking and hiking during the summer. The mainly Uzbek population traditionally made furniture, but felling walnut trees is now banned; there's a community-based project that uses fallen branches to make violins instead. Homestays, trekking guides and horse hire can be arranged through CBT (**m** 77 334 2476; **e** arslanbob_2003@rambler.ru; **w** cbtkyrgyzstan.kg).

in the chaikhana in Babur Park (**$$**). Andijan is also known for offal dishes, *nokhat* (a snack of chickpeas with pepper and raw onion), *mastava* (rice soup) and *siltama* (mutton stew). There are also restaurants at the Elita (page 141) and Vella Elegant (page 141) hotels, though they're fairly uninspiring and often booked out for weddings. The restaurant of the Hamkor Hotel (page 141) is slightly better, however.

✗ **Bosco** 8 Istiqlol; ⏱ 11.00–23.00; **f** Boscores. This is the place for good Russian food, though it is a little more expensive than elsewhere. **$$$**

✗ **Dolma** 43 Kusharik. This is popular with a younger crowd, & on summer evenings it's pleasant to sit outdoors by the fountains. **$$**

✗ **La Veranda Family Restaurant** Navoi; ✆74 223 3434; ⏱ 10.00–23.00 daily. A good modern restaurant serving pizza, pasta & Uzbek food. **$$**

✗ **Gumbaz Parhez Taomlari** 2 Amir Timur; ⏱ 08.00–22.00 daily. Just northeast of the railway station, this large cafeteria has a great range of cheap Uzbek food. **$**

✗ **UzTurk Taomlari** Milliy Tiklanish; ⏱ 10.00–22.00 daily. Just off Babur & south of the Vella Elegant hotel, this serves cheap & very cheerful Turkish food. **$**

SHOPPING The **Eski (or Jahom) Bazaar** (⏱ 09.00–18.00 daily) on Oltinko'l is Andijan's commercial centre, and though it is open daily, it is significantly larger on Sunday and Thursday when the villagers flock into town. Head first to the fringes of the market, where you'll find blacksmiths banging and clanging away in their forges, knifemakers shaping and polishing steel blades, and the occasional dusty

BABUR: UZBEK HERO, MUGHAL EMPEROR

Zahir-ud-din Muhammad (1483–1530), also known as Babur, was a direct descendant of Timur through his father's line, and a supposed descendant of Genghis Khan through his mother. He was born in Andijan, the eldest son of the ruler of Fergana, Omar Sheykh Mirza of the Barlas tribe. He was educated in both Chaghatai Turkish and Persian, and as a young man excelled not only on the battlefield but also as a poet.

In 1495 Babur succeeded his father as ruler of Fergana, but he lacked widespread support. Though he conquered Samarkand in 1497, a rebellion of nobles back in Fergana forced him to abandon his prize, and his troops deserted on the way back. An attempt to retake Samarkand two years later was no more successful, and Babur was forced to retreat to Badakhshan (now in Afghanistan).

Perhaps realising that he was not destined to rule central Asia, he turned his attention south to Timur's other imperial domains: Afghanistan and India. Here he had more luck. He captured Kabul in 1504 and again in 1510, briefly occupied Herat, had one final go at taking Samarkand in 1511, then turned his attention to defeating the Lodi rulers of northern India and seizing their capital, Delhi. En route Babur successfully took Kandahar and the plains of the Punjab, finally winning Delhi at the Battle of Panipat in 1526.

Babur died in 1530, and was succeeded by his eldest son, Humayun. He wished to be buried in Kabul, in his mind a far more civilised city than the cultural wilderness that was India, so after a brief interment in Agra, he was reburied in his garden tomb in Kabul. His descendants, the Mughals (a corruption of Mongols, in reference to their central Asian heritage), would rule much of India and what is now Pakistan until being finally deposed by the British in 1857.

carpentry workshop. Among the craftsmen, keep your eyes peeled for the wizened old pigeon fanciers; their dove-grey birds sit twitching and cooing and watching the world with alert, beady little eyes. The people watching here is unrivalled, and the photographic opportunities somehow sum up life on the Silk Road.

In addition to fresh produce (the melons are enormous!) you can pick up spices, embroidered hats, good silks, embroidered skull caps and the traditional Fergana knives (page 137), all (so long as you haggle) without the usual tourist mark-up.

The **Yangi Bazaar**, south of the station on Babur, is also lively, with lots of cafés nearby, as well as shared taxis to the Kyrgyz border.

OTHER PRACTICALITIES
Communications

✉ **Post office** Uztelecom building; ⏰ 09.00–13.00 & 14.00–17.00 Mon–Fri, 09.00–15.00 Sat. On the northeast cnr of Navoi & Biruni; you can also pay to make long-distance calls in the same building.

❒ **Internet cafés** There was a crackdown on internet cafés in Andijan in the late 2000s & they still seem to get closed down with little reason or notice. You will need to ask at your hotel for the closest option. You have to show your passport when using an internet café in Andijan, & the owner will take a photocopy. You may find that some sensitive sites (including news sites) are blocked, as are their proxy servers.

Money

Cash advances for Visa cardholders, as well as the usual currency exchange services, are available from the National Bank of Uzbekistan (42 Navoi). The following banks do money transfer & foreign exchange:

$ **Asaka Bank** ✆ 74 223 6069; e andijonviloyat@asakabank.uz; ⏰ 09.00–18.00 Mon–Fri
$ **Hamkor Bank** ✆ 74 223 4094; ⏰ 09.00–17.00 Mon–Fri
$ **Savdogar Bank** ✆ 74 225 7895/74 225 2153; ⏰ 09.00–16.30 Mon–Fri
$ **Xalq Bank** ✆ 74 223 9035/74 223 9027; ⏰ 09.00–18.00 Mon–Fri

WHAT TO SEE AND DO Andijan's main sites are clustered around Eski Bazaar in the Old Town. It has a bunch of small museums, the most important of which is the **Babur Museum** (Oltinko'l; ✆ 74 225 7302; ⏰ 09.00–18.00 Tue–Sat; foreigners US$0.75). Babur (see box, opposite) studied in a madrasa on this site, and the design of the heavily rebuilt structure harks back to its original use. When Babur fled Uzbekistan in the early 16th century the building was destroyed and it was 200 years before it was restored, first for use as Andijan's town hall, and then as the private residence of a prominent local family. It opened as a museum in 1990 and the carefully laid-out garden with formal planting also dates from this time.

The exhibits inside the museum celebrate Babur's poetry and prose: his autobiographical chronicle, the *Baburnama*, is one of the most important historical sources we have from the 1500s and he was a fine wordsmith as well as a warrior and statesman. Text displays (which can be a little monotonous) are interspersed with attractive reproductions of miniature paintings and very speculative larger-scale scenes from Babur's life, fleshing out the picture of a man who changed the fate of the Indian subcontinent, as well as his descendants, the emperors Akbar, Humayun, Jahangir, Shah Jehan and Aurangzeb. Babur is also remembered with a statue in **Babur Square** (formerly Lenin Square, facing the station), the site of the 2005 massacre (see box, page 138).

The **Regional Studies Museum** (Oltinko'l; ⏰ 09.00–16.00 Tue–Sun; foreigners US$1) is not in itself terribly exciting, but alongside it is the 19th-century **Juma Madrasa and Mosque** (⏰ 09.00–17.00 Tue–Sun), the only building in the city to have survived the 1902 earthquake. Built as Andijan's chief religious complex in the late 19th century, it's a stocky reddish building with a façade more than 120m long.

There are some attractive vaulted halls, and the traditional portal at the centre of the mosque is crowned with ornamental minarets.

There are two large public parks in Andijan. In **Navoi Park** (Babur Sq), an unexpectedly green haven with numerous trees and boating lakes, there is an elaborate industrialist's house, built in 1897 for the factory-owner Ahmed Beg Khoja who was forced to abandon the building when he fled to China to escape the Bolsheviks. The house was, for a time, a folk museum but now houses the office for Andijan Muslims. During office hours, visitors are permitted to explore living quarters and guest rooms on two of the floors. Inside the park there is also a gaudy modern mosque sponsored by Saudi Arabia, situated on the foundations of an older mosque and madrasa from 1903.

Babur Park is 7km southeast of the city centre (over an hour's walk, or take *marshrutka* 14 from the bazaar). Babur was supposedly fond of coming here (to the hill, not the park); it is said that he stopped atop it, as portrayed in a statue, to get one last, panoramic view of the city before leaving his homeland forever. A new building like an Islamic shrine is to house a **literary museum**, focusing on Babur and two fine poets, his daughter Gulbadan Begum and Nadira Beg (1792–1842), wife of the Khan of Kokand. Earth from Babur's grave in Kabul and from Agra, where he died, was brought here and, like a relic, entombed in marble when the park opened in 1993. The park is at its busiest on Sundays and during holidays, when there are craft stalls, music and dancing; you can also take the somewhat rickety chairlift up to a hilltop fairground.

FERGANA

Founded in 1876 as a Russian garrison town, with a radial-circular plan based on St Petersburg, Fergana has gone through a succession of name changes. From its origin as the less-than-imaginative New Margilan, it became Skobelov in 1907, then finally Fergana in 1924. It is now the capital of Fergana Province and is also a regional centre for oil refining and chemical fertiliser production. The majority of foreigners visiting the town are either here for work reasons, or are passing through en route to somewhere with more cultural capital.

GETTING THERE AND AROUND Fergana's nearest railway station is just north, on the edge of Margilan, and lies on the Andijan–Tashkent line (page 140).

By air Fergana's airport is 5km southwest of the city centre. **Uzbekistan Airways** (page 49) has scheduled departures to Tashkent (1hr) three to four times a week, depending on the season, and also a weekly flight (Wed; 3hrs) to Nukus via Tashkent.

By road Some 350km from Tashkent and 75km from Andijan, Fergana is easily accessible from either direction, should you feel the need: it lies just south of the A373, the main road through the valley. Shared taxis to **Tashkent** leave from the west side of the Yermazar Bazaar (4hrs; US$12), and the minibuses and shared taxis to Margilan (20min; US$0.30/0.70) and Andijan (1¼hrs; US$3/4) leave from the old bus station on Khodjaev, north of the bazaar. For Kokand, minibuses depart from the local bus stand on Kurbunjon Dodkhokh, southeast of the bazaar (2hrs; US$1).

Though Fergana is a fair-sized city, most of the sites you are likely to want to visit fall within a few streets of each other and so are conveniently reached on foot. If you are travelling further afield within the city, buses 6 and 6A run from the airport,

Map legend / map content:

FERGANA

Hotel Makon (5km),
Plov Center (5km)

Margilan (20km),
Rishtan (55km),
Tashkent (320km)

TADBIRKORLAR

Old bus
station

K RAKHIMOV

FERGANSKAYA
TURON
AKHUNBABAEV
Hamkor
KHODJAEV
YUSUPOV

Museum of
Regional History
& Culture

NIYAZOV

Yermazar
Bazaar

KHAMZA

Local bus
stand

Andijan (82km)

KURBUNJON DODKHOKH

MAKSUMOV
OVIR
Vodiy
Sayyox
MURRABIYLAR
Al Fargoni
Park
Stadium
Turon
Kapitalbank

KAMBAROV
YUKSALISHI / KUVASOY

National Bank
of Uzbekistan

AL FARGONI
MARGILONI
MARIFAT

MARUBIYLAR
TURKISTON
SAYILGOH
FAROBIY
KOMUS
MUSTAKILLIK
S TEMUR
NAVOI

BOBUR

Russian fort
(inaccessible)

For listings, see below

Where to stay
1 Asia
2 Sakura Inn
3 Sonya B&B
4 Valentina Guest House
5 Ziyorat

Off map
Club Hotel 777
Hotel Makon

Where to eat and drink
6 Brown Sugar Coffee House
7 Friends Cafe

Off map
Plov Center

N

0 ——— 200m
0 ——— 200yds

Club Hotel 777 (1km),
airport (4km),
Shohimardon (50km)

along Margiloni and eventually to the bazaar and are very cheap. Minibus 22 takes a more direct route from the city centre to the airport.

TOUR OPERATORS   Vodiy Sayyox (43 Al Fargoni; \73 224 2502) offer flight and accommodation bookings, although there is no English spoken.

WHERE TO STAY   *Map, above*

Fergana is a much larger city than nearby Margilan and has a correspondingly greater number of accommodation options. You might, therefore, want to base yourself here, and visit Margilan on a day trip.

Asia Hotel (95 rooms) 26 Navoi; \73 244 1326; e fergana.asia@yandex.ru; w asiahotels. uz/en. Upmarket chain hotel aimed at foreign tour groups. The hotel is large, comfortable & well located but characterless. There is a restaurant on site ($$$) plus ATM, gym & indoor & outdoor swimming pools. B/fast inc. $$$

Club Hotel 777 (16 rooms) 37 Oybek; \73 224 3777. A slightly brash resort hotel for package tourists on coach trips, where you'd expect to fight for a sun lounger by the pool. Facilities are fine; the atmosphere & clientele can be ghastly. $$$

Ziyorat Hotel (72 rooms) 2A Dodkhokh; \73 244 0373; e hotel.ziyorat@mail.ru.Having undergone much-needed renovations, Ziyorat has gone from being a bit of an ex-Soviet dump to a perfectly acceptable (if uninspiring) mid-range option, with an outdoor swimming pool. $$$

145

🏠 **Hotel Makon** (37 rooms) 82 Ferganskaya; 📞73 249 0009. A modern complex with a garden 5km north of the centre, this has a sauna & gym, & you can eat at the adjacent Plov Center (**$**). **$$**

🏠 **Sakura Inn** (7 rooms) 89 Yuksalishi; 📞73 244 2233; m 91 666 2125; e elsevarm@inbox.ru. A very discreet doorway leads to this very friendly & comfortable budget spot above the Kafe Shirin (where b/fast is served). Be sure to book ahead. **$$**

✻ 🏠 **Sonya B&B** 49 Akhunbabaev (or Universitet); 📞73 270 9099/73 224 0325; w sonyabbandtravel.uz. The friendliest homestay in town is with Sonya & her warm & welcoming family. Join them for excellent dinners & comfortable beds in a central location. Highly recommended. **$$**

🏠 **Valentina Guest House** 11 Al Fargoni; m 90 272 4072. A good option especially if you speak Russian; Valentina serves a great b/fast. **$$**

✗ **WHERE TO EAT AND DRINK** *Map, page 145*

For cheap and tasty eats, there are numerous *chaikhanas* and *shashlik* stands in Al Fargoni Park and around the bazaar. Otherwise, we recommend the following:

🍺 **Brown Sugar Coffee House** 4 Farobiy; 📞73 244 0565; 🅵 coffeehousebrownsugar. At the rear of the Asia Hotel, this is a very pleasant place to eat or spend the evening with local beer & wine; however, the Wi-Fi is patchy. **$$**

🍺 **Friends Cafe** 12 Farobiy; m 90 405 3978; ⏲ 10.00–02.00 daily. This scruffy outfit close to the Asia Hotel is a reasonable option, where Fergana's arty types hang out. The espresso is suitably strong; the baristas certainly know their stuff! **$$**

OTHER PRACTICALITIES
Communications
Fergana is better stocked with **internet cafés** than the other cities in the valley, including a couple at the junction of Kambarov & Marifat (⏲ until 23.00). The main **post office** is at 35 Mustakillik (⏲ 07.00–19.00 Mon–Sat).

Money
Fergana has plenty of places to change money & receive Western Union transfers. The most centrally located banks are listed here & shown on the map on page 145, though there are plenty more. None of them have ATMs, although there is a Visa machine inside the Asia Hotel (page 145). Cash advance is available for Visa cardholders at the

National Bank of Uzbekistan (35 Al Fargoni; ⏲ 09.00–17.00 Mon–Fri).

$ Hamkor Bank m 95 401 7175; ⏲ 09.00–17.00 Mon–Fri

$ Kapitalbank 📞73 244 5900; ⏲ 09.00–17.00 Mon–Fri

$ Turon Bank 📞73 224 0617; ⏲ 08.30–17.00 Mon–Fri

Registration
OVIR 36 Akhunbabaev; ⏲ 09.00–17.00 Mon–Fri, 09.00–12.00 Sat. For more information on visas, see page 47.

WHAT TO SEE AND DO To be honest, you don't come to Fergana to see Fergana: you sleep here and make use of the good transport connections to explore other parts of the valley.

Fergana's sole piece of remaining history, a section of the mud-brick walls of its Russian fort, is now sadly hidden from view (and usually inaccessible) inside the army compound on Marginoni.

The **Museum of Regional History and Culture** (26 Murrabiylar; ⏲ 09.00–17.00 Wed–Sun; foreigners US$1.25) is a Soviet relic, and some of the dioramas probably haven't been dusted since then either. It gives some insight into what the USSR felt was important for its citizens to learn about, but once you've seen one museum of this type, you've probably seen them all. The top floor is even duller, if possible, boasting about post-independence Uzbekistan's achievements, and the information is only in Uzbek.

AROUND FERGANA Midway between Fergana and Kokand is the town of **Rishtan,** one of the most important ceramics centres in Uzbekistan. Famed for its blue and green plates, coated with the unique *ishkor* alkaline glaze, it is said that the largely Tajik residents have been making items from the local red clay, decorated with natural pigments, for more than 800 years. Skills and designs are passed down from father to son, although a school of ceramics also opened in 2005.

In 1920, the government collectivised 30 small, artisanal workshops into the **Rishtan Art Ceramics Factory** (6 B Roshidoni; ✆73 452 1549; ⏲ 09.00–18.00 daily; free). Around 2,000 craftsmen now work here, using a combination of modern machinery and traditional techniques to produce around 5 million items a year. Visitors are welcome to watch the craftsmen at work as they throw pots, decorate them with delicate designs and then fire them in the roaring furnace. The showroom sells everything from tea pots to *plov* dishes (which make ideal souvenirs) and, if you fancy having a go yourself, you can do so at the neighbouring **workshop of Rustam Usmanov** (✆ 73 452 1585; m 91 681 2391/94 558 7111; e usmanovd4@ gmail.com/damir74441984@mail.ru), where you'll see a sign reading 'Kulolchilik Ustakhonasi' or 'Ceramic Workshop at 230 B Ar-Roshidoniy'. You can take a free tour (Rustam's nephew speaks good English), and see the collection of old pots, and then of course shop. This is a pleasantly semi-rural private home, there are wheels and kilns here, but most of the painters work at their own homes. Lunch and dinner are available for groups of ten or more – book in advance (**$$**).

Another option is to visit fifth-generation potter **Said Akhmedov**, just off the Fergana road at 8 Amir Timur (m 90 303 0039/90 408 9740; e said_akhmedov@ mail.ru). This is another nice house where you can watch potters at work (no English is spoken) and browse the products laid out in the courtyard. Just show up.

Finally, at the **Koron Works** at 7A Temirov (m 90 274 9305/91 673 4889; e tojiddinov77@mail.ru; w koron.uz; ⏲ closed Sun), just down a side road from the main bus stop in the town centre, Ravshan Tojiddinov employs 60 staff. All are very friendly, and, although no English is spoken, you can watch the process and choose from a wide range of pots in the shop. You can also study the craft here, without charge if it's just for a few days.

MARGILAN

Margilan is the centre of Uzbekistan's silk industry, and much of the silk you see for sale in Samarkand and Bukhara is in fact made in factories here. Like those better-known cities, the population of Margilan is also predominantly ethnic Tajik, which gives it a slightly different feel from other places in the Fergana Valley. It's only a small place, but well worth a few hours of your time.

HISTORY Margilan's history and its name are entwined, for local legend claims that Alexander the Great stopped here on his conquest of central Asia and was fed both *murgh* (chicken) and *non* (flat bread). It was the largest town in the Fergana Valley by the 10th century, in large part due to its location on the Silk Road from Kashgar, and it became famous for both its fruits and its handwoven silks. Industrial silk production became the mainstay of the town's economy during the Soviet period, and Margilan was also noted as a centre for black-market trade; nowadays a limited amount of tourism is boosting the local economy instead.

GETTING THERE AND AROUND A well-maintained road links Margilan with Fergana, 14km to the south (just a 20-minute drive). Fergana is the local hub

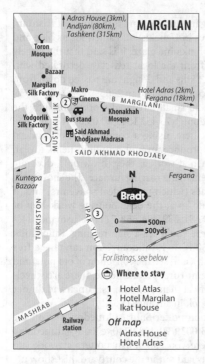

MARGILAN

Adras House (3km),
Andijan (80km),
Tashkent (315km)

Toron Mosque

Bazaar

Margilan Silk Factory

Makro

Cinema

Hotel Adras (2km),
Fergana (18km)

B MARGILANI

Yodgorlik Silk Factory

Bus stand

Khonakhah Mosque

Said Akhmad Khodjaev Madrasa

MUSTAKILLIK

SAID AKHMAD KHODJAEV

Kuntepa Bazaar

Fergana

N

Bradt

IPAK YULI

TURKISTON

0 ___ 500m
0 ___ 500yds

For listings, see below

Where to stay
1 Hotel Atlas
2 Hotel Margilan
3 Ikat House

Off map
Adras House
Hotel Adras

MASHRAB

Railway station

for road and air connections, while the railway runs through Margilan itself.

Margilan's **bus stand** is close to the junction of Mustakillik and B Margilani, just behind the cinema and the Makro supermarket. The ride to Fergana costs US$0.50 by minibus and US$1 by shared taxi.

Margilan's **railway station** (1 Mashrab; 73 237 5728) is on the southern side of the town; see page 140 for an outline of services from Andijan to Tashkent (US$6.50; 5hrs) and beyond.

Once in Margilan, the best way to get around is **on foot**. Almost all of the city's sights are within a few hundred metres of the intersection of B Margilani and Mustakillik.

TOURIST INFORMATION The best way to see the silk factories and workshops are with the guides you will find there, but not many of them speak English. The staff are generally helpful and knowledgeable about the silk industry, as well as having the inside track on what to buy and where (albeit, no doubt, with a hefty commission).

 WHERE TO STAY, EAT AND DRINK *Map, above*
Most people choose to visit Margilan on a day trip from Fergana (page 144), but if you do decide to stay, the hotels listed are fine options.

For **food**, head for the bazaar at the central crossroads, where there are basic cafés and *shashlik* stalls, as well as plenty of fresh bread, tomatoes, cucumbers and fruit.

Hotel Adras (21 rooms) 32 B Margilani; m 91 681 8900; e hoteladras@gmail.com; w hoteladras.uz. Quite a way east of the centre, this is not quite as cheap as you would hope, but it's clean & reasonably new. There is a medium-sized restaurant ($$) serving European & Uzbek dishes & a large conference hall on site. $$$

Adras House 1 Navnikhol; m 91 677 0070/93 974 1919; e adrassilk@inbox.ru. About 3km north in the Joybozor quarter, this is comfortable enough, although internet access is poor & b/fast is a bit chaotic; the attraction is the

loom in a back room & the shop selling *ikat* textiles at very reasonable prices. $$

Hotel Atlas 119 Turkiston; 73 253 3300. A little south of the centre, this is the most reliable budget option. $$

Hotel Margilan 343 Mustakilik; m 95 400 0484. Right in the centre, this old-style Soviet pile isn't refurbished & thus very affordable. Recommended for penniless backpackers. $$

Ikat House 133 Ipak Yuli; m 90 303 3800. This very friendly guesthouse is decorated with local textiles; you can watch weavers at work & even learn how to do it yourself. $$

SHOPPING Buy your silk in Margilan; it would be foolish to do it anywhere else. The **Yodgorlik Silk Factory** (see opposite) has reasonable, though unimaginative, products; the **Margilan Crafts Development Centre** (see box, opposite) and a couple of the guesthouses listed opposite also sell good-value items. If markets are your thing, a visit to the **Kuntepa Bazaar** (see below) is unmissable.

WHAT TO SEE AND DO Put simply, silk, silk and more silk. The **Yodgorlik Silk Factory** (Imam Zakhriddin; \ 73 223 8824; m 90 302 2335; e yodgorlik-factory@ mail.ru; ⊕ 09.00–17.00 Mon–Fri) was established in 1983 in a bid to preserve traditional silk-weaving techniques in the face of industrialisation. The focus on high-quality, handmade goods has clearly paid off as the buoyant factory has now expanded to employ more than 200 workers. All parts of the production process are undertaken here, from the feeding of the big, fat silk worms with mulberry leaves, through dyeing with natural vegetable and mineral dyes, to the weaving of the final cloth, and it is fascinating to follow it through step by step: you'll never look at a silk scarf or tie in quite the same way again. Informative **tours** (US$1, but can be offset against purchases in the shop) are fortunately available upon request in English, French, German and Russian, so you can understand the intricacies of what is going on. The guides are delighted to answer questions and, if you show particular interest in part of the process, they really get into their stride, pull colleagues out of their work to demonstrate things to you, and may even let you have a go yourself.

For its sheer scale, and the contrast in production methods (machines feature prominently), you can also visit the state-run **Margilan Silk Factory** (129 Orol Buyi) on a tour organised by Advantour (page 96). At its peak, this factory employed 15,000 workers, who produced 22 million square metres of silk each year, but the economic downturn and electricity shortages mean the output now is just a fraction of this. If you're curious how centralised planning and mass-production were implemented in Uzbekistan during the Soviet period, this is a prime place to come as little, if anything, has changed since independence.

On Sundays and, to a lesser extent, Thursdays, the **Kuntepa Bazaar** (5km west of the city centre) springs into life: it's one of the most vibrant markets in central Asia and, unusually, is still selling the product that gave the Silk Road its name. It is open all day, but at its busiest in the mornings. The bazaar is a feast for the senses, with glorious textiles not only for sale on the stalls, but also being worn by the traders

4

TURGUNBOY MIRZA AHMEDOV: THE MASTER OF SILK

Silk weaving in Margilan is a family business, the secrets and skills passed down from father to son. Turgunboy Mirza Ahmedov was head of the seventh generation of silk weavers in his family. Born in Margilan in 1944, he was one of the founding members of the Yodgorlik Silk Factory (see above) and created more than 100 designs there. In the 1990s, he was largely responsible for rescuing the *adras* style of weaving, using silk for the warp threads and cotton for the weft, as well as *banoras*, *beak slab* and *shoi*. His work was recognised by UNESCO, which placed atlas and *adras* weaving on its Intangible Cultural Heritage list in 2017.

Keeping the weaving tradition alive, Turgunboy trained his son Rasul to carry on his work, and Rasul begun his own project to reproduce Ala Bakhmal silk, which was last made in Bukhara in 1910 and was even then produced only in tiny quantities for the most elaborate of royal costumes. Rasul is now in charge of the Margilan Crafts Development Centre, a busy co-op in the Said Akhmad Khodjaev Madrasa (page 150), founded by UNESCO in 2007.

and customers alike. Chatter, drink tea, wander around, haggle, drink more tea, buy a hat, engage in yet another complicated conversation of charades, eat *shashlik*, try on something else in silk, then collapse in a heap with yet more tea. This experience cannot be beaten.

Once you're all shopped out (or if silk just isn't your thing), Margilan also has some attractive **religious buildings**. The Khonakhah Mosque (off B Margilani), the city's religious centrepiece, sits behind an impressive pair of minarets (each 26m high), and the main buildings are a showcase for the mastery of Margilan's woodcarvers. The mosque was built in the 16th century and much of the decoration is original. Non-Muslims are welcome inside, providing that they are appropriately attired and behave in a respectful manner.

The elegant Toron Mosque (1840; just north of the central bazaar), has a superb and sensitively restored painted ceiling, as does the Said Akhmad Khodjaev Madrasa, located just off Mustakillik (on Said Akhmad Khodjaev Street, where else!). It was founded at the end of the 19th century by Said Akhmad Khodjaev, a wealthy philanthropist and advisor to the tsarist administration who fled Margilan during the Bolshevik Revolution, first to Afghanistan and then to Saudi Arabia. In the 20th century the building was used first as a jail and then as an office, returning to its original function in 1992, and it now houses the Margilan Crafts Development Centre (see box, page 149).

KOKAND

'The city of winds' is, by Uzbek standards at least, a modern conurbation. Some 230km southeast of Tashkent and close to the border with Tajikistan, it is perhaps the most attractive city in the Fergana Valley. Kokand has maintained much of its rich history, from the vast and sumptuous palace of Khudayar Khan to the Juma Mosque and inevitable (but nonetheless interesting) collection of madrasas, and it's unfortunate that its slightly out-of-the-way location means that many foreign tourists miss it from their itinerary entirely. If you have the time, make sure you visit.

HISTORY Though there has been habitation in this area since the 10th century, as numerous travellers' accounts attest, Kokand village was only fortified by the Shaybanid ruler Shahrukh in the 1730s, becoming capital of the khanate in 1740. As the khanate's influence grew, so did the scale of the city, boasting 35 madrasas and 100 mosques at its peak. Alim Khan brought the entirety of the Fergana Valley under Kokand's control before his assassination in 1809, and the brother who succeeded him, Omar Khan, expanded the khanate's borders as far as Turkestan (now in Kazakhstan).

Kokand's power peaked under the rule of Madali Khan, Omar's debauched son, to whose court came both Russian and British agents, including the ill-fated Captain Conolly (see box, page 240). The Bukharan emir Nasrullah Khan executed Madali in 1842 and seized Kokand, but the people revolted against him, starting two decades of bloody warfare and several short-lived rulers. Political instability fatally weakened the Kokand state, leaving it at the mercy of the Russians.

Khudayar Khan came to the throne in 1845, but lost and regained it four times before he was forced to accept a Russian commercial treaty in 1868, leaving him as little more than a puppet ruler. He continued to live in luxury despite the suffering of Kokand's citizens; insurrections followed and the khan fled into exile in 1875. Kokand was annexed by General von Kaufmann in 1876 and became a province of Russian Turkestan.

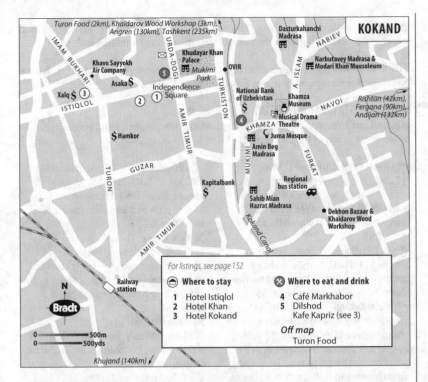

For listings, see page 152

Where to stay
1 Hotel Istiqlol
2 Hotel Khan
3 Hotel Kokand

Where to eat and drink
4 Café Markhabor
5 Dilshod
Kafe Kapriz (see 3)

Off map
Turon Food

Russian rule never sat easily with Kokand's population, however, and in 1917 the revolutionary Mustafa Chokayev seized the opportunity to establish the Provisional Autonomous Government of Turkestan, an Islamic alternative to the Tashkent Soviet. It took just three days for the Red Army to sack and burn the city. Some 14,000 people died and Chokayev fled to Paris, taking with him the Basmachis' greatest hope for an Islamic state in central Asia.

GETTING THERE AND AWAY Kokand's airport is closed, but in compensation there's now a decent **train service** on the Tashkent–Andijan line (page 140). Kokand has a **railway station** (40 Amir Timur), 2km south of the town centre, at the end of Turon and Amir Timur; trains take 4 hours to Tashkent and about 1 hour 40 minutes to Andijan (US$5).

The **regional bus station** is at 102 Furkat by the Dekhon Bazaar. In the daytime, buses leave every 15 minutes to Fergana (2hrs; US$1) and every 45 minutes to Andijan (2hrs; US$1). Minibuses and shared taxis ply the same routes but are slightly faster. Expect to pay twice the bus fare if you go by shared taxi. For Rishtan, shared taxis wait near the Dekhon Bazaar, while minibuses leave from the terminal of *marshrutkas* 14 and 16 on the eastern edge of town.

The fastest way to reach Tashkent, as a rule, is by **shared taxi** (4hrs; US$10–12). These can be picked up from the Tashkent bus station, 5km north of the centre of Kokand, where Turkiston meets the ring road, though it is sometimes possible to get a ride from the regional bus station, too.

Getting around Kokand is straightforward, with lots of **midi-buses**. The most useful are numbers 12, 24 and 33, between the Hotel Kokand and the regional bus station, also passing the Khudayar Khan Palace and the Juma Mosque; numbers

20 and 66 between the railway station and Navoi, north of the bus station; and numbers 25 and 60 between the railway station and the Hotel Kokand.

TOUR OPERATORS For airline tickets and other transport services, try **Khavo Sayyokh Air Company** (9 Imam Bukhari; \ 73 552 3102).

WHERE TO STAY, EAT AND DRINK *Map, page 151*

Kokand has a reasonable selection of accommodation options and places to eat, all within easy reach of the city centre.

Hotel Khan (20 rooms) 31 Istiqlol; \ 73 542 2244; e khudayakhan@mail.ru; w khan.uz. Kokand's best option is this modern hotel with AC. Staff are helpful & will usually change money as well as offering tips on what to see. **$$$**

Hotel Istiqlol (12 rooms) 1 Istiqlol, 1st alley; m 91 140 8000; e info@istiqlol-hotel.uz. A good mid-range option with a pleasant courtyard. It's also the closest hotel to the palace. **$$**

Hotel Kokand 1 Imam Bukhari; \ 73 552 6403; w hotelkokand.uz. Having received a much-needed refurbishment, rooms & public areas are now significantly improved, as are the bathrooms. Even the budget rooms are spacious, although lights & Wi-Fi are unreliable. It's located at the crossroads of the New Town, in the west of the city, with a nice bit of Russian Jugendstil across the road. **$$**

Dilshod 4 Istiqlol; \ 73 552 3078; m 90 550 2300; ⏰ 10.00–23.00 daily. A large hall & a terrace, serving Uzbek & Russian dishes. The handiest place to eat after visiting the Khudayar Khan Palace. **$$$**

Kafe Kapriz 1 Imam Bukhari; ⏰ 08.00–22.00 daily. For something a little more substantial, the Kapriz offers grilled meats & some fairly solid Russian dishes sprinkled amply with dill, to be washed down with plentiful vodka. **$$$**

Turon Food A373; m 91 202 0500; ⏰ 08.00–01.00 daily. Supposedly the best place to eat in Kokand, this modern eatery is out on the northern ring road. **$$**

Café Markhabor Cnr Khamza & Turkiston. Another good option, overlooking the canal. **$$**

SHOPPING As you would expect, Kokand's **Dekhon Bazaar**, the main bazaar, is well stocked with fresh produce and basic household goods. There are some underwhelming souvenir stands chancing it outside the Khudayar Khan Palace, but for something a bit more unusual, try the **Khaidarov Wood Workshop** (67 K Khaidarov, Dangara) where enthusiastic young apprentices will show you their latest woodcarving projects. This is in Dangara, immediately beyond the town's northern ring road.

OTHER PRACTICALITIES

Communications
✉ **Post office** 38 Urda-Dogi

Medical
Kokand has several hospitals, but in an emergency you would need the **Central Kokand Hospital of Urgent Medical Care** (132 Kokandi; \ 73 552 9493; ⏰ 24/7). There are a number of *aptekas* around the hospital & across the city.

Money
Visa cardholders can get cash advances at the National Bank of Uzbekistan. The other banks

listed can send & receive Western Union transfers & exchange money at the official rate.

$ **Asaka Bank** \ 73 542 6101; ⏰ 08.00–18.00 Mon–Fri
$ **Hamkor Bank** \ 73 542 0642/73 553 0573; ⏰ 09.00–17.00 Mon–Sat
$ **Kapitalbank** \ 73 229 7922; ⏰ 09.00–17.00 Mon–Sat
$ **National Bank of Uzbekistan** \ 73 542 0306; ⏰ 09.00–17.00 Mon–Fri
$ **Xalq Bank** \ 255 1868; ⏰ 09.00–13.00 & 14.00–18.00 Mon–Sat

above This mosaic-covered dome is the centrepiece of Tashkent's Chorsu Bazaar (MR/S) page 104

right Round flat breads are served at every meal and are treated almost reverentially (LN) page 73

below left The *chaikhana* at Lyabi Hauz in Bukhara is central to the community (ME) page 240

below right Spices have been traded along the Silk Road since time immemorial (EM/D)

above left It's possible to see Alpine ibex in Ugam-Chatkal National Park (M/D) page 128

above right Uzbekistan is highly fertile wherever there's reliable irrigation (OO/DT) page 6

left Ship skeletons on the bed of the Aral Sea are a poignant memorial to the environmental disaster (DP/D) page 281

below Nomadic herders still live in traditional yurts in the Kyzylkum Desert and around Lake Aidarkul (ME) page 218

above   Lake Charvak glimmers like a turquoise jewel in the Tian Shan Mountains (EK/D) page 126

right   Small ski resorts in the mountains near Tashkent are being developed for modern markets (MM/D) page 129

below   Uzbekistan's foothills are prime areas for trekking and make a cool retreat in the summer months (SS)

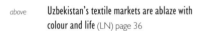

above   Traditional dance shows take place in the madrasa courtyards of Samarkand and Bukhara (OO/DT) page 35

right   The *dutor* is a two-stringed lute used in traditional music across central Asia (M/S) page 32

below   *Kupkari*, Uzbekistan's national sport, is a wild, primitive form of polo (R/S) page 39

above — The ancient city of Mizdarkhan was destroyed by Timur and redeveloped as a cemetery (LN) page 280

left — The Ark fortress is Bukhara's architectural icon (DP/D) page 233

below left & — The Timurid Emperor Ulug Beg was
below right — a notable astronomer as well as ruler (SS); his observatory survived complete destruction and can still be used to survey the stars (E/D) page 174

above left Amir Timur is commemorated in front of the Ak Serai, his palace in Shakhrisabz (p/S) page 188

above right & *right* There would be little reason to come to Nukus at all if it weren't for the Igor Savitsky Museum, an unexpected treasure trove of Soviet avant-garde art from the 1920s and 30s (C/W) & (ME) page 278

below The archaeological site of Kampir Tepe is superbly preserved, and empty of tourists (ME) page 206

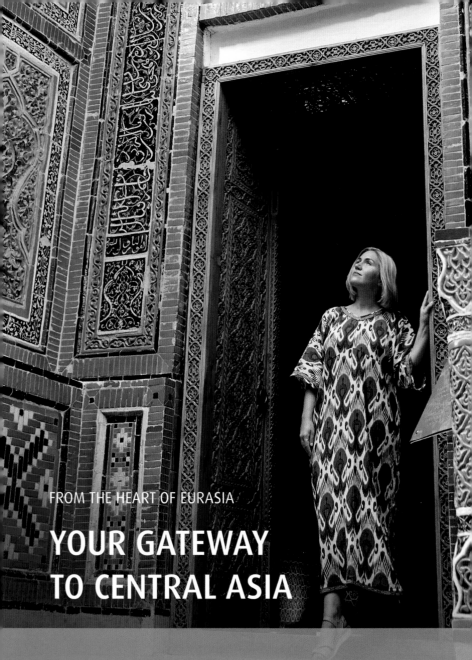

FROM THE HEART OF EURASIA

YOUR GATEWAY
TO CENTRAL ASIA

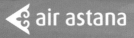

to register here. You have to go to Fergana instead (page 146).

WHAT TO SEE AND DO Without a shadow of doubt, Kokand's most impressive sight is the **Khudayar Khan Palace** (2 Istiqlol; ✎73 553 6046; ⊕ 09.00–17.00 Mon–Sat; foreigners US$2), one of the most glittering royal residences in central Asia and a structure that would make fairytale princesses jump up and down for joy.

In 1863, just before the Russians put paid to his architectural (and political) ambition, Khudayar Khan indulgently commissioned architect Mir Ubaydullo to build a sumptuous palace, also known as the Urda, with 113 rooms set around seven courtyards. His mother lived in one of these courtyards, housed in her very own yurt. The whole wide façade is covered with dazzling mosaic tiles, including an Arabic inscription above the entrance gate reading 'Seid Muhammad Khudayar Khan – the great ruler'.

The entire west end of the palace has been demolished and only 19 of the original rooms remain, but by walking here, in Khudayar Khan's footsteps, you gain a fascinating glimpse into the life of an oriental despot just before everything around him fell apart: it is a palace built on the cusp of history, and you can almost sense the unfulfilled dreams tied up in its walls and furnishings.

Some of the interiors have fortunately survived (some partially restored), however, and these are the palace's real attraction. The craftsmanship is exquisite, and you can clearly see the influence of Russian and European tastes on more traditional Uzbek designs. That said, they're somewhat spoiled by the display cabinets, housing a seemingly random collection (everything from jewellery and weaponry to a beautifully carved hall), probably due to most of the original contents having been dispersed or destroyed in the early years of Soviet rule.

Crossing the first courtyard, your visit starts with the very dated History Department, with relics from the 6th century BC onwards, photos, weapons and musical instruments from the khanate. The nearby Art Department has a bizarre room of European art, including a St Sebastian, works by Russians such as J E Braz and Julius von Klever and what is claimed to be a Honthorst. There's also a room of 18th- and 19th-century Chinese ceramics and another of work by the Rishtan potter Alisher Nazirov.

The museum's English-speaking director gives guided tours (US$3.50) of the site (available upon request), and these are the best way to understand not only the physical building but also the lives and times of Khudayar Khan and his family.

A few general exhibits about life in Kokand have been relocated from the palace to the **Khamza Museum** (2 A Islam; ✎73 552 2329; ⊕ 09.00–17.00 Tue–Sun; foreigners US$2), which commemorates the life of Khakim Khakimzade Niyazi, the Soviet poet, dramatist and propagandist known as Khamza (see box, page 154), and other writers. Built in 1989, it's been scrubbed up recently, along with the adjacent **Musical Drama Theatre**, which has some interesting sculptural window frames.

Rather more worthy of your time are Kokand's religious sites. The **Juma Mosque** (5 Khamza) swings back and forth between being a mosque and a museum; at the time of writing it was (at least partly) the latter. In any case, the building itself was built by Umar Khan between 1809 and 1812, and it was the khan's primary place of worship. The mosque remained shut for most of the 20th century, but reopened after much-needed restoration in 1989. From the road, you can look across the football-pitch-sized courtyard, with its 23m minaret, to the mighty *iwan*, supported on 98 glorious redwood columns, carved and imported from India.

An hour's drive from Fergana, lost among the mountain peaks of the Alai range, is the picturesque resort of Shohimardon. The physical landscape is nigh on perfect: to the south is Lake Kulikubbon (the Blue Lake), reached by a cable car that creaks alarmingly but has breathtaking views, and the Oak-Su and Kok-Su rivers run by. Trekking routes are numerous, as are the picnic spots, and the lake and river waters are clean and fresh for swimming, albeit a little on the chilly side.

Local legend has it that Hazrat Ali, son-in-law of the Prophet Muhammad and the fourth caliph, visited Shohimardon. The name Shohimardon, which is Persian for 'Lord of the People', is in fact a reference to Ali. Ali was assassinated in Iraq, but shortly before his death he is said to have instructed his followers to dig him seven graves in seven places, and to bury parts of his body there. Of these seven graves, three are said to be in Uzbekistan: in Nurata, in Khiva and in Shohimardon. The city is therefore considered to be a sacred place. The Hazrat Ali Mosque and Mausoleum, in the city centre, was destroyed by the Soviets in the 1920s but was rebuilt in 1993 and still attracts a constant stream of pilgrims, in particular barren women.

A second, rather more recent, historical figure is also buried in Shohimardon: the Uzbek poet Khakim Khakimzade Niyazi, known as Khamza. Born in Kokand in 1889, and a key figure in the early development of modern literature, he was stoned to death by Islamic fundamentalists in Shohimardon in 1929. Khamza was an ardent supporter of the communist revolution, and his tomb here is said to be cut from the same pink Pamiri marble as Lenin's tomb in Red Square.

The city lies 80km south of Fergana along a well-maintained road. If you don't have your own vehicle, there are plenty of shared taxis running the route, especially at weekends and other holidays. Taking a private taxi will cost around US$20. Be sure to stop at the village of Vuadil en route, where there's a maple tree with a circumference of nearly 28m that is said to be 800 years old.

For its history and its beauty, Shohimardon should rightly be a key tourist destination in the Fergana Valley. However, thanks to Stalin's meddling with central Asia's borders, it is unfortunately situated in an Uzbek enclave within Kyrgyzstan. Foreigners wishing to visit require a multiple-entry Uzbek visa and a permit from the Internal Affairs Bureau in Fergana (which can be gained from a local travel agent; page 96), and possibly a visa for Kyrgyzstan too.

Two rooms at the rear currently house the less-than-thrilling **Applied Art Museum** (⊕ 09.00–17.00 daily; foreigners US$2), which displays wood carvings by apprentices, 19th-century Rishtan ceramics, paper, manuscripts, looms, skull caps and jewellery.

A short walk west brings you to the **Amin Beg Madrasa** (83 Khamza) which was built in the 1830s for a son of Madali Khan. The madrasa has a particularly attractive tiled façade: indeed, the tilework is so fine that the madrasa is also known as Khomol Khozi Madrasa in honour of the craftsman who restored its ornamental mosaics in 1913. It has recently been restored, and now houses the **Diydor-Shirin chai-khana** (m 90 352 7227).

There are three other madrasas of note in the town: just south of the Amin Beg Madrasa, the 19th-century **Sahib Mian Hazrat Madrasa** (Mukimi) houses a small museum, dedicated to the Uzbek poet Muhammad Amin Mukimi (1850–1903). Just north of the main Chorsu intersection, the **Narbutabey Madrasa** (Nabiev), built in the 1790s, has an attached graveyard (the Dakhma-i-shakhan, or cemetery of the khans) that includes the Modari Khan Mausoleum where Omar Khan and his wife, the poet Nadira Beg, are entombed. Built in 1825, it has a grand entry portal with an ornate mosaic of blue glazed tiles. Finally, a little further north, the **Dasturkahanchi Madrasa** was built (for boys) in 1833, although girls now study embroidery and other sewing skills here.

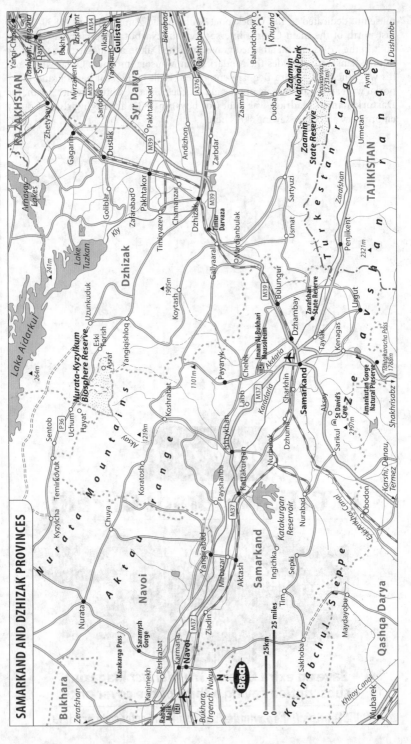

SAMARKAND AND DZHIZAK PROVINCES

5

Samarkand and Dzhizak Provinces

The Samarkand and Dzhizak provinces benefit both from their proximity to Tashkent and from the wealth and variety of tourist sites they contain. The Zaamin National Park and Zerafshan mountain passes of Dzhizak show Uzbekistan's natural landscapes and wildlife at their best; this small province bordering Tajikistan is one of the country's most picturesque and a prime location for climbing and trekking.

A stone's throw away, the manmade wonders of Samarkand never cease to amaze even the most sated of culture vultures. A dynamic city of well over half a million people, Samarkand is quite rightly a must-see stop on every tourist's itinerary. Masterpieces of Timurid architecture soar above the otherwise low-rise Old Town, and surely there's as much archaeological history underfoot as above ground.

SAMARKAND

> For lust of knowing what should not be known,
> We take the Golden Road to Samarkand.
>
> *James Elroy Flecker (1884–1915)*

Buildings of breathtaking beauty in the heart of regal Samarkand caught imaginations long before Flecker's and have continued to do so ever since. Medieval merchants must have marvelled at every sight, from the exotic goods on sale to the spectacular manmade backdrops of madrasas, mosques and mausoleums. Centuries on, visitors are still struck by the beauty, the number and the scale of Samarkand's architectural sites, and are often moved by thoughts of the ambition, dedication and, no doubt, personal sacrifices required to turn dreams into concrete reality.

The Registan Square, with its three exquisite madrasas, is Samarkand's biggest draw and makes for a picture-postcard scene. It's far from the only attraction, however, as the ruins of Afrosiab, the observatory of Ulug Beg and the Shah-i Zinda, the necropolis of the Living King, are sights that you'll never forget. The time of year you visit Samarkand will have a significant impact on your experience: coming out of season, especially in the autumn months, will enable you to get close to the building's physical details and to linger for as long as you like. The city always was a bustling, cosmopolitan place, however, so even if you are sucked into the summertime crowds, your experience will be no less authentic: the residents of Samarkand have for centuries made money from the foreigners passing through.

HISTORY Samarkand's past is built up in myth and legend, its beauty extolled by chroniclers and travellers for two millennia or more. There was certainly a city here from the 6th century BC, around the Afrosiab hill fort (page 172). Two centuries later, when Alexander the Great seized the Sogdian city that the Greeks knew as Marakanda, he is alleged to have said, 'Everything I have heard about Marakanda is true, except that it is more beautiful than I ever imagined.' The city's beauty was not enough to spare its buildings or inhabitants, however, and Alexander's forces torched the citadel to punish the Sogdian general Spitamenes for his resistance.

At a drunken banquet to celebrate the victory, Alexander ended up killing Cleitus, a close friend and senior general, who had been appointed satrap of Bactria but then demoted; after this no-one dared contradict Alexander, and his dazzling successes began to unravel. Five years later, he too was dead.

Samarkand entered a dark age and it was not until the 7th century AD that Silk Road trade returned and the city flourished again. It became one of the most populous cities in central Asia (far larger than it is today), a cultural and mercantile centre whose reputation spread even to Tang China. The Zoroastrian rulers of Samarkand sent luxurious gifts to neighbouring states, which included wild animals, dancing girls, musicians and all manner of natural and manmade curiosities.

As in so many of Uzbekistan's cities, life came to an abrupt halt with the arrival of the murderous Qutaiba ibn Muslim in AD712. Much of the population was killed or exiled, though Qutaiba did thoughtfully compensate the city by building its first mosque in which they could pray for the slain.

In the centuries that followed, Samarkand passed successively through the hands of the Samanids, Karakhanids, Seljuks, Karakhitai and Khorezmshah before being struck down yet again by Genghis Khan in 1220. It is said that the city's irrigation canals ran red with the blood of the people. Those who weren't massacred fled; barely a quarter of the population remained.

Remarkably, Samarkand bounced back. Marco Polo and Ibn Battuta both commented on the city's size and splendour, and in 1370 Timur decided to make it his capital. Samarkand became the epicentre of one of the largest empires the world had ever seen, and to make it great Timur drew on resources both human and financial from as far afield as Damascus and Delhi. He built madrasas and mosques, palaces and *caravanserai*, mausoleums and trading domes. The whole known world brought their goods to sell in Samarkand, and they marvelled at the scale and beauty of the city, and of the speed of its construction.

Timur had put Samarkand on the map, but it made the city a target for any ambitious competitor. Timur's grandson, Ulug Beg, maintained control long enough to build his observatory (page 174), but the power of the Uzbek clans was rising, and they would ultimately chase the last Timurid emperor, Babur, out of central Asia altogether. After twice failing to regain control of Samarkand, he fled south to India and there founded the Mughal Empire instead.

Silk Road trade declined, and Samarkand began to fall into disrepair, especially as Bukhara gained in power under the Uzbek khans, who finally took control of Samarkand in the late 18th century. The Russian General von Kaufmann seized the city with a force of just 3,500 men in 1868; the Russians then set about demolishing the walls, constructing a modern fortress in the citadel and building wide, tree-lined avenues in the European style. The Trans-Caspian railway arrived in 1888, and Samarkand was dragged into the modern age; an earthquake in 1897 further helped the process by destroying some of the taller historic buildings.

In 1917, Samarkand fell to the Bolsheviks with none of the violence seen in Bukhara. It was declared the capital of the Uzbek SSR in 1925 (though only held the title until 1930), in spite of the fact that the majority of its population were ethnic Tajiks, the population swelled to around 400,000 people, and Lenin Square and the Opera House were built atop what was once Timur's Blue Palace. Now, of course, hotels are being built all over the city, though mostly with more regard to the ancient remains.

GETTING THERE AND AWAY

By air Given the ease of road and rail travel between Samarkand and Tashkent, and the relatively short distance involved, it seems unnecessary to fly. However, if you do feel the need, **Uzbekistan Airways** (page 49; see ad, 3rd colour section) flies at least six times a week in each direction. The flight takes 55 minutes and can cost as little as US$10 one-way. Departures are mostly in the early morning. There's also a flight to Nukus on Friday afternoons, and international flights to Moscow,

TRANS-CASPIAN RAILWAY   *Bijan Omrani*

The Trans-Caspian railway was developed as a necessary part of Imperial Russia's conquest of central Asia. At the end of the 1870s, Russia was fighting to overcome the fearsome Tekke Turcomans, but was experiencing serious problems of military transportation across the central Asian deserts. In 1879, their army lost 8,000 out of 12,000 baggage camels in the Karakum Desert, as a result of which they were forced to abandon all the territory they had captured and return across the Caspian. Two years later in 1881, although the formidable General Skobelev was able to break the Turcomans by capturing their stronghold of Geok-Tepe, the Russian Army and camels faced even worse difficulties. At the end of this campaign, only 350 of the latter were left out of an original 12,500. A railway was clearly needed to secure the army's supply routes.

The railway was the brainchild of General Mikhail Annenkov, in charge of the Army Transport Department. He decided that the railway should have a spacious five-foot gauge, and be powered not by burning wood as was common elsewhere on Russian railways, but by naphtha, a by-product of crude-oil refining which was easily available from Baku across the Caspian.

Annenkov had to overcome a range of engineering challenges. Timber, iron and steel had to be imported all the way from central Russia, and stone quarried from the Persian mountains. Although the land was flat, the newly laid tracks could easily be covered by shifting sands, or washed away by flash floods. Nevertheless, when the conditions were favourable the skilled workforce of 1,500 men could lay up to 6km of track a day.

The line was started in 1881, and by 1895 it reached over 1,000km from the Caspian Sea to Bukhara, Samarkand and Tashkent. In 1899, it reached Andijan and in 1906 it connected with the Trans-Siberian Railway at Orenburg. The old Silk Road cities were at first hostile to the line, calling it Shaitan's Arba, or the 'Devil's Wagon'. The strong feelings of Bukhara's citizens caused the Russians to put the station 10km away from the city. However, once the trains started opinions reversed. Locals and merchants flocked to use the new service, and business rapidly drained from the heart of the old cities to cluster around the new railway stations. The initial unwillingness of the people to embrace the new means of transport sapped the dynamism of their old cities, and led to them being treated for much of the 20th century as nothing more than museum pieces.

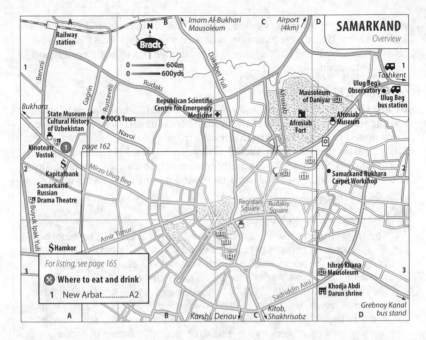

page 162

SAMARKAND
Overview

0 —— 600m
0 —— 600yds

Imam Al-Bukhari Mausoleum

Airport (4km)

Tashkent

Ulug Beg's Observatory
Ulug Beg bus station

Mausoleum of Daniyar

Afrosiab Museum

Afrosiab Fort

Republican Scientific Centre for Emergency Medicine

Rudaki

Railway station

Beruni

Bukhara

Gagrin

Rustaveli

State Museum of Cultural History of Uzbekistan

DOCA Tours

Navoi

Kinoteatr Vostok

Kapitalbank

Samarkand Russian Drama Theatre

Buyuk Ipak Yuli

Mirzo Ulug Beg

Amir Timur

Hamkor

Registan Square

Rudakiy Square

Samarkand Bukhara Carpet Workshop

Ishrat Khana Mausoleum

Khodja Abdi Darun shrine

Sadriddin Aini

Karshi, Denau

Kitob, Shakhrisabz

Grebnoy Kanal bus stand

For listing, see page 165

❌ **Where to eat and drink**

1   New Arbat.............A2

St Petersburg, Kazan, Yekaterinburg and Istanbul. Payments for tickets can only be made in cash or online, and the **airport** is 6km northeast of the city centre on V Abdullo – a taxi will cost around US$1.25.

By rail   Samarkand's **railway station** [160 A1] is 6km northwest of the city centre at the junction of Rudaki and Beruni. It is on the main railway line from Tashkent to Bukhara and Urgench, so it's fast and relatively straightforward to reach the city by rail.

The high-speed **Afrosiyob service** between Tashkent and Samarkand runs three times daily and takes just 2½ hours. Tickets start from US$11. The older **Sharq service** (train 9 or 10 depending on the direction) runs every morning except Tuesdays and has spacious air-conditioned carriages. Tickets begin at US$6. There are also various night trains to Termez, Bukhara, Urgench, Nukus and Fergana, as well as international destinations. These services take between 3 and 4 hours, but the ticket prices are correspondingly lower.

Travelling west from Samarkand, there are twice-daily departures to Bukhara: an Afrosiyob taking 1½ hours and a Sharq taking almost 2½ hours, as well as night trains. Trains to and from Urgench (numbers 56 and 58) run daily apart from Wednesday. Two- and four-berth sleepers are available and they are highly recommended as this journey is about 12 hours' travel in each direction.

For current departure times and ticket prices, see w eticket.uzrailway.uz. Tickets can be bought with cash at the Kassa at the east end of the station, or at the ticket office at the junction of Amir Timur and Bo'stonsaray [162 D2] (⏱ 08.00–13.00 & 14.00–19.00 daily); you can also book online using a credit card. If you are buying your tickets in advance and want them delivered, hassle-free to your hotel, *Caravanistan* (w caravanistan.com) offers a hugely helpful reservations service.

To **reach the station**, you should pay about US$1.25 for a taxi, or take bus 3 or 73 from the Registan. You'll see the new tramlines, but alas these do not lead downtown. However, tram 2 runs from the station to the Siyob Bazaar, within striking distance of the key sights and some of the hotels and hostels.

By road Samarkand is roughly 300km from both Tashkent and Bukhara, an easy 4–5-hour **drive** from either. The roads are surfaced, and vehicles of all shapes and sizes speed along. Samarkand's **Ulug Beg bus station** [160 D1] is 200m east of the Observatory, and it is from here you will pick up most long-distance minibuses and shared taxis. For transport to Bukhara, you need to go a few hundred metres north along the ring road. A seat in a bus or minibus costs US$5 to either Tashkent or Bukhara, and just over twice as much if you travel by shared taxi. You can get to the bus stand by minibus 17 or midi-bus 99 from the city centre.

To travel south to Karshi, Denau and Termez you need the **Grebnoy Kanal bus stand** [160 D3] on the eastern outskirts of the city. Shared taxis to Termez cost around US$17 and take 5 hours. Arrive early and be prepared to wait, as there are frequently more would-be passengers than seats. The bus is cheaper (US$8) but allow twice as long for the journey. It's also possible to take trains on this route (page 190).

Heading east to the Penjikent border, take bus 41 or 74 or a shared taxi from the Suzangaran bus stop [163 G3] (opposite the junction with Karimov) to the Kaftarkhona bus station, then bus 273 or a *marshrutka* (1hr; US$0.70) or shared taxi (40min; US$2.50 pp). For Shakhrisabz, take a shared taxi (US$4) from the Registan stop to Kitob, a few kilometres north of the town (page 185).

If you are driving your **own vehicle** into Samarkand, expect to get terribly lost. The signposts are almost non-existent, and there are so many one-way sections and dead ends it would make the Pope swear. We've found the easiest way is to drive in the general direction of the city centre, then flag down a taxi and pay him to drive in front of you to the Gur-i Amir where there is plenty of free, fairly well-lit parking.

GETTING AROUND Most of Samarkand's important sites are within easy **walking** distance of one another, and hotels tend to be fairly central, too. Karimov has been pedestrianised (and lined with souvenir shops), so walking between the Registan and the Bibi Khanym Mosque and bazaar is particularly straightforward; there's also an **electric trolley** shuttle, costing about US$1, running the length of Karimov.

There is a good network of **minibuses** in Samarkand. Minibus 17 and midi-bus 99 are particularly helpful as they link the bazaar with Ulug Beg's Observatory. Minibus tickets cost US$1.50.

The most useful **bus route** is the 3/73, linking Registan with the train station. Buses 19 and 60 link the airport to the town centre. Bus tickets cost US$0.10 for all journeys.

If you're travelling further afield within the city (for example, to the railway station), you may want to take a **taxi**. There are the usual hail-and-ride options, or you can pre-book a cab with **iTaxi** (✆ 66 235 9999) or **Taxi Co** (✆ 66 727 9064).

Bikes can be rented at weekends in the park near the junction of Navoi and Amir Timur.

TOURIST INFORMATION AND TOUR OPERATORS There's a so-called **Tourist Information Centre** [163 G2] (45 Karimov; m 91 545 0390; ⊕ 09.30–17.00 daily) on the pedestrianised road northeast from Registan Square, but it's basically a souvenir shop. Still, the student volunteers are very helpful, and you can buy a city map and book on to tours, including one to the Hovrenko Wine Factory.

Most **hotels** in Samarkand are able and willing to provide tourist information and make ongoing travel arrangements (including train reservations) on your behalf.

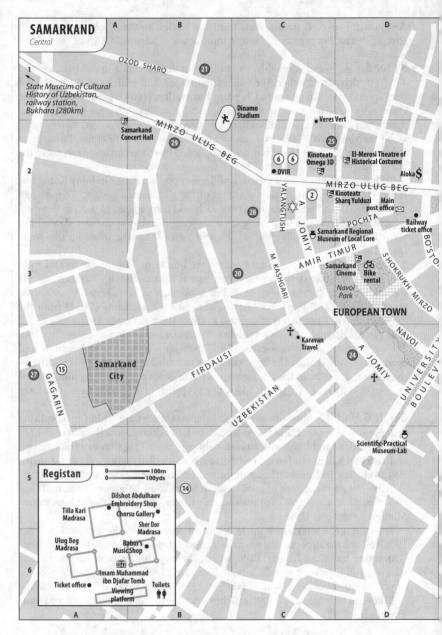

SAMARKAND
Central

State Museum of Cultural History of Uzbekistan, railway station, Bukhara (280km)

OZOD SHARQ

MIRZO ULUG BEG

Samarkand Concert Hall

Dinamo Stadium

Veres Vert

Kinoteatr Omega 3D

El-Merosi Theatre of Historical Costume

OVIR

MIRZO ULUG BEG

Aloka

Kinoteatr Sharq Yulduzi

Main post office

Railway ticket office

POCHTA

Samarkand Regional Museum of Local Lore

AMIR TIMUR

Samarkand Cinema

Bike rental

EUROPEAN TOWN

Navoi Park

Karavan Travel

Samarkand City

FIRDAUSI

UZBEKISTAN

Scientific-Practical Museum-Lab

YALANGTUSH

A JOMIY

M KASHGARI

SHOKRUKH MIRZO

BO'STON

A JOMIY

NAVOI

UNIVERSITY BOULEV.

GAGARIN

Registran

0 — 100m
0 — 100yds

Dilshot Abdulhaev Embroidery Shop

Tilla Kari Madrasa

Chorsu Gallery

Sher Dor Madrasa

Ulug Beg Madrasa

Babur's Music Shop

Imam Muhammad ibn Djafar Tomb

Ticket office

Viewing platform

Toilets

For **tours** around the city, or indeed further afield, there are plenty of options to choose from, including: **Discover Oriental Central Asia Tours** [160 A1] (DOCA; 34A Rustaveli; m 93 352 0044/93 350 2020; w doca-tours.com); **Karavan Travel** [162 C4] (72 M Kashgari; 66 231 1138/66 233 5436; w karavan-travel.com); **Marokanda Citadel** [163 E2] (1A Kuksaroy; 66 235 0475; m 94 539 9616; w marokanda-citadel. com); **Sogda Tour** [163 F3] (38 Registan; 66 235 3609; w sogda-tour.com) and **Zamin Travel** [163 G2] (10 Karimov; 66 210 0811; w zt-ouzbekistan.com).

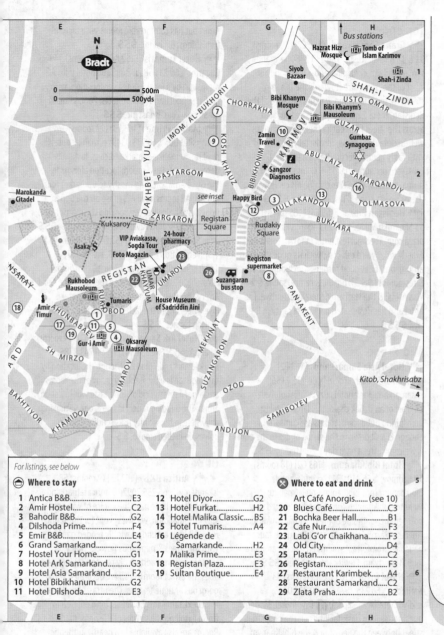

For listings, see below

🏠 **Where to stay**

1 Antica B&B.........................E3	12 Hotel Diyor.......................G2
2 Amir Hostel........................C2	13 Hotel Furkat......................H2
3 Bahodir B&B.......................G2	14 Hotel Malika Classic.....B5
4 Dilshoda Prime...................F4	15 Hotel Tumaris.................A4
5 Emir B&B............................E4	16 Légende de
6 Grand Samarkand.............C2	Samarkande..............H2
7 Hostel Your Home.............G1	17 Malika Prime...................E3
8 Hotel Ark Samarkand.........G3	18 Registan Plaza................E3
9 Hotel Asia Samarkand.........F2	19 Sultan Boutique..............E4
10 Hotel Bibikhanum.............G2	
11 Hotel Dilshoda..................E3	

🍴 **Where to eat and drink**

	Art Café Anorgis........(see 10)
	20 Blues Café........................C3
	21 Bochka Beer Hall............B1
	22 Cafe Nur...........................F3
	23 Labi G'or Chaikhana.........F3
	24 Old City...........................D4
	25 Platan..............................C2
	26 Registan...........................F3
	27 Restaurant Karimbek........A4
	28 Restaurant Samarkand.....C2
	29 Zlata Praha.......................B2

To buy airline tickets, the most central option is **VIP Aviakassa** [163 F3] (38 Registan; ☏66 235 0061).

🏠 **WHERE TO STAY** Samarkand has plenty of places to stay whatever your budget, though the most popular tend to get booked up in high season. The larger hotels typically cater to coach parties, but this means independent travellers can often negotiate a hefty discount on the advertised rate if there are rooms going spare.

Top end

🏠 **Grand Samarkand** [162 C2] (30 rooms)
31 & 38 B Yalangtush; 📞 66 233 2880; e grand-
samarkand@mail.ru; w grand-samarkand.com.
West of the city centre (towards the Dinamo
stadium), but still within walking distance of the
Registan, these 2 modern properties, located
across the street from each other, offer spacious,
well-maintained rooms, comfortably furnished
with fairly neutral décor. There's a pleasant
courtyard restaurant ($$$), swimming pool,
sauna, souvenir shop & exchange office. However,
there's no lift & the b/fast is average. $$$$

🏠 **Registan Plaza** [163 E3] (165 rooms)
53 Shokrukh Mirzo; 📞 66 233 4086; w registan-
plaza.com. The smartest hotel in town, this is not
exactly what you'd call cosy, with its huge yawning
atrium, but it has good facilities (including a bar
& restaurant ($$$), business centre, sauna & 2
Visa ATMs) & the staff are generally attentive. The
hotel also has designated parking, a rarity in the
city. $$$$

Mid-range

🏠 **Hotel Asia Samarkand** [163 F2]
(85 rooms) 50 Kosh Khauz; 📞 66 235 7156;
e samarkand@asiahotels.uz; w asiahotels.uz/
en. Part of an Uzbek chain, this large hotel is
uninspiring but decent; rooms are comfortable
enough & a sit down in the sauna or dip in the pool
is welcome after a hard day's sightseeing. $$$

🏠 **Hotel Bibikhanum** [163 G2] (18 rooms)
10 Karimov; 📞 66 210 0811; e info@hotel-
bibikhanum.com/bibihanim.hotel@mail.ru;
w hotel-bibikhanum.com. Superbly located new
hotel on the south side of the Bibi Khanym Mosque
(there's no access by car, so don't bring too much
baggage); comfortable rooms on 2 floors around a
largish courtyard. Credit cards accepted. $$$

🏠 **Hotel Diyor** [163 G2] (5 rooms) 43
Karimov; 📞 66 235 7571; m 90 212 0743;
e diyorhotel@gmail.com; f Diyorhotel. Modern
guesthouse with basic facilities on the pedestrian
street between the Registan & the Bibi Khanym
Mosque. The location is its best feature. $$$

🏠 **Hotel Malika Classic** [162 B5] (26
rooms) 37 Khamraev; 📞 66 237 0154; e malika-
hotel@mail.ru; w malika-samarkand.com.
The Uzbek-owned Malika chain has 2 hotels
in Samarkand; this one is a little away from
the centre (around 3km southwest of the Gur-i

Amir) but has comfortable rooms with tasteful
furnishings. B/fast inc. $$$

🏠 **Hotel Tumaris** [162 A4] (12 rooms) 149
Gagarin; 📞 66 233 5851. Boutique hotel with AC
rooms run by a local women's association, with
profits supporting social projects. Pool, sauna &
on-site parking. B/fast inc. $$$

🏠 **Malika Prime** [163 E3] (22 rooms) 1/4
Universitet Bd; 📞 66 233 4349; e malika-hotel@
mail.ru; w malika-samarkand.com. Tastefully
decorated hotel in a superb location alongside
the Gur-i Amir, catering mostly to upmarket tour
groups. All rooms have AC; those on the upper
floors have balconies overlooking the mausoleum.
B/fast inc. Discounts available for 2+ nights. $$$

🏠 **Sultan Boutique** [163 E4] (17 rooms)
1 University Bd; 📞 66 239 1188; m 95 507
1707; e infocitysamarkand@gmail.com/info@
citcaféhotel.uz. Ideally located (between the Gur-i
Amir & the Russian quarter), this new hotel is
lovely apart from the lack of a lift; there's an ATM &
rooftop terrace. $$$

🏠 **Hotel Ark Samarkand** [163 G3] (14 rooms)
9 Panjakent; 📞 66 235 6941; m 90 743 8785;
e arksamarkand@mail.ru. Though the location by
the Registan is unbeatable, & many of the rooms
are large, a smattering of good taste would not go
amiss. The building is ugly inside & out & smoking
anywhere in the vicinity risks sending it up in
polyester-fuelled smoke. $$

Budget

✳ 🏠 **Antica B&B** [163 E3] (9 rooms) 58
Iskandarov; 📞 66 235 2092; e anticasamarkand@
hotmail.com. If we have the choice of where to
stay in Samarkand, we always opt for this family-
run B&B built around a lovingly tended garden
with fruit trees & numerous flowers. Many of
the rooms have traditionally painted ceilings (as
does the b/fast room), & all are decorated with
gorgeous antique textiles. The b/fasts are the best
in Uzbekistan – this book isn't long enough to
finish extolling the virtues of the homemade jams.
Rooms are also available in a nearby authentic
19th-century house, where it's possible to eat
dinner (see opposite). $$

🏠 **Bahodir B&B** [163 G2] (16 rooms) 132
Mullakandov; 📞 66 235 4749; m 91 525 8569. A
cheap & friendly B&B in a great location. Dorm
beds cost US$8 including b/fast, & the best of
these is the 4-bed as it has an en suite. Sgls &

dbls are available with & without bathrooms. AC is available & you can request an electric heater in winter. Ask for one of the newer rooms – those away from the courtyard are quietest. **$$**

🏠 **Emir B&B** [163 E4] (8 rooms) 142 Ok Saroy; 📞 66 235 7461; **m** 91 314 0258; **e** muhandis2005@mail.ru; **w** emir.ucoz.net. Well-located Old Town guesthouse with pleasant courtyard & rooftop terrace. Private rooms & dorms with 2 curtained bunks, all AC. **$$**

🏠 **Hotel Dilshoda** [163 B3] (12 rooms) 150 Ok Saroy; 📞 66 239 1318; **m** 90 270 9966/90 603 6565; **e** dil_servis@mail.ru; **w** hotel-dilshoda. uz. On an alley behind the Gur-i Amir, this is really a B&B rather than a hotel. It's basic, clean, comfortable enough & is equipped with Wi-Fi, but lacks the warmth of Antica (see opposite). The newer **Dilshoda Prime** [160 B6], on the same street, has fancier oriental décor but is otherwise similar (**$$**). **$$**

🏠 **Légende de Samarkande** [163 H2] (18 rooms) 60 Tolmasova; 📞 66 235 0543; **e** info@ legendm7.com; **w** legendm7.com. Hidden 10mins' walk from the centre in Samarkand's little-visited Jewish quarter is this 170-year-old property with an airy, double-storey veranda, a lush green courtyard with its own vines, & hundreds of antique fabrics, carpets & intriguing knick-knacks.

It's a hotel with a great deal of character. French & English are both spoken. **$$**

🏠 **Hotel Furkat** [163 H2] (27 rooms) 105 Mullakandov; 📞 66 235 6299; **e** hotelfurkat@ mail.ru. A stone's throw from the Registan, this friendly & comfortable, if rather higgledy-piggledy guesthouse is built around a courtyard where you can relax on the wooden topchan beds. It's definitely worth paying a bit extra for a room with a balcony if one is available, though you can also see the panorama from the rooftop café (**$$**). If your budget is tight, dorm beds in the basement cost US$9 & dinner is US$5 (book before 10.00). Payment is by cash or Visa. **$–$$**

🏠 **Amir Hostel** [162 C2] 45 A Jomiy; **m** 97 916 8899/97 916 6677; **e** info@amir-hostel.com; **w** amir-hostel.com. New in 2017, this small, friendly hostel has AC & private rooms & dorms with a curtain, light, power outlet & locker for each bunk. There's a kitchen & nearby restaurants & good English is spoken. **$**

🏠 **Hostel Your Home** [163 G1] (3 rooms) 2 Kosh Khauz; 📞 66 235 3425; **e** yourhome.info@ gmail.com; **w** yourhome.hostel.com. New in late 2018, this very welcoming hostel is in a modern house with a private dbl & 2 dorms with curtained bunks & bathroom. English, French & German spoken; b/fast inc. **$**

✕ **WHERE TO EAT AND DRINK** For a city with quite so many visitors, it's a shame Samarkand hasn't yet upped its game in the culinary stakes. Hotel restaurants are bland, and the larger restaurants tend to cater mostly to coach parties. You might be privy to an unauthentic belly dance or two, but most of us would happily swap that for a decent meal. Restaurants are open for both lunch and dinner unless otherwise stated, and most remain open during the afternoon, too.

For a more authentic dining experience, the staff at **Antica B&B** (see opposite) can arrange dinner in a traditional 19th-century house with a beautiful painted interior. The menu is set but inevitably tasty, and you will also have the opportunity to try locally produced wine. If you're in luck, the house's owner, a local history expert and curator of one of the local museums, will be present to tell you about her family, the building and its history. What is more, at US$11 per person (plus wine) it is no more expensive than eating at a restaurant in town. Book one day in advance at Antica.

Restaurants and cafés

✕ **New Arbat** [160 A2] 142A Mirzo Ulug Beg; 📞 66 222 1295; **m** 91 550 8111. Ostentatious Neoclassical pillars & a sweeping staircase greet guests at this well-run restaurant favoured by tour groups. Romantic murals of Moscow street scenes grace the walls, it is clean & the Russian menu is tasty. **$$$$**

✕ **Labi G'or Chaikhana** [163 F3] 6 Registan. With its wooden veranda & columns, low tables & kitchen open to the street, this has significantly more character than most. Fresh & tasty *shashlik*, also *plov* (lunchtime only); good but a bit overpriced owing to the location. **$$$**

✕ **Old City** [162 D1] 100/1 A Jomiy; 📞 66 233 8020; **m** 93 346 8020; **e** sam_old_city@mail.ru;

⊕ 10.00–23.00 daily. Always busy with groups, it's well worth a visit for independent travellers, too, with a varied menu of well-prepared Uzbek, Russian & European dishes, including good salads & vegetarian options. Good local wines, too. **$$$**

✖ **Platan** [162 C2] 2 Pushkin; ☏ 66 233 8049; **w** en.platan.uz; ⊕ 10.00–23.00 daily. An excellent Uzbek restaurant (also serving European dishes) with an attractive outdoor terrace where you can enjoy yoghurt & herb soup, *manti* & *shashlik*, as well as a spicy Uzbek–Korean carrot salad. **$$$**

✖ **Registan Restaurant** [163 F3] 5 Registan; **m** 90 742 1548; ⊕ 08.00–23.00 daily. Decorated with *suzanis* & paintings copied from the tilework on the Registan, this restaurant has the best location in town, staring at its namesake across the road. Decent Uzbek food, followed by shisha, if you want. **$$$**

✖ **Restaurant Karimbek** [162 A4] 194 Gagarin; ☏ 66 237 7739; ⊕ 10.00–23.00 daily. Large restaurant at the cnr of Gagarin & A Timur serving Uzbek & European dishes. Uzbek wines, cocktails & draught beers are served at the bar. Live music each evening during summer months. **$$$**

✖ **Restaurant Samarkand** [162 C2] 54 M Kashgari; ☏ 66 233 3591; **m** 95 500 5599; ⊕ 10.00–23.00 daily. Hugely popular with local groups, this restaurant is large & elaborately decorated, albeit with questionable taste, & the music can be too loud in the evenings. Spread over 2 floors, groups tend to be put upstairs, leaving individual guests with the run of the garden & ground floor. Opt for the salads & *shashlik* as the chips are disappointing. **$$$**

✖ **Blues Café** [162 C3] 66 Amir Timur; ☏ 66 233 6296; ⊕ noon–22.00 daily. A suitably dark, atmospheric place with a good choice of music & food – the menu is in Russian, but it offers everything from steak to fajitas & real pizza (they can improvise a good vegetarian version on request). **$$**

✖ **Cafe Nur** [163 F3] 9 Registan; **m** 95 507 0104; ⊕ 10.00–23.00 daily. Fast-food joint with a menu of pizzas, grilled meats & other quick snacks. No Wi-Fi (whatever the sign says). **$$**

☕ **Art Café Anorgis** [163 G2] 12 Karimov; ☏ 66 235 0402; ⊕ 08.00–19.00 daily. Next to Bibi Khanym, with great views from the terrace, this Western-style café serves various salads, soups & cakes (US$0.07) & good Arabica coffee; there's no machine for espresso or cappuccino. The menu is available in English & there's an ATM on the veranda. **$$**

Pubs

🍺 **Bochka Beer Hall** [162 B1] 2 Ozod Sharq; ☏ 66 233 5902; ⊕ 11.00–23.00 daily. The Pulsar brewery, behind the Dinamo stadium, has been working with Czech brewers since the late 19th century & still produces Pilsner, Weissbier & black beer – their brewery tap is the best place to sample it, with sausages & the like to weigh it down, but there are other bars along this street, with *shashlik* & karaoke options. **$$**

🍺 **Zlata Praha** [162 B2] 59 Mirzo Ulug Beg; ☏ 66 233 6639; ⊕ 24/7. Just across the main road opposite the brewery, this is another outlet for their Czech-style beer. It's food-oriented, with 1 room for Uzbek food & another for more international cuisine. **$$**

ENTERTAINMENT AND NIGHTLIFE There is no nightlife in Samarkand per se, but most nights it is possible to watch a cultural performance somewhere in the city. The best of these is at the **El-Merosi Theatre of Historical Costume** [162 D2] (27 Navoi; ☏ 66 233 8098; **e** elmerosi@mail.ru; **w** elmerosi.uz; US$20). Produced with the assistance of the Hermitage in St Petersburg, this historical fashion show takes you through millennia of Uzbek costume, starting with the Scythians and Achaemenids, moving on to the Timurids, and ultimately to clothing of the 19th century. The live performance is accompanied by music and video. It is well produced, and the costumes are historically accurate. Performances take place at 18.00 most nights during the high tourist season. Call the theatre to confirm.

Otherwise, there's the **Samarkand Russian Drama Theatre** [160 A2] (45 Buyuk Ipak Yuli; ☏ 66 221 3315/66 221 0421; **e** info@samrusteatr.uz; **w** samrusteatr.uz) and the modern **Samarkand Concert Hall** [162 A1] out west on Mirzo Ulug Beg.

Cinemas include **Samarkand Cinema** [162 D3] (cnr Navoi & Amir Timur), **Kinoteatr Sharq Yulduzi** [162 C2] (Mustakillik at Mirzo Ulug Beg), **Kinoteatr**

Vostok [160 A2] (99 Mirzo Ulug Beg; m 91 530 0011; e info@vostok3d.uz; w http:// vostok3d.uz) and **Kinoteatr Omega 3D** [162 C2] (34 Mirzo Ulug Beg; m 90 250 1234; w 3dkinoteatr.uz).

SHOPPING Samarkand's commercial centre is the main **Siyob Bazaar** [163 G1] (🕐 05.00–19.00 daily), right next to the Bibi Khanym Mosque. It's primarily aimed at the local market, so although you may not find many souvenirs (particularly on the lower level), it is a good place to pick up a picnic. Having tasted multiple samples, haggle hard for the fruits and nuts, and follow your nose to the stands of flat, fresh bread. Enjoy the people watching.

Samarkand's **Registon supermarkets** (🕐 08.00–23.00 daily) are remarkably big, with a good selection of dried and processed goods – there's one right across Registan from the madrasas [163 G3] (cnr Registan & Suzangaron) and others in the European town.

All over Samarkand are numerous **souvenir shops** selling low-quality and usually fairly samey products. The greatest concentration of these are on Karimov, inside the Tilla Kari Madrasa, and in the cells surrounding the Rukhobod Mausoleum.

If you want something a little different, however, you need to look a little harder. Ethnographer **Dilshot Abdulhaev** sells both antique and modern embroideries from his former teacher's room inside the Tilla Kari Madrasa [162 A5] (at the far side of the courtyard, identified by its numerous bookshelves; e dilsuzani@mail. ru). Abdulhaev speaks good English and is exceptionally knowledgeable about Uzbekistan's textile heritage. His shop is only open April to November as he travels in the winter to textile exhibitions overseas. The **Happy Bird** craft centre [163 G2] (43 Karimov; m 93 720 4215; 🄵 gallerybird; 🕐 10.00–19.00 daily) sells exquisite handmade traditional clothing – the long, striped *chapan* (coats) are dramatic but, for those less keen on drawing attention to themselves in public, also make good dressing gowns.

Tumaris [163 E3] on Rukhobod (look for an arch in the wall with a post office sign) is a bespoke hat maker, though if you are short on time they also have samples ready to wear. Assuming you have no moral objection to wearing wild animal fur, you choose your style, select a pelt and *voila*! You have something unique to keep your ears warm in winter.

Visiting the **Chorsu Gallery** [162 B5] (🕐 erratic) on Karimov is a fascinating experience. Though the contemporary artworks on sale may leave you cold, the building itself dates from the 15th century, but has been thoroughly restored.

The best carpets, both in terms of quality and ethical production, are available from the **Samarkand Bukhara Carpet Workshop** (page 177). The workshop prides itself on having exemplary conditions for its workers and that every carpet here is made by hand.

If you're having a panic that you've come to Samarkand and your memory card is already full, **Foto Magazin** [163 F3] (8 Registan; 🕐 09.00–18.00 daily) will sort you out. They also have batteries, tripods and a selection of old Russian cameras for sale.

OTHER PRACTICALITIES
Communications
Samarkand is well connected with the outside world. In addition to the post office listed below, you can buy stamps from the Tumaris craft shop (see above) by the Gur-i Amir: look out for the post office sign. Many of Samarkand's hotels & restaurants now have Wi-Fi, & this is the most convenient way to get online.

✉ **Main post office** [162 D2] 5 Pochta; 🕐 09.00–18.00 Mon–Fri, 09.00–17.00 Sat, 09.00–16.00 Sun; closed 13.00–14.00 daily. Head here if you want to send postcards. For parcels, **EMS Uzbekistan** (w empost.uz) is also located here.

Medical

Samarkand has several private clinics & hospitals that you could go to in an emergency. For an ambulance, call ☏ 103.

⊞ **Doctor Plus Medical Centre** 6 Lufti; ☏ 66 233 5638
⊞ **Orthopaedic Trauma Hospital** 73 Haliduna; ☏ 66 229 3274
⊞ **Republican Scientific Centre for Emergency Medicine** [160 B1] 18 Vohid Abdullo; ☏ 66 500 7373; ⏰ 24/7
✚ **24-hour pharmacy** [163 F3] 7 Registan. For minor incidents & medication.
✚ **Sangzor Diagnostics** [163 G2] 45A Karimov; ☏ 66 210 1056; ⏰ 09.00–17.00 Mon–Sat. Right in the city centre & akin to a GP practice.

Money

Samarkand suffers from the same ATM shortage as everywhere else in Uzbekistan, but you will increasingly find them in the lobbies of hotels such as the Hotel Asia Samarkand (page 164), Grand Samarkand (page 164), Malika Prime (page 164) & Registan Plaza (page 164).

$ **Aloka Bank** [162 D2] ⏰ 09.00–13.00 & 14.00–18.00 daily
$ **Asaka Bank** [163 E3] ⏰ 09.00–14.00 & 15.00–17.00 Mon–Fri. For Mastercard.
$ **Hamkor Bank** [160 A3] ⏰ 09.00–noon & 13.00–17.00 Mon–Fri
$ **Kapitalbank** [160 A2] ⏰ 09.00–18.00 Mon–Fri, ATM 24/7

Registration

OVIR [162 C2] Cnr Mirzo Ulug Beg & M Kashgari

WHAT TO SEE AND DO For most visitors to Samarkand the challenge is not what to see but what to leave out: the city is packed with fascinating sites from all eras of its history, and unless you have a full week to spend here, you're unlikely to see them all. Below are the city's highlights.

The Registan [163 F–G2–3] (Registan; ⏰ Apr–Oct 09.00–20.00 daily, Nov–Mar 09.00–17.00 daily; US$3) Samarkand's central square will make even the most architecture-weary visitor stand up and take note. Pausing for a minute (and a photo) on the raised viewing platform, the square unfolds below you. An almost infinite number of contrasting patterns swirl and dance on every surface but somehow never clash; the equally garishly patterned textiles worn by Uzbek women walking by appear almost as a continuation of the buildings themselves. The effect is completely mesmerising.

The Registan grew up around the tomb to the 9th-century saint Imam Muhammad ibn Djafar (the tomb can be found in front of the Sher Dor madrasa, but is barely noticeable nowadays), but by the 14th century this was also the commercial heart of the town. Six roads ran through the square, and it was connected directly with Timur's citadel. Imperial decrees were shouted from the rooftops, and people would have gathered here to watch military pageants and other forms of spectacle.

The three magnificent buildings you see today are the successors to this medieval centrepiece. The square was laid out by Timur's grandson Ulug Beg, an intellectual who, sadly for his faltering empire, spent more of his time concentrating on maths and science than he did on affairs of state. He built the oldest madrasa, the **Ulug Beg Madrasa,** on the left of the square, between 1417 and 1420. His love of astronomy is shown in the mosaic tilework above the 15m arch on the main portico: it's a depiction of the sky and the stars.

The madrasa itself measures 56m by 81m and is built around a large courtyard with a high blue-tiled portal on each side. At its peak, some 100 students lived in the 50 cells, many of them making use of the astronomical instruments housed here before the construction of Ulug Beg's Observatory (page 174). Unusually, this was not a religious madrasa: students here studied mathematics and the sciences. For an extra US$2.35 you can climb up the steep and narrow staircase to the top of the right-hand minaret, finally pulling yourself up through the metal hatch and on to the rooftop, 34m above the ground. There's scarcely any room to move and you have to sit in a precarious position with an awfully long drop below, but if you can overcome any fear of heights, this is an exhilarating place from which to view the tiger mosaic on the Sher Dor Madrasa opposite and you feel like you're on top of the world. The minaret of the Ulug Beg Madrasa was jacked up in 1922; it collapsed and was rebuilt, but it still has a clear tilt.

Ulug Beg also built a *caravanserai* and *khanako* (hostel for wandering holy men), but both were replaced by madrasas in the 17th century. The **Sher Dor Madrasa** (the Tiger or Lion Madrasa), built between 1619 and 1636 by Yalangtush Biy, must be one of the most-photographed buildings in existence. There are two ribbed domes (best seen from inside rather than from the Registan Square) and two minarets flank the façade. The elaborate mosaic work on the portico shows two sun gods, two strange big cats each with tiger's stripes but a lion's mane, and two deer, and must therefore contravene so many Islamic prohibitions on art. Despite this, it was a religious building. The mosaic was ravaged over time, but was heavily restored in the 20th century to the condition you see today. Restoration work is ongoing, so parts of the interior courtyard may well be under scaffolding.

The former students' cells now house small souvenir shops and workshops. Among these, the most interesting is **Babur's Music Shop**, where master Babur gives demonstrations of traditional Uzbek instruments including various stringed instruments, tambourines, flutes and trumpets. He explains about each instrument in English, then gives a short performance. This is free to attend, and you can then buy his CDs if you wish. There is no pressure. A music and dance show takes place in the courtyard at 17.00 daily (m 90 324 5888). You'll also see weavers at their looms in the lavishly decorated hall on the left (north) side of the portal.

During the warmer months, there is a spectacular free **sound and light show** in the courtyard at 21.00 (whenever there are enough tour groups booked in), which gives a light (excuse the pun) and rather kitsch overview of the buildings and how they fit into world culture. Crowds gather to watch, standing on and in front of the viewing platform. It is usually in English or French, and you can ask at the Registan's normal ticket office for details.

The third of the madrasas to be built, and the centrepiece of the square, was the **Tilla Kari Madrasa** (Gold-covered Madrasa). When the Bibi Khanym Mosque started to fall into disrepair in the mid 17th century, Yalangtush Biy decided a replacement was needed, so he commissioned this combined mosque- and-madrasa complex on the site of the ruined Mirzoi *caravanserai*. Construction was completed in 1660 after 14 years of hard work; the dome was reconstructed in the 20th century as the original had been destroyed by Nadir Shah's forces in the early 18th century. Though it is easy to get caught up looking at the exterior, this is the one madrasa you must go inside: the golden ceiling of the mosque, to the left of the courtyard, is utterly enthralling, and it is this gilt that gives the madrasa its name. Tour groups inevitably spend a while lingering here and blocking the view, but be patient and wait for space. Position yourself immediately beneath the centre of the golden dome and then look straight up to appreciate the full effect. There's also a small museum on either side of it.

Bibi Khanym Two of the three buildings once associated with Bibi Khanym, Timur's Chingizid senior wife, are still standing. The third, a madrasa with a portico so large that it rivalled that of the neighbouring mosque, was destroyed by Nadir Shah's Persian troops when they invaded in 1740.

The **Bibi Khanym Mosque** [163 G1] (Karimov; ☉ 08.00–19.00 daily; foreigners US$2.50) is one of Samarkand's most impressive sites, but also one of its most controversial owing to the heavy reconstruction that has taken place. It was built between 1399 and 1404, when it was the world's largest mosque. It seems that the speed of the mosque's original construction led to shoddy workmanship, and began to decay not long after completion. What you see now is an almost total rebuild that started in 1974, as much of the original collapsed after an earthquake in 1897. Restoration is still underway, notably in the great western cupola, where huge earthquake cracks are still visible.

It is said that Bibi Khanym built the mosque to be a surprise for Timur while he returned from campaigning in India. The mosque's architect fell deeply in love with her, and when she urged him to hurry to complete the work he demanded he be allowed to give her a kiss. The kiss left a permanent stain on her cheek; Timur saw it on his return and had the architect executed for his insolence. Legend has it that Bibi Khanym was beheaded too, but in fact she outlived Timur by four years. When her grave was opened in the 1950s, her body was remarkably well preserved. She had been buried wearing expensive jewellery (now in the Hermitage in St Petersburg), a nod to her royal Mongol heritage as this was not an Islamic practice.

Building the mosque pushed Timurid engineering to its limits. Skilled workmen were brought from across the empire to design and build the 41m-high cupola, and Indian elephants were purportedly used for the transportation and heavy lifting. The original bronze gates, stolen by Nadir Shah, rung out when struck; the courtyard was floored with marble on which worshippers knelt and prayed. There were 400 marble pillars and the interior was decorated with painted papier-mâché. Sadly, during the 20th century the mosque was used as a storage area for the neighbouring market, and almost all of the papier-mâché decoration was lost when some goods caught fire.

In the centre of this courtyard stands a vast stone Qu'ran stand, under which childless women still occasionally crawl in the hope of conceiving a child. This is where the world's oldest Qu'ran (now on display in Tashkent; page 107) would have been shown on holy days.

The mosque is typically a quiet spot (far more so than the Registan), and at prayer times you may well see both men and women prostrating themselves in the courtyard or immediately outside the mosque's main entrance. Opposite the mosque is **Bibi Khanym's Mausoleum** [163 G1] (foreigners US$2), a simple, brick-built structure with a turquoise dome on top. This building is entirely new, the upper parts having been constructed only in 2007, though the open crypt dates from the 14th century. The graves include those of Bibi Khanym, her mother and two nieces. The interior has some fine decorative mosaics and wall paintings, including a depiction of paradise.

Shah-i Zinda [163 H1] (Shah-i Zinda; ☉ summer 08.00–19.00 daily, winter 08.00–17.00 daily; US$2) The Registan may be Samarkand's poster child, but for us the real star of the show is the line of blue-and-turquoise-tiled tombs known as the Shah-i Zinda. The best time to visit is in the early evening. We had always previously entered through the graveyard and come into the complex at the top of the hill, giving a strange sense of walking back through time, a thousand ghosts your guides through the long grass and headstones; however, this gate is now locked. The main entrance and ticket booth are actually at the bottom of the hill by the street.

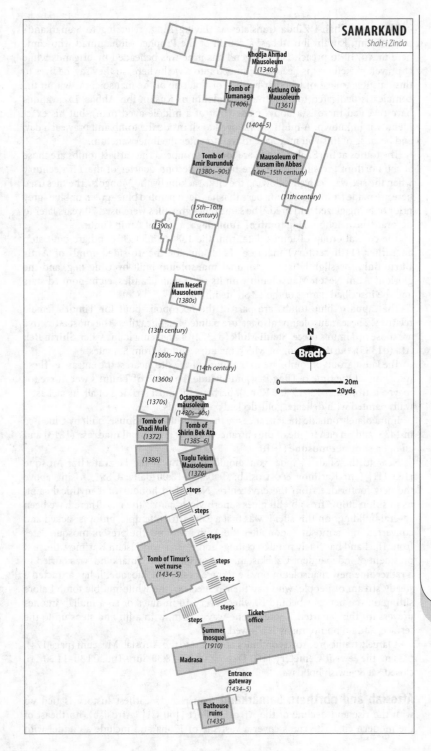

SAMARKAND
Shah-i Zinda

Khodja Ahmad
Mausoleum
(1340s)

Tomb of
Tumanaga
(1406)

Kutlung Oko
Mausoleum
(1361)

(1404–5)

Tomb of
Amir Burunduk
(1380s–90s)

Mausoleum of
Kusam ibn Abbas
(14th–15th century)

(11th century)

*(15th–16th
century)*

(1390s)

Alim Nesefi
Mausoleum
(1380s)

N

Bradt

(13th century)

(1360s–70s)

(14th century)

(1360s)

0 ——————— 20m
0 ——————— 20yds

(1370s)

Octagonal
mausoleum
(1430s–40s)

Tomb of
Shadi Mulk
(1372)

Tomb of
Shirin Bek Ata
(1385–6)

(1386)

Tuglu Tekim
Mausoleum
(1376)

steps

steps

steps

Tomb of Timur's
wet nurse
(1434–5)

steps

steps

steps

Ticket
office

steps

Summer
mosque
(1910)

Madrasa

Entrance
gateway
(1434–5)

Bathhouse
ruins
(1435)

The name Shah-i Zinda translates as 'Living King', referring to Samarkand's patron saint, Kusam ibn Abbas, a cousin of the Prophet Muhammad who came here in AD710 to preach Islam; legend has it he was beheaded by brigands while at prayer, picked up his head and jumped into a well where, so they say, he lives to this day. Regardless of whether he died or not, one of the mausoleums within the complex is dedicated to him: the **Mausoleum of Kusam ibn Abbas**. Excavations have revealed there is a body inside (that of a middle-aged man), but his exact identity is unknown. A mufti is employed to sit inside the tomb and pray each day, and because of this you may have to wait to enter the inner sanctum.

The tombs at the Shah-i Zinda are loosely grouped. The earliest tombs are those at the north of the site, which date from the second quarter of the 14th century when the site was revived following the city's sacking by the Mongols. The tiles used here are made from a terracotta base that has been painted blue–green or blue–grey prior to being glazed and fired. The same blue–grey tiles were used 70 years later to decorate the neighbouring **tomb of Tumanaga**, a wife of Amir Timur.

The central group of tombs date from the 1380s and 1390s and are built atop an earlier (11th century) madrasa. Look out for the 16-sided **tomb of Amir Burunduk**, the slightly later **octagonal mausoleum** built by Ulug Beg, and the glorious **Alim Nesefi Mausoleum** with its relief majolica tiles, eight-pointed stars and the inscribed names of the 12 Shi'ite imams.

The sapphire-blue tombs are part of the necropolis built for Timur's female relatives. These mausoleums also feature painted majolica tiles. The most attractive are those of Timur's niece, **Shadi Mulk** (d1372), and, facing it, his sister, **Shirin Bek Ata** (d1385), the decoration of which includes a quote from Socrates.

The latest group of tombs are to the south of the site, nearest the entrance. These were built at the time of Ulug Beg and include the **tomb of Timur's wet nurse** (or maybe astronomer Kazi Zade Rumi), perhaps the most striking of all, its alabaster walls painted with delicate, gold-flecked palm fronds.

Immediately outside the entrance are the ruins of a **bathhouse**, built by Ulug Beg in 1435, and on either side of the entrance gateway are a small **madrasa** (1813) and an open **summer mosque** (1910).

Near to the Shah-i Zinda, you should also stop at the **Hazrat Hizr Mosque** [163 H1] (cnr Karimov & Afrosiab; ⊕ 08.00–18.00 daily; US$1), rising above the new footbridge from the city centre. Named in honour of a mythical saint, its position atop Afrosiab Hill gives superb views across the city. There have been several buildings on this site. It was first a Zoroastrian temple, but was sacked and converted into a mosque soon after the Arab invasion. The present mosque dates from 1854 and has finely painted ceilings and plasterwork. Islam Karimov, the first president of independent Uzbekistan, who was born in Samarkand, was buried in a rather fine new mausoleum on the terrace beside the mosque. It has attracted a steady stream of people, who pay their respects at the white-marble tomb before sitting on the benches behind it, where every 10 minutes or so a mullah intones prayers for the departed. There's a one-way system, with a lift and steps up to the terrace, and no photography is allowed.

A largely traffic-free road continues northeast to the Afrosiab Museum (page 174), passing the **Jewish Cemetery** [160 D2] (⊕ 08.30–18.30 Sun–Thu, 08.30–14.30 Fri, closed Sat & Jewish holidays).

Afrosiab and northern Samarkand

Samarkand's earliest history is tied up with the rise and decline of the **Afrosiab Fort** [160 C1] (Afrosiab), northeast of the modern city. The ruins cover a vast site of 120ha and include a **citadel** with

REACH FOR THE STARS: ULUG BEG, THE ASTRONOMER KING

Religion disperses like a fog, kingdoms perish, but the works of scholars remain for an eternity.

Ulug Beg

Not content with their earthly domains, kings have often looked to the stars for confirmation of their divine right to rule, and indications of what the future might bring. Their patronage and personal interest in astronomy have driven forward our understanding of not only our own solar system, but also the planets beyond.

Astronomy had been a royal pursuit for thousands of years: the ancient Egyptians aligned their pyramids to the stars and were able to accurately predict the flooding of the Nile by sightings of Sirius and the summer solstice, while the Babylonians were producing star catalogues as long ago as 1200BC. It would be the medieval governor of Mavarannahr, Ulug Beg (1394–1449), who would take astronomy into the modern age, building a vast observatory and producing the most detailed star catalogue before that of Tycho Brahe. The grandson of Amir Timur, he was born in Samarkand in 1394. He lacked the political skills of his predecessors, but instead focused on turning his capital into an intellectual centre for scholars from across the Islamic world. Having travelled to both India and the Middle East as a child, he was well aware of scientific developments in both those regions, and was determined to build upon them in Samarkand. The young Ulug Beg constructed a huge madrasa on the Registan square (page 168) and invited numerous astronomers and mathematicians to study there.

Although Ulug Beg was himself a fine mathematician, his real interest lay in astronomy. The observatory he built, the Gurkhani Zij, contained a sextant, 11m long and with a radius of 40.4m. It was the largest such instrument in the world and had to be kept underground to protect it from earthquakes. Long before the invention of the telescope, this instrument enabled Ulug Beg to accurately position over 1,000 stars, determine the length of the year with such accuracy that it would even surpass Copernicus's calculations, and to work out the exact tilt of the earth's axis.

Given that Ulug Beg and his astronomers were working without optics, the accuracy of their calculations is unnerving. Even today we do not have a more accurate calculation of the earth's axial tilt than Ulug Beg's 23.52°, and his assertion that the year is 365 days, 6 hours, 10 minutes and 8 seconds in length is only 1 minute longer than modern electronic calculations.

Had Ulug Beg and his astronomers had more time to study the stars, they may yet have been more impressive, but fate was to intervene: the observatory was destroyed by religious fanatics in 1449 and would lie forgotten underground until it was rediscovered by an archaeologist in 1908. Ulug Beg himself hardly met a more glamorous fate: he was beheaded by his own son en route to Mecca and his remains were interred in Timur's tomb (page 175).

foundations two storeys deep. Across the road south of the museum, you can easily walk up on to the earthen walls of the Old City; to the north it's possible to cross a wasteland where sheep graze to find archaeologists' abandoned trenches and the mounds of the ancient citadel.

Unlike Samarkand's other sites, the fort has been excavated but not restored, so unless you already have in-depth historical knowledge and a very active imagination, you should first go inside the informative **Afrosiab Museum** [160 D2] (⊕ 09.00–17.00 daily; foreigners US$3). Along with well-laid-out excavation plans, photos and, of course, the archaeological finds themselves (on two floors, including pre-Islamic ritual goods, ceramics, weapons and coins), are a remarkable set of murals found in 1965 – don't miss them; they're half hidden in a central room. Dating from around AD670, each panel is more than 2m high and shows scenes of the Sogdian elite at play: there are hunting scenes, men on horseback and camel, a Chinese princess in a boat, and ambassadors from China, India, Tibet, Turkey and Korea. Their physical appearance and dress show the cosmopolitanism of Samarkand in this period: all the known world is shown coming to trade and play. The murals were painted with vegetable and mineral pigments, including large amounts of lapis lazuli, the precious stone from neighbouring Afghanistan which makes the vivid aquamarine blue.

The best way to understand the murals is to watch the short video in the room alongside their exhibition space, which costs US$1. The voice-over is in English, and computer graphics draw attention to one section of the mural at a time, showing you details that aren't necessarily visible to the naked eye. You also see the archaeologists' idea of what was in the lost sections.

Everyone has heard of Daniel and the lion's den, but few could tell you that his final resting place, the **Mausoleum of Daniyar** [160 D1] (Karimov; ⊕ 09.00–18.00 daily; US$2), is in Samarkand, just beyond the Afrosiab Museum. Daniel (Daniyar in Uzbek) is considered a patron saint and protector of Samarkand, bringing wealth and prosperity to the city, and Timur supposedly brought his remains here from Susa in Iran. It is still a pilgrimage place for the followers of all three Abrahamic religions. Footbridges lead across the river from the car park to a landscaped park, and the steps up to the tomb in a cleft in the cliffs; to the right of the steps is an ancient spring (free access), with water that is said to have healing properties.

The mausoleum is unadorned, and this is even more noticeable given the contrast with the elaborate decoration of Samarkand's other sites. The long, thin brick building, the latest of many on this site, dates from the 19th century and supports five simple domes. Inside is Daniel's tomb; it's a holy site and visitors are not allowed to go inside, but you can stand in the doorway and take photographs.

Local legend has it that despite being dead, Daniel's severed leg continues to grow within his sarcophagus. This unusual miracle has necessitated the lengthening of his white-marble sarcophagus several times during its history. If the leg reaches 18m, the length of the latest sarcophagus, it is said that the world will surely end.

The sarcophagus is covered in green and gold prayer rugs. Green is the colour of Islam; the gold denotes the importance of the saint. It is not only Islam that reveres Daniel, however. If you stand at the entrance way to the mausoleum and look left, you will see a flagpole with a small bundle of horse hair hanging from its top. This is a traditional symbol used by local nomads to denote the burial place of a respected leader. There's also an ancient and sacred pistachio tree on the cliff just beyond the tomb.

Medieval Samarkand was a centre for both religious and secular learning, and its rulers patronised the sciences as well as the arts. **Ulug Beg's Observatory** [160 D1] (Karimov; ⊕ 09.00–18.00 daily; foreigners US$3), the world's largest astronomical observatory at the time it was built, lies a brisk, 10-minute walk beyond Afrosiab by the ring road. The observatory lay forgotten and in ruins for some 500 years prior to its partial restoration, the important work undertaken there remembered only in Ulug Beg's astronomical works, which had been published posthumously in Europe.

The centrepiece of the observatory, rediscovered and excavated by the Russian archaeologist Vladimir Viyatkin in 1908, is part of a quadrant arc 63m in length that was used to chart the progress of celestial bodies across the sky. Using this arc, Samarkand's medieval astronomers produced a star catalogue charting the movements of 1,018 stars, which was used in China and Korea in the 15th century and was published in Oxford in 1648, followed by a fuller edition by the Astronomer Royal John Flamsteed in 1725.

When you first arrive at the site, you'd be forgiven for thinking that there's nothing to see except the museum with its modern madrasa-style portal. The arc itself is sunk below ground, which is the reason it survived when the rest of the observatory was destroyed by fanatics in 1449. Peering into the gloom, you will be struck by the scale of the arc but also the precision with which it was made: tiny niches are cut into the surface for calibrating the once-accompanying astrolabe, enabling exact calculations to be made. In fact, their accuracy would not be beaten until the invention of the computer.

Alongside the arc is the **grave of Viyatkin** and a small **museum** (⏱ 09.00–17.00 Mon–Sat) about Ulug Beg's life and works. It is well worth going inside the museum as the displays are excellent and really help to explain not only the historical context of Ulug Beg's work, but also how he made his calculations. Architectural models, maps and information boards, which include descriptions in English, are well done, and there are a number of replica astronomical instruments, including Ulug Beg's double quadrant and armillary sphere.

The museum and the smaller structure around the entrance to the arc are both modern, as is the large statue of Ulug Beg enthroned that you see on the way up the hill. It was erected only in 2010, on the site of an older statue of Ulug Beg standing. Apparently, he now looks more regal.

The Gur-i Amir and around Amir Timur wanted to be buried in a simple tomb in his home town of Shakhrisabz, but his relatives and advisers had grander plans, for which Samarkand's modern tour guides are no doubt grateful.

THE CURSE OF AMIR TIMUR?

Inside the Gur-i Amir, Timur's final resting place is marked with a single slab of jade, said to be the largest in the world. Brought back by Ulug Beg from Mongolia in 1425, it is inscribed in Arabic calligraphy with the following words: 'When I rise, the World will Tremble.'

The first supposed victim of the curse was the Persian invader Nadir Shah, who carried it off to Persia in 1740 and broke it in two. Nadir Shah's son fell gravely ill, and things started to go wrong to such an extent that his advisers demanded the jade be returned to the tomb. It was brought back, and the son recovered, though Nadir Shah himself met a sticky end just a few years later, stabbed to death in his bed.

On the night of 22 June 1941, a team of Russian scientists began to exhume Timur's remains. Within hours the Nazi tanks had begun rolling into the Soviet Union. Many wondered if this was Timur's curse. The scientists found him to be a tall man, and as his name suggested, lame in the right leg. He had also suffered a wound to the right arm. Analysis complete, Timur's remains were reinterred with full Muslim burial rites, and the Nazis eventually left.

The **Gur-i Amir** [163 E4] (University; ☉ 08.00–19.00 daily; foreigners US$2), a compact but gem-like building, was built for Timur's grandson Muhammad Sultan in 1404. Timur was said to be heartbroken at this loss: he had appointed Muhammad Sultan as his successor and had great confidence in his abilities. When Timur himself died of pneumonia a year later, he was laid to rest in the same tomb, his body covered with a slab of Mongolian jade.

The Gur-i Amir was built in three stages, and you can spot the different periods of construction quite easily. Originally there was a madrasa on this site. The tiled portico belonged to the madrasa, as did the waist-high stonework to the right and left of the main courtyard. Timur destroyed the main part of this to build Muhammad Sultan's tomb, which is the portion of the complex covered by the dome.

The third phase of construction dates from the time of Ulug Beg, Timur's grandson. The original entrance was in the centre of the building, but Timur's religious tutor Abu Said (see below) was buried near to his pupil, and pilgrims therefore trampled over his remains when entering the mausoleum. This was disrespectful, so Ulug Beg created two new wings for the tomb, one to the left of the dome and the other to the right. He added the modest entrance way on the left and blocked up the original door with a latticework screen.

The Gur-i Amir effectively serves as the Timurid dynasty's necropolis, for in addition to Timur and Muhammad Sultan, the bodies of two of Timur's sons, Miranshah and Shahruh, and his grandson, Ulug Beg, are also here. The stone tombs you see are in fact purely decorative, as was traditional: the bodies are in fact interred in crypts beneath the floor.

If you're fortunate enough to step inside the mausoleum after dark, the central chamber sparkles as light flickers from the colossal crystal chandelier hanging beneath the dome. The gilt on the ceiling seems to glow, and it feels like you're in a very holy place indeed. Regardless of the time of day, be sure to also look at the onyx panelling on the walls. The original onyx tiles (the duller green ones) came from Persia; the brighter green ones date from the modern restoration.

Before you leave the complex, stop in the main courtyard and have a look at the stonework beneath the blue plastic shelter in the corner. These pieces were all excavated from the ruins of Timur's Ak Serai palace, now lost beneath modern Samarkand. The large stone block with exquisite carving on its side is thought to have been Timur's coronation stone. At its side, the huge stone font would once have been filled with fresh pomegranate juice, to be drunk by Timurid soldiers.

Hidden in the backstreets, a few hundred metres from the Gur-i Amir, the 15th-century **Oksaray Mausoleum** [163 F4] (Oksaray; ☉ 08.00–18.00 daily; US$1) is plain externally, but has an unexpectedly lovely (if possibly over-restored) interior. Above shoulder height, it's totally covered in blue and golden floral patterns and peacock tails. You can go down to the crypt, with two plain tombs: possibly those of the son of Amir Timur's tutor and of Abd al Latif, responsible for the death of his father Ulug Beg.

The area of the Old Town in front of the Gur-i Amir has been swept away and replaced with a rather sterile park. Diagonally across the car park is the **Rukhobod Mausoleum** [163 E3] (☉ 09.00–18.00 daily; free), Samarkand's oldest surviving monument. Built for Amir Timur in 1380, this simple, cream stone structure marks the burial place of Sheikh Byrhan ad Din Sagarji, a Sufi preacher who spread the message of Islam from central Asia to India and was mentioned by the Arabic traveller Ibn Battuta after they met in the 1340s. Sagarji's son, Abu Said, was Timur's religious tutor and is buried near him in the Gur-i Amir (see above). Though often locked, it is occasionally possible to climb to the upper floors and look back towards the Gur-i Amir. The courtyard now houses a craft centre, with shops selling embroidery, ceramics and costumes.

Other sites in Samarkand Of potential interest to fans of Uzbekistan's literary heritage is the **House Museum of Sadriddin Aini** [163 F3] (7B Registan; 66 235 5153; ☉ 09.00–17.00 daily). Built around a peaceful, whitewashed courtyard just metres from the Registan, the house museum has none of the crowds of its more famous neighbour. It was in these rooms that Aini (1878–1954) wrote his most famous texts, including the novels *Slaves* and *Dokunda*, and the collection includes early editions, photographs and personal papers, as well as lovely pre-revolution interiors and furniture. The elderly curator is passionate about his subject and shows you around the museum with surprising vigour. Sadly, he only speaks Russian, so you'll need a translator to fully benefit from his knowledge.

To see traditional carpet weaving, go to the **Samarkand Bukhara Carpet Workshop** [160 D2] (12A Hujom; 66 235 2273; m 97 455 5777; e badghisia@ hotmail.com; ☉ 08.00–17.00 daily). Established in 1992 in a bid to revive traditional techniques, the workshop is run by the affable and exceptionally knowledgeable Haji Baba (Muhammad Ewaz Badghisi). The workshop produces around 400 handmade carpets a year and prides itself on having exemplary working conditions and benefits for its weavers and dyers. Workers undertake a four-month training programme and work no more than 40 hours a week. All of them are over 18. The plants required to make many of the natural dyes are grown in the workshop garden, which you are welcome to wander around, and the women take painstaking care to show you each stage of the carpet-making process. There is no hard sell, just a fascinating insight into the industry, and if you do decide to buy a carpet, you can either choose from one of those already made, or design one yourself and be confident of having it delivered.

On the outskirts of Samarkand, 3km south of the centre on Sadriddin Aini, lies the **Khodja Abdi Darun shrine** [160 D3]. It's in an active madrasa (☉ daylight hrs), centred on a peaceful little pool, and is slightly dilapidated rather than being heavily restored like many of the city centre's monuments. It's beautifully adorned with fine carved pillars, attractively painted ceilings, and decorative tigers on the doors (likely a model for those later depicted on the Sher Dor Madrasa; page 169).

The buildings you see today date from the 12th to the 19th centuries, and a new madrasa is also under construction on the site. The oldest part was built by the Seljuk sultan Sanjar to be his mausoleum, and it was then reconstructed by Ulug Beg (see box, page 173) three centuries later, who added a khanagha. The water reservoir, mosque and madrasa date from the most recent phase of construction in the 1800s.

Don't miss the **Ishrat Khana Mausoleum** across the road. It is largely derelict but set to be restored by German experts. Completed in 1464, it sat in one of the lost and greatly lamented Timurid gardens and at its peak was one of Samarkand's most remarkable architectural ensembles. There are 20 tombs here, perhaps of noble women.

Last but not least, you may be interested in visiting the **Gumbaz Synagogue** [163 H2] (2 Ilyazarov; 66 223 6516; m 91 552 7268), tucked down an alleyway beside a hammam: you might have to ask to find it. Within the Old City wall, this synagogue was built in 1891 for the Bukharan Jewish community in Samarkand, which today numbers only about 250 people, but has lived in the area for many centuries. It is an interesting place to visit, with old books and a Torah scroll, which was written in the city. It also has a pleasant courtyard.

The European town [162 D3] To the west of the Timurid city (city centre) is the Russian quarter, also known as the European town, laid out at the end of the 19th century. It has been listed as a World Heritage Site by UNESCO since 2001; nevertheless, it is under threat from developers abetted by the city authorities (although the glitzy high-rise Samarkand City development that is under construction is beyond the protected zone). The pleasant Navoi Park abuts the leafy University Boulevard, and there are a couple of interesting museums nearby, as well as Russian Orthodox, Catholic and Armenian churches a little to the west.

Samarkand Regional Museum of Local Lore [162 C3] (51 A Jomiy; \ 66 233 7676; ⊕ 10.00–16.30 Mon–Fri; US$3) This museum occupies the former home of the Jewish merchant Avram Kalendar (1815–78). At the rear of the garden (containing an old tractor and cannon), the archaeology section has some interesting photos of the city's monuments pre-restoration, as well as stone tools that are up to 40,000 years old, Sogdian ceramic ossuaries, coins and weapons, 19th-century carved wooden doors, metal pots, bridal jewellery and textiles, including dervish costumes. It's all rather dated, but there's enough information in English to bring some illumination. Upstairs, the natural history section is even more dated, and there's less English text, although there is a comprehensive, yet rather tatty, collection of stuffed birds and a few reptiles and butterflies. In the south wing, the Jewish section is more interesting, with 19th-century furniture and stoves, as well as lacquered wall coverings and plasterwork, and a prayer hall. There are pictures of musicians and intellectuals, and a section on printing.

State Museum of Cultural History of Uzbekistan [160 A2] (148 Mirzo Ulug Beg; \ 66 234 8215; f samarkandmuseum; ⊕ 09.00–17.00 Tue–Sun; US$2) Founded in 1896, in 2010 this museum was moved from near the Registan to a huge new building out towards the station and now sees very few visitors. It's a great shame as this is a superb collection (with enough information in English), once you get past the displays on the achievements of independent Uzbekistan. The archaeological section runs from Palaeolithic arrowheads via terracotta statuettes from Afrosiab, Gandharan sculpture from Afghanistan, 6th- and 7th-century ceramic ossuaries, and blue-and-white Chinese pots, to attractive 13th-century blue-and-green ceramics, also from Afrosiab. There's also an important collection of ancient coins. Then there are ceramics and metalwork from the 19th and 20th centuries, some very fine and some in folky vernacular style. Up on the third floor are some realist paintings, and there is a great collection of textiles around the gallery, as well as costumes and embroidered boots, kept in side rooms.

Scientific-Practical Museum-Lab [162 D5] (Samarkand State University; 19A University Bd; m 91 542 9965; ⊕ 09.00–17.00 Mon–Fri; free) Here the illustrious history of science in Samarkand is covered, from the madrasas that were offering something similar to university-level teaching by the 10th century, to Ibn Sina (Avicenna), Ulug Beg and his student Ali Kushchi, who moved to Istanbul in 1470 and did much to make his teacher's work known in the outside world. Founded in 1927, the university is directly descended from Ulug Beg's madrasa, but the displays on its recent history are very dull for outsiders.

AROUND SAMARKAND

St David's Cave Just south of the A378, above the village of Aksay and 40km west of Samarkand, pilgrims from all three Abrahamic faiths come to climb the 1,303 steps to a hilltop mosque (it's also possible to ride a horse up a longer track – you'll find them at the bottom, waiting to carry visitors up) and then descend 200 steps to the cave of Hazrat Daud (St David), with marks left by his hands and feet. This is supposedly the King David of the Old Testament (not the patron saint of Wales), although it seems unlikely that he was ever here. In any case, the views from the mosque (at 1,280m) should make the climb worthwhile.

Imam Al-Bukhari Mausoleum (Khoja Ismail village; ⊕ 09.00–18.00 daily; free) Located 25km north of Samarkand, to reach here you need to take a minibus headed to Chelek from the bus stop by the Shah-i Zinda and jump off at Khoja Ismail, 4km before the end of the route.

Al-Bukhari was born in Bukhara in AD810, and at the age of 16 he embarked upon his life's work: scouring the Islamic world for Hadith, the sayings of the Prophet Muhammad. Over the next 16 years, Al-Bukhari collected some 600,000 sayings. The resulting book ran to 97 volumes. Of the six canonical volumes of the Hadith, two were collected by scholars born in what is now Uzbekistan.

The mausoleum complex comprises an impressive gateway, a large courtyard with manicured lawns and flowerbeds, prayer rooms and a water tank, and a minaret. This is in addition, of course, to the tomb itself, which is covered by a blue dome raised upon marble pillars. The symbolic tomb (the actual tomb is in a crypt beneath the floor, as is the case in the Gur-i Amir; page 176) is made of highly polished marble. The inscription on the accompanying gravestone, engraved in Arabic, describes Al-Bukhari's life.

The mausoleum complex is an active religious centre, though non-Muslims are welcome to visit providing they are appropriately dressed (women must cover their heads) and ask permission at the entrance. There is no entrance fee, though you may be asked to make a small donation towards the upkeep of the shrine.

Amankutan Gorge Natural Preserve The 2,158ha Amankutan Gorge Natural Preserve is some 50km southeast of Samarkand, not far from Urgut (known for its large and very cheap Sunday market, and as a base for hiking). It's just off the M39, the road over the Tahtakaracha Pass from Samarkand to Shakhrisabz, and indeed in ancient times the most direct route from ancient Bactria to Sogdiana passed through the gorge. Shared taxis between Samarkand and Shakhrisabz will leave you here, but getting away can be more difficult, as taxis will usually be full and buses don't use this road; you're best off with your own transport. The preserve has been known as a successful conservation site since the late 19th century: mud slides were devastating local villages, so the Russian governor of Turkestan orchestrated an ambitious reforestation programme to counter this. Several thousand trees were planted from 1879, including apricot, almond and walnut – some of these trees still stand today. Their roots bind the soil together, making it less vulnerable to subsidence during the rains, and the trees also offer pleasant shade.

The gorge is famed for its dramatic scenery, as well as being a pristine natural environment (which is sadly a rarity in this part of the world). Emperor tulips (*Tulipa fosteriana*), the ancestor of modern, domesticated varieties of tulips, grow wild here, as do many medicinal herbs such as clary (a type of sage). There are a number of short trekking routes, ideal for day hikes, through the woodlands, where you can see many flowers, birds and butterflies, and you can also hike past a youth camp to visit a cave in which very significant Neanderthal remains (now in the Regional Museum in Samarkand; see opposite) were discovered in 1947.

DZHIZAK

Though many people do pass through Dzhizak (also written Jizzax), and it is a fair-sized town with a long history, for today's tourists it really is just a convenient transit point, mainly for onward travel towards Lake Aidarkul and the Zaamin National Park. You won't want to schedule any time here.

HISTORY Dzhizak grew up as a trading post at the crossroads between Samarkand and the Fergana Valley, a gateway to Western riches. Anxious to control the valuable trade passing through, it was fortified in turn by the Sogdians, the Arabs and the Bukharan Khanate; it was so well defended that it slowed the advance of General Chernyayev in 1866, though the Russians ultimately won out, slaughtering more than 6,000 men.

GETTING THERE AND AROUND Dzhizak is just 203km and 95km from Tashkent and Samarkand respectively, along the M39 or M34 (for details on the route towards Tashkent, see page 92, but note that the M39 bypasses Dzhizak to the east).

If you don't have your own vehicle, getting there can be a bit of a drag on account of the fact that the **Olmazor intercity bus stand** is 10km east of the town at the intersection with the M39 highway. The minibus ride to Tashkent takes 2½ hours and costs US$3; the journey to Samarkand is 2 hours and costs US$2. Shared taxis cost twice as much but reduce the travel time by about a third.

The number 1 minibus frequently plies the route between the intercity bus stand and the town centre, where the Gorod stand is the place for buses to nearby towns and villages. Local minibuses, to get around town, can be picked up from the bazaar or from Rashidov Square.

Dzhizak does have a **railway station** off A Navoi, south of the centre, but relatively few of the long-distance trains stop here. If you do want to take the train to Samarkand, it takes just over an hour. Trains run several times a day, and tickets cost around US$2.

 WHERE TO STAY, EAT AND DRINK Dzhizak is sadly not blessed with many accommodation options as few people visit and even fewer spend the night.

Comfort Continent (9 rooms, 1 apt) 1A S Nasimov; \72 226 2767. Opened in 2012, this mid-range business hotel has large, light rooms with modern bathrooms. There is a bar on site & the best room has a jacuzzi. It also has a convenient bar & restaurant ($$) serving Uzbek & European cuisine. **$$$**

Khalk Markazi B&B 3 Azimov; \72 237 222. Dzhizak's most unusual accommodation option is this somewhat quirky B&B run by the People's Centre, a Sufi group that offers healing & pilgrimages aimed at locals rather than tourists. Facilities are basic but the company is fascinating. **$$**

Sangzor Camp Karasai village. Soviet-style holiday camp close to Timur Darvaza (see opposite). **$**

Amir Timur Karasai village; ⊕ 08.00–23.00 daily. This small restaurant next to the Sangzor Camp (see above) serves salads & other snacks. **$$**

WHAT TO SEE AND DO Almost nothing is left of Dzhizak's past: what you see is a 20th-century industrial town. **Rashidov Square** and the **Rashidov Memorial Museum** (⊕ 09.00–18.00 Mon–Sat; US$0.12) are both named in honour of Sharaf Rashidovich Rashidov (see box, opposite), despite his subsequent fall from favour. The latter houses a fairly underwhelming collection of political memorabilia, including the understandably forlorn stuffed crocodile that was an official gift to Rashidov from Fidel Castro.

AROUND DZHIZAK The two reasons you might come to (or through) Dzhizak are both located out of the city.

Timur Darvaza (Timur's Gates) Located 10km west on the old highway, the narrow opening to the Zerafshan Mountains forms a bottleneck that numerous soldiers have sought to defend (or at least died trying). Ulug Beg left an inscription here to mark his triumphant return home in 1425; other historic inscriptions are sadly hidden among modern graffiti. Although the site itself is in some ways unimpressive (there are no structures to see), it's a place charged with history and you can easily appreciate its strategic importance in keeping invading hordes at bay.

The Dzhizak–Samarkand minibuses pass right by, so it's cheap and easy to jump off, take a look, and hop back on the next one passing through; it's also visible from trains.

Zaamin National Park (◊ 72 392 1212; m 95 503 6633; w zaamin.uz) This national park lies 75km southeast of Dzhizak, along an uninspiring road that traverses a dusty steppe and former collective farms before taking a last-minute turn up into the rolling hills and snow-capped mountains that ring Tajikistan. The oldest national park in Uzbekistan (founded in 1926), it's now fringed by the Zaamin State Reserve, covering a total of 460km^2 of apricot orchards, pine and juniper forests and alpine meadow; it is criss-crossed by four rivers, the Aldashmansoy, Baikungur, Guralsh and Kulsoy.

To reach here, you can take a minibus from Dzizhak (1½hrs) which will drop you at the vast and rather ugly **Zaamin Sanatorium** (Nomalum; m 93 408 2828/95 503 7135; **$$**), where there are various cafés and tourist stalls. If you're looking to stay the night, you can sleep either here or at the **Sharshara Dacha** (m 91 596 6633; **$$**), a popular spot with attractive gardens near the Sharilak Waterfall. Meals are included with the room rates in both cases. Unusually for Uzbekistan, you are also allowed to **camp** in the park, though you will need to bring everything with you and confirm permitted locations at the park office when you arrive; the easiest option is to camp at the sanatorium.

The **park entrance** lies just above a large, manmade reservoir where you can swim and camp in the summer months (mosquito repellent is advised if you do the latter). The **visitor centre** (inside the sanatorium; ✆72 392 1028; page 181) and **park office** lie a short way further on in the Uryuklisai Gorge. Regardless of whether you will be staying in the confines of the park or not, you need to register with this office on arrival. There is no additional fee for entry. At the head of the gorge is one of the park's most striking sites, the 100m Sharilak Waterfall, the course of which was diverted artificially to entertain the demanding clientele of the Sharshara Dacha (page 181), including President Karimov.

The park's true wilderness lies beyond the road and hotel infrastructure, in the alpine meadows over the Suffa Pass, where Kyrgyz nomads make their camp. The ring of peaks, several of which climb to more than 4,000m, make a spectacular setting, especially in the early evening when the sky turns burnt orange and there's not a sound in the air save for the breeze and the twittering of birds. A new observatory is still under construction, and around 150km of designated trails give walkers and wildlife spotters ample opportunity to explore. Route information can be found on the park's website (**w** zaamin.uz). If you leave the trail, keep your eye out for animal tracks and, if you're really lucky and the area is quiet, the animals themselves, including Turkestan lynx, bearded vulture and Asian black bear, can all potentially be spotted. A pair of binoculars will come in useful.

In 2012, a 350m **ski slope** for beginners was constructed close to the sanatorium. Active visitors with a passion for **mountaineering** may also use the park to attempt an ascent on Shaukartau and Tokalichuk, though both climbers and skiers will need to bring their own equipment.

6

Qashqa Darya and Surkhan Darya Provinces

Uzbekistan's two southernmost provinces are little visited by foreigners, especially now that few tourists cross the border with Afghanistan. This is a real pity, however, as the area has some of the country's most attractive natural landscapes, with the Gissar-Alai range providing a dramatic backdrop to any road trip or stay. The cities of Shakhrisabz and Termez, in Qashqa Darya and Surkhan Darya respectively, are both equally rich in history and provide an insight into Uzbekistan's past that is largely devoid of the gloss applied to Samarkand and Bukhara. It is for this reason that you can justify spending several days travelling south to visit them.

SHAKHRISABZ

There has been a settlement here, in the upper reaches of the Qashqa Darya River, for at least 2,700 years. The modern highway from Samarkand overlies a much older route across the mountains, but though it was a well-situated trading post, it would never have come to our notice if it were not for the city's most famous son: the 14th-century emperor, Amir Timur.

Amir Timur dominates Shakhrisabz, and quite rightly so. Join the throngs of wedding goers in Amir Timur Park to have your photo taken with the modern bronze statue of the great man himself and, more importantly, to see what's left of the Ak Serai, his once-mighty palace with its unrestored medieval tilework. Then head through the park to the Dor at-Tilyavat and Dor as-Siadat for the Timurid mosque and family necropolis.

There is very little in the way of practicalities here (including no ATMs). Everything is in limbo until the town recovers from the clearing of the Old Town and redevelopment – until then, bring essentials from Samarkand.

HISTORY Shakhrisabz originated as the Sogdian town of Kesh sometime before the 6th century AD. It survived the Arab invasion but was a place of relatively little importance until the birth of Timur-i Leng (Timur the Lame; see box, page 17) in Khoja Ilgar, a village 12km to the south, in 1336. Though he made his capital at Samarkand, Shakhrisabz was not forgotten: he fortified the town, enlarged his family burial ground, gave the city its present name (which means 'Green City') and began to construct the fabulous Ak Serai (White Palace), whose magnificent gateway remains unrestored but virtually intact to this day. Timur hoped to be buried in Shakhrisabz, in a simple crypt, but his relatives had other

QASHQA DARYA AND SURKHAN DARYA PROVINCES

ideas and he was eventually interred in the sumptuous Gur-i Amir in Samarkand (page 176).

Timur's successors, notably Ulug Beg, continued to build madrasas and mausoleums here, until Shakhrisabz was sacked in the late 1500s by Abdullah Khan II of Bukhara. Under the Kenegesse dynasty, the city regained a measure of independence until finally surrendering to the infamous Nasrullah Khan in 1856. In addition to the city, the emir also seized the ruler's sister; he had her executed on his deathbed, but local legend has it that she had poisoned him by pouring mercury into his ear. Shakhrisabz fell to the Russians 16 years later, and it dwindled into insignificance with neither wealthy patrons nor Soviet governors to steer its development in the 20th century.

The historic centre of Shakhrisabz was added to UNESCO's World Heritage list in 2000, but between 2014 and 2015 the area between and around the monuments was cleared as part of a 'beautification' programme. Though the monuments remain standing, the old streets and courtyard houses, in particular those near the city walls, have been demolished and replaced by a sterile 70ha park. The human context of the *mahalla* or Old Town has been swept away, which President Karimov saw as the way to attract tourists, but in 2016 UNESCO placed the town on its World Heritage in Danger list. Plans for large new hotels in the town centre have thankfully been put on hold.

GETTING THERE AND AROUND Shakhrisabz is 90km south of Samarkand and the **drive** across the mountains takes 1½–2 hours (considerably more if there is snow on the Tahtakaracha Pass, 1,788m above sea level). Coaches and trucks are not allowed to cross the pass for safety reasons, and must therefore take a longer route around the mountains. **Minibuses** from Samarkand run from the Suzangaran stop, across the road from the Registan, to Kitob (2hrs; US$4) from where you have to take a local *marshrutka* for the last few kilometres. **Shared taxis** are faster but cost about twice as much. There are two **buses** a day on the same route (4hrs; US$3), as well as direct minibuses from Tashkent (8hrs; US$6). To reach Bukhara, get a shared taxi first to Karshi and change there; the total journey takes 5 hours (excluding waiting around for your connection) and costs US$12–14.

A daily Afrosiyob high-speed **train** also runs from Tashkent via Samarkand and Karshi (a very long way around) to a station in Kitob, from where you can take a taxi or minibus to the historic centre of Shakhrisabz. The train leaves Tashkent at 08.00 daily, taking 4½ hours, and returns at 15.43; fares start at US$21.

Once you've reached the city, Shakhrisabz is best explored **on foot**; all the sites listed here are within 5–10 minutes' walk of one another along Ipak Yuli, now a pedestrianised boulevard in the new park, although electric trolleys also trundle up and down the traffic-free zone (US$1).

🏠 WHERE TO STAY *Map, page 186*

Shakhrisabz is just a few hours' drive from Samarkand (page 157), so it's easily done as a day trip. If you want to have a little longer to look around, however, or are travelling the long way to Bukhara, there are various options, with more set to open.

🏠 **Hotel Shakhrisabz Yulduzi** (50 rooms) 2 Ipak Yuli; 🖀 75 521 0554; e shakhrisabzstar@inbox. ru. Opened in 2009, this is Shakhrisabz's best hotel, though don't expect 5-star standards. Overlooking the city walls, it is clean, comfortable & all rooms have AC. The swimming pool is welcome in summer. Unusually for Uzbekistan, some rooms have access for travellers with disabilities. There is a restaurant on the roof ($$) & a souvenir shop & small art gallery in the foyer. Service is slow & lacklustre. **$$$**

🏠 **Kesh Palace** (30 rooms) 1 Fusunkor; m 91 216 8111. A modern hotel 10mins east of the centre, with comfortable rooms & a restaurant (b/fast inc). **$$**

🏠 **Orient Star** (54 rooms) 26 Ipak Yuli; m 93 500 5931. This large modernised block has a restaurant ($$), bar & business centre. **$$**

🏠 **Ulug Beg Hotel & Spa** 98 Ipak Yuli; 🖀 75 522 0440. A large modern hotel with an indoor pool & spa, plus restaurant ($$), bar & café. **$$**

🏠 **Bek** (10 rooms) 58/1 Ok Saroy; 🖀 75 522 4700. The town's best budget option is located 2km east of the centre (take *marshrutka* 9). It has simple rooms & an attractive courtyard. **$**

✗ WHERE TO EAT AND DRINK *Map, page 186*

Various pleasant *chaikhanas* were demolished along with the rest of the Old Town and replacements have been slow to emerge. There are various cafés dotted around the new park, but for a meal your best bet seems to be **Maysa** (186 Ipak Yuli; $), serving Uzbek food by the southern entrance to the park, or one of the touristy places across Taragay Bahodir to the north of the Ak Serai.

In a circular water reservoir (*sardoba*) just north of the Dor as-Siadat, the **Coffee House Sardoba** (Khovuzi Mardoi; $), in a circular water reservoir (*sardoba*), promises treats such as espresso, cappuccino and lattes.

SHOPPING Shakhrisabz is known for crafts, including *suzanis*, carpets and skull caps; although it lacks the variety of souvenirs you'll find in Samarkand, the quality is reasonable and the prices are relatively low. Inside the Dor at-Tilyavat and Dor as-Siadat complexes (page 187), you'll find various stands selling embroidered bags,

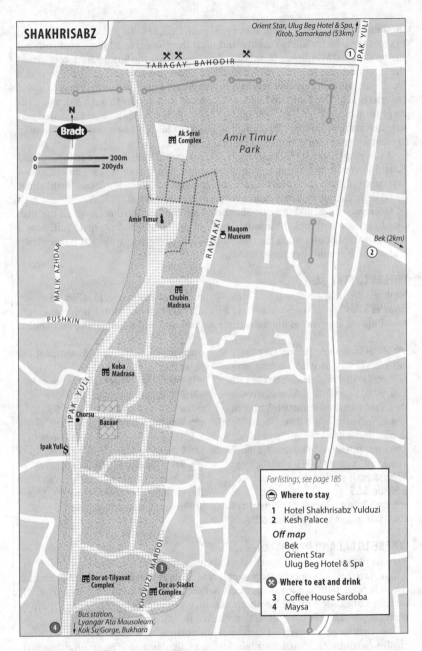

SHAKHRISABZ

Orient Star, Ulug Beg Hotel & Spa,
Kitob, Samarkand (53km)

IPAK YULI

TARAGAY BAHODIR

N
Bradt

0 ——— 200m
0 ——— 200yds

Ak Serai
Complex

Amir Timur
Park

MALIK AZHDAR

Amir Timur

RAVNAKI

Maqom
Museum

Bek (2km)

2

PUSHKIN

Chubin
Madrasa

Koba
Madrasa

IPAK YULI

Chorsu

Bazaar

Ipak Yuli $

For listings, see page 185

🛏 **Where to stay**
1 Hotel Shakhrisabz Yulduzi
2 Kesh Palace

Off map
Bek
Orient Star
Ulug Beg Hotel & Spa

✖ **Where to eat and drink**
3 Coffee House Sardoba
4 Maysa

KHOVUZI MARDOI

Dor at-Tilyavat
Complex

3

Dor as-Siadat
Complex

Bus station,
Lyangar Ata Mausoleum,
Kok Su Gorge, Bukhara

4

hats, socks and other gift items. The same is true at the Ak Serai, where there are a number of stalls and also usually artists displaying their paintings. One of these artists also has a gallery inside Hotel Shakhrisabz Yulduzi (page 185).

WHAT TO SEE AND DO Shakhrisabz has a wealth of historical sites, and they are far less visited than the big-name draws of Samarkand and Bukhara. All of the sites mentioned here are open between 09.00 and 18.00, unless otherwise stated. All of Shakhrisabz's tourist sites are in the new pedestrian park, stretching from the Dor at-Tilyavat Complex to the Ak Serai. Half-day tours cost around US$15 per person and can be booked through Hotel Shakhrisabz Yulduzi (page 185).

Dor at-Tilyavat Complex (US$1) This holy site (its name means Abode of Reverence) dates from the 1374 construction of the tomb of Sheikh Shamsiddin Kulyol, a revered Sufi teacher who is credited with converting the Chagtai tribes to Islam; he was joined by various other holy men, and this became an important destination for pilgrimages. On the left/east side of the courtyard (lined with craft stalls) are two heavily restored blue-domed mausoleums (known as the Kosh-Gumbaz or Double Dome): the **Mausoleum of Shamsiddin Kulyol** to the left, and the **Gumbazi Seidon** (dome of the Sayyids) to the right, marking the graves of various Timurid-era reverends.

The aptly-named **Kok-Gumbaz** (Blue Dome), on the right side of the courtyard, was built by Timur's grandson Ulug Beg in 1434–35, not long after his father had moved the centre of Timurid power from Samarkand to Herat, and is the town's main mosque. On the site of an older, Karakhanid-era mosque, it once had a dome larger than that of the Bibi Khanym Mosque in Samarkand, as well as 40 domed galleries to house additional worshippers. The original dome collapsed in the late 18th century, but was rebuilt 200 years later.

On either side of the Kok-Gumbaz are are two porches with vaulted ceilings on whitewashed pillars; a few traditional stonemasons may be working here when you visit, mostly producing elaborately carved headstones, some of which include realistic depictions of the deceased. Watching them work is mesmerising and the chink-chink of their chisels against the marble echoes back from the curved roof. Removing your shoes and stepping across the threshold, you'll find the interior mosque of the complex cool and calm, particularly when compared with the heat of the courtyard outside. The interior decoration, showing signs of damp in places, may come across as a little garish, but it should not be forgotten that it would always have been brightly painted and tiled; the only change is in the quality of the workmanship and its maintenance.

Dor as-Siadat Complex (Free) Just east of the Dor at-Tilyavat stands the Dor as-Siadat (Abode of Might), the family necropolis built by Timur himself when his eldest son, Jahangir, died in 1376. It's a pleasant spot with plenty of mature trees. Construction of the necropolis took 25 years, and a second son, Omar, is also buried there. It is thought that Timur also wished to be entombed here, and a crypt discovered by archaeologists beneath the floors of the memorial mosque supports this idea, though he was ultimately interred at the Gur-i Amir in Samarkand (page 176). It's a fairly plain edifice, with most of the external tiling missing.

On the mausoleum's northern side is the **Hazrati Imam Mosque**, a 19th-century building with an attractive wooden *aivan* (veranda). Though it is not explicitly named in honour of one particular man, the inscription across the doors perhaps links it to Abu Abdulla Muhammad ibn Nasr al Keshi, a local holy man in the 9th century.

Ak Serai Complex At the northern end of Ipak Yuli is Timur's Ak Serai (or Ok Saroy; White Palace), quite possibly the largest and most impressive building he commissioned. The portal alone would have reached 50m in height and been flanked by a pair of tapered minarets, each 65m tall. Construction of the palace

6

began in 1380 and it took the labourers and artisans, drawn from across the Timurid Empire, 24 years to complete. According to the Castillian ambassador Clavijo, the rear courtyard was 300 paces wide (in all an estimated 1.6ha) and the reception halls were painted azure blue and richly gilded. It must have been quite a sight.

Envisaging the scale and might of this structure today requires a little imagination. In their attempt to wipe out memory of the Timurids (the legend is that Abdullah Khan was fooled by the size of the building and his horse died of exhaustion before he reached it, leaving him furious), the Shaybanids destroyed many of the original structures, leaving just 38m of the central gateway intact. This may not sound a great deal, but it still rises dramatically above the surrounding parkland and is visible from quite a distance. Unlike many of Uzbekistan's other historic sites, very little restoration work has been done here, and UNESCO's emphasis seems, quite rightly, to be more on shoring up the building than touching up its magnificent (albeit time-ravaged) tile work. This approach enables you to appreciate what is original and what is a modern interpretation of the site, far more so than is possible in Samarkand.

Immediately in front of the gates is Shakhrisabz's modern **statue of Amir Timur**. It's big, it's brash and it probably looks nothing like the man himself, but every bride and groom in the vicinity, plus their inebriated entourages, are clamouring to have their photos taken alongside. If you stray too close, expect to be enveloped into the fold and to have a glass thrust into your hand: foreigners are popular additions to wedding photographs, it seems, even if you've previously never met.

A small section of Shakhrisabz's mud-brick **city walls** has been rebuilt just behind the gateway. Originally at least 8m thick and 11m high, and broken up with a tower or archway every 50m, they must have been an imposing prospect for any would-be invader. The buildings abutting the walls have largely been demolished and more sections are being rebuilt as part of the town's beautification programme, but a relatively authentic section survives just east of the gateway.

Other sites in Shakhrisabz Three other sites in the city are worthy of mention. In the middle of the park is the **Chorsu**, a trading dome built in 1602 that was still in use until the bazaar was cleared away in recent years. The external dome covers an octagonal hall, which is surrounded by four smaller domes, each with its own portal.

Closer to Ak Serai, the **Chubin Madrasa** (3 Ipak Yuli; ℡ 75 522 0837; w shahrisabz.parusinfo.com/en; ⊕ 09.00–18.00 Tue–Sun; US$2) dates from the late 17th century. It was restored in the 1990s, the theological students and their teachers long gone; in their place is a small history museum with local archaeological finds including rather fine relics from a Zoroastrian ossuary, a war drum, a medieval polo mallet and ball, and a scale model of Shakhrisabz as it would have looked in its Timurid heyday.

A little to the north, the communist Palace of Culture now houses the **Maqom Museum**, dedicated to Uzbek classical music; it officially opened in September 2018, but we were unable to get in when we visited the following month.

AROUND SHAKHRISABZ In the Kok Su Gorge, 60km south of Shakhrisabz, is the **Langar Ata Mausoleum**, the final resting place of 15th- and 16th-century sheikhs from the Iskiya order, rivals to the dominant Naqshbandi order, who drove them out of Samarkand during the Timurid period. On a hilltop above the small village of Langar, the mausoleum is clearly visible from all around, and the mosque by its side once held both an early Qu'ran and a cloak said to belong to the Prophet

THE GISSAR STATE NATURE RESERVE

The Gissar State Nature Reserve (75 522 7669; w hisor.uz/en) is an 80,000ha site in the Gissar-Alai range at the western end of the Pamir-Alay mountain system, which begins around 40km to the east of Shakhrisabz. Since 2008, it has been on UNESCO's Tentative List for inclusion as a World Heritage Site on account of its combination of unique geological outcroppings, biodiversity and ancient historical sites.

The territory of the reserve, which was formed in 1985 when the Kyzyksui and Mirakin reserves were merged, comprises gorges, caverns, small glaciers, streams and waterfalls, so it is exceptionally photogenic. There is very little human habitation in this part of Uzbekistan, so the indigenous wildlife thrives: there are snow leopards (which have been successfully photographed with the use of camera traps), marmots, Tolai hares and porcupines. The mixed habitats – forest, shrub, grassland, rocky areas and wetland – attract diverse birdlife, including large birds of prey. You can expect to see Himalayan snowcock, Hume's lark and yellow-billed chough, and may be lucky enough to spot the endangered saker falcon and near-threatened cinereous vulture and Himalayan griffon.

To date, more than 800 species of flora have been recorded in the reserve, and experts estimate that there may be as many as 300 more to find. Scientists working in the reserve are collaborating with the National University of Uzbekistan, as well as local universities in Samarkand and Karshi, to create a gene pool of the reserve's flora and fauna. They are also monitoring changes in the reserve's ecosystem, and trying to identify unique and fast-disappearing species.

Of historic interest (and hence of interest to UNESCO) are a dinosaur's footprint, a pilgrimage site dedicated to the Muslim saint Khodji Daud and a vast subterranean lake in a natural cavern, which was settled in the Stone Age and occupied until about the 3rd century BC. All of these sites are accessible if you have a knowledgeable guide (page 96) and are prepared to hike.

There is currently nowhere to stay within the reserve, and no public transport to reach it. You will need to travel to Shakhrisabz (page 184), and then hire a taxi to take you on to the reserve. The journey to the edge of the park will take about an hour.

The UNESCO bid also includes the **Kitob State Geological Reserve**, in the mountains to the northeast of Shakhrisabz, which features beautiful mountain scenery including waterfalls and caves, rare varieties of tulips, and eagles and bears.

Muhammad. These artefacts have sadly long since been removed, but it's still worth stopping off for half an hour, if only to break the journey south. You'll need your own transport to reach here – turn off the M39 to the southeast after around 20km.

KARSHI

The capital of Qashqa Darya Province, this small city of 200,000 people is a regional hub owing to the proximity of natural-gas plants and the numerous cotton fields that surround it, all of which are irrigated with water diverted from the Amu Darya. The city has Sogdian roots, but it is the surviving medieval madrasas, mausoleums and mosques, not to mention a reputation for producing finely worked flat-weave carpets, that attract an occasional tourist.

HISTORY There have been three cities on this site: Sogdian Nakhshab, the Arab Nasaf, and lastly Karshi, which took its name from the two 14th-century palaces built by the Mongol khans. Timur erected the city's citadel and protective moat in 1364; successive rulers extended the city walls and constructed *caravanserais*, gardens and religious buildings.

Karshi was annexed by the Russians in 1868, and the documents reducing Bukhara to merely a Russian protectorate were signed in the city five years later.

After a long hiatus, Karshi emerged briefly to international attention following the US invasion of Afghanistan as the site of the Khanabad airbase, needed to supply US troops. This was forced to close in 2005 following US criticism of the Andijan massacre (see box, page 138) and was replaced with the Manas airbase outside Bishkek in Kyrgyzstan.

GETTING THERE AND AROUND Karshi is 455km southwest of Tashkent (an 8-hour **drive** via Samarkand) and 160km southeast of Bukhara. The road to Bukhara is slow, and in parts rough. The **main bus station** is about 5km southwest of the city centre on Nasaf, a few hundred metres east from the first lights north of the station. It is reached by minibuses 20 and 32 from the city centre, and from here there are regular buses, minibuses and shared taxis to Bukhara, Shakhrisabz and Termez. By shared taxi, expect to haggle hard and end up paying US$8–10 to Bukhara (2hrs), US$6 to Shakhrisabz (1hr) and US$10 to Termez (4hrs); as ever, buses and minibuses are much slower and much cheaper. Minibuses and shared taxis for Samarkand and Tashkent (4hrs; US$15) wait at the junction of the A378 and A380, 3km north of the centre. From the bazaar, minibus 12 runs past the war memorial and the Kok Gumbaz Mosque.

The **train station** is at the end of Karimov (formerly O'zbekiston), 5km south of the centre and reached by bus number 1. There are daily departures to Samarkand (1½hrs), Tashkent (3½–6hrs), Shakhrisabz (1hr) and Termez (7hrs).

Flying used to be an option, but the introduction of high-speed trains has led to the abandonment of flights from Tashkent (although Ural Airlines and Nordwind fly weekly from Moscow; page 49). The airport is in the southwest of the town, past the railway tracks, and is reached by minibus number 4. The Karshi–Khanabad military airbase is just east of town, and it's possible that the civil airport may move there.

TOUR OPERATORS
Avia Marka 2 Mustakillik; m 93 722 0900. Airline tickets & other transport bookings.
City Tour 216 Karimov; ✆ 75 221 3003; m 91 462 3003. Basic travel agency. No English is spoken.

Nasaf Travel Company 245 Karimov; ✆ 75 225 0665; m 97 318 3777; e nasaf.travel@gmail.com. The owners of Hotel Nasaf Travel (see opposite) also run this small, professional outfit & can arrange guided tours, onward transport & make hotel bookings.

WHERE TO STAY, EAT AND DRINK Don't expect to be impressed by Karshi's hotels and restaurants: they're functional, but certainly nothing special.

The easiest places to eat are the **restaurants** at the Nasaf Travel, Sultan and Afsona hotels ($$; see opposite), where food is inevitably bland but at least predictable. The Afsona's restaurant does a reasonable selection of salads, which goes down well if you've had your fill of *shashlik*. There are a number of unnamed *chaikhanas* in the bazaar and also to its east on Nasaf. Follow your nose and expect to eat either standing or squashed on a bench with a stranger at busy times.

🏠 **Hotel Nasaf Travel** (80 rooms) 245 Karimov; 📞 75 225 0665; e nasaf.travel@gmail. com. Renovated hotel south of the city centre. All rooms have AC, satellite TV & slow Wi-Fi, & a large restaurant ($$). **$$$**

🏠 **Sultan** (34 rooms) 254A Karimov; 📞 75 225 1010/75 225 3322; w hotelsultan.uz. This mock château, opened in 2017, is not quite as grand as it seems, but the facilities are good, with a restaurant & ATM. **$$$**

🏠 **Asila** (25 rooms) 430 Karimov; 📞 75 226 4424. The only hotel north of the centre towards the Samarkand bus station, this is an identikit modern block with comfortable rooms & a restaurant ($$). **$$**

🏠 **Hotel Afsona** (40 rooms) 5A Sherkulov; 📞 75 771 0091. Modern hotel with a candyfloss-pink exterior that would make Barbie proud. Bedrooms are a little on the small side, as are the bathrooms, but it's clean enough. Note that it is in the business district rather than the city centre. **$$**

🏠 **Hotel Sarbon** (18 rooms) 10A, Microrayon 4; 📞 75 223 0808. Comfortable hotel located south of the centre, just off Karimov. Clean AC rooms, a restaurant ($$) & bar, & a swimming pool. Good b/fast. Probably your best option in Karshi, with the adjacent (& similar) **New Sarbon** added in 2016. **$$**

OTHER PRACTICALITIES
Communications
✉ **Central post office** 19 Mustakillik; 🕐 09.00–18.00 daily. In addition to the regular postal service, you can also courier letters & parcels with EMS Falcon from here.
UCell 49 Karimov; 🕐 09.00–17.00 Mon–Sat

Medical
In addition to the options listed below, there are lots of pharmacies in town.

✚ **Multidisciplinary Medical Centre of Qashqa Darya Region** 413 Karimov; 📞 75 226 1760/75 226 0059. Your best bet for general medical issues.
✚ **Republican Centre of Science of Emergency Medicine** 5 Bashir; 📞 75 227 6616. For emergencies.

Money
$ **Agrobank** 2 Navoi; 📞 75 771 1560; 🕐 09.00– 16.00 Mon–Fri
$ **Asia Alliance Bank** Cnr Karimov & Juraev; 📞 75 225 1991/75 225 0414; 🕐 09.00–13.00 & 14.00–18.00 Mon–Fri
$ **Ipak Yuli Bank** 18 Mustakillik Sq; 📞 75 221 449; 🕐 09.00–22.00 Mon–Fri
$ **Microcredit Bank** 3 Mustakillik Sq; 📞 75 221 1364; 🕐 09.00–17.00 Mon–Fri
$ **National Bank of Uzbekistan** 219 Karimov; 📞 75 221 0077; 🕐 09.00–16.00 Mon–Fri
$ **Uzpromstroibank** 2A Khonobod; 📞 75 223 0683; 🕐 09.00–16.00 Mon–Fri

WHAT TO SEE AND DO Karshi's medieval heart is centred on the bazaar, though you have to look past the wide boulevards and the 20th century's less tasteful architectural creations if you're to get a sense of what historic Karshi would actually have been like. The well-stocked **Eski bazaar** makes a good, central spot for people watching; on Fridays you'll see numerous men flitting through in long black *chapan* coats and embroidered skull caps on their way to the Kurgancha and Chakar mosques.

Across Karimov to the southeast of the bazaar, the 16th-century Odina Mosque is built on the site of a Mongol palace and later served as a prison. Recently restored, it houses Karshi's **Regional Museum** (🕐 09.00–17.00 Tue–Sat; foreigners US$1), though this is rather underwhelming: it is the building's domed exterior that is the main attraction, though you may also want to take a look inside the *sardoba* or circular covered pool nearby as this would have been the mosque's main source of water, essential for the faithful to perform their pre-prayer ablutions.

Elsewhere on the same square are the **Bekmir** (or Rabiya), **Kalizbek** and **Khodjaev Abdul Aziz madrasas** (all built between 1904 and 1915). These somewhat forlorn structures are caught in limbo due to the government's policies on religion: they can no longer function as religious buildings, but are surplus to other requirements and hence generally lie empty, collecting dust and pigeons where once their students trod. If you ask their guardians, they will be happy to let you inside to look around, and they may even give you a tour. These buildings were more fortunate than the 18th- and 19th-century Shir-Muhammad, Khodja-Kurban and Sharap-Khodja madrasas, which were once also located here, but demolished by the Soviets, so that only the foundations remain.

A 5-minute walk southwest from the bazaar along Nasaf brings you to the attractive **Kok Gumbaz** (Blue Dome). This late-16th-century mosque is richly tiled and not dissimilar to those built by the Timurids in Shakhrisabz, though it is less heavily restored than similar mosques elsewhere.

A couple of kilometres further southwest along Nasaf (or take the number 12 minibus) is a sprawling **war monument** that remembers the Soviet casualties of the Great Patriotic War (World War II). One of the largest such monuments in central Asia, it's an eclectic mix of plaques, walkways, an eternal flame and a red star-topped tower with a series of stained-glass windows. Karshi's students tend to hang out in the square, and you'll need to co-opt one of them to locate the elderly guardian with the key to the upper levels of the tower and show you the stained-glass scenes, contrasting images of children harvesting wheat and soldiers departing for the battlefield.

Just south of the bazaar on Karimov (and opposite a striking modern swimming pool) a fort-like **military museum** is under construction; an array of jets and tanks as well as a helicopter and a YAK-40 airliner are already in place outside, and the Vatanparvlar Park is nicely planted out. The park is open to all, not just museum goers. Apparently, ice cream used to be sold from the airliner, but it remains to be seen whether that will continue. It's also worth taking a look at the 16th-century bathhouse immediately northwest of the museum, once the city's male social centre which, legend has it, was magically heated by the warmth of a single candle. It now seems to be out of use.

AROUND KARSHI On the road northwest to Bukhara, about 15km from Karshi in Fudina, is the **Khasim Ata Mosque Complex**. Entrance is free, but donations for the site's upkeep are welcome. Centred on the Mausoleum of Hazrati Khasim Ata, an 11th-century Islamic missionary and teacher, it is unusual in Uzbekistan by virtue of the fact that it is still an active religious site: the mosque is functional, and pilgrims still come to the tomb to pray. The building, which includes additional tombs from the 13th and 14th centuries, is rundown and definitely in need of repair, but the fact that it still has life makes it a welcome contrast to so many madrasas left empty and purposeless by the government's continuing crackdown on religious establishments.

Half an hour southeast of Karshi towards Termez is a second, better-preserved architectural site: the **Sultan Mir Haydor tombs**. Nearby is a medieval **covered reservoir**, the 17th-century **Namazgokh Mosque**, and a series of decorative brick-built tombs, the earliest dating from the 1200s. The tombs can appear as a land that time forgot: white-bearded men who seem almost as old as the architecture linger in the courtyard, waiting for goodness know's what.

BOYSUN

About 200km southeast from Karshi towards Termez, after crossing the southwestern spur of the Gissar Mountains, there's a left-hand turning to the small town of Boysun. Travel another 25km east and you'll reach the centre of a fascinating region that is only slowly becoming known to the outside world.

Boysun **station** is 15km southwest from the town on the Karshi–Termez railway; the day and night trains between Tashkent and Termez stop here and you'll usually find a car there waiting for passengers. For getting around, there's a central taxi rank on At-Termisi and you can also ask your hosts about hiring a car and driver.

There are few **accommodation options**, but tour companies (page 96) can book you into private homes, such as the **Abdusalom-aka Guesthouse** (Pasurkhi district, 1km south of the centre; **$**), which of course gives visitors the closest contact with local culture. If you're travelling independently and want to stay here, ask around town. The **Hotel Gaza** (10 rooms; Gaza Mahalla; m 90 912 4666; w boysun-gaza.uz; **$$**), about 1.5km from the centre on the eastern edge of town, is small and simple, but it has decent en-suite rooms, and a restaurant (**$**). The **Hotel Ferdaus** (19 Olmazor; \ 76 335 2763; m 91 909 0584; **$$**) is another decent option. A few kilometres further east (take a taxi from the town centre for US$0.40), there's a large **spa hotel** at the Omonkhona cave, known for its healing waters since perhaps the time of Alexander the Great.

It is possible to explore the villages and sites surrounding Boysun by either speaking to a tour operator (page 96) or the host at your accommodation (see above). The whole area was listed by UNESCO in 2008 as a Masterpiece of the Oral and Intangible Heritage of Humanity, owing to its well-preserved folk traditions (notably unique songs and legends) and crafts (ranging from the making of carpets, ceramics and wooden boxes to musical instruments and even yurts).

The region also has great natural and scenic value, with both Uzbekistan's highest point, **Hazrat Sultan Khan** (4,643m) and its lowest, at least 1,158m down in the **Boyundov cave**. Other caves held Palaeolithic tools and rock paintings, most notably the **Zarautsoy cave**, just south of Kyzyl Alma village. The nearby Kyzyl canyon is spectacular, as is the Derbent canyon (close to the Karshi–Termez road). You'll find rare varieties of tulips in springtime.

There's a lot more to be seen by serious hikers, or those with access to a 4x4 vehicle, such as the stunning **Hodja Gur Gur Ata escarpment**, some 30km long and dotted with caves. The huge Dark Star and Festivalnaya systems are gradually being explored by international teams, who hope they will turn out to be the world's deepest caves. It's said that all of the Boysun villages are small museums, but there is a proper museum (small, but interesting) in the **Centre for National Applied Art Centre** in Boysun itself. The **Boysun Spring festival** (🕑 late Apr or early May) is fast becoming a very important gathering, with tens of thousands of people assembling in a natural bowl of hills above the town to enjoy folk music, dance and sports (such as wrestling), and the traditional costumes and contemporary fashion inspired by folk traditions.

DENAU

After Termez, Surkhan Darya's second town is Denau, also known as Denov. It is the border town with Tajikistan when entering into the west of the country for Dushanbe and the Pamir Highway, and transiting between the two countries is the most likely reason you'll find yourself here.

The valley around Denau has a subtropical climate, which has enabled it to become a relatively successful wine-producing area and also to support a wide range of non-native plants in the R Shreder Dendrarium. The archaeological remains of two important Kushan-era cities, Kalchayan and Dalverzin Teppe, are also within easy reach of here.

GETTING THERE AND AROUND

By rail Denau is on the railway route from Tashkent to Tajikistan. Day and night trains run daily from Tashkent via Samarkand, Karshi and Denau to the border town of Sariosiyo (14½hrs; US$24). You don't have to change, just be very patient. The **railway station** is just east of the town centre, a short walk down Mustakillik.

By road Denau is well connected with other cities in Uzbekistan. Most arrivals from Tajikistan (see box, opposite) will be heading by shared taxi or minibus along the picturesque road through the hills **to Samarkand** (5hrs; US$18) via Shakhrisabz or **to Bukhara** (6hrs; US$22) via Karshi. These prices are for journeys by shared taxis; minibuses are slower and about 30% cheaper. There is also a daily bus **to Tashkent**, but it will easily take you 12–14 hours; shared taxis and minibuses are also available. Shared taxis run down the valley **to Termez** (2hrs; US$5), as do regular minibuses (2½hrs; US$2). All these options leave from Denau's bus station, 2km south of the bazaar on Rashidov. For the shared taxis you will need to haggle to get a fair price (those included above are guide prices). When in town, all the main sites are within walking distance of one another.

WHERE TO STAY, EAT AND DRINK Visitors have a distinctly limited choice of places to stay in Denau; indeed, if possible, it is best to continue on to your next destination rather than try to find a bed here. The **Hotel Denau** (cnr Mustakillik & Rashidov; **$**), is a miserable hole of a place, with horrid bathrooms and no breakfast, but it is very central. Decent mid-range options include the **Turon** (m 91 511 1131; **$$**), just south of the station on Erkliyurt and the **Asomiddin** (m 90 568 0358; **$$**), just south of the Dendrarium (west of Rashidov). About 3km north from the town centre along Rashidov, the **Hotel Euro-Asia** (\ 76 412 8002; **$$$**) is flashy and ungracious, but more comfortable.

Denau's **bazaar** is a lively place and well stocked with foodstuffs and crafts from both Uzbekistan and Tajikistan. In addition to fresh produce there is the usual array of *shashlik* stands and *chaikhanas*, all of which serve hot, tasty food for a dollar or two.

The valleys around Denau are known for their **winemaking**, in particular using the local Novbakhor and Morastel varieties of grape. Rum is also produced using sugarcane. Your best chance of tasting Denau wines or rum is in someone's home, though it is also worth asking for it in the bazaar.

OTHER PRACTICALITIES

Medical
There are plenty of pharmacies in town.

✚ **District Hospital** S Otaboev. A small hospital with only basic equipment that cannot be relied upon for emergency care.

Money
Denau has several banks that exchange money & provide Western Union services. The most conveniently located are listed below.

$ Hamkor Bank 255 Rashidov; \ 76 413 1991; ⏱ 09.00–18.00 Mon–Sat
$ National Bank of Uzbekistan 47 Mustakillik; \ 76 413 1026; ⏱ 09.00–18.00 Mon–Fri

WHAT TO SEE AND DO In the centre of Denau, close to the bazaar, the **Sayyid Atalik Madrasa** (cnr Mustakillik & Nozim Mirzoiev) dates from the 16th century and is one of the largest madrasas in central Asia. Its scale and elegant symmetry are more than ample compensation for the lack of ornamentation. The madrasa has officially been closed for renovation since 1997 but, at the time of writing, was supposedly going to reopen in 2019; however, if, when you visit, it still hasn't opened, ask at the gate for the director, Murat, who will show you every last fascinating corner. You are likely have the site to yourself; the atmosphere is somewhat eerie, as if echoing that a generation of students is missing and mourned.

A surprising discovery, just south of the centre on S Rashidov, is the **R Shreder Dendrarium** (m 94 205 4229), an arboretum with more than 1,000 species of plant brought here by scientists and official visitors from around the world. Among the more common trees, flowers and herbs, many of which are native to Uzbekistan, are also imported varieties including kauchuk, bamboo and sequoia. The arboretum also has a notable collection of persimmons: more than 200 species are represented in the garden. Stop here for an hour or two if you've overdosed on madrasas and ruins: the plants will refresh your mind.

AROUND DENAU The hinterland around Denau contains a number of intriguing sites which, though probably not worth a visit on their own, can be combined into a worthwhile day trip (arranged with a tour operator or a local driver; page 199), particularly if you are already in the area.

The ruined Fortress of Yurchi, 8km north of the city on the road from Termez, dates from the 10th century, and the author Colin Thubron visited the village while researching *The Lost Heart of Asia* in the hope of finding the burial place of the Basmachi leader and World War I Turkish war minister, Ismail Enver Pasha (see box, page 196). Thubron failed to find a trace of Enver (who likely died and was buried across the border in Tajikistan), but instead found in the village the grave of Licharov, the regional Bolshevik commander who was killed here in 1924.

Kalchayan, 10km northeast of Denau, is a Graeco-Bactrian city first settled in the 4th century BC. The Soviet archaeologist Professor Galina Pugachenkova led extensive excavations here in the mid 20th century, and found a large number of Kushan-era sculptures, many of them particularly lifelike. The variety of dress, hairstyles and ethnic features displayed in the figures reveals both the diversity of people living and trading in ancient Kalchayan, and the skill of the city's artisans. The most important finds have been taken from the site and are now displayed in the Termez Archaeological Museum (page 202) and the State Fine Arts Museum in Tashkent (page 114).

It's well worth continuing northwest up the Sangardak (or Kyzyl-Su) Valley to the 150m-high Sangardak Waterfall, located 50km from Denau near Nelu village. The highest in Uzbekistan, this is a popular picnic spot at weekends and holidays.

6

Heading south from Denau towards Termez, it's about 30km to the small town of Shurchi and neighbouring archaeological site of **Dalverzin Tepe**, a Kushan-era (1st–4th century AD) settlement that was once an important defensive site on the Surkhan Valley branch of the Silk Road. The settlement, which was protected by walls 10m thick, housed an important and wealthy Buddhist complex; archaeologists have unearthed the remains of a *stupa*, prayer hall and also the so-called King's Room, a hall richly decorated with sculptures that show both Buddhist and Hellenistic influences. The neighbouring complex contained a Bactrian temple, numerous statues of the Buddha and bodhisattvas and, remarkably, a treasure hoard of gold and silver items, many of them set with precious stones. The total hoard weighed in at 36kg, and the most important items are now exhibited at museums in Tashkent and in Russia.

The Dalverzin Tepe site is rather better preserved than Kalchayan; significant portions of the city wall are still clearly visible, as is the Buddhist temple and part of a Bactrian shrine. There's no charge to enter and no set opening times, though you'll need to go during daylight hours to stand a chance of seeing anything.

ENVER PASHA

In the dying days of the Ottoman Empire, a young revolutionary called Ismail Enver cut his military teeth fighting guerrillas in the Balkans, then played a key role in the Young Turks Revolution of 1908; now known as Enver Pasha, he rose to prominence as a rather ineffective minister of war during World War I. His rallying cry to his troops was 'war until final victory'.

When the Russian Revolution took place in 1917, Turkey's Committee of Union and Progress (CUP), of which Enver was a founding member, befriended the Bolsheviks and sent their own troops into the Caucasus, where a power vacuum had been created by the withdrawal of tsarist forces. Enver named his new army the Army of Islam.

Enver's fortunes changed with Turkey's defeat in World War I. He fled into exile, was court-martialled *in absentia* for acting beyond his official remit (by instigating the genocide of Armenian troops in the Ottoman army), and condemned to death. Enver went first to Germany, was rejected by Mustafa Kemal's Turkish revolutionaries, then offered his services to the Bolsheviks, hoping to incite the Muslim world to join the revolution.

Lenin dispatched Enver first to Bukhara in 1921, to help defeat the Basmachi revolt. Driven by his pan-Turkic dreams, Enver switched sides and joined the Basmachi in the hills of Surkhan Darya. He led a number of successful attacks (notably on Bukhara and Dushanbe), proving far better as a leader of guerrillas than he had been of regular armies, and became the Basmachis' military commander (1921–22).

Styling himself Emir of Turkestan, in effect a rival to the Emir of Bukhara, Enver soon lost the support of his men and was cornered and killed by the Bolsheviks in the summer of 1922, probably in what is now Tajikistan. A truce had been called for Eid, but an informant betrayed Enver's location. He attempted to defend himself with a single machine gun but was shot by a sniper's bullet. The Basmachi hid his body to prevent its capture, and it is likely that it was buried more than once. A body thought to be Enver Pasha's remained in Tajikistan until the Turkish government carted it back to Istanbul for a state funeral in 1996.

TERMEZ

The city of Termez is the final frontier. Few foreigners venture this far south, save those heading across the border into Afghanistan, and so making the journey seems like quite an adventure regardless of whether you are continuing across the border or not. The city is home to a population of 15,000 people, including large numbers of Tajiks and Afghans, and its history stretches back some 2,500 years. From ancient Buddhist monasteries to medieval mausoleums, there is plenty to see, all nestled in the sweeping curve of the mighty Amu Darya.

HISTORY Termez marks the border between Uzbekistan and Afghanistan, and its history is therefore inevitably caught up with developments in both territories. In the wake of Alexander the Great's conquest, Greek troops built a line of fortifications along the banks of the Oxus, and Termez grew up at a crossing point on the river. A Graeco-Bactrian city, it thrived financially, culturally and spiritually at the meeting point of Mediterranean, Indian, Persian, Chinese and central Asian civilisations. Termez became a centre for Buddhism and for Gandharan art, a fusion of Indian and Hellenistic styles.

The Bactrian state eventually fractured and slid into decline, torn apart by warring factions. The Arab general Musa ibn Qasim seized Termez in AD689 and proclaimed himself king, only to be overthrown by Caliph Uthman in AD704. From then on, Termez began to look north to central Asia rather than south to Afghanistan.

In the 12th century Termez slipped swiftly through the hands of the Karakhanids, Seljuks, Ghaznavids, Gurids and Khorezmshah and thence into the clutches of Genghis Khan. A census was taken of the population, and every man, woman and child listed on it was killed. The bulk of the city walls was demolished and flung into the Oxus. Old Termez would never recover.

New Termez rose up in the 14th century: Ibn Battuta visited here on his travels, Timur built a line of pontoons across the Oxus to boost trade (and allow it to be taxed) and the city's perfume and soaps were particularly valuable commodities.

The third and final city of Termez was created after 1894, a Russian garrison town on the southernmost border of the Russian Empire. A naval base was built on the river at nearby Chardzhou, and military boats monitored the border closely. The military would remain Termez's *raison d'être*, first as the entry point for the Soviet invasion of Afghanistan in 1979 and then for fuel, supplies and aid crossing the railway bridge after the US-led invasion in 2001.

GETTING THERE AND AWAY Termez is an intriguing destination, but a long way from anywhere, and this will inevitably influence your itinerary and preferred mode(s) of transport. For reference purposes, it is 375km from Samarkand, 380km from Bukhara, 676km from Tashkent, 855km from Khiva, and a whopping 1,100km from Namangan.

By air There are five direct flights a week to Tashkent with **Uzbekistan Airways** (1hr 20min; US$40; see ad, 3rd colour section), with reasonable connections across the rest of Uzbekistan and to Russia (page 49). The **airport** is a 20-minute drive northeast of the city, and can be reached either by taxi or by taking minibus number 11 from the bazaar on Termezi.

Tickets are available from Aviakassas in the town centre and the ticketing desk at the airport.

ALEXANDER THE GREAT AND UZBEKISTAN   *Bijan Omrani*

Alexander the Great spent around two years in Uzbekistan during his conquest of the Achaemenid Persian Empire. He experienced there not just some of the most difficult fighting of the entire campaign, but also some of the most remarkable events of his expedition into Asia.

Through 330BC, Alexander had chased the Persian nobleman Bessus around Afghanistan. Bessus was leading the Persian resistance to Alexander, and Alexander had to capture him to ensure the complete submission of the Persian Empire. In 329BC, Alexander crossed the Oxus after leaving the Afghan city of Balkh, and was shortly able to capture and execute Bessus.

However, Alexander remained in the region to consolidate his power. Perhaps foolishly, he did not make use of his natural allies in the region. Shortly after crossing the Oxus he discovered a town that was inhabited by Greeks, who welcomed him wholeheartedly. However, on discovering that they had collaborated with the Persians when they had invaded Greece in 480BC, he executed the entire settlement and levelled it to the ground. Proceeding northward, he captured Samarkand (page 158) and then reached the Syr Darya (River Jaxartes) where he founded Alexandria Eschate, 'Alexandria-the-Farthest', modern-day Khojend in Tajikistan.

Despite this immediate success, there was considerable disquiet in the area. Alexander faced a number of uprisings from the indigenous Sogdians and Scythian tribesmen. They were able to employ guerrilla hit-and-run tactics, again relying on their mastery of horsemanship and archery to strike at his columns

By rail Termez's **railway station** is at the northern end of Termezi, an easy walk from the town centre. Buy tickets from the Kassa to the left (west of the station) (⏱ 08.00–13.00 & 14.00–20.00 daily). Train 379/380 (depending upon the direction of travel) runs overnight to Tashkent (13½hrs; Platskartny tickets from US$10) and stops en route at Karshi and Samarkand. There are also two local trains a day to Denau and Sariosiyo (4hrs; US$2), where you can cross the border into Tajikistan.

By road Termez's **main bus station** is just west of town on the road towards Karshi; it's reached by minibuses 2, 7 and 8 from the centre. The city is pretty well connected with other destinations in Uzbekistan, though the journeys are inevitably long.

Buses leave early in the morning to Samarkand (8hrs; US$8) and Tashkent (16hrs; US$17) and **shared taxis** run the same route throughout the day in half the time but at twice the price. To reach Bukhara, you'll need to take a shared taxi to Karshi (4hrs; US$8) and pick up westward transport there. Beyond Karshi, the road is slow, and in parts rough. Even in your own vehicle, you will should allow at least 8 hours for the drive. Heading northeast to Denau (for Tajikistan), you have the choice of a minibus (US$2) or shared taxi (US$5), both taking around 2 hours.

GETTING AROUND Termez's **public transport** system is actually quite well organised, with buses, minibuses and minivans linking most parts of the city where you're likely to venture. It costs around US$0.30 to reach the mausoleum, and less for travel around town. The following minibus routes are most helpful for visitors:

Minibus 4   Along Termezi to the train station
Minibus 11   Yubileyniy Bazaar to the airport

from a distance. Alexander had not faced this sort of warfare before, and he had to develop new tactics to defeat the nomadic warriors, including the combined use of catapults and archers, as well as hunting his opponents down to their fortresses and carrying out a conventional campaign of sieges. Despite being badly injured and suffering from dysentery, Alexander was able to lead his men to a notable success against the Scythians on the Syr Darya River.

As Alexander gained the upper hand, his opponents rallied at a fortress called the Sogdian Rock on top of a large escarpment. Its site is not known for certain, but it is thought to be near Samarkand. They thought it impregnable, and taunted Alexander that he would need soldiers with wings to capture it. Alexander was so irked by their jibes that he called for volunteers to scale the sheer cliffs up to the fortress. Three hundred men came forward and, using ropes and tent pegs, they made the ascent in the dead of night. Although 30 were lost in the climb, by morning they were inside the fortress. Alexander's herald shouted that they had found the soldiers with wings, and the defenders, amazed, surrendered immediately.

According to Greek historians, Alexander met on the rock a princess named Roxane, the daughter of one of the local rulers, Oxyartes. They record that he fell in love with her on sight and arranged a marriage with her. Having made such an alliance, he was ready to proceed out of Uzbek lands on his attempt to conquer India. The legend of Roxane still lives today, and many distinguished families in the region claim descent from the union of Alexander and Roxane.

| **Minibus 265** | Yubileyniy Bazaar to Namuna (for the Sultan Saodat Mausoleums) |
| **Minibuses 12 & 305** | Yubileyniy Bazaar to the Mausoleum of al Hakkim al Termezi, via the rail and bus stations |

So long as the weather is not too hot (temperatures here sear in the summer months), it is also quite feasible to explore the central areas of Termez **on foot**. Hotel Asson, the bazaar and the Termez Archaeological Museum are just a couple of blocks away from one another, and if you walk through the park rather than around it, it is only another 5–10 minutes on to Hotel Meridian.

Travel agents (see below) in the town can arrange a **car and driver** if you want private transport to get between the outlying historical sites, but it doesn't come particularly cheap: budget US$50–60 per day depending on your itinerary.

TOUR OPERATORS Various companies can provide guided tours in a variety of languages, can make transport and accommodation bookings, and should be able to arrange permits to visit sites in the border zone.

Asia Termez Travel 168 Sultan Saodat; m 91 585 3551; w http://asiatravel.ws/en

Termez Turism Travel 16 A Navoi, flat 7; m 93 798 5000; w termeztravel.com

 WHERE TO STAY *Map, page 201*
Termez is surprisingly well equipped with hotels, and some of them are even quite pleasant places to stay: no mean feat for a provincial town without a significant footfall of tourists!

Hotel Asson (85 rooms) 27 Termezi; 76 224 4366; w asson-hotel.com. Next to the archaeological museum, the Asson has perhaps a little more character than the Meridian (see below) & is easier on the pocket. It is, however, rather dark & gloomy & no English is spoken. The outdoor swimming pool is a real bonus in summer, even if it looks rather rundown. Non-residents can pay to use the pool or sauna. **$$$**

Hotel Meridian (54 rooms) 23 Alpomysh; 76 225 1286; m 95 502 4555; e meridian_hotel@mail.ru; w hotelmeridiantermez.uz. The best hotel in Termez is this modern, mid-sized option with large, clean (but somewhat tired) rooms. All rooms have AC, which is essential in summer & there is a shower over the bath in the bathrooms. It was founded by a German company, so the staff speak a few words of German & other European languages. There is a mediocre restaurant in the lobby & a bar & gym. Take your drink up on to the rooftop terrace for views across Termez. **$$$**

Hotel Sharq 28 Barkamol; 76 223 4613; e mmz.uzb@inbox.ru. Soviet-era hotel that has fortunately undergone a thorough renovation. All rooms have AC & the dbl rooms are large: you might think about taking one even if you're on your own. B/fast isn't great, but there's a sauna. **$$**

Hotel Ulugbek (37 rooms) 13 Barkamol; 76 223 1692; e hotel_ulugbek@mail.ru. Comfortable, family-run hotel with large, clean AC rooms & helpful staff. **$$**

Surkhon (95 rooms) 9A Termezi; 76 224 0101/76 224 1717; e surxonhotel@mail.ru; w surxonhotel.uz. A fairly grand tower block (refurbished in 2018) with 4 classes of room (all AC), restaurant (**$$**) & a terrace bar. **$$**

Tennis Court Rooms 29B Termezi. The sports centre opposite the archaeological museum (page 202) may have very basic dorm beds available (ask at the more modern sports hall on the east side of the tennis club). It is targeted at athletes & students rather than tourists, so there's no service to speak of, but it's the cheapest option in town. **$**

✕ WHERE TO EAT AND DRINK *Map, opposite*

The restaurant at Hotel Meridian (see above) is open 24/7, so if you're craving something bland covered in mayonnaise at 03.00 then this is the place for you (**$**). At more sociable hours it's a better bet to wander out into the city, as prices tend to be lower and flavours a little more distinct. There's a row of clean, modern fast-food places opposite the bazaar on Termezi, such as **ASL Burger** (**$**), **Lavash Center** (**$**) and **City Burger** (**$**), but we particularly recommend the following:

✕ **Malika Gold** A Navoi; ⊕ 11.00–23.00 daily. Large, clean restaurant popular with tour groups, with a private dining room seating 14. The menu includes good, fresh salads, *manti*, noodle soups & tasty kebabs, all of which can be washed down with beer or vodka. **$$$**

✳ ✘ **Azizbek Restaurant** 48 A Navoi; ☏ 76 225 2034; ⏱ 11.00–23.00 daily. Our favourite place in town is this sprawling restaurant with indoor & outdoor space & even its own (slightly seedy) disco. Grab a patio chair & table, order a Baltica beer & choose from a wide menu of salads, different *shashliks*, cutlets & other mixed grills. English isn't spoken, but it is easy to make yourself understood: if you're really struggling, just point to the neighbouring table's dinner & tuck in to the same. Whatever it is, it'll surely be tasty. **$$–$$$**

✘ **Chorsu Oshkhasi** Cnr Termezi & Jurabaev; ⏱ noon–22.00 daily. A classic *plov* place, this is rather more rough & ready than Azizbek (see left), but unless you're staying at the Hotel Meridian, it's undoubtedly in a better location, & you can recline on tea beds out front. **$$**

☕ **Feredun Café** 16/7 Navoi; ☏ 76 225 1188; m 90 294 3638; ⏱ 08.00–22.00 daily. A relatively glitzy Western-style café-restaurant, all glass & stainless steel – come for coffee, snacks or a light meal. **$$**

☕ **Choixona** Dostlyk Park. If you just want a tea, coffee or small snack, try this friendly café on the edge of Dostlyk Park. It's shady & a very pleasant spot to relax for an hour or more. **$**

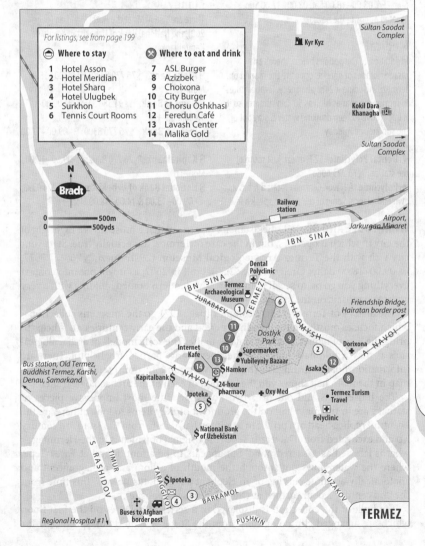

For listings, see from page 199

🛏 **Where to stay**
1 Hotel Asson
2 Hotel Meridian
3 Hotel Sharq
4 Hotel Ulugbek
5 Surkhon
6 Tennis Court Rooms

✘ **Where to eat and drink**
7 ASL Burger
8 Azizbek
9 Choixona
10 City Burger
11 Chorsu Oshkhasi
12 Feredun Café
13 Lavash Center
14 Malika Gold

TERMEZ

SHOPPING The main **Yubileyniy Bazaar** is on Termezi, very close to Hotel Asson but on the opposite side of the street. It's primarily for the local population rather than tourists, so most of the shops sell foodstuffs and household goods. On the left-hand side of the bazaar there is also a large, Western-style **supermarket**, which is a good place to go if you want to buy bottled water and soft drinks, packeted goods, fresh bread, etc. Unlike in the bazaar, prices in the supermarket are fixed.

OTHER PRACTICALITIES
Communications
✉ **Central post office** Cnr Taraggiyot (formerly Tashkent) & Barkamol (formerly Xo'jaev); ⏱ 08.00–noon & 13.00–17.00 Mon–Fri
🖥 **Internet Kafe** Termezi; ⏱ 08.00–22.00 Mon–Fri, 08.00–18.00 Sat, 08.00–17.00 Sun. Located opposite the bazaar.

Medical
In addition to the options below, there's an insane number of *aptekas* opposite the market on Termezi, including a 24hr pharmacy. Temperatures in Termez can soar as high as 50°C in summer, so it is imperative to keep drinking water & stay out of the sun around midday.

✚ **Dental Polyclinic** 12 Termezi, just south of the station; ☎76 223 6066
✚ **Polyclinic** A Navoi. Centrally located & has its own ambulance. Some of the doctors speak a few words of English, & though conditions are very basic, the standard of care provided is admirable.
✚ **Regional Hospital #1** 2 Chanishev; ☎76 223 6203. The main hospital.

Money
There are Visa ATMs at the Hotel Meridian (page 200), the National Bank of Uzbekistan & outside Kapitalbank.

$ **Asaka Bank** ☎76 770 8220; ⏱ 09.00–16.00 Mon–Fri
$ **Hamkor Bank** m 91 580 3159; ⏱ 09.00–18.00 Mon–Fri
$ **Ipoteka Bank** ☎76 770 8300; ⏱ 09.00–17.00 Mon–Fri
$ **Kapitalbank** ☎76 770 8202; ⏱ 09.00–17.00 Mon–Fri
$ **National Bank of Uzbekistan** ☎76 224 0398; ⏱ 09.00–13.00 & 14.00–18.00 Mon–Fri

WHAT TO SEE AND DO In Uzbekistan, it's rare to say that a museum is a highlight of the city in which it operates, but in the case of Termez, it is actually true. Start your city visit with the **Termez Archaeological Museum** (29 Termezi; ☎ 76 227 3017; ⏱ 09.00–18.00 daily; foreigners US$2.50), built in 2002, as it will put into context everything you go on to see. It is an impressive modern domed building with a very attractive mosaic on the façade.

The history of Termez is quite complex (page 197), so the museum's collection – which focuses mostly on the Buddhist period and the early centuries AD – helps to bring the lists of names, places and dates to life. The scale models of archaeological sites as they would have looked in their heyday are particularly helpful. There are information boards in English (but with very random transliteration) and a 3D map in the main hall shows you the location of each of the archaeological sites.

The museum is laid out over two floors, and the most impressive pieces of statuary are in the main hall on the ground floor. Key items to look at here are the beautiful replica head of a prince in a pointed hat, dating from the 1st to 3rd century AD and excavated from Dalverzin Tepe (the original of which is in the Hermitage); what is labelled as a 'sacred pond' but appears to be a font, found at Fayaz Tepe, where the water flows out through the mouth of a lion; and a magnificent and anatomically accurate carving of an elephant among lotus flowers, this time from the 2nd century AD, unearthed at Old Termez (see opposite).

The bulk of the collection is displayed in a series of galleries on the first floor, which are arranged chronologically from the Stone Age on. Look specifically for the well-preserved Bronze Age ceramics from Buston and Jarkutan; head, hand and foot fragments of Buddhas from Fayaz Tepe; and the stone statuette of a Bactrian virgin (2nd century AD). There are also small pieces of the gloriously vivid wall paintings recovered from Balalyk Tepe and Tavka Kurgan: they're remarkable for their clarity and state of preservation, as well as for the insight they give into life on the Silk Road in the 5th and 6th centuries.

Fired up and inspired (and hopefully a little better informed), it is time to get out of the modern city centre. **Old Termez** is 6km to the northwest, just off the main road to Karshi and accessible by the minibuses listed on page 198. Only small sections of the walls of the early medieval citadel remain – the Mongols certainly knew how to raze a town – but you can still get an idea of the scale and strength of this settlement, which once hosted not only houses, shops and bazaars, but also a mint, *caravanserais*, orchards and a sophisticated network of irrigation canals.

Also in Old Termez is the 15th-century, mud-brick-built **Mausoleum of al Hakkim al Termezi** (🕐 daily; free), a Sufi saint, jurist and writer who died in Termez in AD859. Much of what you see here was built at the instigation of Timur's son, Shah Rukh, though there have been a series of structures on the site since at least the 10th century. A 5-minute drive north of Termez's main bus station, a tree-lined road leads through fake historic walls to a car park and a porch, into shady and beautifully maintained **gardens**: a popular destination for young couples and families that has recently been massively expanded. After you've passed the museum (US$1), an outpost of the main archaeological museum in town (see opposite), turn left towards the plain brick mausoleum itself, replete with a large, marble tombstone (a 15th-century replacement) and 14th-century extensions. A large chunk of the tomb is missing, purportedly taken by British archaeologists for display in the British Museum.

If you come on a Wednesday, expect to find the site packed as the faithful (and also the peckish) come to pray to al Hakkim (meaning 'the wise') and to eat the free mutton and tea doled out for them at lunchtime. The food is sponsored by local businessmen and you are welcome (and indeed encouraged) to join them in this feast. Expect to be fed until you're ready to burst, to be grilled mercilessly on your home, your family and what you earn, and to have your picture taken with absolutely everyone. There is, as they say, really no such thing as a free lunch.

A further 2–3km along the main road (with regular minibuses and taxis) brings you to **Buddhist Termez**, which also spreads out a little to the east; drivers in the mausoleum car park will offer to bring you out here. The oldest of the three sites (and possibly the oldest building in Uzbekistan still standing) is the **Zurmala Tower**, a brick-built structure 16m high that dates from the 1st to 2nd century AD. It is the only remaining part of a vast Buddhist *stupa* (mound containing relics) that would originally have been clad in stone and richly decorated, an expensive and labour-intensive design that demonstrates the significance of Termez as a Buddhist centre. There is no road access to the tower, and the closest stopping place on the road is about 200m away, with a potentially waterlogged cotton field in between. If you want to get up close, therefore, be prepared for wet feet and muddy trousers.

Caught in the riverside border zone just north of the mausoleum is **Kara Tepe**, a rock-cut Buddhist temple complex that is unique in this region. It was founded in the early 2nd century AD, on three low hills – there are cave cells and the remains of others built of mud bricks, as well as some small *stupas*. It was abandoned from the 4th century on, and the caves were used for burials. Owing to its sensitive location (emphasised by the presence of an intimidating electric fence) you should apply for a permit at least 40 days in advance, through a tour company (page 199). You can also ask the Termez Archaeological Museum (page 202) for an update on the current situation. If you are prevented from going, a short video of the site is online at **w** tours-tv.com/en/kara-tepe_monastery.

The same applies to the **old port**, to the south of the mausoleum, for Termez took advantage of water trade on the Amu Darya as well as caravans travelling by road. Unfortunately, the new security wall prevents you from accessing the site, though in places you may be able to see across the wall. The archaeological remains here include an expansive wharf, customs house and rest house. Owing to the proximity of the border and consequent sensitivity of the site, assess the situation carefully before taking a picture and keep your camera out of sight.

Rather more accessible, and fortunately no less interesting, is **Fayaz Tepe** (open access), a slightly grander Buddhist monastery and temple complex. Though the majority of the site dates from the 3rd century AD, the oldest part – the *stupa* protected beneath a modern dome and visible only through the window – is probably 400 years older than that. The *stupa*, which is a fraction of its original size (only the inner part survives) stood on the northern side of the temple courtyard, which was flanked to the east by the main refectory, and to the west by the monks' living quarters.

Among the usual artefacts excavated here (many of which are on show in the Termez Archaeological Museum, along with a model of the site; page 202), archaeologists discovered the remains of a 2km-long aqueduct that would once have carried water to the monastery straight from the Amu Darya River. Fragments of pottery containing Brahmi, Punjabi, Kharoshti and Bactrian scripts confirm that this was a truly international site, with visitors to the monastery coming from across the known world.

A visitor centre explaining the significance of both Kara Tepe and Fayaz Tepe is planned and is likely to be funded and executed by UNESCO and the Japanese government. There is, however, as yet no scheduled date for this to happen.

AROUND TERMEZ
Kyr Kyz Just before the airport, to the northeast of Termez, is the intriguingly named Kyr Kyz: the 40 Girls Fortress. The story behind the name has sadly been lost in the mists of time, but the options include 40 daughters, 40 virgins or 40 girls in a harem variously abstaining, avenging or procreating depending on the fantasy of the particular storyteller. Let your imagination run wild.

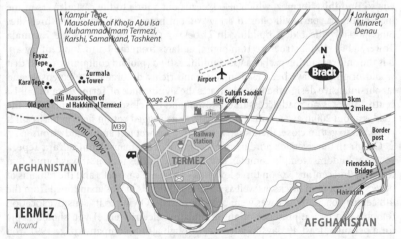

Regardless of quite what they were up to, the Kyr Kyz dates from the 9th century, and it is not actually a fortress at all: archaeologists believe it was either a substantial *caravanserai*, or a Samanid-era summer palace. The architecture is typical of structures built in this region just prior to the Arab invasion. Thick, mud-brick walls ran 54m on each side of a square and encompassed some 50 rooms over two floors. Enough remains that you can wander from one obvious room to the next and get a sense of the impressive scale of the place. One section of the façade has been restored, so you can compare easily the old and the new. Kyr Kyz attracts few visitors, so it is likely that you will have the site to yourself. It's about 200m south of the minibus route to Sultan Saodat (number 265; 10–15min), a short distance west of the Kokil Dara turning.

Sultan Saodat Complex Slightly further out on the same road is the Sultan Saodat Complex, the family necropolis of the Termez Sayyids, supposed descendants of Ali. They were politically powerful, exceptionally influential in religious matters, and wealthy to boot, enabling them to leave this lasting legacy. To reach it, it's a 15-minute walk down a side road, clearly signposted from the *marshrutka* route. Mausoleums line a short street, not dissimilar to the Shah-i Zinda in Samarkand (page 170), housing 120 graves, mostly dating from the 9th–16th centuries. A portico at the end gives on to the tombs of Sultan Saodat, 30 others to the right and a very simple mosque to the left.

Unlike the Shah-i Zinda, this was the burial place for holy men, not royal family members, and so the decoration is much simpler. There is some decorative brickwork, especially in the main mausoleum, where the symbolism of the star-like motif on the columns pre-dates the arrival of Islam: it is a Zoroastrian symbol of infinity and fertility. The mud bricks from which the complex is made are not held together with conventional mortar but rather with a durable mixture of clay, egg yolk, camels' blood and milk. Cement was clearly used in the 2002 restoration, which may not last as well.

Timur visited Sultan Saodat to pay his respects to the saints buried here, and also because he had a practical use for the Sayyids: when he planned to attack a town he would send one ahead to convince the local people to surrender, and said that doing so was the Islamic thing to do. Timur used similarly persuasive tactics to encourage newly conquered peoples to pay taxes without rebelling. His grandson, Khalid Sultan, thanked the Sayyids for their contributions by erecting the elegant portico, the only tiled part of the complex, between the mosque and the main mausoleum. It dates from the 15th century (and was restored at the same time as the rest of the site in 2002). It's a striking focal point among the otherwise mud-brown façades.

A short distance to the west (10 minutes south of the road between Sultan Saodat and Kyr Kyz) is the Timurid **Kokil Dara Khanagha** (⊕ daylight hrs; free). Built by Abdullah Khan II of Bukhara in the 16th century as a resting place for itinerant Sufi dervishes and other holy men, the building's design owes much to cultural links with Afghanistan, especially in the styling of its vaulted ceilings. The tall, symmetrical portico appears imposing even now: it must have made quite an impression on early visitors.

It's a simple structure – it was never decorated – and the domed interior was unique within Uzbekistan, as normally the portal opens on to a courtyard. Here there isn't one. This khanagha was a space for meditation and debate. The different orders of sufis have their own ways of meditating: the dervishes here didn't whirl, unlike their counterparts in Turkey – they preferred to meditate quietly and alone. Today, there are no dervishes at all in Uzbekistan; they are banned by the government.

Jarkurgan Minaret Continuing beyond the airport on the road to Denau, don't miss the Jarkurgan Minaret, raised in 1109 in Minor village (also known as Kommunizm Kolkhoz), 38km (45min–1hr) from Termez. Though a truncated version of its former self (only the first 22m of an estimated 50m remain intact), it is remarkable for the wave-like shape in its brickwork: it appears to be made from a rounded concertina of herringbone-patterned bricks, broken up with occasional Kufic inscriptions. The minaret narrows towards the top, cheating the perspective to make it appear taller than it is.

Kampir Tepe About 30km (40mins' drive) northwest of Termez is the Buddhist site of Kampir Tepe, a thriving city on the banks of the Amu Darya from the 3rd century BC for about 400 years, until the river changed its course and the city's inhabitants had to move on. Built on the riches of both river and overland trade, there were *stupas*, temples and monasteries, as well as civic buildings and common homes. You need your own transport to get here, but it is well worth the cost of a taxi, either from Termez or from Angor, which is closer and easily reached from Karshi or Termez.

The site was first discovered in 1972 during a survey of the Amu Darya riverbank, and the fortress (also known as the Kafir Qala) was excavated in the 1980s. The excavations lasted seven years and unearthed one of the most complete Kushan-era settlements ever found.

THE OXUS TREASURE

On rare occasions, all that glitters is indeed gold, as Captain F C Burton, a British political officer in Afghanistan, discovered when he rescued a group of merchants from bandits on the road from Kabul to Peshawar in the spring of 1880. Intrigued by the treasure the merchants carried, Burton purchased from them a gold lion- and griffin-headed armlet and alerted colonial colleagues to scour the bazaars of Rawalpindi where the merchants were thought to be headed.

Major General Sir Alexander Cunningham, Director General of the Archaeological Survey of India, and Sir Augustus Wollaston Franks, a curator of the British Museum, managed to reunite around 170 gold and silver artefacts from the original treasure hoard, including vessels, coins, armlets and rings, and a beautifully intricate figurine of a chariot with its driver, a government official and four horses.

The Oxus Treasure is the most important surviving collection of Achaemenid Persian metalwork and it dates from the 5th–4th centuries BC when the Achaemenid Empire stretched from Egypt in the west to the Indus Valley in the east. Though the exact site of its discovery is unknown, it is always thought to have been found accidentally somewhere along the banks of the Amu Darya. Archaeologists have subsequently hypothesised that it would have originally been collected and stored at the Oxus Temple in Takht-i Sangin (now in Tajikistan), though subsequently dispersed, buried for safe keeping, and lost.

Today, the Oxus Treasure takes pride of place in the Ancient Iran gallery at the British Museum, to which it was bequeathed by Franks upon his death in 1897. Tajikistan's President Rahmon called for its return to central Asia in 2010, but this is unlikely to occur.

You should park some distance from the core of the site and walk across the plateau to appreciate the scale of the city. Looking carefully at the hillocks you'll see they are in fact mud-brick ruins, melted over the past two millennia back into the earth from which they came. Underfoot you'll see plenty of terracotta pottery shards, and occasional pieces of glass.

One section of wall has been rebuilt around the main excavation site, so it is easy to spot where you are heading for: it stands out considerably taller than anywhere else on the site. Behind this, the original walls are still at least waist-high, and sometimes reach well above your head. Rooms and alleyways are clearly visible, and you can also pick out the wells and pantries. Larger pieces of pottery, possibly from heavy terracotta storage jars, lie here, too.

Standing atop the reconstructed wall gives you a superb view of the labyrinthine site, and thence across the irrigated fields to the Amu Darya and, on the horizon, the hills of Afghanistan. Devoid of visitors, it can feel slightly eerie, but the sense of history and its lingering ghosts makes this one of our very favourite places to go in Uzbekistan.

Mausoleum of Khoja Abu Isa Muhammad Imam Termez

Continuing along this road, close to the town of Shirabad, is the Mausoleum of Khoja Abu Isa Muhammad Imam Termezi (AD824–92). A significant figure in Islam, he travelled across the Islamic world for 30 years collecting sayings of the Prophet to contribute to the Hadith, the holiest book after the Qu'ran (page 179). The tomb is less impressive than one might expect given his importance, but it is still an important pilgrimage site and was restored between 2016 and 2017. It has a plain brick exterior, but a finely decorated interior.

Friendship Bridge

Travelling east from Termez for 10km brings you to the Afghan border at Hairatan and this ironically named bridge, over which Soviet tanks and troops poured into Afghanistan in 1979.

The bridge's name is something of a misnomer. Built by the Soviets in 1982, it was required to supply the invasion of Afghanistan, an act that was far from friendly. It links Termez with the town of Hairatan in Balkh, spanning the Amu Darya.

The bridge closed in 1997 when the Taliban seized Mazar-i Sharif, and as it was (and remains) the only road and rail link between Uzbekistan and Afghanistan, the border remained shut until after the US invasion in 2001. It is the main transport route for imports into Afghanistan, and the railway is currently being extended south from Mazar towards the Iranian border, which will ease congestion on the road. A free-trade zone (including a hotel and restaurant) was opened near the bridge in 2019.

Somewhere along this stretch of riverbank must also have been discovered the Oxus Treasure (see box, opposite), though quite where nobody is sure. If you find the spot, then let us know: we wouldn't mind having a hunt for some more!

6

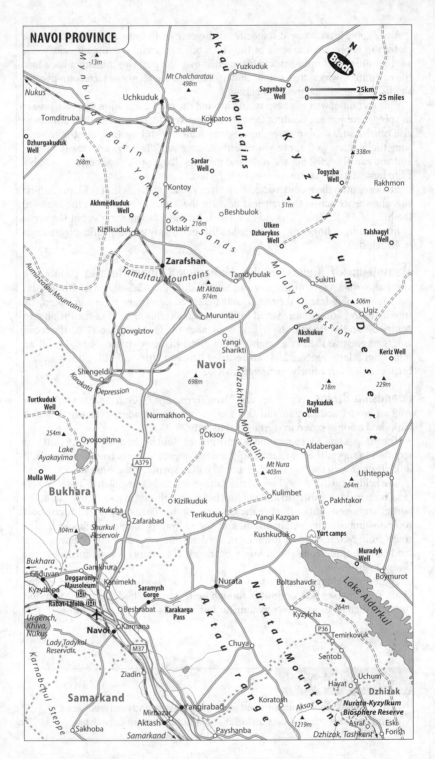

NAVOI PROVINCE

Nukus

Mynbulak Basin
-13m

Tomditruba

Dzhurgakuduk
Well

268m

Kizilkuduk

Uchkuduk

Mt Chalcharatau
498m

Shalkar

Kontoy

Akhmedkuduk
Well

Oktakir
216m

Yuzkuduk

Sagynbay
Well

Kokpatos

Sardar
Well

Beshbulok

Ulken
Dzharykos
Well

Zarafshan

Tamditau Mountains

Mt Aktau
974m

Muruntau

Dovgiztov

Yangi
Sharikti

Shengeldi

Karakata Depression

Turtkuduk
Well

254m

Oyokogitma

Lake
Ayakayima

Mulla Well

Bukhara

Kukcha

304m

Shurkul
Reservoir

Bukhara
Gijduvan

Kyzyltepa

Rabat-i Malik

*Urgench,
Khiva,
Nukus*

Navoi

Lady Tadykol
Reservoir

M37

Ziadin

Samarkand

Sakhoba

Samarkand

Karnabchul Steppe

**Deggaroniy
Mausoleum**

Kanimekh

Beshrabat

Karmana

Mirbazar
Aktash

Yangirabad

Payshanba

Garikhura

Saramysh
Gorge

Karakarga
Pass

Zafarabad

Kizilkuduk

Terikuduk

Aktau

Nurata

Koratosh

Aksay

1219m

Tamdybulak

Sukitti

338m

Togyzba
Well

Rakhmon

51m

Talshagyl
Well

506m

Ugiz

Akshukur
Well

Keriz Well

218m

229m

Raykuduk
Well

Aldabergan

Mt Nura
403m

Ushteppa

264m

Pakhtakor

Kulimbet

Yangi Kazgan

Kushkuduk

Muradyk
Well

Yurt camps

Boltashavdir

Lake Aidarkul

Boymurot

Kyzylcha

264m

Temirkovuk

Sentob

Uchum

Hayat

Dzhizak

**Nurata-Kyzylkum
Biosphere Reserve**

Asraf

Dzhizak, Tashkent

Eski
Forish

Chuya

range

Nuratau Mountains

Aktau

Navoi
698m

Kazakhtau Mountains

Molaly Depression Desert

Kyzylkum

Aktau Mountains

Yamankum Sands

Auminzatau Mountains

Shengeldi

Nurmakhon

Oksoy

A379

Tomditau Mountains

P36

Bradt

N

0   25km
0   25 miles

Nukus

Samba005

Mulla Well

Beshbulok

Kizilkuduk

7

Navoi Province

The vast province of Navoi (pronounced Navo-ee) covers almost a quarter of Uzbekistan's territory but includes just a fraction of the country's population, as much of the region is covered by the inhospitable Kyzylkum Desert. Despite the arid climate, cotton is still grown here, though Navoi's real wealth comes from what lies beneath the ground: natural gas, oil and precious metals.

For short-term visitors (and those without a few billion dollars handy to invest in a gold mine), Navoi Province offers camel trekking and desert safaris, Bronze Age petroglyphs and medieval *caravanserais*. The Nuratau-Kyzylkum Biosphere Reserve is one of the most important conservation sites in Uzbekistan, there are hikes of all difficulty levels among the mountains, and Lake Aidarkul is a fine spot for birdwatching, especially in the spring. If you've had enough of hotels and towns, plan a few days in the biosphere reserve, staying in a family homestay and learning to appreciate rural Uzbekistan.

NAVOI

Both the province and the provincial capital take their name from the Timurid poet and politician Alisher Navoi (see box, page 116), although it's unlikely that he came here. Navoi is a small, modern city, founded only in 1958 as an annexe to the existing town of Karmana. It's a low-density sprawl, with enough parks to ensure you have to take a taxi to get almost anywhere. It makes its money from mining and processing minerals (including gold), natural gas, and producing chemical fertilisers. The majority of foreigners coming here are on business, though you may also pass through en route to Nurata.

GETTING THERE AND AROUND Navoi is situated quite centrally within Uzbekistan, 435km from Tashkent, 155km from Samarkand and 115km from Bukhara.

By air Navoi Airport (w navoi-airport.com) is 25km west of the city, 300m south from km174 on the road to Bukhara. It is becoming somewhat of a regional hub, especially for cargo, and passenger flights operate to Tashkent (1hr; 3 per week with Uzbekistan Airways; see ad, 3rd colour section), Moscow (4hrs; 1 per week with each of Ural Airlines & Red Wings) and St Petersburg (8hrs 45min; 1 per week with Rossiya).

From here, it is a 25-minute drive into the city centre, and taxis wait by the terminal around the clock (Navoi's taxi drivers are some of the pushiest we've ever encountered); they cost around US$1 each way, while minibuses, which also wait by the terminal, run from 06.00 until 19.00 and cost US$1.

There is a **ticket office** at the airport (✆ 79 539 3523), though you might find it more convenient to book online, at an Aviakassa in town, or by going to the Uzbekistan Airways office in the city centre (52 Karimov; ✆ 79 223 3471).

By rail Navoi is on the rail route from Tashkent and Samarkand to Bukhara and high-speed trains between these cities stop here (3hrs 20min), as do long-distance trains that run overnight to and from Urgench (7hrs 20min), Khiva (8hrs) and Nukus (12hrs) in the west of the country and on into Russia. The railway station is at the southern end of Galaba; buy tickets at the Kassa to the left of the station building.

By road If you're travelling with your own vehicle, the main road (M37) between Samarkand and Bukhara passes through Karmana (referred to as 'the Old Town'), and Navoi is clearly signposted 4km to the south.

Travelling by **minibus** or **shared taxi**, you will need the bus station in Karmana, which is at km159 (indicated by a marker near the road) on the M37, just north of central Navoi. Local minibuses link the two. From here, you can easily find onward transport to Bukhara (every 1½hrs; 1hr; US$0.50), Samarkand (2hrs; US$1) and Tashkent (5hrs; US$8). Buses are marginally cheaper, but take longer. Taxis also run around the clock to Bukhara and cost US$3 per vehicle (one-way), or US$4.50 one-way to Samarkand. They are the fastest way to travel.

Within the city centre, the price of minibus rides varies depending on distance, but is always very cheap. The most useful routes run from the railway station north along Galaba, passing the bazaar and continuing on to Karmana and the intercity bus station (a good 10km), or west from the bazaar along Amir Timur.

TOUR OPERATORS **Sputnik Navoi** (16/14 Matvienko; m 95 225 5417) can help with ticket and accommodation bookings.

WHERE TO STAY Owing to its position as a business centre, Navoi has a number of upmarket hotels with price tags to match, both in town and near the airport. Fortunately, however, there are also a few reasonable budget options for those of us not travelling on a company expense account.

Grand M Hotel (33 rooms, 3 apts) 77A Kharimov; 79 770 3737; e info@grandm-hotel.uz; w grandm-hotel.uz/en. Navoi's newest business hotel opened in 2011 & it is a step above the other options in town. The architecture may not be to everyone's taste, but service is of a high standard, the outdoor pool is huge & the 2 restaurants' ($$) menus include both continental & Uzbek dishes. Apts are available for long-term rent. $$$$

Silk Road Palace (66 rooms) Malik Rabot; 79 780 2000; e info@silkroadpalace.uz. Technically, the Silk Road Palace is in Karmana, but it is so close to the airport that we've included it here. It's a well-run, mid-size business hotel with its own bar & restaurant ($$), conference facilities & fitness centre. The hotel also has designated parking. $$$$

Hotel Kamilla (27 rooms) 2/2 Ahkunbayaev; 79 223 1473; e info@hotel-kamilla.uz; w hotel-kamilla.uz. One of the more surreal designs for a hotel interior that we've come across: there's a tree growing through the staircase & some of the public spaces look like a set from *Day of the Triffids*. Plants aside, the rooms are large & clean with new linens. Restaurant ($$) & small conference hall on site. $$$

Zarafshan Grand Hotel (38 rooms) 8 Navoi; 79 573 5111; w zarafshan-grand.com. Easily confused with the Zarafshan Hotel (see below), this solid brick building has been well refurbished & offers parking & a decent restaurant ($$). $$$

Zarafshan Hotel (58 rooms) Free Industrial Economic Zone; 78 770 2020/78 770 2550; e elegant5@mail.ru; w hotel-zarafshan.com. West of the city (km178 on the M37) & close to the airport & cargo zone, this modern business hotel has immaculate bathrooms, a conference centre, swimming pool & gym. B/fast buffet served until 11.00. $$$

Hotel Yoshlik (43 rooms) 138 Karimov; 79 224 4021; e info@hotel-yoshlik.uz; w hotel-yoshlik.uz. Centrally located mid-range option surrounded by parks with friendly, helpful staff & a relaxed atmosphere. There is a fitness centre & *banya* on site, & they offer good tours. Recommended. **$$**

🏠 **Maximum Plaza** (22 rooms) 9 Galaba;

m 95 603 0077; e maximum.hotel@inbox.ru; w maximum-hotel.uz. Just north of the station, this rather US-style new hotel is fairly simple but has a cellar restaurant-bar (**$**), outdoor pool, sauna & gym. **$$**

✗ **WHERE TO EAT AND DRINK** Navoi has a large number of restaurants serving a selection of European and Uzbek dishes. Their primary clientele are a mixture of businessmen and wedding parties, but there are usually a few extra tables even if a party is in full swing. The hotel restaurants at Grand M and Silk Road Palace (both **$$$–$$$$**; see opposite) are also pretty good, and the staff don't fuss around you while you're eating. You can also get a drink at their bars and take it outside, which is ideal on a summer's evening.

✗ **Richard** Microdistrict 6; ☎79 223 3581. Probably the best restaurant in town, if a little removed from the centre (to the south of Amir Timur). Indoor & outdoor tables & a mixed menu of European & Uzbek dishes. **$$$**

✗ **Vstrecha** 57A Karimov; ☎79 225 0327. A particular favourite with the Korean Air staff from the cargo centre, Vstrecha prides itself on its chicken dishes. **$$$**

✗ **Shams Fast Food** 52 Karimov; ☎79 770 3030. High-calorie snacks delivered to your table at

speed. The pizzas are the pick of the dishes, though the doner kebabs aren't bad either. **$–$$**

🍺 **Yoshlik Cafe** 4B Zarapetyan; ☎79 223 1886. Although Yoshlik does have indoor seating, the café's main attraction is its garden. Sit back & enjoy a cold beer & salads in the shade of the trees. **$$–$$$**

🍺 **Khoja Nasriddin** 2 Abduramoanova. *Shashlik*, *manti* (steamed dumplings) & *plov* are the mainstays on the menu at this bustling Uzbek café. The *plov* is the best in the city. Ignore the monstrous mock-stone interior – the food is better than the décor. **$**

ENTERTAINMENT For a provincial city with no major tourist traffic, the cultural scene in Navoi is surprisingly vibrant.

The **Alisher Navoi** (cnr Ibn Sino & Janubiy) and **Uzbekistan** (west of Karimov, near the Grand M Hotel) cinemas have regular showings of Russian and Uzbek blockbusters. The **Farkhad Cultural Centre** (cnr Karimov & Tolstoy; ☎ 79 223 4261) and the **Jewish Cultural Centre** (5A Kurilish; ☎79 225 2627) have occasional recitals, film showings, plays and exhibitions. Call in for programme details.

SHOPPING Navoi's **Central Mall** (⊕ 08.00–20.00 daily) is on Karimov, just south of the main post office. The **Central Bazaar** is by the roundabout at the eastern end of Amir Timur, and this is the best place to pick up fresh produce, bread and snacks.

OTHER PRACTICALITIES
Communications
✉ **DHL** 44A Karimov; ☎79 770 2117. The most reliable option for international shipments.
✉ **Main post office** 3A Karimov (on the cnr of Amir Timur); ⊕ 09.00–17.00 Mon–Fri, 09.00–14.00 Sat. Located at the city's central crossroads.

Medical
General ailments can be diagnosed & treated at either of the polyclinics listed here.

✚ **General Urban Polyclinic** 5A Yujnaya; ☎79 223 7182. A private establishment.
✚ **Polyclinic #1** 3A Yujnaya; ☎79 223 1588
✚ **Republican Scientific Centre of Emergency Medicine** 27 Ibn Sina; ☎79 223 1341; ⊕ 24/7

Money
The following banks are centrally located.

$ **Aloka Bank** ☎79 223 4140; ⊕ 09.00–18.00 daily

$ **Asaka Bank** ✆ 79 770 2129; ⏰ 09.00–16.00
Mon–Fri
$ **National Bank of Uzbekistan** ✆ 79 227 8384;
⏰ 09.00–18.00 Mon–Fri

$ **Turon Bank** ✆ 79 224 2108/9; ⏰ 09.00–17.00
Mon–Fri

Registration
OVIR 4 Matvienko; ✆ 79 223 6081

WHAT TO SEE AND DO Navoi grew out of the desert in the 20th century, so there's unfortunately little to see within the city itself. You can take a walk in **Victory Park** (block north of Tolstoy & Galaba) or around the manmade Lake Navoi in **Alisher Navoi Park**, where there is also a statue of the great man himself. For more options, you'll need to head to Karmana (see below) and beyond.

KARMANA

These days, Karmana and Navoi run into one another, but you'll notice the difference between the two: while Navoi is modern and includes far too much concrete, large parts of Karmana are still made from traditional mud brick, and the pace of life seems slower.

HISTORY Karmana is old Navoi, and it was probably founded around the time of the Arab invasion. The town lay within an independent kingdom, Karmana and Paikend, one of several such kingdoms within the Bukhara Oasis, the rulers of which had the right to mint their own bronze and copper coins. The town was a stopping point on the Silk Road – as testified to by the *caravanserais* and *rabats* that remain – and it was the significant trade wealth that made it a target for Arab invaders seeking plunder. Karmana and Paikend fell to the Arab forces in AD706, before experiencing a prolonged period of decline.

Karmana's fortunes slowly revived from the 11th century onwards, when the area became a popular hunting ground for the Karakhanid rulers and, for some, also their final resting place. Their mausoleums (see opposite) attest to the wealth and status of Karmana during the medieval period. Wandering dervishes and itinerant holy men walked along the same routes as the merchants, and this is why the Kasim Sheikh Khanagha (see opposite) was erected here in the 16th century.

Karmana sank into commercial and political obscurity following the establishment of Navoi in 1958, but it retains a certain charm and there are several historic sites of note.

GETTING THERE AND AROUND The main **bus station** for both Karmana and Navoi is technically in Karmana, immediately east of the junction between the M37 and the A379, the road through the desert to Nurata. For destinations and journey times, as well as air, rail and local minibus options, see page 210. From the bus station it's possible to walk to the bazaar and the nearby sights, otherwise you'll need to flag down a minibus or taxi.

WHERE TO STAY, EAT AND DRINK The best accommodation options and restaurants are in Navoi (page 210), though it is possible to get a *shashlik* (or three) and a cup of tea in one of Karmana's *chaikhanas* if you need a break from exploring the sights. **Chahalpak Café** ($$) is the best located, next door to the Kasim Sheikh Khanagha (see opposite).

WHAT TO SEE AND DO Life in Karmana still centres on the main bazaar, located about 1km southeast of the bus station. When we visited in November, the watermelons were the size of beach balls, and the pomegranates incredibly sweet and pink. Eating a pomegranate requires patience and a certain amount of skill, especially if you want to do it without getting covered in the sticky red juice, but it's definitely worth the effort. You can buy them one at a time or, more commonly, by weight.

About 1km south of the bazaar is the **Mir Said Bakhrom Mausoleum**, an 11th-century brick-built tomb that, with its dome and monumental portal, served as an architectural model for many later structures, probably including the Ismail Samani Mausoleum in Bukhara (page 237). The portico is decorated with a Kufic inscription but, unusually, this is not made from mosaic or painted on to larger tiles, but rather depicted with certain bricks raised out from their surroundings. The mausoleum was added to the tentative list of UNESCO World Heritage Sites in 2008 in recognition of its importance as an architectural prototype. Between the Navoi River and the cemetery (which includes a Polish Catholic section) is the **Kasim Sheikh Khanagha**, a 16th-century hostel built by the Bukharan emir Abdulla Khan II for itinerant holy men. The turquoise dome atop a lapis lazuli-coloured drum still stands, and the latter is strikingly decorated with calligraphy, stars and floral motifs. The khanagha is still in daily use, though now as the town's main mosque; the chambers echo in a spine-chilling fashion with the sound of the muezzin's voice if you are fortunate enough to be present as he calls the faithful to prayer.

AROUND KARMANA West of Karmana, 26km along the road to Bukhara and not far beyond the airport, is the **Rabat-i Malik**, an ambitious and heavily fortified *caravanserai* built by the Karakhanid ruler Abu'l Hasan Shams al Mulk Nasr in the late 11th century. After an earthquake in 1968, only the portico remained fully intact: it is 12m tall, domed and with an impressive façade of embedded columns, connected at the top with arches. The only other example of this particular style is the Jarkurgan Minaret in Surkhan Darya (page 206). Behind the portico are the recently restored foundations of a large complex of cells, stables, guardhouses and storerooms around a courtyard; there are also new gardens in front and a car park with toilets to the west. Across the highway you can also look at a *sardoba* or covered water tank.

About 4km further west on the M37, it's also worth turning north for 5km to see the **Deggaroniy Mausoleum**, the 11th-century burial place of the theologian Mavlono Orif Deggaroniy (1313–76), teacher of Khoja Bahauddin Naqshbandi (page 245). Built of plain brick with low domes, it's a restful spot nowadays.

North from Karmana on the road to Nurata, about 40km from Navoi, the **Saramysh Gorge** sits hidden among the Aktau Mountains, just before you reach the Karakarga Pass. Cones of volcanic rock rise up around an oasis, and on their surface is a gallery of more than 4,000 petroglyphs that give a panoramic view of life from the 9th millennium BC right through to the 18th century AD, when wandering Sufis are thought to have taken refuge here. Most, however, date from the Bronze Age (3000–900BC). The number of petroglyphs, their variety, and their state of preservation, is truly remarkable. They have both been painted on to the cave surfaces and hewn out of the rock with stone chisels and other basic tools. In addition to the usual figures of hunters, horses and deer, there are also dancers, strange camels with three humps, and even stranger men with two heads. Engaging a guide from a tour company (page 210) is the best way to get the most out of the site, as the finest petroglyphs are not always that easy to find. There's a children's camp (Lager Sarmysh) at the start of the gorge, so it's best to avoid the area in July and August when the security guard may not allow you through – although you should be OK if your guide has called ahead.

There's also a good new **yurt camp** at the top of the gorge beyond the petroglyphs (Sarmish Soy; 🕻79 220 6037; m 95 603 6163; w sarmishsoy.uz; **$$**).

NURATA

Nurata City is surrounded by the Nuratau Mountains and is home to not only a fortress supposedly built by Alexander the Great, but also a medieval pilgrimage site supposedly linked to Hazrat Ali. The city also serves as the transport hub (and occasional overnight stopover) for those camel trekking in the Kyzylkum Desert or trekking and birdwatching in the stunning and remarkably unspoilt Nuratau-Kyzylkum Biosphere Reserve.

HISTORY Local people believe that Nurata was founded as Nur by Alexander the Great in 327BC. They credit Alexander with building the hilltop fort (see opposite) and also the *kariz*, a complex water system that brought drinking water several kilometres from a spring right into the centre of the citadel.

Nurata became important again at the start of the Islamic era as Hazrat Ali, son-in-law of the Prophet Muhammad, is said to have struck the ground here with his staff, and the Chashma Spring spurted forth (it may also have been caused by a meteorite strike). The 10th-century Bukharan chronicler Muhammad Narshakhi recorded people having visions of the Prophet in Nurata, and hence it became an important regional pilgrimage centre, with all the mosques, resthouses and other supporting structures you would expect.

GETTING THERE AND AROUND From the main bus station in Karmana, shared taxis run to Nurata, 65km to the northeast (1hr; US$2.50, or US$1.50 & slower by minibus). They'll take you to the Chashma Complex, around the Chasma Spring, but to leave Nurata you'll have to go to the bus station, a couple of kilometres north; luckily there is an occasional minibus service running between the old and new parts of the town.

If you are travelling on to Lake Aidarkul and the yurt camps, you will need a private car or taxi. Expect to pay around US$20 each way.

TOUR OPERATORS There are no travel agents actually in Nurata itself. However, there are a number of small companies in the surrounding towns and villages that specialise in camel trekking, home and yurt stays and wildlife watching in the biosphere. All of them can provide suitable transport and guides, as can companies in Samarkand and Bukhara (pages 162 and 226).

Kyzylkum Safari Dungalak village, Kanimekh district; m 90 732 4393. Guided tours on foot & by 4x4. Homestay bookings possible.
Narzullo Musaev Hayat; m 97 325 0407; e narzullo-musaev@mail.ru. This very welcoming family have a couple of excellent guesthouses (see box, page 217) & will also feed & entertain you & take you hiking.

Responsible Travel 34 Amir Timur, Yangiqshloq; 🕻72 452 1200; m 90 265 0680. The very helpful Sherzod Norbekov can book homestays & organise transport & guides, as well as yurt stays & camel riding by Lake Aidarkul.

WHERE TO STAY, EAT AND DRINK There is only one decent modern hotel in Nurata. If you have the choice, stay in one of the safari camps in the surrounding desert (page 218) or in a homestay within the biosphere reserve (see box, page 216).

Nurota Hotel ✆ 79 523 2627; m 97 281 1911. A much-needed new place by the Chashma Complex, with modern facilities, including Wi-Fi, coffee machines, satellite TV in all rooms & a restaurant ($$). **$$**

Guesthouse Ruslan Nurata & Tours (4 rooms) 2 Akhunboyev; m 95 607 2027/93 661 1013; e ruslan.nuratau@mail.ru. A short distance north of the Chashma Complex, this is run by a very friendly family who serve delicious meals. Ruslan Rakhmonov is a local guide who speaks English, French & Farsi & can arrange hiking, cycling & camel trips plus stays in mountain villages & desert yurts. **$**

OTHER PRACTICALITIES
Medical
Nurata has a small & overstretched **district hospital**, but in a serious situation you would still need to get to Navoi & seek treatment at the emergency hospital there (page 211).

Money
There is no ATM in Nurata, but the National Bank of Uzbekistan can theoretically advance money to Visa cardholders.

$ Agro Bank 10 Amir Timur; ✆ 79 523 1903; ⏰ 09.00–17.00 Mon–Fri
$ National Bank of Uzbekistan 49 Rashidov; ✆ 79 523 1651; ⏰ 09.00–18.00 Mon–Fri

WHAT TO SEE AND DO First and foremost, you will want to visit **Alexander's Fort** (⏰ 24/7; free). It is strategically located on the top of a hill to the south of the town, and Uzbek sources suggest that Alexander instructed one of his generals to build an impenetrable fortress here while he continued his conquest of Bactria and Sogdiana. When Alexander returned, his troops could neither break down the gates nor scale the walls, such was the strength of the construction.

We first came to the fort one Sunday afternoon in September, expecting it to be a visit of an hour or so. We stayed until nightfall, necessitating a scramble back down in the dark. It is a steep climb to the top of the site. What appears to be clay underfoot is, in fact, adobe bricks, compacted by thousands of sandalled feet and the elements over two millennia. In places you can still make out their individual shapes, and it's slightly eerie if you're on your own to think of the men who built it, lived and worked here. It's timeless. The central citadel, once measuring half a kilometre in each direction, has long gone, but one glance at the view, across the mountains and across Nurata itself, reveals exactly why Alexander (if indeed it was he) chose this spot, and why it was such a good decision.

Down below the fort, close to the modern town, is the **Chashma Spring** (open access), which is linked with Hazrat Ali (see opposite and page 154). The centre of the complex is a pool where the faithful come to bathe, have their children blessed or collect water to take to sick relatives and friends. Regardless of the time of year, the mineral-laden spring water is said to remain at a consistent 19.1°C. The population of *marinka* fish in the pool is thriving as it is considered a holy spot, and hence no-one is allowed to catch them.

The whole area around the spring was tidied and organised during 2017 and 2018, and the area of the Old Town immediately to the north was cleared and replaced with a sterile park and a new hotel (see above).

By the spring is the Chilsutun (Panjvakt) Mosque, built in the 16th century with one large dome. Just to its north is the larger **Namazgokh Mosque**, built in the 10th

This reserve was established in 2001 to protect the fragile ecosystems of the Nuratau Mountains, preserving both the diverse natural landscapes and the numerous varieties of wildlife the land and waters support (most importantly Severtsov's sheep, the westernmost sub-species of the argali or mountain sheep, *Ovis ammon*). For several years, the United Nations Development Programme funded a community-based tourism initiative, and consequently the biosphere now has the best-developed tourism infrastructure of any nature reserve in Uzbekistan. If you've had your fill (quite understandably) of mosques and madrasas, a few days in Nuratau are the perfect antidote. One of the highlights of visiting the reserve is the option to stay with a family in their home, which could be a house or a yurt (on the shores of Lake Aidarkul; see opposite).

To **reach the reserve**, road P36 runs west from Dzhizak to Nurata, south of Lake Aidarkul; after 67km it passes through Yangiqishloq (formerly Forish and Bogdon), home to the offices of the Nurata Nature Reserve (72 452 1165; m 97 342 6098; e nurota@urmon.uz; w elyor-mustafaev@inbox.ru) and of Responsible Travel (page 214). From the central bus station in Dzhizak (page 180), shared taxis and minibuses run to Yangiqishloq (US$0.60–0.80 pp), from where you'll need a taxi (US$0.60–0.70) to Asraf, Hayat or Sentob (50km; under 1hr). There's also a daily bus from Tashkent bus station to Yangiqishloq (4½hrs, leaving 14.00 or sooner if full, returning at 05.30; US$0.80).

To the west of Yangiqishloq, largely unpaved roads lead a few kilometres south to villages nestling where streams emerge into the desert from the Nuratau range. There are guesthouses in most of these (see opposite), but the only way to really get into the mountains is to take the road from km107.5 to Uchum and then fork right to Hayat, where Nazrullo (see opposite) can organise accommodation and activities.

It is possible to take a **hike** in the area, but trails are as yet unmarked, so you are advised to take a local guide (US$25/day, plus US$5 for a donkey & US$5 or US$10 for a horse). At the top of the delightful village of Hayat, paths lead to the fenced-off core of the reserve, from where you may be able to see Severtsov's sheep, as well as raptors such as lammergeier, golden eagle and Eurasian griffon. It is a birdwatcher's paradise (with 314 species recorded), especially in the spring when the migratory birds arrive, so make sure you bring your binoculars and a camera. Around the villages 'forest orchards' have developed. Walnut, almond and mulberry trees are the most common, but fruit trees, sycamore and white poplar can also be found; pistachio, Zarafshan spruce and other trees grow higher up.

Other hikes from Hayat or Sentob take you through dramatic mountain peaks to see waterfalls, petroglyphs and archaeological ruins. If you have particular interests in spotting flora and fauna, guides will do their best to accommodate this, though sightings are inevitably seasonal and do require an element of luck.

century and rebuilt several times; the current structure (mostly late 16th century) has 25 small domes supported on 16 columns.

There is also a small **museum** (08.00–17.00 Tue–Sun; US$0.25) on the site and a mausoleum, which dates from the 9th century and is said to cover the grave of either a Muslim preacher or one of Alexander's generals who died here while on campaign.

If you have the time and stamina for a full-day hike, one of the most rewarding options that you can take is south from Sentob to Lake Fazilman (22km return; 10hrs; it's long but not difficult). Highlights of the route include the Chavaksoy Valley, where you'll meet local families transporting firewood and fodder by donkey; crossing the Gaukum Pass; and picnicking on the lake shore (at 1,650m). Again, you will get the most out of the trek if you go with a local guide, although guesthouse owners will be able to give you some further information.

Horse trekking from Asraf to Sentob is also an option, and guides are able to tailor itineraries according to your level of fitness and the amount of time available.

On spring and autumn weekends there may be games of *kupkari* (the Uzbek variant of *buz kashi* or 'dead goat polo'), much to the delight of spectators. The horses sprint and sweat, the men shriek and fight, and both ride high on adrenalin. You'll need to keep your wits about you, even if you're only standing on the sidelines, as in all the excitement it's not uncommon for men and beasts to come thundering off the pitch, scattering the crowd in their wake. If you're particularly brave (and/or foolhardy) they'll even let you join in.

 WHERE TO STAY, EAT AND DRINK Homestays and guesthouses, located within the biosphere reserve, are listed village by village from east to west; expect to pay US$25 pp full board for a night (**$$**). One or two other options are also available in most villages.

Porasht Guesthouse (2 rooms) Eski Forish (1km south from km98). A simple guesthouse with space for 6 & a basic wash block. The hospitable hosts grow most of the food you'll eat.

Zamira Homestay (2 rooms) Eski Forish (2.5km south from km98); m 90 265 0680. Built in 2009, Zamira Homestay sleeps up to 6 guests. A solar panel provides hot water for the shower & there's a flushing toilet. Zamira's son is a qualified mountain guide.

Yahshigul Homestay (4 rooms) Asraf (3.5km south from km103); m 94 191 7967; w yahshigul.com. Larger homestay sleeping 16 guests, with 2 showers & flushing toilets. Drinking water comes from the spring, there's a wonderful orchard & musical entertainment can be arranged on request. Yahshigul & Bobojon's son Rahmat speaks English & is a hiking guide.

Narzullo Musaev (9 rooms) Hse number 71, Hayat (9km south from km107.5); m 97 325 0407; e narzullo-musaev@mail. ru. This very welcoming family have a couple of comfortable guesthouses & will provide food, activities & transfers from Samarkand or Bukhara.

Komil Homestay (3 rooms) Sentob; m 90 265 0680. Sentob's newest homestay was built in 2012 & sleeps 9. There's an outdoor shower in summer & a hot hammam in winter. Meals are prepared with vegetables grown in the garden & there's a waterfall a short hike away.

Rahima's Homestay (4 rooms) Sentob (6.5km south from km118). A very hospitable family with a lovely house & garden & very sociable kids; excellent, largely homegrown food, with vegetarian options easily found.

LAKE AIDARKUL AND AROUND

Nurata is a stone's throw from the **Kyzylkum Desert**, which can be accessed from shared taxis from Karmana, although most visitors come here on trips organised by a tour company (pages 96, 162 and 226). Named after its red sand, it is the world's 15th-largest desert, and spreads across northern Uzbekistan and up into neighbouring

The camel may be the pin-up of the Silk Road, but the two-humped Bactrian camel, with its scrawny legs, ungainly walk and hairy humps, is far from a sexy beast.

A fully grown adult camel can stand well over 2m tall, but chooses to mate on its knees. The male has a large, inflatable sack in its neck, an organ called a dulla. When in rut it extrudes from his mouth like a long, swollen, pink tongue in a bid to assert dominance and attract the glances of a passing female. When he finally catches her eye (possibly having pursued her at speed across the steppe: be warned if you're riding on top), they mate kneeling; in a single mating session, the male ejaculates three or four times in succession.

It's not only their sexual habits that make camels intriguing; they also have a number of physiological adaptations to help them live in dry climates. Camels' humps don't actually contain water, as was once commonly believed, but concentrated body fat. When this fat is metabolised, it releases more than 1g of water for every gram of fat. Unlike other mammals, a camel's red blood cells are oval rather than circular, which helps them flow when the body is dehydrated and also makes them less likely to rupture when large quantities of water are finally consumed. Consequently, a camel can drink as much as 70 litres of water per minute, taking on 200 litres in total. Camels rarely sweat, even when temperatures reach 50°C, and when they do sweat they can lose up to 25% of their body weight before circulatory disturbance results in cardiac arrest. When a camel breathes out, water vapour is trapped in its nostrils and is then reabsorbed. They can, in fact, ingest sufficient moisture from eating green foliage to remain hydrated without drinking water at all.

Kazakhstan. Between March and May, and September and October, you can trek a circuit on foot or by camel from the village of Yangi Kazgan, just west of Lake Aidarkul; **camel treks** of two days or more include accommodation in the camel-hair yurts belonging to local Kazakh nomads. Expect to enjoy the best of local hospitality, from homemade bread dipped in still-steaming camel milk, to hunks of camel meat. Beds are made up on the floor from piles of rainbow-coloured blankets and rugs, and you'll often sleep cheek-by-jowl with other guests. You'll never forget the experience, and certainly won't get cold at night.

You can arrange camel trekking through a tour company (pages 96, 162 and 226) or, alternatively, by approaching the camel camps directly. The first two camps to be opened, both inland from the west end of the lake near Kushkuduk and providing a high level of service, were **Sputnik Camel Camp** (✆ 79 223 8081; e sputnik-navoi@yandex.ru; w camping.uz) and the nearby **Yangi Kazgan Yurt Camp** (✆ 79 225 1419). A couple of newer options, located close to the lake at Eski Dungalok, are **Aidar Yurt Camp** (m 97 929 9922) and **Qizilqum Safari** (m 95 610 4455/94 372 4455; e qizilqum-safari@mail.ru; w nuratau.com/yurt-camp), which have permanent yurts on concrete bases, good wash blocks, electricity and hot water; a local musician usually plays by a campfire (followed by a noisy party if there's an Uzbek group staying – beware). The latest addition, on the south shore of the lake near Uchum, is **Oxus Adventure Eco-Resort** (km107 of the Dzhizak–Nurata road; m 90 908 1177 (Tashkent)/97 921 0190 (Samarkand)/95 280 1122 (camp); e office@tour-orient.com/booking@oxus-travel.com; w https://oxus-adventure.uz), which has wooden cabins as well as yurts.

In all of these cases you'll pay about US$40 per person per day for accommodation, meals and a short camel ride (where you will be led, at least to begin with). The local Bactrian camels are far more comfortable to ride than Arabian dromedaries, although it's all relative. Don't expect to get too fond of your mount; camels are surprisingly hard creatures to love when you get up close and personal. Wet wipes will undoubtedly come in handy.

If you wander into the dunes around the camps you may see ground squirrels, skinks, hares and tortoises among the scrubby saxaul bushes, along with birds such as warblers, whitethroats, shrikes, sparrows, coveys of partridges, and with some luck the Turkestan ground-jay, and raptors such as snake-eagles and long-legged buzzards. In spring and autumn, you may see migratory species such as demoiselle cranes, bustards and black vultures. It's a short drive down to the lake (your camp will be able to take you), where over 100 species of waterbird can be seen, and there's commercial fishing for species such as catfish, carp, snakehead and zander. There are also real beaches; walking along the shore is very pleasant, although some private resorts have been fenced off.

8

Bukhara Province

You come to Bukhara Province for Bukhara itself. Whether you are drawn to the Ark, the city's medieval mud-brick citadel, and the grisly history of its Registan and prison, or to the majestic beauty of the Kalyon Mosque and the buildings of Lyabi Hauz reflected in the gently shifting waters of the tank, everything you see is a treat for the eyes. Many people will, quite understandably, spend their entire stay wandering the labyrinthine streets of the Old Town, savouring each sight, sound and smell.

Those who do venture a little further afield will not be disappointed, however. The Mausoleum of Bakhauddin Naqshbandi outside the modern city's confines is considered among the holiest sites in central Asia, and huge numbers of visitors come both on pilgrimage and to admire the *mazar*. Close by is the Sitorai Mokhi Khosa, the summer palace of Alim Khan, which gives a poignant insight into the last days of the Bukharan emirate before the Bolsheviks took control, and also the town of Gijduvan, famous for its finely painted handmade ceramics.

BUKHARA

In our minds, Bukhara is the undisputed pearl (or perhaps that should be sapphire, given that its dominant colour is blue) of Uzbekistan. Samarkand and Khiva both have their charms, but they seem but pale mirages when you are standing alone on a late autumnal afternoon staring up at the Kalyon Minar, the most prominent sight on Bukhara's skyline, and with the vast and unbelievably sumptuous 16th-century Kalyon Mosque at your side.

HISTORY The founding of Bukhara is cloaked in mystery, the creation myths as rich and elaborate as the façade of Lyabi Hauz. The famed Persian epic, the *Shahnama,* tells us the city was founded by Siyavush, a Persian prince from the Pishdadian dynasty. Accused by his wicked stepmother of seducing her, he was forced to undergo a trial by fire but emerged from the flames unscathed and crossed the Amu Darya in search of new lands and fortune. In Samarkand, he wed the princess Farangis, daughter of King Afrosiab, and her dowry included the vassal state of Bukhara.

The story did not end there, however, as Siyavush was later accused of plotting to overthrow Afrosiab. Afrosiab had him executed in front of Farangis, and his head was buried beneath the Ark's Kalyon Gate, a permanent message to the citadel's residents to remember their place and not to threaten the sovereignty of Samarkand.

Situated near a crucial crossing of the Amu Darya between Merv (now in eastern Turkmenistan and one of the largest cities in the ancient world), Herat and Samarkand, Bukhara was in a prime location to benefit from Silk Road trade. It was already flourishing by the 6th century BC when it was sacked by the Achaemenids, becoming a satrapy of the Persian Empire. The evident wealth of Bukhara would

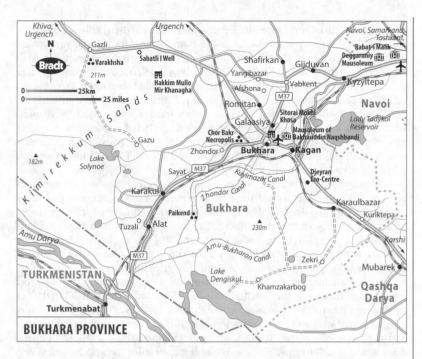

in many ways prove a curse, attracting the unwanted attentions of Alexander the Great in 329BC, then the subsequent invasions of the Seleucids, Graeco-Bactrians and the Kushans.

Bukhara became a centre of worship for the Iranian goddess Anahita, and devotees flocked to the city each year to exchange the idols they believed would ensure the fertility of their fields. The city also attracted Nestorian Christians and Manicheans, followers of a gnostic religion originating in Sassanid-era Babylonia, who were persecuted elsewhere in the Sassanian Empire but able to flourish in Bukhara.

When Arab invaders came to Bukhara in the 7th century, the residents were initially able to spare themselves by paying an annual tribute. Relations deteriorated, however, when 80 Bukharans were kidnapped and committed mass suicide en route to Medina, depriving their captors of slave profits they felt to be rightfully theirs. The crusading Qutaiba ibn Muslim arrived in AD709 and violently asserted direct control. The religious diversity for which the city was famed was quashed almost overnight and by the time Bukhara became the capital of the Samanid dynasty (819–1005), the city was known as Bukhoro-i Sharif (Bukhara the Noble) and 'The Pillar of Islam'.

The 9th and 10th centuries were a golden age for Bukhara. The Samanid ruler Ismail ibn Ahmad (who moved the capital of Maveranahr here from Samarkand in AD892) maintained the political stability required for trade to flourish, and with his wealth he patronised some of the greatest intellectuals and artisans in the Islamic world. The scientist, philosopher and physician Ibn Sina (known in the West as Avicenna), the Persian poets Ferdowsi and Rudaki, and the chronicler al Beruni all thrived in the city and completed their most important works here.

The fall of the Samanids resulted in 200 years of attacks on Bukhara. The Karakhanids invaded in AD999, the Karakhitai attacked in 1141, the Khorezmshah in 1206 and, most catastrophically of all, Genghis Khan and the Mongol horde rode into town in 1220. Every one of Bukhara's 30,000 troops was slaughtered, the city was torched, the civilian population (including women and children) killed or enslaved, and the Great Khan himself stood in the Namazgokh Mosque and proclaimed himself the 'Scourge of God'. The city was utterly decimated and when the Arab traveller Ibn Battuta visited nearly 150 years later, he described it as still lying more or less in ruins. Under the Timurids, Bukhara saw a limited recovery, but it remained an Islamic centre rather than the economic or political capital of Maverannakh.

Bukhara's revival continued when an Uzbek tribe, known as the Shaybanids, established a khanate here in 1500. Abdullah Khan II (who ruled between 1583 and 1598) united the Uzbek clans to resist the Shi'ite Safavids (Bukhara's rulers were Sunni), and artisans captured from the Safavid city of Herat (now in western Afghanistan) were instructed to rebuild Bukhara.

Bukhara once again became a regional religious centre, with some 150 madrasas and nearly 300 mosques within the confines of the city, each more ornate and better endowed than the last. In 1747, the Mangit dynasty established itself in power, calling themselves emirs rather than khans from 1785 to stress their religious credentials. During this time, Bukhara was struggling economically as trade took a back seat to religion and goods formerly traded along the Silk Road were now being transported along maritime routes, skipping central Asia entirely. Bukhara's rulers became known for their barbarism and for their religious extremism; the most notorious of them was 'the Butcher' Nasrullah Khan, who murdered 31 relatives (including three brothers) to ascend to the throne in 1826, and later cut his chief advisor in half with an axe. A succession of British and Russian officers, diplomats and spies trooped through Bukhara in this period, including Alexander 'Bukhara' Burnes, and it is Nasrullah Khan who was responsible for the imprisonment and execution of the British officers Conolly and Stoddart (see box, page 240).

ALEXANDER 'BUKHARA' BURNES

The dashing captain, Sir Alexander Burnes FRS (1805–41), cousin of the Scottish poet Robert Burns, joined the East India Company's army at the tender age of 16 and set off to make his fortune. He learned Hindustani and Persian fluently while in service in India, and in 1831 he travelled up the Indus River to Lahore to deliver a gift of horses from King William IV to Maharaja Ranjit Singh, the Lion of the Punjab.

Burnes got a taste for adventure and decided to continue north into virtually unchartered territories, arriving in Bukhara in 1832 disguised as an Afghan trader. His command of Persian must have served him well. Burnes hoped to meet with Emir Nasrullah Khan in person but, probably fortunately for Burnes, he never got further than the Grand Vizier. Burnes collected as much information as he could about the city (particularly things of strategic importance) and left, his neck intact, a month later.

Returning to London, Burnes wrote *Travels into Bokhara*, which overnight became a publishing sensation. The first edition earned him £800 (a significant sum at the time) and a gold medal from the Royal Geographical Society.

With his new-found fame, Burnes was appointed to the court of Sindh and then as political agent to Kabul. He was assassinated in Kabul in 1841, quite possibly by the irate husbands of Afghan women he'd slept with, but not before he'd killed six of his assailants and earned, at least as far as the British were concerned, a heroic reputation.

Few characters in Uzbekistan's history are more colourful than Joseph Wolff (1795–1862), a German-born Cambridge oriental scholar and Jewish-Christian missionary who wound his way to central Asia in the mid 19th century.

Wolff began his wanderings in Egypt and the Holy Land in the 1820s, working as a Christian missionary. He returned to England in 1826 and became obsessed with the idea of finding the Lost Tribes of Israel, a journey which took him through Turkey and the Caucasus, to Afghanistan and then on to India. Subsequent travels took him to Africa and the Americas (where he was ordained as a deacon), and back again to the Middle East.

Wolff set out for Uzbekistan in the 1840s wondering if the Jews of Bukhara were one of the Lost Tribes. He arrived at the court of Nasrullah Khan dressed in full canonical garb (clerical gown, academic hood and shovel hat), much to the surprise of everyone around him: they had never seen anything quite like it. Having heard that Conolly and Stoddart had been imprisoned (but not, alas, that they had already been executed; see box, page 240), he attempted to negotiate their release; he escaped with his life only because the emir was so entertained (and, no doubt, bemused) by Wolff's appearance, and by his styling himself 'Grand Dervish of England, Scotland, and Ireland, and the whole of Europe and America'.

Wolff wrote and published two volumes of *Narrative of a mission to Bokhara, in the years 1843–1845, to ascertain the fate of Colonel Stoddart and Captain Conolly* in 1845 and despite its lengthy title, the book was a huge success, running to no fewer than seven editions in as many years. When nearly 100 years later diplomat and writer Fitzroy Maclean visited central Asia, he retraced Wolff's journey and wrote about him in his own memoirs, *Eastern Approaches* and *A Person from England*.

After military victories in 1866 and 1868, Russia gained trading concessions in the Bukharan emirate and, though remaining nominally independent, it was essentially a Russian protectorate. The Trans-Caspian railway arrived in 1888, physically linking the city to Russia.

The Emirate of Bukhara finally ended with the Bolshevik Revolution. The Bolshevik governor of Tashkent, Kolesov, came to Bukhara to request a peaceful surrender from Alim Khan, but the emir arranged a violent mob to slaughter both this emissary and the Russian detachment that followed. Ethnic Russians living in the city were also killed. Some 15 unfortunate Bolshevik spies were caught and dispatched, one by one, but this was to be the emir's swan song: in 1920, General Mikhail Frunze marched his troops into the city. Large parts of Bukhara were destroyed during four days of fighting, the emir fled to Afghanistan, and by the end of it the Bolshevik flag flew from the Kalyon Minar.

The Bukhara People's Republic was born, and within a matter of weeks the local Communist Party had 14,000 members. The republic joined the Uzbek SSR in 1924, and the transformation of Bukhara from a religious centre to a museum city began: the population halved between 1917 and 1926 (owing to residents moving to new suburbs); mosques were converted into offices and workers' associations; *mullahs* were purged and exiled and madrasas became stables and storage yards. Bukhara was largely left to decay until the 1950s, when the walls were demolished and wide boulevards were driven through the maze of winding alleys and courtyard houses.

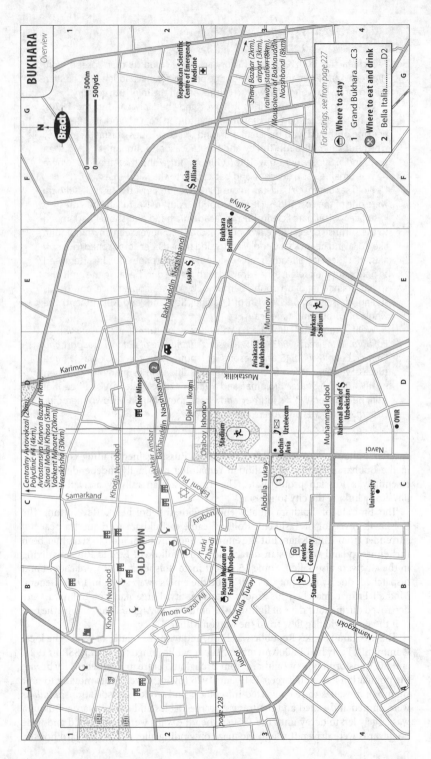

BUKHARA
Overview

N

Bradt

0 ——— 500m
0 ——— 500yds

For listings, see from page 227

Where to stay
1 Grand Bukhara......C3

Where to eat and drink
2 Bella Italia..........D2

Republican Scientific Centre of Emergency Medicine

Shad Bazaar (2km),
airport (3km),
railway station (8km),
Mausoleum of Bakhauddin
Naqshbandi (8km)

Asia Alliance

Zulfiya

Bukhara Brilliant Silk

Asaka $

Bakhauddin Naqshbandi

Muminov

Aviakassa Mukhabbat

Markazi Stadium

Mustakilik

Karimov

Chor Minor

Djaloli Ikromi

Otaboy Ishonov

Bakhauddin Naqshbandi

Mekhtar Ambar

Stadium

Uztelecom

Lochin Avia

Muhammad Iqbol

National Bank of $ Uzbekistan

Navoi

OVIR

Abdulla Tukay

Centralny Avtovokzal (2km),
Polyclinic #4 (4km),
Avtostansiya Karvon Bazaar (4km),
Sitorai Mokhi Khosa (5km),
Vabkent Minaret (20km),
Varakhsha (30km)

Samarkand

Khodja Nurobad

Khodja Nurobad

Espani Pir

OLD TOWN

Arabon

Turki Zhandi

House Museum of Faizulla Khodjaev

Imom Gazoli Ali

Abdulla Tukay

Jewish Cemetery

Stadium

University

Namazgokh

Jubor

page 228

page 228

However, because most buildings were abandoned rather than being demolished, later restorers have had plenty of original material to work with.

In recent years, tourism has fuelled the city's revival, and new hotels have been integrated into the existing urban fabric more successfully than in Samarkand.

GETTING THERE AND AWAY

By air Bukhara's **airport** is 5km east of the city centre. Getting there takes 10 minutes by taxi, and only slightly longer by public transport (midi-bus number 100, 06.30–21.30 daily; US$0.10). There are one or two flights a day to Tashkent (1hr 10min; US$30) and weekly services to Moscow, St Petersburg and Krasnodar.

Tickets are available from the **Uzbekistan Airways** desk at the airport, and also from their ticketing office in the city centre (15 Navoi; ✆ 65 223 5060). For other departure points, including for international flights, Aviakassas include **Lochin Avia** (20/1 Muminov, 15 Navoi; ✆ 65 223 5060) and **Aviakassa Mukhabbat** (2 Muminov; ✆ 65 223 2484).

By rail The **train station** [224 G3] (✆ 65 524 6593) is not actually in Bukhara at all but in Kagan, 10km to the southeast. You can get there by taking minibus number 378 from Bakhauddin Naqshbandi (the airport road) or 236 from the Karvon Bazaar. The station is known as Bukhara-1; nearer town, Bukhara-2 was the terminal of the Emir's private branch but is now only used for freight. Note that the district Bukhara-2 is located in a district known as Vokzal (Station), which can cause confusion.

A taxi from the station to the centre should cost about US$1.50; a seat in a shared taxi will cost around US$0.60.

The fastest trains to Samarkand and Tashkent are the **Afrosiyob** high-speed trains that leave at 04.55 (train 765) and 15.48 (train 761), returning from Tashkent at 07.30 (train 762) and 18.50 (train 766). These travel the 592km journey to Tashkent (Samarkand is 249km away) in around 3 hours 50 minutes; prices start at US$4. There's also the daily **Sharq** service (trains 009/010; 09.13 from Tashkent, 16.10 from Bukhara, doesn't run Tue) which takes 6 hours (calling at other stations such as Dzhizak en route) and costs from US$7. There are also much slower **sleeper trains** (including one that continues to Alat, near the border southwest of Bukhara). These run daily (trains 073/4).

At the end of 2017, a new line opened between Bukhara and Urgench, with an overnight train running from Tashkent (20.30), Samarkand (00.39) and Bukhara (04.15), arriving at Urgench at 10.07; in 2018 this line was extended to reach Khiva at 10.52. The service returns from Khiva at 14.28 and from Urgench at 15.25 and reaches Bukhara at 22.30, Samarkand at 02.30 and Tashkent at 07.00. Bukhara–Urgench fares start from US$3.50 for an unreserved seat (not advised) or US$10 for a Coupé berth. To reach Nukus, you'll have to travel to Navoi (towards Samarkand and Tashkent; page 210) and change there.

Current departure times and fares for all services are listed at w uzrailpass.uz. If you haven't bought your ticket online, you can get it from the Kassa to the right of the train station or from the ticket office on Bakhauddin Naqshbandi (at the bus stop opposite the Restaurant Sezam, halfway to the airport). The station is a bit less palatial than some, but has a decent buffet, an exchange desk, and fast Wi-Fi (accessed through a code sent to a mobile phone).

By road The M37 east of Bukhara to Samarkand and Tashkent is well maintained and a fairly fast drive on smooth tarmac. Travelling west to Khiva, the road was being upgraded (with resulting delays) at the time of going to print, but the much-improved highway should be up and running during the lifespan of this edition noticeably reducing the journey time.

Bukhara has three bus stations; which one you need is dictated by your destination. The **Centralny Avtovokzal** [224 C1] (central bus station) is on Gijduvan Ko'chasi, 3km north of the city centre, and serves Samarkand (6hrs; US$2) and Tashkent (12hrs; US$4), departing in the morning – minibuses to the same destinations cost slightly more but take approximately half as much time, while shared taxis take 4 hours to Samarkand (US$4) and 8 hours to Tashkent (US$8).

The **Avtostansiya Karvon Bazaar** [224 C1], 1.5km further along the same street, has transport to local towns and (around the corner by the westbound carriageway) to Urgench (bus 9hrs, US$9; minibus 7hrs, US$10; shared taxi 6hrs, US$13).

Shared taxis go from the **Sharq Bazaar** [224 G3], 4km east of the city on the road to the railway station, to Karshi (2hrs; US$10) and Shakhrisabz (5hrs; US$14). Minibuses to local destinations also leave from here.

If you are arriving with your own vehicle, bear in mind that there is limited **parking** in the city centre, particularly in the Old Town. Unless your hotel tells you otherwise, you will need to park in the few dozen parking spaces on the edge of Lyabi Hauz, pay an attendant, and then walk to your final destination from there.

GETTING AROUND The best way to explore the centre of Bukhara is **on foot**: indeed, some sections of the Old Town are pedestrianised, and others have a confusing one-way system, so at times walking may be your only option. Cycling also works; bicycles can be hired from East Line Tours (see opposite) for US$10 a day and the Ziyo Baxsh hotel for US$1.25 an hour.

If you are travelling a little further afield, for example to the train or bus station, you can hail one of the city's **yellow taxis** (US$1 for short trips) or, for a cheaper ride, take a **minibus** or **bus**. It's most likely that you'll catch a white midi-bus, costing US$0.10, as few buses run right into the centre nowadays. That said, midi-bus routes 8 and 9 turn around just south of the Hotel Asia (check which direction it's continuing in with the conductor or a passenger). Most routes run north-south along Karimov, just east of the Old Town, and many come from the Karvon Bazaar, the main transport hub north of the centre; they either continue south on Mustakillik or head east on Bakhauddin Naqshbandi towards the airport and Kagan. A few run along Muminov, just south of the centre, ending up just south of the Ark; others run to the west, from the Markazi Bazaar and left (north) past the Ark. The following bus and midi-bus routes are the most useful for tourists:

Midi-bus/Bus 100	North of the centre (various stops) to airport
Midi-bus 236 & 477	Karvon Bazaar and Bakhauddin Naqshbandi to the railway station
Midi-bus 378	Ark and Bakhauddin Naqshbandi to the railway station
Bus 9	Karvon Bazaar to Sharq Bazaar (via centre)
Bus 17	Vokzal and Karimov to Sitorai Mokhi Khosa
Bus 60	Ark to Bakhauddin Naqshbandi Mausoleum

TOURIST INFORMATION AND TOUR OPERATORS There are a couple of tourist information kiosks (⊕ 09.00–22.00 daily) in the centre, and at the airport and railway station, which should give you a free city map.

The following outlets can also assist with tickets, transport, accommodation and guided tours:

East Line Tours [228 F3] 98 Bakhauddin Naqshbandi; ☎65 224 2269; e ru@eastlinetour.uz; w eastlinetour.uz. Professionally run outfit founded in 2004. They offer private, tailor-made tours of the city with bilingual guides & can also arrange excursions further afield.

Komil Travel [228 F4] 40 Barakiyon; ☎65 221 0800; e info@komiltravel.com; w travelbukhara.com. Charming Komil Kadirov arranges cultural tours of Uzbekistan & also more unusual trips such as camel safaris in the Kyzylkum Desert. He speaks good English & is particularly keen to show off the highlights of his home town, Bukhara.

Minzifa Travel [228 F4] 9 Khamza; m 93 659 1107; e travel@minzifatravel.com/sales@minzifatravel.com. Located at the Minzifa Boutique (page 229), the Minzifa team are keen to offer easy-going but educational tours that also benefit the community.

Sarrafon Travel [228 E4] 4 Sarrafon; ☎65 221 0502; e info@sarrafon-travel.uz; w sarrafon-travel.uz. Abdurakhmon Abdullaev is an attentive host (page 230) & guide. He has a detailed knowledge of Bukhara, can make bookings for onward travel & makes reliable accommodation recommendations for other cities in Uzbekistan.

WHERE TO STAY The competition for tourists' business has significantly improved the quality and quantity of accommodation options in Bukhara; there has been a veritable revolution among the budget options, with the city now proudly boasting some of the best guesthouses in the country. There's still a divide between the more sterile, package-tour-focused hotels and the characterful options serving independent travellers, but it is horses for courses: period buildings are not always easily adapted to offer all mod cons. New hotels are limited to three storeys and have been remarkably well designed to fit in to the historic centre, as a rule.

Out of season, particularly from mid-November, most of the hotels in Bukhara are half empty, and you can consequently negotiate a significant reduction in price. The same is true at other times in the larger hotels: if they have groups staying but a few rooms spare, they'll often offer them to individual travellers at the knock-down commercial rate.

Top end

Hotel Asia Bukhara [228 E3] (95 rooms) Mekhtar Ambar; ☎65 224 6431; e reservation.bukhara@asiahotels.uz; w asiahotels.uz. One of the city's largest hotels, this offers a range of facilities, from a swimming pool, sauna & gym to a conference centre & restaurant (page 230). It lacks the character of some older properties, but it is efficiently run & easily caters to large groups. B/fast & Wi-Fi inc. **$$$$**

Hotel Malika [228 E3] (35 rooms) 25 Gavkushon; ☎65 224 6256; e malika-bukhara@mail.ru; w malika-bukhara.com. Part of the well-run Malika chain, the Bukhara property is in a great location midway between Lyabi Hauz & the Kalyon Minar. It's clean & quiet with a gym, sauna & a good restaurant ($$$). **$$$$**

Omar Khayyam Hotel [228 E2] (75 rooms) 7 Haqiqat; ☎65 221 4707; e omar.bukhara@gmail.com; w hotelomarkhayam.com. Tucked immediately behind the Mir i-Arasb, this large, modern hotel is a favourite of European tour groups. The hotel was extended in 2014 & older rooms were renovated at the same time, so it is absolutely immaculate. Rooms are large with spotless linens, satellite TV & AC. The courtyard restaurant ($$$) is gorgeous for b/fast & evening meals (it is too hot at lunchtime). Staff speak English & are exceptionally helpful. **$$$$**

Mid-range

✳ **Amelia Hotel** [228 G3] (11 rooms) 1 Bozor Khoja; ☎65 224 1263; e info@hotelamelia.com; w hotelamelia.com. Even if you have the budget for a top-end option, book yourself into this atmospheric boutique hotel instead – it soundly trounces places twice the price. The rooms are beautifully decorated with relief plasterwork & the modern conveniences (including immaculate bathrooms) integrate sensitively with the old building (a 19th-century Jewish merchant's house). It's in a good location & the staff are warm & attentive. Excellent b/fast. In short, this hotel is a Bukharan gem. **$$$–$$$$**

Devon [228 F3] (32 rooms) 20 Eshoni Pir; ☎65 224 2524; m 93 658 0005; e devontravel@

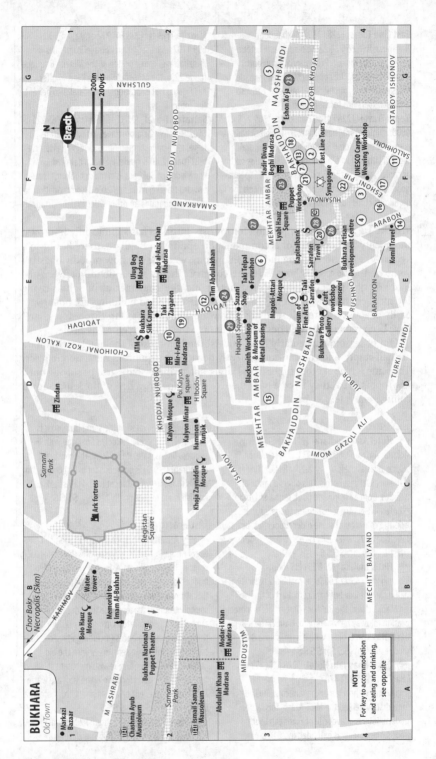

BUKHARA
Old Town

● Markazi
1 Bazaar

Chashma Ayub Mausoleum

Ismail Samani Mausoleum

Bolo Hauz Mosque

Memorial to Imam Al-Bukhari

Water tower

Bukhara National Puppet Theatre

Chor Bakr B
Necropolis (5km)

M ASHRABI

KARIMOV

Samani Park

Registan Square

Ark fortress

Zindan

Samani Park

Khoja Zayniddin Mosque

8

Kalyon Mosque
Kalyon Minaret
Poi Kalyon square
Hammom Kunjak
H'bodov Square

ATM $
Bukhara Silk Carpets

Taki Zargaron

Mir-i-Arab Madrasa 10

19

Ulug Beg Madrasa
Abd al-Aziz Khan Madrasa

Tim Abdullakhan

12

Suzani Shop
Haqiqat Square
Blacksmith Workshop
Museum of Metal Chasing

Taki Telpal Furushon

6

27

Museum of Fine Arts 9
Magoki-Attari Mosque
Taki Sarrafon
Bukhara Photo Gallery
Craft workshop caravanserai
Bukhara Artisan Development Centre

15

Abdullah Khan Madrasa
Modari Khan Madrasa

MIRDUSTIM

MECHITI BALYAND

IMOM GAZOLI ALI

BAKHAUDDIN NAQSHBANDI

MEKHTAR AMBAR

JUBOR

K RUSHNOI

BARAKIYON

TURKI ZHANDI

Komil Travel 14

ARABON

16

4

3

26
20
28 Ⓔ
Sarrafon Travel
Kapitalbank $

Lyabi Hauz Square
Puppet Workshop
25

Nadir Divan Beghi Madrasa

Mekhtar Ambar

18
13
7
21
22
23
1
5

Synagogue

Eshon Xo'ja

BOZOR KHOJA

NAQSHBANDI

BAKHAUDDIN

HUSAINOVA

ESHONI PIR

UNESCO Carpet Weaving Workshop
17
11

East Line Tours
2

SALLOHXONA

OTABOY ISHONOV

GULSHAN

KHODJA NUROBOD

SAMARKAND

HAQIQAT

TADIQAH

CHOIHONAI KOZI KALON

KHODJA NUROBOD

ISLAMOV

N

Bradt

0   200m
0   200yds

NOTE
For key to accommodation and eating and drinking, see opposite

228

mail.ru. Perhaps the most successful of the Old Town's new hotels, fitting unobtrusively into the historic setting. Around the courtyard, there's a restaurant (**$$$**), terrace & lounge & rooms with satellite TV &, in some cases, a balcony. **$$$**

🏠 **Grand Bukhara** [224 C3] (148 rooms) 8 Muminov; 📞65 223 1236/65 223 1604; e info@ bukharatourist.com. Vast, Soviet-era hotel in the government area south of the centre that was (fortunately) renovated in 2009 & handed over to new management in 2018. Service can still be patchy & it is rather overpriced, but there are 2 bars & a restaurant (**$$**), gym & sauna on site. The rooftop bar is a fab spot from which to watch the sun go down. **$$$**

🏠 **Hotel Amulet** [228 G3] (8 rooms) 73 Bakhauddin Naqshbandi; 📞65 224 5342; e tashrif@bu.uzpak.uz. In a converted madrasa (built in 1861), this atmospheric boutique hotel has cosy rooms in former student cells & a good b/fast is served in the courtyard. A nice mix of old & new; rooms have AC & satellite TV. **$$$**

🏠 **Hotel Asl** [228 F3] (12 rooms) 100 Bakhauddin Naqshbandi; 📞65 224 5839; e hotel. asl@gmail.com. Right on Lyabi Hauz, Hotel Asl & the neighbouring (& slightly more expensive) Sultan & Kabir hotels have one of the best locations in the city. Tour groups dominate the clientele, but if they have space then independent travellers can negotiate a discounted rate. B/fast inc. **$$$**

🏠 **Hotel Caravan** [228 C2] (28 rooms) 8 Khodja Nurodod; 📞65 224 6144. Right beside the Ark Fortress, the Caravan has a convenient location & the views from the rooftop across the Old City are impressive. Rooms are clean & unfussy, if a little characterless. B/fast inc. **$$$**

🏠 **Hotel Shakhristan** [228 E2] (18 rooms) 53 Haqiqat; 📞65 224 2108; e shakhriston@yahoo. com; w shakhristan.narod.ru. Overlooking the Toki Telpak Furushon trading dome, this mid-size hotel has large, clean rooms with innocuous décor & AC. **$$$**

🏠 **Kabir Hotel** [228 F3] (15 rooms) Bakhauddin Naqshbandi; m 91 408 3883; e kabir_hotel@mail.ru. Behind a rather unprepossessing façade on the corner of Lyabi Hauz, the Kabir's interior is loosely modelled on a traditional Bukharan house, with large, clean & comfortable rooms. The rooftop bar has panoramic views of the Old City, but b/fast is served in the basement. **$$$**

✳ 🏠 **Komil Boutique Hotel** [228 F4] (29 rooms) 40 Barakiyon; 📞65 221 0800; e info@ komiltravel.com; w travelbukhara.com. A restored merchant's home, just south of Lyabi Hauz, this lovely place has a 19th-century dining room & rooms decorated in a 19th-century style (but with AC & satellite TV), set around a series of courtyards with decorative pillars & plasterwork. Komil (who speaks English & German) also organises tours to the Nuratau Mountains & Lake Aidarkul (see box, page 216 & page 217). Massages available for an additional cost & a set dinner (US$10 plus alcohol), with vegetarian options available. **$$$**

🏠 **Minzifa Boutique** [228 F4] (12 rooms) 63 Eshoni Pir; 📞65 221 0628; e minzifa_inn@ mail.ru; w minzifa.com. Just south of Lyabi Hauz, Minzifa is a modern building, but you wouldn't know it; it's been carefully designed to recreate the architecture of 19th-century Bukhara. Antique wooden gates open on to a courtyard, the perfect place to take tea. Rooms are all decorated with

---

BUKHARA *Old Town*
For listings, see from page 227

🏠 **Where to stay**

⊗ **Where to eat and drink**

local textiles & paintings. At the time of writing, the hotel was planning on expanding into the Minzifa madrasa next door; they also own the nearby but less attractive **Minzifa Hotel ($$$)**, along with Minzifa Travel (page 227) & the Minzifa Restaurant (see below). See ad, page 219. **$$$**

🏠 **Sultan Hotel** [228 F3] (12 rooms) 100 Bakhauddin Naqshbandi; 📞65 224 2435; e hotelsultan@gmail.com. Right on Lyabi Hauz, there's little to choose from between the Sultan & neighbouring Hotel Asl, though the Sultan is a little more expensive. **$$$**

🏠 **Hélène Oasis** [228 F4] 9 Arabon; 📞65 221 0622; m 93 960 5181; e heleneoasis@mail.ru; w heleneoasis.com/en. Delightful French-owned guesthouse with rooms on 2 floors along the long courtyard & a tasty b/fast served in the lovely dining room of a Jewish merchant's house. Not the fanciest, but nicely decorated & very welcoming. **$$–$$$**

Budget

🏠 **Hotel Orom** [228 D2] (11 rooms) 9 Haqiqat; 📞65 224 6498; e hotel-orom@yandex. ru. Small, conveniently located hotel with an attractive interior courtyard decorated in traditional style. **$$**

🏠 **New Moon** [228 F3] (10 rooms) 8 Eshoni Pir; 📞65 224 4442; e xilol@newmoon-hotel. com; w newmoon-hotel.com. Large rooms & a convenient location, all at an affordable price. **$$**

🏠 **Sarrafon B&B** [228 E4] (5 rooms) 4 Sarrafon; 📞65 221 0502; m 91 402 0641; e info@ sarrafon-travel.uz. The best of Bukhara's budget

options, Sarrafon is comfortable & well located with friendly, accommodating staff, AC & private bathrooms. It's also possible to share rooms, hostel style. B/fast inc. **$$**

Hostels and homestays

🏠 **Madina & Ali's Guesthouse** [228 D3] 18 Mekhtar Ambar; 📞65 224 6162; m 90 512 5820; e madina.hotel@mail.ru; w madina-ali.blogspot. com; 📘 madinaandaliguesthousebukhara. A lovely family guesthouse with both private rooms (en suite & shared bathrooms) & shared rooms (US$10–12), all with Wi-Fi. Great b/fast & other good meals (especially *plov*) are available for guests. Fairly central (look for a blue door down an alley on the south side). **$$**

🏠 **Guesthouse Gulnarakhanum** [228 F4] (5 rooms) 8 Eshoni Pir; m 93 620 7884/93 622 6717; e mehrinigorkarimova776@gmail.com. A simple guesthouse & hostel with an attractive little courtyard & AC rooms. **$**

🏠 **Hostel Rumi** [228 F4] 19 Sallohhona; 📞65 221 0621; m 90 637 0545; w hotel-rumi.business. site. A traditional family home with a mix of dorms & private rooms, aimed at overland travellers & other skinflints. Located on the southern edge of the Old Town, towards the stadium. There's parking available here. B/fast inc. **$**

🏠 **Umarxon Hostel** [228 F4] 44 Eshoni Pir; 📞65 224 3734; m 91 417 3734. A welcoming, family-owned home with shared & private rooms; they'll cook a great dinner with a bit of advance notice. **$**

✕ **WHERE TO EAT AND DRINK** With a significant footfall of tourists, Bukhara is bound to have plenty of places to eat and drink. That's not to say that they all offer quality food, or value for money, as often their reason for staying in business is that they can seat an entire coach party at once. These are all open from mid morning until around 22.00, unless specified otherwise. Bukhara is known for its *shashlik* and for Jewish dishes, such as stews cooked slowly overnight for the sabbath.

Restaurants

✕ **Asia** [228 E3] Mekhtar Ambar; 📞65 224 6431; m 91 445 8230. The restaurant inside Hotel Asia Bukhara (page 227) has a bland menu of European dishes targeted at coach parties, but is redeemed by the nightly dance shows & 10 varieties of tea. **$$$$**

✕ **Bella Italia** [224 D2] 125 Bakhauddin Naqshbandi; 📞65 224 3346; m 93 383 4700; 🕐 11.00–23.00 daily. With a menu that

offers such culinary delights as 'horse flesh & bear-battered fish', you might be forgiven for wondering what you've let yourself in for. Fortunately, it's a laid-back place with a good selection of salads, & freshly prepared pizza & pasta dishes. The garlic bread is pretty tasty. 15% service charge. **$$$$**

✕ **Minzifa Restaurant** [228 E4] 6 Khoja Rushnoy; 📞65 221 0175; m 90 718 5798; 🕐 11.00–23.00 daily. Up the steps just east of the Sarrafon baths, this has a pleasant rooftop terrace looking over the hammam's domes. It offers a fusion of local & European cuisines with a reasonable range of vegetarian options, & an efficient service that slows down dramatically when a group arrives. $$$$

✖ **Dolon** [228 E3] Northeast cnr Haqiqat Sq; m 90 274 5366; ⏰ 10.00–midnight daily. Take lunch on the roof of this centrally located restaurant for a fabulous new perspective on Bukhara. The Uzbek food is passable, but your attention will be on the views. $$$

✖ **Old Bukhara** [228 F3] 3 Samarkand; m 90 185 7077; ⏰ 10.00–23.00 daily. One of the best places in town for classic Uzbek food such as *shashlik, plov* & salads; there's an attractive rooftop terrace & rooms are decorated with *ikat* & pottery. Not particularly expensive. $$$

✖ **Saroy Restaurant** [228 F4] Bakhauddin Naqshbandi; m 90 744 1034/97 304 4454; e mirshod.saroy@gmail.com; ⏰ 12.30–23.30 daily. On the cnr of Sarrafon, this small but atmospheric restaurant has tasty dishes & efficient service. $$$

Cafés, tea houses and bars

🍵 **Café Wishbone** [228 E2] Tim Abdullakhan market; m 93 658 4050; w cafe-wishbone-bukhara.uz; ⏰ 09.00–20.00 daily. For those craving a decent coffee & a small selection of homemade cakes (both sadly rarities in Uzbekistan), this German café is an absolute godsend, even without Wi-Fi. The domed interior is simple & cool & there is a small terrace for the warmer months. English & German are spoken. An espresso or matcha chai will cost you US$1, & a slice of apple strudel to go with it US$1. The café is within a stone's throw of the Kalyon Minar. $$$

🍵 **Malika Tea House** [228 E3] 25 Garkushon; 📞 65 224 6256. Traditional-style tea house-restaurant on the 2nd floor of the Hotel Malika (page 227), decorated with wall paintings & silk hangings. The wooden beams supporting the roof were hand carved by local craftsmen in 2007. Enjoy your tea with a view of Bukhara's Old Town. $$$

🍵 **Silk Road Tea House** [228 D3] 5 H Ibodov; 📞 65 224 2268; w silkroadspices.co; ⏰ 09.00–19.00 daily. Run by the proprietors of Silk Road Spices, who claim to have been in business since 1400, the numerous teas & *tisanes* on the menu certainly suggest a long history in the spice trade. Coffee & cardamom, saffron tea & ginger tea all feature on the menu (which is available in English) & can be enjoyed with the accompaniment of sticky sweets such as *halva* & *nabat*. Everything is also available to take away. $$$

🍵 **Chinar Chaikhana** [228 G3] Bakhauddin Naqshbandi; m 91 446 2227/97 488 4349; ⏰ 11.00–23.00 daily. A busy place that serves good Uzbek food for a fair price, considering how many tourist groups eat here. $$

🍵 **Lyabi Hauz Chaikhana** [228 F3] Lyabi Hauz. On the edge of the reservoir, this must have the best location of any *chaikhana* in Uzbekistan. Though it is crowded with tourists in summer, out of season things are rather more relaxed & you'll be sitting alongside local chess players drinking endless bowls of tea. The food is good too, with *shashlik*, salads, soup & vegetarian dishes; you can get beer from a stall by the pool. $$

🍷 **Under the Moon** [228 F3] ⏰ 19.00–midnight daily. The Hotel Asia Bukhara's (page 227) rooftop bar, also known as the Sky Bar or even 'the aircrew bar', is an unmissable place for a drink, with a view over Old Bukhara. $$

ENTERTAINMENT AND NIGHTLIFE Bukhara isn't exactly renowned for its nightlife, but during the high season there are various evening entertainment options that draw in the tourist crowds.

The annual **Silk & Spice Festival** takes place on (or close to) the last weekend of May and aims to preserve the city's artistic heritage with a programme of music and dance performances and craft exhibitions held at various central sites. On around the third weekend of October, the **Bukhara City Festival** is more for the locals – it's lively, with food, drink and raucous music, but the noise dies down by about 20.00.

Other options for an evening's fun include taking in a performance by the **Bukhara National Puppet Theatre** [228 B2] (Nadir Divan Beghi Khanagha; ⏰ summer 18.00 & 19.00 daily, rest of year 17.00 & 18.00; US$5) or the **Bukhorcha Song and Dance Group** (Nadir Divan Beghi Madrasa; ⏰ summer 19.00 daily;

US$5). Neither of these shows is particularly highbrow (or authentic), but they tend to be good fun and well attended nonetheless.

SHOPPING

Souvenirs Souvenirs are, quite predictably, everywhere in Bukhara, but their quality is hit and miss. Expect to haggle hard, and don't be afraid to walk away if you think you're being fleeced, as you probably are. There are numerous souvenir stalls in Bukhara's madrasas and the three restored 16th-century trading domes: **Taki Sarrafon** [228 E4] (the money changers' dome); **Taki Telpal Furushon** [228 E3] (the hat makers' dome); and **Taki Zargaron** [228 E2] (the jewellers' dome). Much of what they sell is uninspiring and probably made in China, but they are well worth a visit for the impressive (and historically significant) buildings that house them. Taki, incidentally, means dome or arch.

Metal working and jewellery making have long been important here, thanks to the gold washed from the mountains by the Zerafshan ('gold-bearing') River. Carpets, *ikat* textiles, woodwork (including musical instruments), hats and miniature paintings are also made in the city. A pure wool carpet might cost in excess of US$250, or about half that price if woven on a cotton base; a pure silk carpet could cost ten times as much. Many of the carpets for sale here are actually made in Turkmenistan. Bukhara is also the best place to find antique *suzanis* (see box, page 78).

The following options are friendly, knowledgeable about their products and will always haggle in a good-natured manner.

Blacksmith Workshop & Museum of Metal Chasing [228 E3] 12 Haqiqat Sq; \ 65 224 5765; ⊕ 09.00–18.00 daily. At the exit from the Taki Telpak Furushon, opposite Silk Road Spices, you can watch craftsmen at work &, of course, shop.

Bukhara Artisan Development Centre [228 F3] Lyabi Hauz; ⊕ 09.00–18.00 daily. The cells of this restored *caravanserai* (& a similar centre west of the Taki Sarrafon [228 E4]) house the numerous workshops of miniaturists, embroiderers, decorative metalworkers & weavers. You can watch them work (the embroidery with golden thread looks particularly striking, if not to everyone's taste), hear them explain about their crafts &, of course, buy directly from the producers. Handwoven *ikat* scarves, fresh from the loom, so to speak, cost US$15.

Bukhara Brilliant Silk [224 F3] 256 Bakhauddin Naqshbandi (entrance around the cnr on Zulfiya); m 91 443 9449; e bbsilk@mail.ru; w uzbbsilk. com.You can take a factory tour (available on request) & buy carpets here.

Bukhara Silk Carpets [228 D2] Khodja Nurobod; \ 65 722 0220; m 90 513 4824; e Muhammad. mk@mail.ru; ⊕ 09.00–19.00 daily. The lovely Sabina runs what is one of Bukhara's largest carpet shops. There is a wide range of styles, sizes & prices as carpets cover every surface, including the walls,

& the staff are up front about which carpets are handmade & which are not. Some are now made in Turkmenistan, & it's possible that some actually come from China. You can watch carpets being woven in the shop by a gaggle of young women sat cross-legged & simultaneously knotting & gossiping at the looms in the corner.

Puppet Workshop [228 F3] Lyabi Hauz; e puppets@rambler.ru, w bukharapuppets.net; ⊕ 08.30–12.30 & 13.30–19.00 daily. At the cnr of Husainova, the alley south to the synagogue, this has remarkably good displays on the walls & you can watch papier-mâché puppets being moulded, sanded, painted & costumed & buy your own.

Suzani Shop [228 E3] Haqiqat Sq. A mother & her teenage daughter run this Aladdin's cave of textile treasures. In addition to the usual *suzanis* & scarves (some old, some new) is a small but beautiful selection of traditional costume pieces that include *chapans* & short, embroidered jackets: it is a rail of these that will most likely catch your eye outside. Vazira, the daughter, speaks English well but is still keen to practise while you haggle for the inevitable discount. We left with a free gift, too.

Tim Abdullakhan [228 E2] Haqiqat Sq; \ 65 190 3720; e samira_fayz@mail.ru. Once the Tim-i Kalan (the Great Market), silks & other textiles have been traded in this covered marketplace since

1577. A large number of quality carpets & *suzanis* are for sale inside the beautiful historic building with its cupolas, galleries & niches. Visit as much for the surroundings as for the stock, & be prepared to drink endless bowls of tea while making your final selection.

UNESCO Carpet Weaving Workshop [228 F4] 57 Eshoni Pir; ⏲ 09.00–17.00 Mon–Sat. No longer run by UNESCO, despite its name, this workshop, located in a former madrasa, produces traditional carpets using natural dyes.

Food To buy picnic items, bottled water and snacks, go to **Eshon Xo'ja** [228 G3] (cnr Bakhauddin Naqshbandi & Eshoni Pir), a well-stocked convenience store located just 2 minutes from Lyabi Hauz, but far friendlier and less overpriced than the food shops there. Otherwise, the main food markets are the Markazi and Karvon bazaars (pages 237 and 226).

OTHER PRACTICALITIES
Communications
Many of Bukhara's hotels & cafés now have **Wi-Fi** & it's usually free if you're staying there or buy a coffee. If you're without your own laptop or smartphone, there are also a few internet cafés to the southeast on Mustakillik, charging US$0.10 an hour.

✉ **Post office** [224 D3] 8 Muminov; ⏲ 09.00–17.00 Mon–Fri. Opposite the stadium. Counters can also be found at Hotel Grand Bukhara (page 229) & the airport.
Uztelecom [224 C3] 8 Muminov; ⏲ 24/7. In the same building as the post office. For telephone & telegraph service. For courier services, **EMS** is also found here.

Medical
For general aches, pains, stomach upsets & mild injuries, head to either of the polyclinics listed below.

✚ **Polyclinic #2** [224 G3] 61 Bakhauddin Naqshbandi; ✆65 223 0503. Just east of the centre.
✚ **Polyclinic #4** [224 C1] 80 Gijduvani Ko'chasi; ✆65 224 8374. On the main road north beyond the Karvon Bazaar.
✚ **Republican Scientific Centre of Emergency Medicine** [224 G2] 159 Bakhauddin Naqshbandi; ✆65 225 1026; ⏲ 24/7. For medical emergencies. Well equipped by Uzbek standards but still not really comparable to a Western hospital.

Money
If you have a Visa card, Kapitalbank has quite a few yellow ATMs for you across the city, both in hotels & on the street. There are exchange offices in the Asia & Grand Bukhara hotels (pages 227 & 229). Otherwise, you can withdraw money from the following:

$ **Asaka Bank** [224 E2] ✆65 770 0506; e buxoroviloyat@asakabank.uz; ⏲ 09.00–17.00 Mon–Fri
$ **Asia Alliance Bank** [224 F2] ✆65 223 0408; ⏲ 09.00–13.00 & 14.00–18.00 Mon–Fri; 24hr ATMs on the west side of Lyabi Hauz, at Sitorai Mokhi Khosa, 15 Murtazayev & 11 M Iqbol
$ **Kapitalbank** [228 E3] ✆65 770 1224; ⏲ 09.00–17.00 Mon–Fri; ATMs on Khodja Nurobod (by Bukhara Silk Carpets) & in the Grand Bukhara & Malika hotels
$ **National Bank of Uzbekistan** [224 D4] ✆65 223 7098; ⏲ 09.00–18.00 Mon–Sat

Registration
All of Bukhara's hotels should register you automatically, but head to the OVIR if you need to register yourself.

OVIR [224 D4] 10/3 Murtazaev. Just northeast of the junction with Navoi.

WHAT TO SEE AND DO
The Ark [228 C1/2] (Registan Sq; ⏲ 09.00–19.00 daily; adults US$2, includes entry to the Archaeology & Local History museums) The mud-brick walls of the Ark fortress grace almost every postcard of Bukhara: it is to this city as the Eiffel Tower is to Paris, or Tower Bridge is to London. It's both an architectural icon and, if we're truly honest, a slightly overrated tourist spot.

The exact origins of the Ark are lost in the mists of time, but archaeologists believe it to have first been built sometime between the 5th and 6th centuries AD. The original structure covered a roughly rectangular site of some 3ha and included a palace, Zoroastrian fire temple, administrative areas and guardrooms; the main functions of the town all took place within these city walls so that they could more easily be defended in the case of attack. The earliest structure recorded in local histories, built by Bukhar Khudat Bidun in the 7th century AD, collapsed and so did its successors. It was only when the fortress was reconstructed to reflect the shape and orientation of the constellation Ursa Major (the Great Bear) at the suggestion of a local seer that the gods were satisfied and the structure stood firm (at least for the time being).

The Arabs built Bukhara's first mosque in the confines of the Ark in AD713; they set it atop the smouldering ruins of the earlier Zoroastrian temple to assert physically and metaphorically the power of Islam over other faiths and their adherents. The site was heavily fortified by the Samanids and Karakhanids between the 9th and 13th centuries, during which time the vast, sloped ramparts were added, only to then be razed by the Karakhitai, the Khorezmshah and, last but certainly not least, the Mongols.

Most of what you see still standing at the Ark today dates from the 16th-century Shaybanid dynasty, with later additions from the Mangits (1753–1920). Under Shaybanid rule the Ark was expanded to accommodate not only the royal family, but also a population of some 3,000 people, their homes, workplaces and mosques. Everything from the royal mint and treasury to the dungeons and slave quarters were within the citadel's walls.

A similar-sized population was still living in the Ark in 1920 when a fire ripped through the site, destroying as many as 80% of the buildings. The fire was no accident, though no-one is really sure whether it was the Bolsheviks (allegedly dropping bombs from planes) or the ousted, and understandably irate, emir who was responsible for striking the match. Derelict and blackened, the corpse of the Ark was an easy target for Soviet propaganda, and it continued to disintegrate throughout the 20th century, the only pitiful use of its remaining, decaying buildings being to house Bukhara's history museum and archives. Thankfully, the front part of the Ark has now been restored and reopened to the public, and an ongoing renovation project will bring back to life other parts of the site one section at a time.

Your visit to the Ark will inevitably begin with the **Registan** [228 C2], the vast square outside what is now the Ark's main gate. Historically, it served as both a slave market and public execution ground, though now it lies empty save for tourists posing for photos with camels.

To picture the square at its height requires you to use your imagination: Soviet demolition crews made sure of that. Stand in the square facing the citadel walls and envisage the luxurious home of the *tupchi bashi*, the city's chief of artillery, surrounded by cannons seized in battle from the Kokand khanate. To your left would have stood a line of mosques and madrasas equal in beauty to those surrounding the Registan in Samarkand. The square itself would have been heaving: you'd have been jostled from every angle by courtiers and street hawkers, slave traders showing off their wares, and an occasional dervish spinning through on his way to the khanagha. When the drumbeat was heard from atop the city walls, the crowd would have surged forward for a grisly hour's entertainment: the ground would run red with the blood of publicly executed prisoners.

Entrance to the Ark is through the **Western Gate**, an imposing entrance way built by Nadir Shah in 1742. The second, southern or Kalyon Gate has long-since been destroyed. Two important items once hung from this gateway: a *khamcha* (six-stranded whip) to remind the people of the emir's power; and a mechanical clock made by an Italian clockmaker, Giovanni Orlandi, who was captured by Turkmen slave traders in Orenburg, Russia in the mid 19th century. Orlandi earned himself a temporary reprieve by offering to make the clock (at the time the only mechanical clock in Bukhara) for Nasrullah Khan but once it was completed, Orlandi was caught drunk and this gave Nasrullah the excuse he wanted to sentence the Italian to death. The skin on his neck was sliced off, and he was then beheaded.

Climbing the steep stone ramp through the gateway brings you to an entry passage lined with historical photos, weapons and Chinese pots: a taster for the displays of the regional history museum dotted around the citadel. There is a definite sense of shades of former glory, though as the renovation programme continues and as more areas are restored and opened to the public, you should get a picture of what life inside the citadel was like. You will come across a number of restored structures in a tightly contained area: first the 18th-century **Jome mosque**, which now houses a small exhibition of calligraphy, including early Qu'rans and illuminated works of poetry; then, down an alley to the left, the Kush Begi Complex (the prime minister's residence).

This complex comprises three *khanas*: the **elchi khana**, an administrative building that contains underwhelming archaeological displays and ethnographic and nature sections; the **salam khana** (courtyard of greetings) where Conolly made his infamous (and ultimately fatal) error of judgement, off which is the display of Ancient and Medieval History of the Bukhara Oasis, which actually covers older archaeology than the previous section; and the 17th-century **kurinesh khana** (throne hall), actually a courtyard, where the emirs were crowned and lifted on to a marble throne (dating from 1699) while sitting on a silk carpet. You will also see some fine royal costumes (including the emir's coronation robes and an accompanying 20m-long turban) and illuminating photographs of the Ark when it was still inhabited.

The neighbouring courtyard overlooks the two-storey orchestra pit, the **nagora khana**, from which the court's musicians serenaded (or at least so he claimed) Joseph Wolff with a rousing rendition of *God Save the Queen* (see box, page 223). External wooden stairs lead up to the History of the Bukhara Khanate and Emirate section, holding ceramics, weapons and photos; a further flight leads up to a display of coins and inscriptions spanning 2,000 years.

For those with an interest in the Great Game (see box, page 19), the most important, and also most harrowing, sight is the **zindan** (just northeast of the Ark), the 18th-century jail in which the unfortunate Conolly and Stoddart (see box, page 240) were kept prior to their execution. This is accessed around the back of the Ark and requires a separate ticket (US$1.25). This is technically called the Museum of History of Law and Court System of Bukhara, and there are a few weapons on display along with information on the legal system, rather confused by the fact that 'Qozi' is translated as jury when it in fact means judge. Even now the jury system has barely arrived here. Off the guards' cell is the notorious Bug Pit, with some feeble mannequins 6m below where wretched men, starving and chained by the neck, were abandoned to be tormented by snakes and scorpions. The exhibits inside include a few items relating to torture, photographs of victims, and some more models of prisoners, forever trapped in the gloomy cells.

Across the road from the Ark, a former **water tower** (built in 1927 by the constructivist architect Vladimir Shukhov) has been rebuilt, with a modern lift alongside (US$4). It opened in 2019 as a café (**$$**), and offers the best views of both the Ark and the city.

Samani Park and around In and around **Samani Park** [228 B2] (cnr S Murodov & M Ashrafi), west of the Ark, are three exceptionally important structures, often overlooked by tourists in their bid to take in the big-name sites emblazoned on postcards and souvenir tea towels. The first is the **Chashma Ayub Mausoleum** [228 A2] (M Ashrafi; ⊕ 09.00–18.00 daily; US$1.10), which purportedly marks the spot where the Prophet Job struck the arid ground and a spring of pure drinking water miraculously burst forth, saving his followers when those around them were dying of thirst. The city grew up around this holy site, and this may be a reason why the city's early Jewish community (page 244) chose to settle here.

First erected in the 11th century, the plain and slightly austere mausoleum you see today was raised by Timur in 1380 to protect the sacred tomb below. It is not known who is buried here, but it certainly isn't Job. On the roof are three domes, each one unique and dating from a different period of the building's construction.

ABU IBN SINA (AVICENNA)

Medieval Bukhara was a hotbed for intellectuals from across the Islamic world, and one of its most remarkable sons was Abu ibn Sina (AD980–1037), known in the west as Avicenna.

Born in the village of Afshona, north of Bukhara, the son of an Ismaili scholar from Balkh, ibn Sina gained a rigorous education in Bukhara, which was then the capital of the Samanid Empire. According to his biographers, he had memorised the entire Qu'ran by the age of ten, and he read Aristotle's *Metaphysics* more than 40 times during his teenage years. Ibn Sina then turned his attention to medicine, studying medical theory but also experimenting with his own treatments and remedies.

His appointment as court physician at the age of 18 gave ibn Sina access to the Samanid royal library, a treasure trove of scholarship. Ibn Sina was able to immerse himself in books, further educating himself in logic and astronomy. He remained in Bukhara until the fall of the Samanids in 1004, whence he travelled to Urgench, Merv, Tehran and Isfahan. In every place he sought more knowledge, and lectured on what he knew.

Throughout his life, ibn Sina wrote extensively. His most important works are in the fields of philosophy and medicine. His treaties on metaphysics and logic were written in Arabic and attempted to reconcile Aristotelianism and Neoplatonism; Avicennan philosophy became the leading school of medieval Islamic thought, and was also influential in Europe.

Ibn Sina's 14-volume *Canon of Medicine* was a standard medical textbook in European universities as late as the 18th century. He made original observations on conditions from diabetes to facial paralysis, classified diseases and their causes, and laid down methodology for testing the efficacy of new medications. More importantly, he adopted ideas from the ancient Greeks about contagious diseases, leading to germ theory and the adoption of quarantine (and eventually the spread of hospitals to western Europe after the Crusades). Ibn Sina was the first person to use a cannula to open the windpipe of a choking patient, and he recognised the importance of diet, exercise and psychology in good health.

The **Avicenna Museum** was opened in Afshona to mark the 1,000th anniversary of his birth, but it is not of interest to general visitors and few of the exhibits are marked.

The shape of one of the domes, atypical in the region, is thought to have been derived from the roof of a Khorezmian nomads' tent.

Inside the mausoleum you will find a small **museum** (⏰ 09.00–18.00 daily; US$1) dedicated to Bukhara's water supply. There are displays on irrigation, hammams and water carrying, including a few photographs.

Immediately opposite the mausoleum is the modern **Memorial to Imam Al-Bukhari** [228 B1]. Born in Bukhara in AD810, Al-Bukhari (page 179) collected 97 volumes of Hadiths, the sayings of the Prophet Muhammad.

Across the road to the north is the **Markazi Bazaar** (Central Market) [228 A1], where it's great to wander through the alleyways and soak up the atmosphere; domestic animals are sold here daily until noon, including pigeons and songbirds.

More elaborate, and of great historical importance, is the early 10th-century **Ismail Samani Mausoleum** [228 A2], which gives the park its name. It is the oldest Islamic monument in Bukhara, a perfect cube of seemingly woven brickwork that marks the grave of the founder of the Samanid dynasty as well as his father, nephew and other family members. Pilgrims have been drawn to Ismail Samani's tomb for more than a millennium: it was one of the holiest sites in Bukhara, the final resting place of ancient kings. It sits by a pool, a 5-minute walk west into the park towards a Ferris wheel.

Striking in its simplicity, the design incorporates aspects of Sogdian architecture, newer mathematical developments and even Sassanid fire temples. The cubic shape harks back to the Kaaba in the Masjid al-Haram in Mecca, and the dome above it represents the heavens. The complex patterns in the brickwork add texture to the four equal façades, enticing visitors to run their hands across the grainy surface. There are two reasons for its unusually good state of preservation: it is made from fired bricks instead of sun-dried mud bricks; and it was partially buried beneath the sands until the 1930s. This protected it from both the wrath of Genghis Khan and the Bolsheviks and the erosion of time and weather. When it was discovered in 1934 by Soviet archaeologists it was fully excavated, and the graves relocated. Only the dome has had to be rebuilt.

Poi Kalyon Square [228 D2]
The Poi Kalyon square is the star in the Bukharan sapphire, the beating heart of the Old Town, and the visual high point (both literal and metaphorical) of the city's skyline. The name, which means 'at the foot of the Great', is derived from its place at the foot of the Kalyon Minar, the tapering, mud-brick tower which rises gracefully some 46m above the city.

Kalyon Minar (Great Minaret) The minaret was built in 1127 and it was, so an inscription tells us, the work of an architect named Bako. He ordered that the foundations be dug some 13m deep, and demanded the labourers use a special mortar that was mixed with bulls' blood, camel milk and eggs, which took two years to set. The exact original height of the minaret is unknown, but it is thought to have been the tallest free-standing tower in the world. The uppermost section appears to have been lost (possibly due to an earthquake) and the part below reworked.

Bako died not long after the minaret was completed, purportedly broken hearted that it had failed to live up to his dreams. Genghis Khan looked upon it a little more favourably in the following century, however, and, having seen it for miles as he rode across the steppe and been suitably impressed, he spared the tower when all around it was razed. It used to be possible to climb the 104 steps of the spiral stairs to the top, where the Mangits were fond of tying their prisoners up in sacks and chucking them off the top, a grisly but no doubt effective punishment that endured well into the 1800s (and again in 1917–20), much to the disgust of Lord Curzon (see box, below). Now, however, there's only access for researchers.

Kalyon Mosque (Great Mosque; ⊕ 08.00–20.00 daily; US$0.75) In the sundial-like shadow of the Kalyon Minar, the Kalyon Mosque stands on the foundations of the earlier, 8th-century mosque in which Genghis Khan ordered that the pages of the Qu'ran be trampled beneath the feet of his horses and the entirety of Bukhara (with the exception of the Kalyon Minar) be destroyed. The mosque was burnt to a cinder.

This replacement, a worthy successor, is also known as the Juma or Friday Mosque and was built by the Shaybanids in 1514. An inscription on the mosque's façade attests to this completion date. Since then it has served as the city's main mosque: there is space for more than 10,000 worshippers to pray, the entire male population of the city at the time of its construction. Passing through the eastern gate on Poi Kalyon, you enter a truly breathtakingly beautiful courtyard surrounded by 208 columns and 288 domes; the numerous pillars, forming triple aisles on either side, evoke the legendary court of Solomon and are an evocative statement in mosques and palaces from the Alhambra in Moorish Spain, to the forts and palaces of emperors in Mughal India. At the far (western) end of the plaza is the turquoise-tiled **Kok Gumbaz** (blue dome), an architectural bubble, the shape of which belies its weight and width. Beneath it lies the mosque's wonderfully gilded *mihrab* and an unusual octagonal structure designed to improve the building's acoustics,

LORD CURZON IN UZBEKISTAN   *Bijan Omrani*

In the summer of 1888, the Honourable George Nathaniel Curzon – Old Etonian, classical scholar, precocious modern linguist, Fellow of All Souls College, Oxford and 29-year-old Conservative MP – set out for central Asia. At that time the Great Game was in full swing, and debate in England about the intentions of Russia was at its height. Many believed that having taken over central Asia up to the northern borders of Afghanistan, Russia was now preparing to launch an attack on India. Few Europeans or non-Russians had been to central Asia, so Curzon wanted to visit the region and judge the situation for himself.

Curzon travelled along the newly built Trans-Caspian railway to Tashkent, where it then terminated, and from there by horse-drawn *tarantass* to Bukhara. The following year, he published his observations in a consistently entertaining 478-page work entitled *Russia in Central Asia and the Anglo-Russian Question*.

Curzon asserted in his introduction that his purpose was to write a work primarily dedicated to the problems of politics and foreign relations. However, he also admitted travelling at a 'unique' moment, when the railway had made travel suddenly easy, but had not yet changed the ancient way of life in the region, which he could see it would soon do. When he travelled, criminals were still hurled to their death from the great minaret of Bukhara, the city centres still bustled with their ancient trades and craftsmen, and the old rulers were still maintained (albeit as Russian puppets) in the medieval magnificence of their courts. Hence, Curzon's work is not only a well-informed assessment of Russia's objectives in the region, but also a compelling snapshot of the old Silk Road cities before the railways changed them forever.

amplifying the voice of the imam as he speaks his Friday sermon. The inscription on the dome itself, a spider-spun web of Kufic calligraphy, reads 'Immortality belongs to God'.

Having been used as a warehouse during the Soviet period, the Kalyon Mosque reopened to worshippers in 1991. It continues to be a place of prayer, albeit on a fraction of the scale for which it was originally intended, but visitors and their cameras are welcome to come inside providing they are appropriately dressed and behave in a respectful manner.

Mir-i Arab Madrasa Opposite the mosque is the Mir-i Arab Madrasa, constructed, so they say, with the profits from the sale of 3,000 Persian slaves. Its benefactor, the Shaybanid Khan Ubaidullah, clearly felt a need to salve his conscience, and hence in 1530–36 he endowed what is considered one of the most important educational establishments in the Islamic world. With the exception of a 21-year period of closure from 1925 to 1946, it has remained fully functional, including throughout the Soviet period, and today around 120 students are studying here. They take a demanding four-year programme of Arabic and Qu'ranic studies, the first step on the path to becoming imams. There is limited access for tourists to the madrasa: you can enter the foyer and look into the inner courtyard but, theoretically at least, can go no further. However, if you ask nicely and there is an appropriate guide present, you may also be permitted to view the tombs, under the left dome, of Sheikh Abdullah of Yemen (also known as Sayyid Abd Yamaniy or Mir-i Arab, the prince of the Arabs), a close friend of Khan Ubaidullah who directed the madrasa's construction. The tombs are marked with a white flag and a goat's tail, the traditional signs of saints, and of Khan Ubaidullah himself.

Lyabi Hauz Square [228 F3] The heart of Old Bukhara is the photogenic Lyabi Hauz Square on Bakhauddin Naqshbandi, centred on an **artificial reservoir** (a *hauz* in Persian) constructed on the orders of the Grand Vizier, Nadir Divan Beghi, around 1620. The surrounding mulberry trees predate the construction of the *hauz* by 150 years, suggesting the square has long been a shaded focal point in the city. Early visitors recall the presence of jugglers, storytellers and dancing boys, musicians and magicians, and even the occasional Indian snake charmer. It's a far cry from the serene, almost sleepy spot we see today.

The reservoir, which measures 42m by 36m and is 5m deep, is fed by a water channel known as the Shah Rud (the Royal Canal), that was built at the same time to be both the city's main water supply and its drain. It was built with stone steps to allow the city's water carriers to easily fill their leather buckets, regardless of the reservoir's current water level, though it's unlikely you'd actually have wanted to drink the water: until the Soviets drained, restored and refilled the pool in the 1960s, it was stagnant and infested with all manner of worms and fleas, a perfect breeding ground for waterborne diseases.

On the east side of the pool is a modern statue of **Hodja Nasruddin**, the homespun philosopher and humourist on his donkey. Elsewhere in the world he is generally accepted as Turkish (dying around 1280), but Uzbeks claim he was born in Bukhara and is one of their own. At family gatherings and parties, they still tell well-worn stories about him that contain typically Sufi insights.

Also around the reservoir, and beyond the statue, are the **khanagha** (☏ 65 224 4548; ⏱ 09.00–18.00 daily) to the west and **Madrasa of Nadir Divan Beghi** (⏱ 09.00–18.00 daily; US$1) to the east, which are roughly contemporaneous with the reservoir. The khanagha, with its elegant portal reflected in the surface of the

In 1838, as Britain was embarking on its first ill-fated invasion of Afghanistan, Lieutenant Colonel Charles Stoddart was sent as an envoy to Nasrullah Khan, the Emir of Bukhara. The British authorities wished to assure Bukhara's ruler that they had no intentions of marching beyond Afghan territory, and also to suggest measures, such as the abolition of slavery, which would make the Russians less likely to attack Bukhara.

Stoddart was admired as an army officer, but possessed no diplomatic training. Unaware of the niceties of central Asian royal protocol, he caused offence as soon as he arrived by failing to dismount before the emir outside the *arg*, or palace. On entering an official audience shortly afterwards, he compounded his offence by failing to make a symbolic gesture of respect. When a courtier tried to correct the mistake, Stoddart thought the official was attacking him and knocked him down. The emir, who had a volatile temper, was outraged and ordered Stoddart be thrown into a dungeon known as the Bug Pit (page 235).

The pit was notorious as one of the worst punishments in Bukhara. It was dark, 6m deep and crawling with rats and scorpions. Stoddart's first fellow inmates there were two thieves and a murderer. He was on occasion allowed out and kept under house arrest, but thrown back into the dungeon without any reason or notice.

The British government sent notes of protest to Nasrullah, but he failed to respond. Even the Russians attempted to free Stoddart, but Nasrullah ignored

water, was a place where Sufi dervishes could stay and meditate. At the centre of the building is a mosque with a *mihrab* decorated with coloured stalactites in crimson red, ultramarine blue, a vivid green and gold. Around the mosque are two storeys of *hujras* (cells) in which the holy men would have slept. They've been replaced by souvenir sellers.

The madrasa, on the opposite side of the square to the khanagha, was intended as a *caravanserai*, but Khan Imam Kuli mistook its elaborate façade for a madrasa, and Nadir Divan Beghi felt compelled to change its function. This unplanned change of use accounts for the absence of typical madrasa features such as a mosque and teaching hall. There's now a *chaikhana* ($) in the courtyard, where you can listen to wood- and metalworkers tapping away industriously.

The mosaic of two *simurgh* (flying creatures from Persian mythology) and two deer on the madrasa's façade is one of the finest examples of figurative tile work in Uzbekistan. It makes for a truly dramatic scene, especially when you consider that it flies in the face of the widely accepted Islamic prohibition on figurative art. The Mongol sun, replete with human face, must have horrified orthodox visitors.

The **Kulkedash Madrasa**, across the road on the north side of Lyabi Hauz, pre-dates all three of Nadir Divan Beghi's constructions, having been built between 1568 and 1569 by the Kulbaba Kulkedash (foster brother) of Abdullah Khan II. Its footprint measures 86m by 69m, which makes it one of the largest madrasas in Bukhara, and the building includes 160 *hujras*. The madrasa's most famous student was the writer Sadiriddin Aini (1878–1954; page 177), and a couple of cells at the rear of the courtyard now constitute the **Bukhara Literary History Museum** (⏲ 09.00–18.00 daily; US$0.60), with displays (not in English) on writers such as Aini, Abdurauf Fitrat (1886–1938) and Ahmad Donish (1827–97). Bending low to get into the split-level cells, you'll get at least a sense of how life was for students here.

them too. The Russians had just failed in an attempt to capture the city of Khiva, and were not in a strong bargaining position. The British were reluctant to mount an expedition to save their countryman as they were bogged down in Afghanistan and could not extend themselves any further. When Stoddart's imprisonment had continued to the autumn of 1841, a fellow army officer, Captain Arthur Conolly, decided to stage a desperate attempt to rescue him. He was outraged not only by the British government's failure to act, but, as a devout Christian, by a report that Stoddart had been forced to convert to Islam. A failure in love, it seems, also drove him to this act of reckless courage. Conolly arrived at Bukhara in November 1841. He possessed rather greater diplomatic talents than his brother officer, and he negotiated for Stoddart, who was by then badly malnourished and ill from fever, to stay with him in better lodgings above ground. Yet, this happier situation did not last for long. At the beginning of 1842, when news came that the British garrison in Kabul had been annihilated, Nasrullah felt emboldened to defy Britain. Stoddart and Conolly were relegated to the dungeon, and then executed around the middle of June. They were forced to dig their own graves before their heads were cut off.

The murders marked a lull in the Great Game, as both Britain and Russia suffered serious setbacks in their central Asian engagements and drew back from serious endeavours in the region until the 1860s.

During the Soviet period, the madrasa was used for a variety of purposes, including as a hotel and a Soviet-era women's centre, a deliberate slight, one would assume, to those who believed the madrasa to be the realm of men. The Kulkedash Madrasa has now been restored to its original condition, if not its original function, and you can step inside the cool interior to admire the vaulted ceilings, colourful tile work and, of course, the numerous *hujras*.

Other madrasas

Kosh Madrasa [228 A3] (Tinchlik & Mirdustim; ⊕ 09.00–18.00 daily) Located southwest of the Registan, Kosh Madrasa is in fact two madrasas (*kosh* meaning twin): the small **Modar-i Khan Madrasa** built by Abdullah Khan II for his mother in 1566, and the rather more impressive **Abdullah Khan Madrasa** that Abdullah built for himself in 1590. You can see where his priorities lay. The architecture of this building was controversial (one might go as far as to say heretical) as, rather than being orientated towards Mecca, it was placed so that its façade mirrored that of the Modar-i Khan Madrasa opposite. Inside, the mosque is set at an odd angle to the rest of the building so that the mihrab is oriented to Mecca, as traditional; the building, one might argue, was laid out not for the glory of God, but for the convenience of Abdullah Khan.

Ulug Beg Madrasa [228 E2] (Khodja Nurobod; ⊕ 09.00–18.00 daily; combined charge of US$0.50 to visit both this & the Abd al-Aziz Khan Madrasa; page 242) East of the Poi Kalyon, this madrasa was built by Timur's grandson in 1417. It is the earliest of three such madrasas (the others being in Samarkand and Gijduvan; pages 168 and 248) and one of the oldest madrasas in Bukhara.

Ulug Beg (see box, page 173) was an intellectual as much as a king, and it should therefore come as no surprise that the inscription over the madrasa's main door reads 'Aspiration to knowledge is the duty of each Muslim man and woman'. The architect's name, Ismael, is also inscribed among the tile work, the star patterns of which surely reflect Ulug Beg's love of studying the heavens. Inside the madrasa is a small mosque, library and the **Museum of the History of Bukhara Calligraphy** (🕐 09.00–17.00 daily; US$0.60), which includes manuscripts and some costumes.

Abd al-Aziz Khan Madrasa [228 E2] (Khodja Nurobod; 🕐 09.00–18.00 daily; combined charge of US$0.50 to visit both this & the Ulug Beg Madrasa, page 241) Immediately opposite the Ulug Beg Madrasa, this unrestored madrasa was built in 1652. Modelled on the Mir-i Arab Madrasa (page 239), it was constructed for Abd al-Aziz after his defeat of the Mughal army in Balkh. The madrasa's footprint measures 60m by 48m, and the entire site is sumptuously decorated with mosaics in riotous colours and equally bright ganch stalactites. One side of the courtyard is unfinished and unadorned, the rest seemingly more spectacular for the contrast.

Chor Minor [224 D2] (1 block north of Mekhtar Ambar) Located to the east of the Old Town, this is a stubby, brick-built structure with four turquoise domes. The uncharitable have described it as looking like an upturned chair. The name Chor Minor, meaning 'four minarets', is a misnomer, however, as though the towers look like minarets, they were never designed (or used) as a location from which the muezzin could call the faithful to prayer. There's now a laughable plastic nest, decorated with storks on one of them, to deter the real ones from nesting, and a souvenir shop inside.

Built in 1807, the Chor Minor is the only known building in Uzbekistan in this style, though it was possibly inspired by the Char Minar Mosque in Hyderabad, India, where its patron, the Turkmen merchant Khalif Niyazkul, is thought to have travelled. It is said that the four towers, each subtly different from the next, represents his four daughters. The front-left minaret collapsed completely during an earthquake and so has been rebuilt; the other three have also been heavily restored. If you look closely at the tiles on the domes, you'll see each dome has a date: this is the date it was restored.

Originally the gatehouse to a madrasa that has now disappeared, the Chor Minor housed a library, accessed via the staircase in the front right tower. Students would take their books to read in the cells on either side of the building, several of which still survive. You can climb the same staircase on to the roof (US$0.50), though in all honesty you can't see very far.

Before you leave, take a look at the stone barleycorn columns either side of the Chor Minor's front and back doors. No-one knows exactly where these came from, but they appear much older than the rest of the structure and were likely incorporated from an earlier building.

Other mosques
Magoki-Attari Mosque [228 E3] Central Asia's oldest surviving mosque is situated between the Taki Sarrafon and Taki Telpal Furushon trading domes (page 232). Prior to the Arab invasion there was a Buddhist monastery and then a Zoroastrian temple on the site; it was only revealed in the 1930s when archaeologists excavated the site down to a depth of 6m in order to get to the bottom (literal and metaphorical) of its 2,000 years of history.

The mosque you see today was founded sometime in the 9th century and gained its name from the herbalists (*attars*) trading in the bazaar next door. It was burned down and rebuilt in the 10th century, and again 200 years later, though the portal from the first structure remains. There is some suggestion that the columns at the sides of this portal may in fact be pre-Islamic, a tantalising suggestion of the appearance of the destroyed Zoroastrian temple. The domed portal on the eastern side is a relatively recent addition: it dates from 1547. It now houses the dull **Museum of the History of Carpet Weaving** (US$1).

Bolo Hauz Mosque [228 B1] One of the most elegant mosques in Bukhara stands on the west side of the Registan. The 12m-high pillars, 20 in all, that support the *aivan* are so slim that they look like super-sized chopsticks. They are made from elm, poplar and walnut wood. Built in 1712, the Bolo Hauz Mosque is the only historic building on this side of the square to survive: all the others were destroyed in the early 20th century by the Soviets, and the mosque itself was turned into a working-men's club. This did, at least, save it from a far worse fate, and both the pool that gives the mosque its name (*hauz* meaning reservoir or pool) and the brightly coloured paintwork have been sensitively restored.

The interior of the mosque is less interesting than the outside, though as it is free to go inside, you might as well. Take your shoes off and put them on the rack by the door. The original painted *mihrab* is quite attractive; the modern chandelier hanging from the dome is hideous and out of keeping. If you want to take photos inside, put something in the donation box, to be used for the conservation of the building.

Khodja Zayniddin Mosque [228 C2] (Khodja Nurobod) Among the various ruined mosques and madrasas in the backstreets south of the Ark, there survives one jewel that is still worth seeking out. Behind the superb *aivan* (porch) of this mosque is some of the best mosaic and ganch (plasterwork) found anywhere in Uzbekistan. Built in the 1540s and 50s, it's small but boasts a central dome that's 8.2m across and rises 16m above the ground.

Other museums

Museum of Fine Arts [228 E3] (41 Bakhauddin Naqshbandi; ☏ 65 224 2107; ⏰ 09.00–17.00 Thu–Mon, in theory; US$0.50) In a Tsarist bank building just west of the Lyabi Hauz (and actually above the Shah Rud channel), this is only erratically open, but it's worth checking the door whenever you pass. The first gallery contains little other than a good collection of historical postcards (in chronological groups). From here you'll be led down an alley to a gallery of art for sale and Soviet medals, and then, at last, upstairs to the main collection, where the work of Russian-born artists such as Venkov, Kurzin, Tansikbayev and Tatevosyan and local Bukharan

Bukhara Province **BUKHARA**

8

artists, including the miniaturist Sadriddin Pochchayev, is displayed. If you show enthusiasm, another ground-floor gallery may be unlocked, showcasing Uzbek art from the 1980s; overall, there's a range of art here: some good, but none outstanding.

Bukhara Photo Gallery [228 E4] (70 Bakhauddin Naqshbandi; m 90 715 1236; e buxarchik@gmail.com; f shavkatboltaev12; ⏰ 09.00–19.00 daily; free) In the 19th-century Olimjon Caravanserai, the excellent local photographer Shavkat Boltaev displays mesmerising photos of local life, including Bukhara's Jews and gypsies.

House Museum of Faizulla Khodjaev [224 A2] (70 Abdulla Tukay; ↘ 65 224 4188; ⏰ 09.00–17.00 Mon–Sat; US$1.50) One of Bukhara's most spectacular 19th-century houses, this retains its original carved wooden entrance way, wall paintings and separate living areas for male and female members of the family; few such properties remain, and there are probably no others in such good condition. It was the home of the Bolshevik revolutionary Faizulla Khodjaev (see box, page 243), but the displays on him are less interesting than the house itself.

Other sites As in cities across the Roman Empire, bathing in historic Bukhara was a communal affair; you could drink tea, do business and gossip while having a rub in the communal tub. Several of the medieval bathhouses remain operational, though these days visiting is more of a novelty than an essential component of public hygiene. Our favourites (both dating from the 16th century) are the **Bozori Kord Bathhouse** [228 E3] (Taki Telpal Furushon; ↘ 65 301 1133; ⏰ 06.00–15.00 men only, 15.00–19.00 mixed; US$12 including massage) and the **Hammon Kunjak** [228 D2] (4 Ibodov; ⏰ 07.00–18.00; US$12 including massage), a women-only bathhouse just west of the Kalyon Minar. In both cases you can bathe and/or have a massage, and should expect to go *au naturel*.

South of Lyabi Hauz is Bukhara's **Jewish quarter**. Although only a fraction of the city's Jewish population remains (the majority having emigrated to Israel and the US since the 1970s), it is possible to visit the 16th-century **synagogue** [228 F4] on Husainova and, around 300m further out, the **Jewish cemetery** [224 A3] (Arabon). Yura, the synagogue caretaker, is very happy (once you've put a donation in the chest) to tell you about the history of the Jewish community and how their school is still the most esteemed one here, even though few of its pupils are now Jewish.

AROUND BUKHARA The outskirts of Bukhara house some other intriguing sites, including a summer palace and a mausoleum to the city's patron saint. Birdwatchers will also be interested in the area's many wetlands, some of which are being considered for designation as RAMSAR sites.

Sitorai Mokhi Khosa (⏰ 09.00–17.00 Thu–Tue; US$2) Just 6km north of the town centre (about 500m east of the M37, just inside the city limits), this was the summer palace of Bukhara's emirs. Built in 1911 for the last emir, Alim Khan, the three-building compound incorporates elements of both Russian and traditional Bukharan architecture, and it now houses the Museum of Applied Arts. You can get here with minibuses 17, 37 and 53 (but not routes 33 and 72 which go to the Mohi Khosa Sanatorium, just south).

The **inner courtyard** was the location for the First Congress of the Bukharan Soviet in 1920; around it is a U-shaped palace where you'll see the mirrored White

Hall, a chess room and a banqueting hall. These have quite extraordinary mirrored and painted interiors, original chandeliers, and some fine furniture and Chinese and Japanese porcelain.

The **museum** includes collections of costumes (in the Guest Hall) and needlework (in the harem, with a superb collection of *suzani*), which are worth 20 minutes or so of your time. Basic descriptions are in English. Check out the *paranja*, a heavy and itchy horse-hair robe akin to a *burqa* that would have been worn by high-class womenfolk, and also the wedding robes. There are some beautiful embroidered boots and hats and jewellery.

The palace compound must once have been the most wonderful **garden**, shaded beneath hundreds of persimmon and quince trees. The aviaries are now empty, but there are still peacocks strolling about. It's a bit of a wilderness, but still attractive in its way, and you should take the time to wander through to the pool by the harem and its neighbouring folly, a pair of wooden towers linked by a bridge at the top. The emir used to select his companion for the night by throwing her an apple. The girl had to catch it and then take a bath in donkey's milk before being permitted to enter the royal bedchamber.

Mausoleum of Bakhauddin Naqshbandi (⊕ 09.00–18.00 daily; donations welcome) This mausoleum is 10km outside the city to the northeast, in the village of Kasri; the easiest way to reach it is by taxi, but you can also catch midi-bus 60 from Bakhauddin Naqshbandi (where else?). Muhammad Ibn Burhanuddin Muhammad Bukhari (1318–89) was the main teacher (though not actually the founder) of the most important Sufi order in central Asia, the Naqshbandis. His teaching is summed up in the saying 'The heart for God, the hands for work'. As Bukhara's unofficial patron saint, it should come as little surprise that his birthplace and tomb is the holiest site in the Bukhara region.

Naqshbandi's tomb is part of an extensive complex of park, gardens, tombs and shrines. His *mazar* (shrine), encases a black *dakhma* (tombstone), which pilgrims circumnavigate, or just sit near and pray, and have their photo taken with. They used to be able to kiss the shrine as well, but a cordon now prevents them getting that close. The shrine lies in a lovely courtyard with tapered wooden columns and exquisitely painted ceilings. Allow plenty of time to sit here, look up and take in the details.

Within the complex are 20 other graves, including that of Abdullah Khan II, two mosques (one for women and the other for men) and a 16th-century khanagha with a striking, 30m-high dome. Local tradition has it that if you are sick, this is the place to come: those with bad backs should climb above the small basin in the main courtyard, touching their back against its roof, to be cured. If you have any other condition, including an inability to conceive, there is a long-dead mulberry tree towards the back of the site, under which you once had to wriggle three times for the saint to answer your prayer; it's now roped off, but women still leave notes in its cracks.

There's a small **museum** (US$1.10), housed in a 17th-century madrasa building, with a pretty random collection of ceramics, tools, costumes, blocks for printing cloth, a dervish's begging bowl, tools for food preparation (eg: rolling noodles) and finely carved wood panels. Captions are in English, but the main texts are not.

Chor Bakr Necropolis In the village of Sumitan, 5km or so west of the city, is the Chor Bakr Necropolis, where Imam Sayid Abu Bakr, a direct descendant of the Prophet, was buried in about AD970, followed by three family members (*chor bakr*

meaning four brothers). The site was adopted as sacred by a sect of Sufi dervishes who were also buried here.

In 1560 Abdullah Khan II commissioned a khanagha, mosque and madrasa here, enabling the necropolis to operate as a fully fledged pilgrimage centre, and many local sheikhs, as well as Bukharan khans, were laid to rest in the vicinity. The crumbling streets, lined with 20 mausoleums, sprawl out from the central square, largely decaying and forgotten. The gatehouse through which you enter the site, and also the twin façades of the mosque and khanagha, which mirror one another, are in somewhat better repair, with beautiful mosaics and Qu'ranic verses covering the façades.

Minibuses from Bukhara's Markazi Bazaar to Alat, Jondor and Karakul all stop in Sumitan, though if you expect to be travelling back later in the day you may prefer to go by taxi and to get the driver to wait for you: it's not always an easy place to get back from!

Vabkent Minaret In the village of Vabkent, 20km northeast of Bukhara, is this 39m-tall Karakhanid tower, built by Bukhari ad-Din Ayud al-Aziz in 1196–98. The second-largest minaret in the Bukhara Oasis after the Kalyon Minar, it was originally part of a Friday Mosque complex. Following this taller, slightly earlier model, the Vabkent Minaret tapers towards the top and has a lantern-like crown, its base decorated with stalactites. The trunk of the minaret is divided into eight ornamental bands, each decorated with calligraphy. It's briefly visible to the north of the M37 highway, at about km239.

Varakhsha Moving a little further afield, 30km northwest of Bukhara is Varakhsha, founded between the 4th and 3rd centuries BC, which medieval sources described as the biggest city along the Bukhara to Khorezm trade route. It was a well-fortified, important military outpost and an agricultural area, as well as being a major centre of crafts. One of the major towns of the Hephtalite civilisation in the oasis of Bukhara, it was the final retreat for the local kings when the Arab armies advanced. The **Varakhsha Palace**, home to the rulers of Bukhara, was built in the 7th century AD and is situated at the southern fortress wall. The palace was rebuilt a number of times, but was finally abandoned in the 11th century, and now all that remains is ruins. Excavations began in 1937 and were continued in 1947–53, when archaeologists unearthed three halls with an extensive courtyard area. The walls of the hall were highly decorated with exquisite frescoes showing scenes of hunting wild and fantastic animals. The mound is visible today from quite a distance but the excavations comprise only a small area around the citadel. Huge adobe fortifications with arched gateways and high walls may be seen. The site is open air, and has no guardian or entry fees. Varakhsha is on UNESCO's Tentative List for World Heritage status.

If you are travelling in your own vehicle to Varakhsha, it is well worth making a short stop at Chilangu, 20km outside Bukhara's city limits, to visit the 17th-century Hakkim Mullo Mir Khanagha (no entry fee but donations welcome). Originally a hostel for dervishes on pilgrimage to saints' graves and other holy places, this khanagha was built in honour of Sheikh al-Islam Emir Hussein Mullo Mir, who died in 1587. From the entry portal staircases lead up to the roof of the four-storey building; in the central courtyard is a mosque, allowing easy access from the pilgrims' cells at prayer time.

The best time to visit is on a Friday afternoon, when prayers are followed by a feast, which modestly dressed visitors are welcome to partake in.

The large Djeyran Eco-Centre is 40km southeast of Bukhara, and since the 1970s it has been an important conservation site for the flora, fauna, and landscapes of the southwestern Kyzylkum Desert. The reserve includes a wildlife sanctuary, where injured animals are cared for prior to re-release into the wild, and there is also a respected breeding centre for Persian gazelle, Przewalski's horse, the Turkmenian kulan, and the Houbara bustard.

You can reach the reserve easily on a day trip from Bukhara, which is advisable as there is nowhere locally to stay. The best time to visit is in the spring or autumn, when the temperatures are pleasant, there are plenty of flowers, and the wildlife is easier to spot. Binoculars and a camera are advisable, as are hiking boots if you're intending to cover any distance as the going is rough underfoot.

Paikend Along the length of the Silk Road were a series of oases, which became prosperous trading hubs. Although many of these have survived and are still populated, others were utterly destroyed by marauders or became uninhabitable owing to climatic change and drought. The remains of Paikend, 60km southwest of Bukhara, founded by the 4th century BC, are slowly being recovered from the desert sands and are revealing many fascinating clues about the Sogdian period, when Paikend was at its height. This was the last stop before the Kyzylkum Desert for the large numbers of merchants from Afghanistan, China, and India, who traded with each other and also with the craftsmen of Paikend itself, who produced fine glassware, ceramics and armour. This golden period was brought crashing to an end by invasions, first by the Arabs and then the Mongols; crops were abandoned and the starving populace abandoned the city.

The city's wealth is evident from the recent archaeological finds (many of which can be seen in the Ark in Bukhara; page 233): inside its massive fortifications were sizeable buildings, notably a minaret taller even than the Kalyon Minar in Bukhara, and central Asia's oldest-known pharmacy. There's also a Zoroastrian burial site. Clearly, Paikend has substantial potential for tourism, and UNESCO is advising the government on how to develop the site sustainably – it will be some time before this plan comes to fruition, but you can easily drive to the site or take a taxi from Bukhara (US$10–12 return, including waiting time). Alternatively, there is a small museum on the outskirts of Sayat village (head east across the railway), the director of which may also take you on a tour of the ruins.

GIJDUVAN

Historically Gijduvan was a cultural, mercantile and religious centre in the region, though today little of this is on show. The city makes its money from cotton production, though there has also been a revival of traditional crafts (particularly ceramics), which are then sold in the tourist centres of Samarkand and Bukhara. It's a pleasant place for a short excursion, especially if you are interested in visiting the many craft workshops.

GETTING THERE AND AROUND Gijduvan is 48km northeast of Bukhara on the M37 towards Samarkand, so it is best visited as a brief stop en route between those two cities. Although trains do not stop here, buses, minibuses and shared taxis (page 226) pass through Gijduvan, and there are frequent *marshrutkas* from Bukhara's Karvon Bazaar. The town itself is small enough to explore **on foot**.

WHERE TO STAY, EAT AND DRINK It is recommended that you stay at a hotel or guesthouse in Bukhara (page 227) and visit Gijduvan on a day trip, although the simple **Hotel Marvarid** (just north of Yuusuf Hamandoniy; m 91 312 5545/98 180 5588; **$$**) is now available. There are also guest rooms at **Gijduvan Ceramics Museum** (**$$**; see below) for those wanting to study there.

Food, fortunately, is a different matter entirely. Gijduvan is famous within Uzbekistan for its cuisine: the *shashlik* and fried fish are said to be the best in the country, and there are plenty of *chaikhanas* and cafés where you can indulge.

SHOPPING The finest **ceramics** in Uzbekistan come from Gijduvan, so it would be churlish not to come away with a plate or three. It is best to buy direct from the craftsmen, especially as you can also see them at work and learn about their techniques. The best place to go is **Gijduvan Ceramics Museum** (55 Kimsan; 90 718 3060; w folkceramics.uz), the home and craft centre of sixth-generation master-ceramicist Abdullo Narzullaev. Here, you will meet members of the family (and their gorgeous donkey, who is instrumental in preparing the clay), and can watch them making both painted ceramics and hand-sewn *suzanis*, for which they also produce the natural dyes. The Narzullaevs are keen to pass on their expertise and welcome guests.

OTHER PRACTICALITIES
Medical
There is no proper hospital in Gijduvan.

✚ **District health centre** 5/1 Sharq; 65 572 5656

Money
As ever, there is no ATM here, but money can be withdrawn at the following:

$ **Agro Bank** 5B Naqshbandi; 65 572 1793; ◷ 09.00–17.00 Mon–Fri
$ **National Bank of Uzbekistan** 45 B Naqshbandi; 65 572 4551; ◷ 09.00–18.00 Mon–Fri, 09.00–16.00 Sat

WHAT TO SEE AND DO Other than the ceramic workshops (see above), Gijduvan has two sights of interest to tourists. The third of **Ulug Beg's madrasas** was built here in 1433, and though less impressive than those in Samarkand (page 168) and Bukhara (page 241), it is still an attractive building with a striped minaret by its entranceway, an ubiquitous turquoise dome and a lapis lazuli blue-tiled portico. It's on the west side of the park in the city centre (just north of the central bazaar).

Though built as a madrasa, in practice it functioned more as a khanagha for those visiting the **Mazar of Abdul Khaliq Gijduvani,** which sits within the madrasa's courtyard and was the reason why Ulug Beg selected this particular site. Gijduvani (1103–79) was a Sufi saint, an Islamic teacher whose pupils included Bakhauddin Naqshbandi (page 245), and he founded his own Sufi order, the Khodjakhon, which later became better known as the Naqshbandi order. The *mazar* (tomb) is a simple structure, and unlikely to be of particular interest to non-pilgrims: it is the surrounding buildings you should come to see.

9

Khorezm Province

Khorezm can only exist because it's an oasis, a fortunate strip of fertile land in the Amu Darya delta that is sandwiched between the Karakum and Kyzylkum deserts. The region has at least 57,500 years of known human history, starting with the Mesolithic Keltiminar (5500–3500BC) and moving through Bronze Age and Iron Age cultures to the Scythians, Achaemenids and Sassanids. An independent state was established here by the 4th century BC, surviving until AD712, when the Arab Ummayads conquered the region. Such fascinating history has left rich pickings for visiting culture vultures: desert fortresses, some 2,500 years old; ancient palaces; royal citadels; and the remains of fire-worship temples.

And then, of course, there's Khiva, the caravan stop turned religious centre turned UNESCO World Heritage Site supposedly founded by Shem, son of Noah. This museum city, frozen in time behind its crenellated, mud-brick walls, seems to contain more historical sites per square metre even than mighty Bukhara. Ignore the distances it takes to get there: it is absolutely not to be missed.

URGENCH

Konya-Urgench, the historical city, is now in Turkmenistan, but its newer incarnation, the Soviet city of Urgench, dismal and concrete though it is, remains significant as the gateway to Khorezm Province and thus offers access to sights you'd actually want to see.

HISTORY The UNESCO World Heritage Site Konya-Urgench (Old Urgench) lies just across the Uzbek–Turkmen border from Urgench. One of the greatest cities on the Silk Road, it was founded during the Achaemenid period and reached its peak under the Khorezmshahs in the 12th and early 13th centuries, when its only possible rival in the region was Bukhara. Konya-Urgench's fortunes changed suddenly, however: in 1221 Genghis Khan oversaw one of the bloodiest massacres in history, after demolishing a wooden dam to wash the city away. As if this was not bad enough, the Amu Darya then changed its course, leaving the city without water. Life became untenable, and the city's surviving inhabitants were forced to up sticks and move.

The new settlement, also on the banks of the Amu Darya, was at first simply a small trading town in the Khanate of Khiva. The arrival of the Trans-Caspian railway at the end of the 19th century made it viable as an international trading post, however, and during the Soviet era the city was heavily industrialised. The Soviets introduced cotton, motifs of which decorate buildings across Urgench, and this cash crop remains the mainstay of the local economy to the present day.

GETTING THERE AND AWAY Urgench is a long way from anywhere other than Khiva, and so taking a flight or the sleeper train is a sensible option, at least in one direction, if you are likely to be short of time.

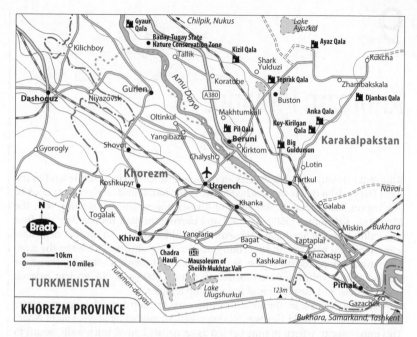

Map labels (clockwise / by region):

Gyaur Qala, Chilpik, Nukus, Lake Ayazkol, Kilichboy, Baday-Tugay State Nature Conservation Zone, Tallik, Kizil Qala, Ayaz Qala, Kukcha, Shark Yulduzi, Koratobe, Toprak Qala, Zhambakskala, Gurlen, A380, Buston, Djanbas Qala, Dashoguz, Niyazovsk, Makhtumkuli, Anka Qala, Oltinkul, Pil Qala, Koy-Kirilgan Qala, Yangibazar, Beruni, Kirktom, Big Guldursun, Karakalpakstan, Gyorogly, Shovot, Chalysh, Lotin, Koshkupyr, Khorezm, Turtkul, Navoi, Urgench, Togalak, Khanka, Galaba, Khiva, Yangiariq, Bagat, Taptaplar, Miskin, Bukhara, Chadra Hauli, Mausoleum of Sheikh Mukhtar Vali, Kashkalar, Khazarasp, 0 10km, 0 10 miles, Turkmen-deryasi, TURKMENISTAN, Lake Ulugshurkul, 123m, Pitnak, Gazachak, KHOREZM PROVINCE, Bukhara, Samarkand, Tashkent

Amu Darya

By air Given that it is 1,050km from Tashkent to Urgench, many visitors choose to fly, at least in one direction. Urgench's airport (Al Khorezmi; ☏ 62 780 3236; e urgench.airport@uzairways.com) is 5km north of the city centre. There are two daily flights to Tashkent (1hr 35min; US$50), and two flights a week to Bukhara (1hr; US$40) with Uzbekistan Airways. It is also possible to fly direct to Moscow (3hr 50min; 5 flights/week with Uzbekistan Airways & 3/week with S7) or St Petersburg (4hr 40min; 3 flights/week with Uzbekistan Airways & 2/week with Ural Airlines).

Uzbekistan Airways also operates popular charter flights direct from France, Italy and Germany (page 49) to Urgench and has a ticketing office in the city centre (28 Al Khorezmi; ☏ 62 226 8860), as does S7 (13B Beruni; ☏ 62 223 0104; m 98 277 2791; ⏱ 09.00–18.00 daily).

By rail The train station (☏ 62 225 6111) is at the southern end of Al Khorezmi. New lines give direct access to Khiva, and to Bukhara, Samarkand and Tashkent without the need to transit through Turkmenistan.

Trains run overnight between Tashkent and Urgench. Train number 56/58 departs Tashkent at 20.30 (Thu–Tue), reaches Samarkand just after midnight and Bukhara at 04.15, then continues to Urgench, arriving at 10.07. In 2018, this was extended to reach Khiva at 10.52, returning at 14.28 from Khiva and 15.25 from Urgench and reaching Bukhara at 22.30, Samarkand at 02.30 and Tashkent at 07.00. A sleeper berth from Tashkent to Urgench starts from US$22, and a reserved seat from US$15. For more information on tickets and reservations, see page 65.

Trains north to Nukus and Moscow go less frequently and need to be booked well in advance, as they are invariably oversubscribed. They pass through Turtkul, just east of Urgench. You can make a booking through a local travel agent, or on the *Caravanistan* website (w caravanistan.com), and then take a taxi from Urgench to Turtkul (allow at least 1hr).

By road The road between Bukhara and Urgench is in terrible condition, but is gradually being replaced by a new, multi-lane highway. This is a major infrastructure project, however, and very slow going; although the central 270km was open at the time of writing, there is still quite some way to go.

Urgench's **bus station** (\ 62 225 5440) is on Al Khorezmi, just north of the train station, and both minibuses and shared taxis congregate here, too. There are cheap buses **to Bukhara, Samarkand and Tashkent**, but they take significantly longer (Urgench to Tashkent is 25 hours, for example) and are less frequent than the minibuses travelling the same routes, so avoid them unless you are exceptionally strapped for cash. There are regular minibuses to Bukhara (6hrs; US$10), and less frequent ones to Samarkand (9hrs; US$12) and Tashkent (18hrs; US$20), though it may be faster to go to Bukhara and change there. Shared taxis for Bukhara and Tashkent also wait at the corner of Mustakillik and Samarkand, a few hundred metres east of the big new Jame Mosque.

Shared taxis **to Nukus** (2½hrs; US$10) leave from the northeast side of the Olympic Stadium on Gurlenskaya. They travel via Beruni, so if there is a shortage of vehicles heading to Nukus, you can always make for Beruni and change there.

Getting **to Khiva** is more straightforward: there are plenty of options. Shared taxis leave from Beruni, close to the main bazaar (30–40min; US$0.60); the trolley bus (1hr; US$0.30) also runs (every 20–30min) down Beruni, one block west of the post office, or you can take a taxi for US$3 per seat. If you pick up a taxi from the airport or train station, you'll have to haggle hard for a reasonable fare, but from the bazaar there's a flat rate.

GETTING AROUND Urgench is a relatively large city, but there are a limited number of places you'd want to go, and all of them can be reached by public transport. Minibus numbers 3 and 13 go from the airport and along Al Khorezmi (the main drag), while minibus number 19 links the bazaar and the train station.

It is usually easiest to hire a car and driver to reach the Khorezm fortresses (page 270), and a 4x4 is preferable for the more remote sites. The tour operators below all keep a list of reputable drivers. The cost will depend on the distance you travel; expect to pay between US$50 and US$80 if you are travelling out from Urgench.

TOURIST INFORMATION AND TOUR OPERATORS **Green Globus** (33 Al Khorezmi; m 93 770 5050) and **Zukhro Travel** (42/25 Pahlavan Makhmud; \ 62 228 5678; w zukhrotravel.com) can arrange guided tours of Khiva and the Khorezm fortresses, as well as making onward travel and hotel bookings. **Ayaz Kala Tour** (G Gulom, Buston; \ 61 532 4361; e ayazkala_tour@mail.ru) and **Turtkul Travel** (Kirkkiz, Turtkul; \ 61 221 0707) are based outside Urgench but specialise in desert fortress tours and yurt-camp stays.

 WHERE TO STAY *Map, page 252*
Personally, we don't like staying in Urgench: the accommodation options are uninspiring and generally overpriced. If you can, it is far better to travel straight on to Khiva, where there are many nicer places to choose from (page 256).

Hotel Khorezm Palace (103 rooms) 2 Beruni; \ 62 224 9999; e khorezmpalace@mail.ru; w khorezmpalace.uz. Urgench's most expensive accommodation option is a soulless place, aimed at business travellers. It has all the facilities you'd expect, but customer service (&

the concept of smiling) appears anathema to them. The travel desk & ATMs (one each for Visa & Mastercard customers) may be of use to non-guests. **$$$$**
Hotel Fayz (37 rooms) 66/1 Al Khorezmi; \ 62 228 8444; e fayzhotel@gmail.com;

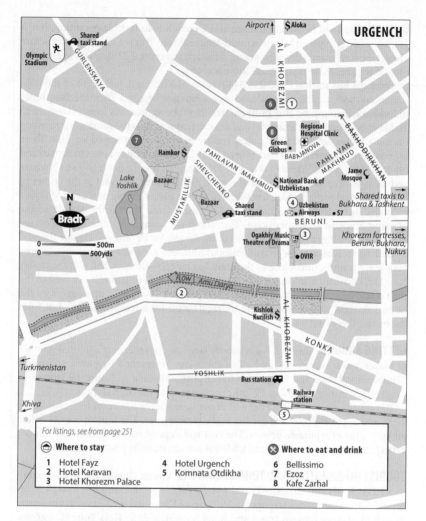

For listings, see from page 251

Where to stay

1 Hotel Fayz
2 Hotel Karavan
3 Hotel Khorezm Palace
4 Hotel Urgench
5 Komnata Otdikha

Where to eat and drink

6 Bellissimo
7 Ezoz
8 Kafe Zarhal

w fayzhotel.uz. Comfortable, mid-range hotel with its own restaurant (**$$**) & bar. Rooms are somewhat on the small side, especially if there are 2 of you, but it's clean. B/fast inc. **$$$**

🏠 **Hotel Karavan** (36 rooms) Konka; ☏ 62 226 0606; m 91 429 9777; e karavanhotel. uz@gmail.com. This big, modern place near the station has friendly staff, clean, comfortable rooms (some with a view of the Amu Darya) & a decent restaurant (**$$**), plus free bikes & sauna/ massage. **$$$**

🏠 **Hotel Urgench** (65 rooms) 27 Pahlavan Makhmud; ☏ 62 226 2022; e 2116663@mail. ru. Concrete Soviet block in need of rather more renovation than has so far taken place. Prices start at ridiculous levels but come down quickly if you hold your ground: aim for around US$40 for a twin. The beds are predictably narrow & lumpy. **$$**

🏠 **Komnata Otdikha** Train station, Al Khorezmi. The cheapest option in town is just about bearable if you use your own sleeping bag. Dorm beds only. **$**

✘ WHERE TO EAT AND DRINK *Map, above*

If you happen to find somewhere decent to eat in Urgench, please tell us about it. The best options currently are probably the **Kafe Zarhal** (77 Al Khorezmi;

62 228 8098; **$**), near the Hotel Fayz, and the **Bellissimo**, around the corner on Bakhodirkhan. There's also the **Ezoz restaurant-*chaikhana*** (m 91 997 5777; **$**) at the western entry to Amir Timur Park, for beer and *shashlik*.

ENTERTAINMENT If you happen to be stuck in Urgench overnight, for example while waiting for onward transport, your stay may coincide with a performance at the **Ogakhiy Music Theatre of Drama** (32 Al Khorezmi; 62 226 6264), one of Uzbekistan's better regional theatres. You will need to pop in, or ask an Uzbek speaker to phone up, to find out what's on, and when. Tickets will be cheap.

OTHER PRACTICALITIES
Communications
✉ **Main post office** 1 Beruni (cnr Al Khorezmi); 09.00–17.00 Mon–Fri. The telephone & telegraph office & a couple of internet terminals are in the same building.

Medical
✚ **Regional Hospital** 1 Babajanova; 62 226 2110

Money
There are ATMs for Visa & Mastercard holders at the Hotel Khorezm Palace (page 251), & the banks below will change money. The National Bank of Uzbekistan will also arrange a cash advance on foreign debit cards, which is especially useful when the hotel's ATMs are out of order.

$ Aloka Bank 62 228 8201; ⊕ 09.00–18.00 Mon–Sat
$ Hamkor Bank 62 228 5923; ⊕ 09.00–17.00 Mon–Sat
$ Kishlok Kurilish Bank 62 227 2790; e info. xorazm@qqb.uz
$ National Bank of Uzbekistan 62 226 9050; ⊕ 09.00–18.00 Mon–Fri, 09.00–16.00 Sat

Registration
OVIR 28 Al Khorezmi; 62 227 1840; ⊕ 09.00–13.00 & 14.00–17.00 Mon–Fri

KHIVA

It is rare to come across an entire city that is a museum. Though Bukhara is packed with remarkable sites it is still nonetheless a living, working city. Khiva, however, is more akin to a film set, the local population, rightly or wrongly, sidelined in order to preserve historic buildings and present a manicured scene to tourists.

Whatever you feel about such a policy, Khiva remains one of the greatest cities on the Silk Road: the Ichon Qala in particular is a labyrinth of madrasas and mosques, minarets and trading domes that, at least on the surface of it, look just as they would have done at the end of the 19th century before Soviet town planners, demolition crews and modernist architects got their hands on Uzbekistan. On a cold winter's evening, after the wedding parties have departed and the few tourists are enjoying their supper, you can be entirely alone with the ghosts of the past, wandering the narrow streets and soaking up the atmosphere. Which decade, indeed which century, you care to imagine yourself in is entirely up to you.

HISTORY In October 1997, Khiva celebrated its 2,500th birthday. Archaeological digs in the Ichon Qala during the 1980s and early 90s uncovered a wealth of material as much as 7m below the modern ground level, and the earliest finds from these excavations suggest that the town was first inhabited between the 6th and 5th centuries BC. Legend has it that the city was founded long before this, however, as Shem, son of Noah, is said to have first marked out the city's walls.

Khiva rose in importance and was fortified sometime after the 4th century BC as the Khorezmians attempted to fend off Achaemenid incursions from Iran.

A double wall provided physical protection for the city and its inhabitants, and archers were stationed in turrets more than 20m high. The encroaching desert continually eroded these first walls, however, and by the early centuries AD a second wall and citadel had to be constructed. The new walls were between 7m and 9m thick. This incarnation of the city survived until AD709, when it was razed to rubble by the Arab governor Qutaiba ibn Muslim in his conquest of central Asia.

Khiva became part of the Samanid Empire and the city grew rapidly through the 9th and 10th centuries, becoming a regional economic and cultural hub. It is thought that in the 9th century the city's population may have been as high as 800,000. The city was sacked again by Genghis Khan in 1220–21, but thanks to its reputation for craftsmanship (in particular pottery and tile making), it was able to recover relatively swiftly. The walls of the current Ichon Qala were erected in the 14th century, and Khiva's population again became wealthy, exporting their ceramics and trading all manner of goods along the Silk Road.

In 1505, Khiva was conquered by Mahmoud Sultan on the orders of his brother, Shaybani Khan. When the latter was killed near Merv (now in Turkmenistan) five years later, however, the entire Khorezm state briefly broke away from Shaybanid rule. Military expansionism on both sides during the early 16th century saw numerous battles between the rulers of Khiva and their rivals in Bukhara, even more so after Khiva replaced Gurganj as the capital of Khorezm towards the century's end, after the Amu Darya changed its course again. The entire population of Gurganj was forcefully moved to the city, and construction boomed. Under the rule of Abu'l Gazi Bahadurhan (1643–64), Khiva became a major cultural centre. The rulers funded not only religious buildings, but also bathhouses, civic buildings and irrigation canals.

In 1717, Tsar Peter of Russia had sent a 4,000 strong force to Khiva to investigate rumours of Khorezmian gold and a maritime route to India. After an initial warm welcome, they were slaughtered. Prince Alexander Bekovich, who led the expedition, was flayed alive in punishment. At the time, the Russians could do little to avenge this slight, but they did not forget the insult; in the 19th century they would return with vengeance, and this time they would stay.

Two decades later a second force, that of the Iranian Nadir Shah, met with greater success. As he advanced on central Asia in 1740, Khiva and Bukhara initially joined forces in resistance, but Bukhara's rulers then switched sides. Khiva was yet again conquered. As if this wasn't bad enough, plagues and famines followed.

The restoration of Khiva began in the late 18th century. Under the rule of Muhammad Amina-inak (r1752–90), the various tribal factions in the area were united, and each community given a voice in the running of the city. A reformed tax system was introduced, as was a customs service, diplomatic relations with Russia and other neighbouring powers were strengthened, and trade thrived. The wealth of this era is reflected in its architecture: a significant number of the buildings you see within the Ichon Qala today date from the late 18th and early 19th centuries when Muhammad Amina-inak and his descendants ruled.

For centuries Khiva had been famed for its slave market (see box, opposite), and though the plundering of caravans and abduction of traders may have been lucrative, it eventually brought the Khivans into direct conflict with tsarist Russia. In the winter of 1839 General Perovsky led 5,000 troops across the desert in a bid to rescue 3,000 Russian slaves said to be held within the city's walls. The snows came early, devastating Perovsky's forces and his camel train, and the Russians were forced to admit defeat. It was not until 1872 that the Russians finally entered Khiva and halted the trade of slaves.

In the 18th and 19th centuries, the names of Khiva and Bukhara would have simultaneously struck both fear and wonder into the hearts of Silk Road traders. While the cities were deposits of almost unimaginable wealth, and every conceivable good was traded within their bazaars, one of the most lucrative trades was in slaves, and no passing caravan was safe from the Turkoman slavers' raids. The Russians believed they'd lost in the region of 5,000 nationals into slavery, and though the Great Game was in full flow, even British officers interceded with the khans in a bid to have Russian citizens released.

The Khivan slave market was an interesting example of the free market economy at work. Slaves were traded exactly as if they were livestock, with the finest physical specimens commanding the highest prices. A strong, Russian male would cost you the equivalent of four camels, or two good horses. They were more expensive than either women or other races. When slaves were in ready supply (for example after a battle or particularly successful raid), prices fell. At other times you'd be able to haggle to get a substantial discount. Slaves with deformities, or who had been branded in punishment for a previous escape bid, were already marked down in price.

Slavery was officially outlawed in Bukhara in 1863 and in Khiva shortly afterwards. In reality it persisted, though less openly than before, with the elite maintaining extensive harems and everyone who could afford to do so keeping household staff.

To a greater or lesser extent, the Russians were in Khiva to stay. A series of rebellions weakened the khanate and, as it entered the 20th century, Khorezm was a shadow of its former self. Isfandiyar Khan was assassinated in 1918; his successor, Abdullah Khan, abdicated two years later. The Khorezm People's Republic was declared in 1920 and, despite a valiant struggle to reclaim Khiva by 15,000 Basmachi, Khorezm was promoted to a Soviet Republic in 1922 and incorporated into the Uzbek SSR in 1924.

Khiva was proclaimed an open-air museum by the government in 1967 and the Ichon Qala was recognised by UNESCO as a World Heritage Site in December 1990. Hotels and museums were opened in some madrasas, and in December 2018 President Mirziyoyev announced that the Old Town's remaining inhabitants would be moved out to new apartments to make rooms for more tourist accommodation. Quite apart from the human rights aspect, this risks turning the city into a Disney-esque theme park.

GETTING THERE AND AROUND Urgench is the regional transport hub, and wherever in Uzbekistan you are coming from, you will pass through there (see page 250 for details). However, in 2018, **trains** began running from Tashkent, Samarkand, Bukhara and Urgench to Khiva's new station, about 1km east of the Old Town. For details of schedules and prices, see page 250.

From **Urgench to Khiva** it is just 35km, and by car it takes just 30–40 minutes. You will pay around US$12 for a taxi, and US$2 for a seat in a shared taxi or minibus. You can pick these up from Beruni in Urgench; they drop you at the North Gate of Khiva's Old Town.

Once in Khiva, you'll explore the Ichon Qala **on foot**, as much of it is pedestrianised and the alleys are too narrow for a car. Much of the Dishon Qala can also be seen on foot, though it is also possible to pick up minibuses (US$0.06) from the bazaar if you want to travel a little further. Local taxis are available; there is no set fare, but you should be able to negotiate a rate of around US$0.35 per hour within the city limits. Longer distances will depend on the mileage.

TOURIST INFORMATION AND TOUR OPERATORS As well as those listed here, there is a second information centre inside the Allah Kuli Khan Madrasa, and a helpful travel desk at the Orient Star (see opposite).

Bek Tour 14 R Majidiy; 62 375 2455; e info@ bektour.uz; w bektour.uz. Professionally run travel agency with its head office in Khiva. In addition to the usual accommodation booking & escorted tours, Bek Tour can also arrange helicopter transfer to the Aral Sea & invitations to attend an Uzbek wedding.

Khiva Information Centre 41 A Boltaev; 62 375 6928; e info@khivamuseum.uz; w khivamuseum.uz; ◷ 08.00–19.00 daily.

Khiva's main tourist information centre is inside the Ichon Qala, close to the West Gate. It has information about the main sites, sells tickets for trains, planes, dance performances & film showings, & can arrange bilingual guides (US$30/day) & tours to the Khorezm fortresses. There are also a couple of internet terminals here.

Zafarbek Travel 28 Toshpulatov; 62 375 8485. Basic escorted tours, guides & reservations.

WHERE TO STAY *Map, page 261, unless otherwise stated*

The most attractive of Khiva's hotels are inside the Ichon Qala, putting you right at the heart of the action. Large hotels (with bigger rooms and baths) that are popular with groups are found just outside the southern gate. There's little reason to stay anywhere else.

Top end

Asia Khiva [map, opposite] (127 rooms) 1 K Yakubov; 62 375 2098; e hotelasiakhiva@ rambler.ru; w asiahotels.uz/en. Modern, functional hotel just outside the Ichon Qala's walls that's mostly frequented by tour groups. A 5th block should have been completed in 2019 (advertised as 127 rooms), making this the city's biggest hotel. All rooms have AC, there is a large restaurant (**$$$**) & gardens with a superb outdoor pool to cool down in at the end of a long, hot day. **$$$$$**

Mid-range

Arkanchi B&B (41 rooms) 10 Pahlavan Makhmud; 62 375 2974; e info@hotel-arkanchi. uz. Near the West Gate, this mid-sized hotel has comfortable rooms & its own restaurant (**$$**), sauna & gym, though it could do with some updating. The parking immediately outside makes it a particularly good choice if you have your own vehicle (they also have good bikes available). More expensive at w/ends & for 1-night stays. **$$$**

Hotel Hayat Inn [map, opposite] (38 rooms) 71 K Yakubov; 62 375 7571; m 94 316

4035; e hotelhayatinn@mail.ru. Opened in 2011 (in a former carpet factory), this large hotel caters predominantly to tour groups. It's also good for those who don't like small rooms; apts cost US$120 & are ideal if you're staying a while. **$$$**

Hotel Shaherezada Khiva (16 rooms) 35 Islam Khoja; 62 375 9565; m 91 572 7070; e tionshaherezada@mail.ru. Small & friendly hotel in a new building designed in an old style. Rooms are large, quiet & clean. Excellent b/fast inc. **$$$**

Malika Kheivak (22 rooms) 11 Islam Khoja; 62 375 7610; e booking-malika@mail.ru; w malika-khiva.com. The Malika Hotel Group now has 3 properties in Khiva. Slap bang in the middle of the Ichon Qala, the Malika Kheivak's location is unparalleled. Rooms are immaculately clean & comfortable but, oddly, the hotel feels a little sterile & empty even when it's not. B/fast inc. Also has a decent restaurant (page 258). **$$$**

Malika Khiva [map, opposite] (39 rooms) 19A P Kori; 62 375 2665. This hotel is opposite the city's main gate, the Ata Darvoza. AC rooms give on to a slightly barn-like atrium (with a giant chess set). **$$$**

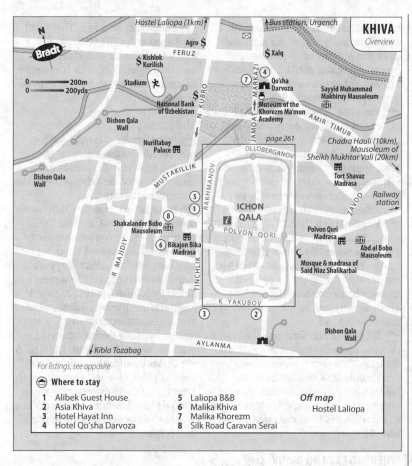

Hostel Laliopa (1km)

KHIVA
Overview

Bus station, Urgench

N

Bradt

Agro $
FERUZ

$ Xalq

Kishlok
Kurilish $

$ N KUBRO

Qo'sha
Darvoza

Sayyid Muhammad
Makhiruy Mausoleum

0   200m
0   200yds

Stadium

National Bank
of Uzbekistan

Museum of the
Khorezm Ma'mun
Academy

Dishon Qala
Wall

AMIR TIMUR

page 261

*Chadra Hauli (10km),
Mausoleum of
Sheikh Mukhtar Vali (20km)*

Nurillabay
Palace

OLLOBERGANOV

MUSTAKILLIK

RAKHMANOV

Tort Shavaz
Madrasa

Dishon Qala
Wall

ICHON
QALA

Railway
station

ZAVOD

Shakalander Bobo
Mausoleum

POLVON QORI

Polvon Qori
Madrasa

Abd al Bobo
Mausoleum

R MAJIDIY

Bikajon Bika
Madrasa

TINCHLIK

Mosque & madrasa of
Said Niaz Shalikarbai

K YAKUBOV

Dishon Qala
Wall

AYLANMA

Kibla Tozabag

For listings, see opposite

Where to stay

1 Alibek Guest House
2 Asia Khiva
3 Hotel Hayat Inn
4 Hotel Qo'sha Darvoza
5 Laliopa B&B
6 Malika Khiva
7 Malika Khorezm
8 Silk Road Caravan Serai

Off map
Hostel Laliopa

Malika Khorezm [map, above] (32 rooms) 5 Centre; 62 375 5451; w malika-khiva.com. Malika's third property is in a rather ugly modern building not far outside the Ichon Qala. Some rooms are a little small, so do ask to see them before you check in. Bedrooms, however, are immaculate, & there is a reasonable restaurant ($$$) & parking. The AC is welcome in summer. $$$

Orient Star (78 rooms) 1 Pahlavan Makhmud; 62 375 4945; m 93 922 0787; e orientstarkhiva@mail.com; w hotelorientstar. com. The most atmospheric hotel in Khiva, if not the whole of Uzbekistan. Situated, somewhat controversially, inside the 19th-century Muhammad Amin Khan Madrasa, each of its simple rooms is made from a former student's cell. Note that the rooms have no windows, though there are AC units to keep them cool. There's a tea house in the courtyard & a restaurant (page 259)

in a neighbouring madrasa with equally beautiful tiling, & both buildings are in the shadow of the Kalta Minar. B/fast inc. $$$

Budget
Alibek Guest House [map, above] (8 rooms) 17 Rakhmanov; m 91 437 9673. Just outside the main gate, this friendly place has simple AC rooms (some with shared bathrooms). Good b/fasts, shared kitchen, free parking. $$

Hotel Islambek (21 rooms) 60 Toshpulotov; 62 375 3023; e islambekhotel@nm.ru. One of the cheapest options in this price bracket, the friendly Islambek is northeast of the Ichon Qala & has good views from the rooftop terrace. B/fast inc. $$

Hotel Qo'sha Darvoza [map, above] (8 rooms) 1 Amir Timur; 62 375 3060; m 90 187 2651; e oltintoj@mail.ru. This very friendly family-run hotel, at the Qo'sha Darvoza Gate just north of the Old Town, was built in 1905 as a guesthouse for the khan & later served as a pharmacy & army barracks; restored in 2014, it now makes a comfortable base for tourists, with AC rooms around a peaceful courtyard. **$$**

Meros B&B (6 rooms) 57 Boltaev; `62 375 7642; m 94 315 3700; e meroskhiva@gmail.com; w meroskhiva.com.` Manager Jaloladdin Matkarimov & his team create a hospitable atmosphere in their beautifully decorated home with simple, spacious rooms. The rooftop terrace offers unobstructed views of the Ichon Qala & simple, cheap meals are available on request. **$$**

Mirzaboshi B&B `62 375 2753; e mirzaboshi@inbox.ru.` Small, central B&B with 2 sites in the pedestrianised section of the Ichon Qala (the main site is at 24 Toshpulatov): bear this in mind if you're carrying a lot of luggage. This family-run place is exceptionally friendly, & the dinners are pretty good, too. Non-guests can book in for dinner (**$$**). **$$**

Silk Road Caravan Serai [map, page 257] (10 rooms) Bikajon Bika Madrasa; `m 94 315 5678.` Opened in 2018 in a former women's madrasa dating from the 1890s, some cells have been knocked together to create comfortable dbl rooms while some remain as cosy sgls; there's also a large tpl next to reception. Good location west of the Old Town. **$$**

Laliopa B&B [map, page 257] (5 rooms) 11A Rakhmanov; `62 375 4449; e laliopa@mail.ru.` Simple rooms in 'Granny Opa's' house overlooking the Ichon Qala's walls. Bikes available for guests. Great b/fasts; dinners (**$$**) are provided on request. Dorm beds US$8. **$–$$**

Shoestring

Hostel Farrukh (5 rooms) Polvon Qori; `m 97 362 1005.` Primarily a tea house (see opposite), the very friendly owners have a few simple rooms with shared bathrooms; the location is unbeatable at the price. **$**

Hostel Laliopa [map, page 257] (4 rooms) Obvodnaya; `62 375 4449; m 91 998 8999; e laliopa@mail.ru.` A proper backpackers' hostel (with a relaxed common area & kitchen, but b/fast starts rather late…), this is more spacious than Laliopa B&B (see above) & has a garden & parking; the downside is that it's a 20min walk from the Old Town (free bikes available, or take minibus 4 from outside the city walls). The hostel organises tours to the Khorezm fortresses for guests & a daily transfer to Bukhara (US$10 pp). **$**

Otabek Guesthouse (3 rooms) 68 Islam Khoja; `62 375 3968.` More of a homestay than a guesthouse, Otabek is understandably popular with backpackers & the home cooking is delicious: if you have a choice, request the pumpkin *manti*. Dorm beds only. **$**

✕ WHERE TO EAT AND DRINK *Map, page 261*

For a city that attracts so many tourists, Khiva has frustratingly few good places to eat. Until now, almost none of them stayed open in winter; thankfully, that is beginning to change.

If you are staying in a hotel or bed and breakfast that can provide evening meals, your best bet will be to eat there. Even if dinner is not advertised, it's still worth putting in a polite request as most places are more than happy to oblige. The home cooking in the bed and breakfasts tends to be particularly good, and you'll get to sit down and chat with the family or other guests. When the electricity is off, prepare to have something cooked solely on the hob.

The following restaurants and cafés are viable alternatives if you don't have the choice of home cooking.

✕ Café Kheivak Restaurant 11 Islam Khoja; ⏰ high season 18.00–22.00 daily. The Malika Kheivak hotel (page 256) has a small, rather dark restaurant inside & this far preferable patio with a few shaded tables. Uzbek & European dishes, including pizza, which makes a nice change if you've been travelling in Uzbekistan a while, are available. Book at least 2hrs ahead by calling the hotel. **$$$**

✕ Khorezm Art Restaurant Allah Kuli Khan Madrasa; `62 375 7918; m 95 606 9270;` ⏰ 11.00–23.00 daily. The outdoor patio here has one of the best locations in Khiva, though if it's too cold to stay outside there is an indoor section to the restaurant as well. They claim their green noodles topped with an egg & soured cream or a meaty stew, or the *tuhum barak* (egg dumplings), can only be had here, but they are in fact available at other Old Town restaurants. They are tasty, if a little on the costly side, but then what you're really paying for is the view. **$$$**

✕ Matinyaz Divanbegi Polvon Qori; ⏰ 18.00–22.00 daily. Behind the Kalta Minar in a former madrasa, this is the restaurant of the Orient Star hotel (page 257). It has an impressive exterior & the interior is not bad either. Service is excellent, but the Uzbek food can be bland. **$$$**

✕ Yasavul Boshi Yasavul Boshi Madrasa, 1 Boltaev; ☎ 62 375 2456; **m** 91 278 9991; **e** yasavulboshi-restaurant-khiva@mail; ⏰ 11.00–21.00 daily. In the covered courtyard of the renovated madrasa of the same name, the menu includes some pretty good fresh salads, tasty soups & crêpes stuffed with minced mutton. **$$$**

✕ Zarafshon Café Tolib Maxsum Madrasa; ☎ 62 375 7051; **m** 91 434 9817; **e** cafezarafshonkhiva@mail.ru; ⏰ all year 08.00–22.00 daily. The covered courtyard of this former madrasa (built in 1908), this offers a great range of tasty local dishes, with plenty of vegetarian options such as *plov*, pumpkin *manti* & green noodles. There's also a lovely, summer-only terrace. **$$$**

✕ Bir Gumbaz Pahlavan Makhmud; ⏰ all year 09.00–18.00 daily. Behind the information centre, this stocky, domed structure is home to a pleasant tea house with Wi-Fi & English-speaking staff. It is possible to get a proper coffee (quite a novelty in Uzbekistan) & also standard Uzbek dishes, including *lagman* & *plov*. **$$**

☕ Terrassa Café 7 Boltaev; **m** 91 993 9111; **w** terrassa-cafe.com; ⏰ 10.30–23.00 daily. A great place to stop for drinks (including espresso, ginger tea, cognac tea & ice tea) & sandwiches, salads, *shashlik* & cake, not to mention cocktails. The balcony & rooftop terrace are recommended in the daytime, but it's better to go elsewhere for dinner. **$$$**

☕ Teahouse Farrukh Polvon Qori; ⏰ 11.00–18.00 daily. Shady courtyard *chaikhana* with low tables. Serves Turkish coffee (US$0.80), tea & Uzbek dishes such as plov & *manti*. Rooms are also available (see opposite). **$$**

SHOPPING Unsurprisingly, there are souvenir shops and stalls everywhere in Khiva, the majority of them selling a fairly similar selection of wooden Qu'ran stands, postcards and hats. *Suzanis* are for sale in every hotel reception, at what seem to be pretty fair prices.

The **Khiva Silk Carpet Workshop** (Pahlavan Makhmud; **w** khiva.info/khivasilk; ⏰ 09.00–18.00 Mon–Fri) is the star shopping attraction; its story is told in Chris Alexander's excellent book *Carpet Ride to Khiva*. An English-speaking guide is available in high season to talk you through the processes of dyeing and weaving; Jaloladdin, who runs the Meros B&B (see opposite), is another good contact for this. On the same street you'll also find the **Khiva Suzani Workshop** (⏰ 09.00–18.00 Mon–Fri), another NGO-backed initiative that produces high-quality silks and other textiles. The *suzani* workshop may be shut in September if its workers are required to go out and pick cotton.

The **bazaar** in the Dishon Qala is lively and well stocked with food and practical goods. Prices here are significantly cheaper than for goods sold within the Ichon Qala.

OTHER PRACTICALITIES
Communications
Khiva has embraced the internet wholeheartedly, & there is no shortage of **Wi-Fi** spots in hotels & cafés. If you need a computer as well as an internet connection, the information centre (page 256) has several.

✉ **Post and phone offices** 23 Amir Timur; ⏰ 09.00–noon & 14.00–17.00 Mon–Fri. North of the North Gate, actually off the main road by the canal.

Money
It's best to bring plenty of cash to Khiva, as there are few ATMs here, & even those may be out of cash. That said, there are Visa ATMs at the Orient Star and Asia hotels (pages 256 & 257), & 1 for Mastercard/Maestro at the Arkanchi (page 256).

$ Agro Bank ✆62 223 1359; ⊕ 09.00–17.00 Mon–Fri
$ Kishlok Kurilish Bank ✆62 375 3181

$ National Bank of Uzbekistan ✆62 375 4930; ⊕ 09.00–18.00 Mon–Fri, 09.00–16.00 Sat
$ Xalq Bank ✆62 375 4288; ⊕ 09.00–17.00 Mon–Fri

WHAT TO SEE AND DO Khiva's tourist sites are divided between the Ichon Qala (the medieval walled citadel) and the Dishon Qala (the mostly 19th- and early 20th-century outer walled city). Visitors tend to spend most of their time in the former (the 'Museum City'), but the Dishon Qala is not without its own considerable charms. Most of the surviving buildings date from between the invasion of Nadir Shah (in 1740) and the Russian takeover, although some are older, and some major buildings such as the Islam Khoja madrasa and minaret and the Nurullabay Palace were built between 1874 and 1920.

You are free to wander around both the Ichon Qala and the Dishon Qala and to enter some of the buildings. A single entrance ticket (US$12 for two days) covers a total of 15 small museums, mosques, etc, and is available from an unmarked door (⊕ 09.00–18.00 daily) in the Ata Darvoza (West Gate). There's also a one-day ticket (US$5) available, which covers only the Tash Khauli Palace, the Ark and the Juma Mosque. One camera permit (US$1) allows you to take photographs inside all the monuments and is available from the same place; there is no need for a permit if you want to photograph only the exteriors of the buildings. Where additional charges are levied (eg: at the Islam Khoja Madrasa), they are mentioned in the text below.

Ichon Qala [map, opposite] The heart of the Museum City, the Ichon Qala seems like a time warp. Listed as a UNESCO World Heritage Site since 1990, it is devoid of cars in its central areas, and with most of the modern infrastructure hidden from view, if you wake up and get out early, or take a walk late in the evening once the crowds have gone, then you'll capture a glimpse of Khiva in a bygone age, albeit rather cleaner. The density of sites, in particular the madrasas, means you're unlikely to be able to take everything in, and regular refreshment breaks will certainly be in order. We've tried to provide a list here of the most important sites, though as seemingly every building has a story to tell, there's no doubt you'll chance upon plenty of others as well.

Walls The crenellated city walls were Khiva's first line of defence from medieval raiders. Some 2.2km (1.4 miles) surround the city centre, and at their most impressive point they are 10m high and 8m thick. Built from adobe mud bricks, the oldest remaining sections of the walls date from the 5th century AD, though much of what you see is of far later (17th century) construction. Four substantial gateways allowed access through the walls; the sentries posted here would have been heavily armed, and closely monitored everyone and everything entering and leaving the city.

KHIVA *Ichon Qala*
For listings, see from page 256

⬤ **Where to stay**
1 Arkanchi B&B
2 Hotel Islambek
3 Hotel Shaherezada Khiva
4 Hostel Farrukh
5 Malika Kheivak
6 Meros B&B
7 Mirzaboshi B&B
8 Orient Star
9 Otabek Guesthouse

✖ **Where to eat and drink**
10 Bir Gumbaz
    Café Kheivak (see 5)
11 Khorezm Art
12 Matinyaz Divanbegi
    Teahouse Farrukh (see 4)
13 Terrassa Café
14 Yasavul Boshi
15 Zarafshon Café

Though they look as historic as the walls, the gateways you see today were rebuilt in the 19th and 20th centuries. The Ata Darvoza (Father's Gate or West Gate) is the main gate and was rebuilt in 1975 following its predecessor's demolition in the 1920s. Just to its right before you enter the Ichon Qala is a large bronze statue of the 9th-century mathematician Muhammad ibn Mūsā al-Khwārizmī, born in Khorezm, who discovered algebra. The Baggcha Darvoza (Garden Gate or North

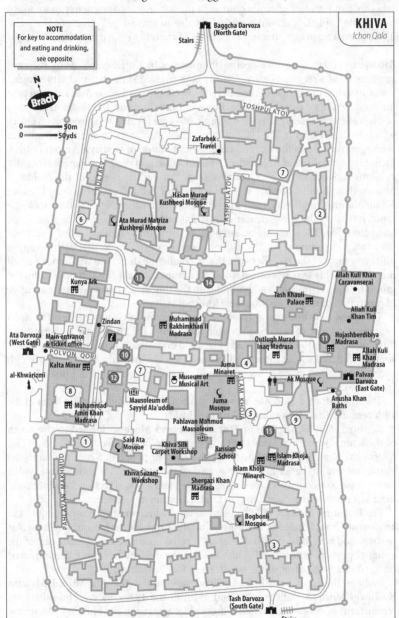

NOTE
For key to accommodation and eating and drinking, see opposite

KHIVA
Ichon Qala

Baggcha Darvoza (North Gate)

Stairs

TOSHPULATOV

Zafarbek Travel

BOLTAEV

Hasan Murad Kushbegi Mosque

Ata Murad Matriza Kushbegi Mosque

TASHPULATOV

Kunya Ark

Zindan

Muhammad Rakhimkhan II Madrasa

Tash Khauli Palace

Allah Kuli Khan Caravanserai

Allah Kuli Khan Tim

Hojashberdibiya Madrasa

Ata Darvoza (West Gate)

Main entrance & ticket office

POLVON QORI

Kalta Minar

al-Khwārizmi

Qutlugh Murad Inaq Madrasa

Juma Minaret

Museum of Musical Art

Muhammad Amin Khan Madrasa

Mausoleum of Sayyid Ala'uddin

Juma Mosque

ISLOM KHOJA

Ak Mosque

Palvan Darvoza (East Gate)

Anusha Khan Baths

Allah Kuli Khan Madrasa

Said Ata Mosque

Khiva Silk Carpet Workshop

PAHLAVAN MAKHMUD

Pahlavan Mahmud Mausoleum

Russian School

Islam Khoja Madrasa

Khiva Suzani Workshop

Islam Khoja Minaret

Shergazi Khan Madrasa

Bogbonli Mosque

Tash Darvoza (South Gate)

Stairs

0 — 50m
0 — 50yds

Gate) is another 19th-century construction and would have been used by customs officials to collect duty from caravans entering the city from Urgench; the Polvon Darvoza (Warriors' Gate or East Gate) dates from 1806 and was once the entrance to the slave market; and finally the Tash Darvoza (Stone Gate or South Gate), rebuilt during the reign of Allah Kuli Khan, contained a guardhouse and customs office. Rough staircases at the north and south gateways bring you on to the walls, where you can spot invaders advancing through the suburbs (or, fortunately more likely, take photographs). It should soon be possible to make a full circuit of the walls. There's also a surprising amount remaining of the outer ring, dating from 1842.

Mosques There were once nearly 100 mosques in Khiva, emphasising the city's importance as a religious centre. Usually built from mud or clay bricks, they didn't stand up well to the ravages of time and so were continually knocked down and rebuilt on the same site, or heavily restored. Below, they are listed in chronological order.

The oldest mosque in Khiva is the **Juma Mosque** (Friday Mosque; Polvon Qori), which has its origins in the 10th century, albeit with many later additions. It was the largest mosque in the city and caught the attention of medieval Arab travellers, including Al Istahri and Al Makdisi. Around a dozen of the 213 *karagacha* (the elm columns supporting the roof) survive from this earliest period of the building's history, though most of what you see is from the rebuild undertaken in 1788 for Khan Abdurakhman Mekhtar. The pillars are fascinating: at first they look the same, but as you look closer, you realise that each one is unique in its size, shape and patterning. The stone blocks supporting them, many of which are also carved, vary too, compensating for the differing lengths of timber so that each complete pillar can support the roof. Between the wood and the stone, you will notice a small metal cuff, inside which is camel wool. This innovation absorbs humidity from the ground, deters termites from chomping on the timber, and may even give a degree of protection during an earthquake. How cool is that?

The mosque is unusually simple in its design and as you step into the open courtyard, a sense of calm washes over you, even if the crowds are jabbering and hustling outside. The hand-carved pillars and doors and the marble plaque on the south wall detailing the mosque's land holdings are the main attractions, though the mosque also provides access should you wish to climb the Juma Minaret (page 265).

The small, domed **Said Ata Mosque** was built for Yar Muhammad Divan in the 18th century. There is nothing really to see inside.

Restored in 1997, the **Hasan Murad Kushbegi Mosque**, located in the north of the Ichon Qala, dates from 1800 and was the joint endeavour of Kushbegi and his cousin, Shah Niyaz. Kushbegi was the chief of police in Khiva and amassed significant wealth, hence his ability to endow the mosque. The mosque is divided into two parts, an open area for use in summer, and a closed section for winter, and there is a small, whitewashed minaret in the northeastern corner.

The **Bogbonli Mosque** (1809) seems to serve as an unofficial monument to the artisans of Khiva. Funded by two horticulturalist brothers, the mosque is rectangular in shape and is decorated with domes and carved pillars. A stone plaque east of the entrance portico remembers Pakhlavan Quli, the mosque's architect, and engraved on the doors is the name of the woodcarver, Ruz Muhammad.

Perhaps the most beautiful of Khiva's mosques is the **Ata Murad Matriza Kushbegi Mosque**. Built in 1800 and again in the 1830s, its graceful pillars are reminiscent of chopsticks. When a breeze blows through the building you realise how well it is designed for hot weather.

The **Ak Mosque** (White Mosque) was founded in 1657 but the current building dates from 1838–42. The domed hall is surrounded on three sides by an open terrace, and inscriptions name the artisans responsible for the elegant columns: Nur Muhammad, Kalandar and the sons of Adin Kalandar and Sayyid Muhammad. Stop here to admire the finely carved doors and also the diminutive minaret.

Madrasas At the start of the 20th century there were 65 madrasas in Khiva, 54 of them within the city walls. The city was a hotbed for religious education and religious debate, and its wealthier residents bid to outdo each other by building larger, richer and more elaborate madrasas. A selection of the most interesting examples is mentioned here, though there are plenty more you'll find while wandering through the streets. Below, they are listed in chronological order.

The oldest madrasa in Khiva is the **Hojashberdibiya Madrasa** (near the Polvon Darvoza), parts of which date from 1688. A major rebuild for Allah Kuli Khan in 1834 divided the site in two, and the new layout was said to resemble a saddlebag: it was consequently nicknamed *hurjun* (the saddlebag), and this name is still occasionally used today. It's now a craft centre, meaning there are lots of stalls inside.

The imposing **Shergazi Khan Madrasa** (in the south of the Ichon Qala) was built by 5,000 Persian slaves captured by Shergazi Khan on a raid at Meshed in 1718. The slaves were promised their freedom once the madrasa was complete, but fearing (probably quite rightly) that he would renege on the deal, they took out their anger on the project manager and murdered him inside the unfinished madrasa in 1720. An inscription over the madrasa's door remembers what purportedly were his final words: 'I accept death at the hands of slaves'. The madrasa's most famous student was the Turkmen poet Makhtum Kuli (1724–83).

Qutlugh Murad Inaq, an uncle of Allah Kuli Khan, had the madrasa bearing his name constructed between 1804 and 1812 and hoped to be buried beneath its floors. When he died (murdered by a rival) outside the city walls, it was thought to be inauspicious to bring the body through one of the gateways, and his family sat scratching their heads. Thinking outside the box, someone suggested the drastic step of demolishing a section of the eastern wall so that the madrasa straddled both the Ichon Qala and the Dishon Qala. The deed was done, and Qutlugh was buried beneath his madrasa's entrance way.

Further demolition was required to accommodate the **Allah Kuli Khan Madrasa** in 1834–35. Space was at a premium inside the citadel, so the external wall had to be removed to enable the city to expand. Some 99 student cells were constructed (this was an auspicious number), and the building also housed the municipal library, acquisitions for which were funded by profits from the Allah Kuli Khan Tim (page 268). The façade is richly decorated with dark blue, light blue and white majolica tiles.

The largest madrasa in Khiva (near the Ata Darvoza) is the two-storey **Muhammad Amin Khan Madrasa** (1851–53), which now houses the Orient Star hotel (page 257). Some 250 students once studied here and it was considered a luxurious place to live: student cells had two rooms rather than the usual one, and they looked outward at the world rather than into the courtyard. The High Muslim Court once had its registry office here, and held sessions in the central courtyard.

Muhammad Amin Khan was one of Khiva's most illustrious rulers, a strong leader who built effective alliances with neighbouring tribes but was also not above beating them bloodily into submission. He commissioned a number of buildings in Khiva, including both this madrasa and the Kalta Minar (page 265), but his life

THE MADRASA

Madrasas are to Khiva as university colleges are to Oxford or Cambridge. As with the colleges, they were higher education institutions endowed by wealthy benefactors where teachers and students lived and worked together.

Endowing a madrasa was an expensive business. In addition to the construction costs for the buildings, benefactors were expected to donate enough land or property to support the students and teachers and to pay for the building's upkeep. The upside for the donor was that, as the madrasa bore his name, he would have a lasting legacy in the eyes of Khiva's population and, it was hoped, be looked upon favourably when he finally had to account for his deeds before God.

The curriculum in the madrasas included both secular and religious subjects. Arabic grammar, sharia, and Arabic and Persian literature were taught to the youngest students, who could enter the madrasa at the age of 15; older students also studied logic and law. Classes took place four days a week throughout the year, and students were expected to pass an exam before taking their degree and being given an appropriate job by the khan.

The buildings themselves were divided into public and private areas. Public rooms included the mosque, an audience hall and teaching rooms, and to the rear of the madrasa were typically the students' *hujras* or cells where they slept. In addition to the students and their teachers, the madrasa's community included an imam, a muezzin to call the residents to prayer, a *mutavalli* (similar to a bursar), cleaners, barbers and water carriers.

and the construction of the minaret were simultaneously cut short in a rather grisly fashion in 1855 when he was beheaded by a Turkmen horseman. If you wish to climb the Kalta Minar, access is from the northeast corner of this madrasa.

The most fabulous tile work is to be found on the **Muhammad Rakhimkhan II Madrasa**, built in 1871 and restored in 1992. The blue-and-white majolica is set off by terracotta, and the resultant façade is sumptuous, particularly when viewed in the early evening. Inside, you'll find a museum of the history of the Khivan Khanate that is essentially about Muhammad Rakhimkhan II, replete with flags, photographs, armour and robes. Performances of dance and circus acts occasionally take place in the courtyard on summer evenings.

Muhammad Rakhimkhan (1847–1910) was an intriguing character: he was a fine poet and printed his work on his own printing press under the pseudonym Feruz; he admired Russian culture, smoked cigars and dressed his harem in corsets and crinolines; and when pressure from Russia mounted and he had to cede control to the tsar, he willingly gave up power and joined the army as a major general. He was a man whose rule straddled two markedly different eras and, as the photographs on display in the madrasa's right-hand mosque show, Muhammad Rakhimkhan did a remarkably good job of reconciling them.

The striking turquoise **Islam Khoja Madrasa** is a surprisingly late construction: it was completed only in 1908. Its founder, Islam Khoja, was grand vizier to the khan and an active educationalist. He introduced several educational reforms, endowed schools and hospitals, and his *pièce de résistance* is this building. Sadly, the completion of the project is tied up in tragedy: Islam Khoja was assassinated in 1913 and the madrasa's architect was buried alive by Emir Isfandiyar Khan as a potential witness to the murder.

The 42 rooms of the madrasa now house the Museum of Applied Arts (🕐 09.00–18.00 daily). Though the selection of artefacts is not of such high quality as in similar museums in Tashkent and Bukhara, there are still some interesting examples of royal costume, metalwork, leather goods, tiles and carved marble.

Minarets Fourteen minarets have survived in the centre of Khiva (we only mention the most striking here). They were constructed so that the muezzin might climb the stairs to call the faithful to prayer five times each day, his voice carrying on the breeze across the city.

The oldest, the **Juma Minaret** (Polvon Qori), dates from the 10th to the 13th centuries and has distinctive turquoise stripes around its otherwise sand-coloured cylinder. If you have a head for heights (or want a bird's-eye view of the city), you can climb the 81 steps to the top (US$2). You can see a lot from 33m up!

Every postcard of Khiva seems to be illustrated with a photo of the **Kalta Minar.** This stumpy, but still eye-catching, green-and-turquoise landmark was intended to be the tallest minaret in central Asia: its patron, Muhammad Amin Khan, planned for it to be at least 70m tall, allegedly so that you could see Bukhara from the top. Sadly, it was not to be. Muhammad was murdered (page 263) before the minaret was complete and the architect responsible for the project fled.

Rather more graceful looking is the **Islam Khoja Minaret** (1910), which adjoins the Islam Khoja Madrasa (see opposite) in the south of the Ichon Qala. Almost 57m tall, it looks even taller due to the tapered shape and the varying widths of the yellow and blue-green stripes. It is possible to climb the 120 steps to the top, following in the footsteps of the city's watchmen (US$1.10). It is said that the minaret was used as a radio tower to summon air support during the 1924 assault on Khiva, though sadly this is probably a myth.

Mausoleums The burial places of Sufi holy men were not simply tombs, but also pilgrimage places. As pilgrims gave donations as well as prayers, it was possible to build elaborate mausoleums, sometimes centuries after the holy man's death, and so to not only immortalise his memory but also ensure a constant stream of pilgrims (and their money) in the future. Despite the best efforts of the Soviet state to wipe out such practices completely, pilgrims do still occasionally come to the mausoleums to pray, and so you should act in a respectful manner and remove your shoes before entering the burial chambers.

The oldest surviving building in Khiva is the **Mausoleum of Sayyid Ala'uddin** (just inside the Ata Darvoza). The earliest part of the mausoleum, the domed burial vault, was built in 1303 and contains a stunning blue and green majolica tile-covered casket. It is thought that the tiles were made in Konya-Urgench (page 249) prior to the city's relocation. Ala'uddin was a holy man from the Naqshbandi order of Sufis (Islamic mystics).

Originally similar in size and style, the **Pahlavan Mahmud Mausoleum** (also known as Palvan Pir; US$1) marks the final resting place of Pahlavan Mahmud (1247–1326), a local wrestler, poet and furrier who unexpectedly became a revered saint. The cemetery was expanded substantially in the 17th and 18th centuries, and Muhammad Rahim Khan I built the mausoleum in 1810.

You enter the complex through an 18th-century portal that opens out on to a pleasant courtyard framed by a khanagha and *hujras*, the summer mosque and well. Each surface is exquisitely decorated in every imaginable shade of blue, blue-green and turquoise, and a vast blue dome, restored in 1993 after it was brought down by unexpectedly heavy snowfall, looms above it all. Pahlavan Mahmud is buried behind a screen inlaid with ivory, local folk motifs decorating his eternal chamber, and the tomb of Muhammad Rahim Khan I (d1825) is in a niche. In 1825 an east wing was added, housing the tomb of Allakuli-khan (d1842), and the tombs of other significant Khivan figures can be seen outside the main mausoleum, including Abdul Gazi Khan (d1664), and the mother and son of the assassinated Isfandiyar.

Palaces Khiva's rulers and merchants may have spent vast sums endowing mosques and madrasas, but they also built luxurious, lavishly decorated homes in which they could entertain guests and enjoy themselves. Palaces (and, indeed, smaller houses) were divided into public areas for feasting, hosting guests and doing business, and private, residential areas where the family lived and the harem was kept out of view.

Kunya Ark (immediately north of the Ata Darvoza) This fortified palace was built in 1686 (on older foundations) by Arangan Khan, son of Anusha Khan. It was a town within a town, with its own defensive walls, mosques and offices, factories and stables, arsenal and mint as well as residential areas. A single gateway in the eastern wall gave access to the complex, which was guarded with copper cannons.

Sadly, few of the Ark's original structures remain: when the khans moved into the Tash Khauli (see below), their former home fell into disrepair, and many of the buildings you see date just from the 19th century. An attractive courtyard is surrounded by the winter and summer mosques, complete with blue and white floral tiles laid out to resemble creeping ivy, and the royal mint, built for Muhammad Rakhimkhan II. This holds a collection of coins, medals and silk and paper money, mostly from the 20th century, and a diorama of a primitive mint, just like a blacksmith's shop.

It's also possible to visit the Kurinish Khana (throne room), behind a grand tiled portico on the second courtyard; built by Iltuzar Khan in 1804 to replace the earlier throne room destroyed during the Persian invasion, it's surprisingly small and somewhat gloomy. This was the public audience hall, and the khan's throne, made from wood covered with thin sheets of engraved silver, would have stood beneath the sumptuous painted ceiling. Sadly, the throne was taken as booty by the Russian army and is now in the Armoury at the Hermitage Museum in St Petersburg: the one you see is a copy. The emir received his most important visitors here, including the Russian Captain Muraviev, or alternatively inside a yurt erected specially for nomadic guests on the round platform in the middle of the courtyard. The smaller rooms around the throne room would have housed the Treasury and valuable manuscripts, and also have given the khan a quiet place to retreat to when required.

A narrow passage leads to the harem and the stairs to the Ak Sheikh Bobo Bastion, the Ark's fortified heart and the oldest place in Khiva; its foundations are contemporaneous with the Toprak Fortress in Khorezm. Later in its history the bastion was used as a hermitage, a watchtower and an arsenal.

If you want to climb up on to the walls and ascend the tower for views across Khiva and thence to the desert (best late in the day when the light is not so bright), it is possible to do so. There is a separate charge for this of US$1.10, payable as you go up.

Tash Khauli Palace (near the Polvon Darvoza) This newer palace was commissioned by Allah Kuli Khan in 1830. Construction of the 160-plus rooms took eight years and was undertaken by more than 1,000 slaves; the project's first architect was impaled for daring to suggest (correctly, so it later turned out) that the project might not be completed on time.

The oldest part of the palace is the harem, built around a **courtyard**. On the southern side of the courtyard are four open areas, one for each wife, and the more elaborate area on the eastern side was the summer living area of the khan himself. You can step inside his sumptuous bed chamber, where his wives and concubines would have presented themselves. The rooms on the opposite side of the courtyard would have been occupied by the concubines in the summer months. They shared the hall at the far end of the complex in winter. Life as a Khivan concubine was tough. Girls, usually slaves, came into the harem around the age of 12 and, if they were lucky, lived here until about 30. Only wives of the emir were allowed to bear his children, so those concubines unfortunate enough to conceive were subjected to forced abortions, which were often fatal for the concubine, too. When the emir died, all of his concubines were evicted from the harem and resold in the slave market as a son could not inherit his father's wives or concubines.

The blue-and-white tiles that decorate the harem are absolutely stunning, and the proportions of the courtyard are most unusual. The ceilings are painted with an almost psychedelic abstract detailing. It is thought they were prepared in a workshop and then lifted into place once complete. There is a small Museum of Handicrafts (entrance included in the Ichon Qala ticket price) in the harem, which has dusty dioramas and photos, but it's not really worth more than a cursory glance.

A long corridor once linked the harem with the **Ishrat Khauli** (public court), though visitors are now required to take a more circuitous route, going outside and re-entering on the south side. This is where the khan would have received envoys and other guests. As in the Kunya Ark (see opposite), there is space to erect a yurt in the courtyard; the throne room was on the upper floor. In addition to geometric majolica tiles you should also take a look at the calligraphy; the words are taken from the poet Ogahi.

The third courtyard is the **Arz Khana** (law court). Larger than the Ishrat Khauli, this was where the most important affairs of state took place. Allah Kuli Khan would have presided here for 4 hours each day and been expected to dispense justice. Defendants would exit the courtyard through one of the two gateways: the first was for those acquitted, the second led to the executioner. The tiles in this courtyard are considered among the finest in Khiva. Indeed, they were made by Abdullah the Genius, who was given this particular moniker after completing his work on the palace.

As you leave the Arz Khana, look left to see the emir's carriage. Made in St Petersburg, this was an official gift in 1876 and somehow has survived intact.

During the summer season, dinner shows with traditional music and dance take place in the palace courtyard. Details and bookings are available through the information centre (page 256).

Museums Khiva's museums are a mixed bag: indeed many visitors are so focused on the architectural masterpieces that they understandably feel little need to venture inside the small, somewhat dated museums. The best is in the New Town (page 269), while the pick of those in the Old Town are the **Museum of Musical Art** and the **Museum of Applied Arts** (⊕ 09.00–18.00 daily; included in the Ichon Qala collective museums ticket). The former is in the Qozi Kalyan Madrasa (1905) and covers the musical traditions of Khorezm, with a number of instruments on show and photos of famous Uzbek musicians – but there's no information and no music! The latter, in the Islam Khoja Madrasa, has a reasonable collection of regional costumes, carpets, saddlebags, ceramics, metalwork, tiles and carvings, and manuscripts. In addition, the **Russian School**, not far south of Polvon Qori,

(1912) exhibits black-and-white photographs of Khiva and its inhabitants by Khudaybergen Divanov (1878–1938), who studied in St Petersburg at the expense of Muhammad Rakhimkhan II and was shot in the purge of 1938 (page 34).

Other structures Behind the Ak Mosque are the **Anusha Khan Baths** where, for more than 300 years, the ordinary citizens of Khiva could take a dip. As with their Roman predecessors, these baths had underfloor heating, and the baths themselves were sunk into the ground to conserve as much heat as possible. They belonged to the khan, and access was prohibited for women, non-Muslims and, sensibly enough, anyone with a contagious skin disease.

The cupolas of the **Allah Kuli Khan Tim** (trading dome) link the Ichon Qala with the **Allah Kuli Khan Caravanserai**. Both structures date from the 1830s and would once have been the commercial heartland of the Ichon Qala, selling everything from Siberian furs to Persian carpets, Indian spices to Turkish sweets. The goods these days are a little less exotic, and sadly lean towards overpriced plastic imports from China. Take note of the *caravanserai's* two-storey design: the upper level would have served as a budget hotel for merchants and enabled them to keep a close eye on their goods at night.

Khiva's most gruesome site is the **zindan** (the city's dungeon). Though less notorious than Bukhara's zindan (it's all relative; page 235), prisoners condemned to death would have been held here. They were executed into a pit immediately outside, so that those inside could hear the screams and be continually reminded of what awaited them. The current building dates from 1910 and showcases a range of manacles and torture implements (flailing, beating and stuffing the mouth full of salt were especially popular), as well as artistic but still gruesome paintings of torture and executions. Look for an unmarked door immediately south of the Ark.

Dishon Qala The 5.6km (3.5 miles) of city walls of the Dishon Qala were erected in 1842 by Allah Kuli Khan. Unlike the mud bricks of the Ichon Qala, these walls are made of clay mined north of Khiva at Ghovuk Kul. Local legend has it that clay from the same source was also used to build Medina, though there is no scientific or historical evidence to support this claim. Some 200,000 people purportedly worked on the walls' construction (many of them slaves), and there were once ten gateways, though today only three remain. The domed **Qo'sha Darvoza** (Twin Gate), on the road north, has attractively patterned tilework; it is so-called because its forward-thinking architect designed it so that traffic could enter and leave the city simultaneously rather than creating a choke point on the road.

Madrasas There are half-a-dozen or so madrasas in the Dishon Qala, listed here chronologically. Close to the Polvon Darvoza of the Ichon Qala are the **mosque and madrasa of Said Niaz Shalikarbai**, a rice merchant (*shalikar* meaning 'rice grower') who endowed the building in the 1830s. It was completed in 1842. Still in use as a place of worship, it is Khiva's largest mosque after the Juma Mosque and the only place in the city where the muezzin still calls the faithful to prayer. Listen out for his dulcet tones from the minaret in the early morning and at dusk. The mosque's nine domes shelter worshippers during the cold winter months; in summer they can pray in the courtyard and in the shade of the four-pillared veranda.

The beautiful **Tort Shavaz Madrasa** (1885; Ollobergenov) has an open-sided, columned hall, green chequered minaret and tree-lined garden. Four tombs belonging to Yafandiyar I and three of his generals are also within the complex, and this gives the site its name (*tort shavaz* meaning 'four brave ones'). The Hungarian traveller Armin Vambery stayed in the madrasa's khanagha in 1863, dressed as a wandering dervish to avoid attracting attention. Following his time in central Asia, Vambery published a number of illuminating accounts including *Sketches of Central Asia* (1868) and *Manners in Oriental Countries* (1876).

Also of note are the **Bikajon Bika Madrasa** (1894), whose construction was halted for seven years following a dispute, believe it or not, over planning permission, and the robust-looking **Polvon Qori Madrasa** (1905), built by a Khivan merchant with profits from his trade with Russia and Turkey.

Mausoleums There are also several noteworthy mausoleums to keep an eye out for. The **Abd al Bobo Mausoleum** holds the grave of Palvan Ahmad Zamchiy (known as Abd al Bobo), a supposed descendant of Ali and an Islamic missionary in the wake of the Arab invasion. This is also the site of Khiva's original, infamous slave market, though there's little sign of this history now. The **Shakalandar Bobo Mausoleum's** simple, mud-brick structure remembers the Sufi Sheikh Kalandar Bobo and his two dervish brothers. Muhammad Khan, Muhammad Rakhimkhan II, Isfandiyar, Islam Khoja and a number of royal wives, mothers and children are buried in the much later and far grander **Sayyid Muhammad Makhiruy Mausoleum** (Amir Timur); although on the site of an earlier sheikh's tomb, it is, in essence, a 19th-century royal family crypt.

Museum of the Khorezm Ma'mun Academy (1 Jamoat Markazi; w mamun. uz; ⊕ 09.00–17.00 daily; US$0.60) The museum of the academy founded by Ali ibn Mamun II (d1017) is little-known but excellent. Upstairs, in a modern building to the north of the Old Town, the displays (with good information panels in English) start with Palaeolithic and Neolithic stone weapons from the 7th to 4th millennia BC and bronze pieces from the 3rd millennium BC, followed by the Suyargan and Amirabad cultures in the 2nd millennium BC. Until the time that Achaemenids invaded in the 6th century BC, primitive states established themselves here, building solid forts and minting coins. Despite the Arab and Mongol invasions, the area became wealthy from Silk Road trade and produced great scholars such as Muhammad ibn Mūsā al-Khwārizmī (783–850), the discoverer of algebra, the great polymath Abu Rayhan Beruni (973–1050), and the poet and philosopher Pahlavan Mahmud (1247–1326).

Nurillabay Palace (Kubro; ⊕ 09.00–19.00 daily; US$6) Muhammad Rakhimkhan II began building the vast Nurillabay Palace in 1906 following a visit to St Petersburg. He hoped that the palace, which was intended for his son, would incorporate many of the architectural features he'd seen in Russia. Behind the imposing defensive wall with its towers and buttresses were more than 100 rooms; the cost of construction nearly bankrupted the state. Parquet flooring was delivered from St Petersburg, fireplaces were installed in many of the rooms, and Tsar Nikolai II sent two chandeliers as a gift to mark the palace's completion. The first parts you come to, the courtyard, madrasa and reception hall, were preserved because of their importance to Soviet history: the last khan, Isfandiyar, was murdered here in 1918; the first people's government was established here in 1920; and the first statue of Lenin in central Asia was raised in the palace's courtyard (it has since been displaced by a modern statue of Muhammad Rakhimkhan II). The rest of the sprawling site was left to decay until very recently, but has now been very well restored. It's expensive, but you can spend an hour or two nosing around and coming across unexpected treasures, such as a **gallery of contemporary Uzbek art** (with a few good pieces), another of well-presented old photos of Khorezm, taken by Russian visitors in 1858, 1873 and 1903, and by Khudaybergen Divanov (page 268). The Gallery of **Traditional Crafts of Khorezm: History & Modernity**, displays excellent old and new ceramics, as well as metal- and woodwork (including musical instruments), coats and carpets. There are also shops selling art (poor) and crafts (much better), and the gardens are lovely.

AROUND KHIVA

Kibla Tozabag (New South Garden; ⏰ 09.00–17.00 daily) The Kibla Tozabag was built in 1897 as the summer residence of Muhammad Rakhimkhan II. Its 0.5ha plot is 2km southwest of the city centre (accessible by taxi), and its design incorporates both central Asian and Western features. Though the verandas are open in the traditional style, the palace also has large, European windows made by artisans in St Petersburg, and the first of its three courtyards is laid out with flowerbeds and a fountain. The buildings are made from fired bricks, in some places decorated with plasterwork and gilt, and the wide wooden doors were carved by German craftsmen. The palace was restored in 1992 to mark the 150th anniversary of its founder's birth, but it's rarely visited by tourists and you may well have the site to yourself.

Mausoleum of Sheikh Mukhtar Vali The extraordinary 13th-century Mausoleum of Sheikh Mukhtar Vali, a Sufi hermit and saint who was a rival of Pahlavan Mahmud (page 265), is 20km east of Khiva (you can take a shared taxi or minibus to Yangiariq, then find a taxi to take you 5km to the southwest to Ostana). The sheikh died in 1287 and is buried alongside his brother-in-law, Sayyid Ata, a follower of Khoja Ahmed Yassaui of Turkestan (now in southern Kazakhstan). The mausoleum complex, which was expanded and restored in 1807, is a local landmark, rising 22m above the surrounding landscape. In the past it offered pilgrims a place of refuge from Turkmen slave traders, and though that threat has thankfully now passed, you'll still be invited in for tea.

On the way to the mausoleum, you can stop (halfway along the road between Khiva and Yangiariq) at **Chadra Hauli**. This peculiar stepped tower, four storeys high, may at first look like a minaret but was in fact the summer residence of a local merchant, probably built in the late 18th or early 19th century. His simple living quarters, with open balconies to catch the breeze, are perched atop stables and storage rooms, and the caretaker will happily unlock the building for you to look around. Tip him a dollar (or the som equivalent) for his trouble.

THE DESERT FORTRESSES OF ANCIENT KHOREZM

Although the desert fortresses of ancient Khorezm lie mostly in Karakalpakstan (page 273), the majority of visitors will access them from Urgench and Khiva rather than from Nukus, and we have therefore listed them here.

The Kyzylkum Desert was not always so dry: as recently as the early centuries AD this was fertile agricultural land, supporting the stable and centralised kingdom of Khorezm. The area's traditional name, Elliq Qala (the 50 fortresses), gives a stark indication of what lies beneath the desert sands, and UNESCO and local tour companies have worked closely to promote the itinerary they call 'The Golden Ring of Ancient Khorezm'. A detailed, illustrated guide to the main sites has been produced by UNESCO and can be downloaded free at w http://bit.ly/khorzem.

You will need your own transport to visit the forts as there is quite some distance between them. To hire a car and driver, or to arrange a tour, contact one of the operators listed on page 251. If you're looking to self-drive here, ensure that you have a GPS and a really good map (page 70). To explore them properly, and drive between, you will want to schedule no more than three into a day. Eight major forts remain sufficiently intact to be of interest to the casual visitor.

First on the alphabetical list is **Anka Qala**, a 5th-century fort that later became a 12th-century fortified *caravanserai*, built on a square with double adobe walls and a central courtyard with a well in the middle. A narrow corridor ran between the walls, of which the outer one would originally have been 7–8m high.

Far more impressive, however, is the **Ayaz Qala**, a 'must-see' on every Kyzylkum Desert itinerary. The external walls, built upon a flat hilltop, have stood since at least the 4th century BC, and you can clearly see the scale of the site: the fort's footprint was a remarkable 182m by 152m, and even today sections of wall survive that are 10m high. The Ayaz Qala would once have been a very wealthy place with sophisticated inhabitants. At least ten major structures have been identified within the complex, and archaeologists have unearthed everything from early wine presses to golden statues. Ayaz Kala Tour (page 251) is able to arrange camel trekking (US$10) and a yurt stay (US$50 FB; **$$$**) overlooking the fort: each yurt sleeps two to six people in comfort. The two bathroom blocks are basic but clean, with cold showers. Tasty meals are served, and the lighting is solar powered.

Fortress three is **Big Guldursun**, a 7th- to 8th-century AD fort built atop an earlier (1st- to 4th-century) structure. With walls 15m high, this was a purely defensive structure, with a garrison rather than a town inside. The walls were 15m high, but ultimately these were not enough to protect it, as legend has it that Princess Guldursun fell in love with a Kalmyk warrior and opened the gates to him. Once inside, he cast her aside, his troops killed everyone they could find, and they reduced the buildings to ruins. Note to romantics: if you're going on a first date, pick somewhere public just in case that tall, dark, handsome stranger turns out to have homicidal tendencies.

One of the earlier forts is the **Djanbas Qala**, construction of which was started in the 4th century BC. Unlike Khorezm's other fortresses, Djanbas never had any towers; the garrison of 2,000 soldiers was obviously felt sufficient to keep invaders at bay. Within the fort's walls were organised blocks of housing, wide streets and a fire temple.

The **Gyaur Qala** is quite a way from the other forts – it's near the Amu Darya River and the road northwest to Nukus. We arrived late in the day; the long shadows it cast were both dramatic and slightly eerie. One of the so-called Hellenic fortresses on account of the Greek influence at the time of its construction (3rd to 2nd century BC), it continues to cut an imposing figure on the horizon long before you reach it.

Kizil Qala (meaning 'Red Fortress'), about 30km north of the Beruni bridge, dates from the 1st and 2nd centuries AD and was restored in the 12th and 13th centuries against the threat of Mongol invasion. It forms a square with sides of over 60m in length and its walls are 8m thick and up to 16m in height. The interior is in good condition, but you should not try to get into the lower level owing to the number of resident snakes.

Similar in age to the Djanbas Qala is the **Koy-Kirilgan Qala**, the tastefully named Fort of Dead Rams. It's probably a reference to pre-Islamic sacrifices that took place here. This was a round fortress with a 90m diameter. The inner citadel (the oldest part of the site) was a royal burial ground; beyond this were rooms for servants and artisans; and lastly you reached the outer wall with its nine imposing towers. The Koy-Kirilgan Qala was inhabited as late as the 4th century AD.

The walls of the **Pil Qala,** dating between the 4th and 2nd century BC, were more than 6m thick and sloped to make it hard for invaders to attack. It was built by the Afrigids, rulers of Khorezm at the time, roughly on a square and was designed with double walls with a narrow space so that archers could stand between them shooting out at the advancing enemy.

We've saved one of the best for last. The **Toprak Qala** covered a site 500m long and, at its peak in the 1st century BC, accommodated a population of 2,500 people. It was both a city fortress and an important religious centre, and the 1ha citadel at its heart was a royal residence: archaeologists have identified a throne room, a fire temple and an armoury. The three main halls were spectacularly decorated with murals of both Greek and Zoroastrian deities, as well as kings and soldiers. The wall paintings are now preserved in the Hermitage collection in St Petersburg. There is a small, very basic **yurt camp ($$)** next to the car park of the fortress. Contact a tour company (page 251) if you would be interested in staying here. From here, it is a steep climb to the top of the site, from where you'll get excellent views across the plain.

Finally, easily visible to the south of the road and railway west to Nukus (it looks like a mesa in the bad lands of Arizona), the **Chilpik hill** [map, page 274] is topped by a roofless structure, 65m across, that was built more than 2,000 years ago as a Zoroastrian tower of silence, a place for dead bodies to be left and eaten by birds. It's possible to reach the base of the hill on dirt tracks and climb up to the entry on the west side, through a gap in the clay walls that still stand up to 15m high; however, there's nothing much to see inside.

10

Republic of Karakalpakstan

In the far northwest of Uzbekistan, this huge tract of desert is in fact an autonomous republic. It is theoretically sovereign (with the exception of the right to secession), and political decisions impacting upon it are made jointly by the Uzbek government and the Karakalpak legislature in the republic's capital, Nukus.

If you go back 2,000 years, Karakalpakstan was a fertile agricultural region, a far cry from the desert it is today after centuries of gradual climate change. Its indigenous inhabitants, the Karakalpaks, were nomadic herders and fishermen, fishing not only in the rivers, but also in the southern parts of the Aral Sea. The area was nominally a part of the Khanate of Khiva, but was ceded to the Russian Empire in 1873. The Soviets considered it first as an autonomous part of Kazakhstan, then as an autonomous state within Uzbekistan from 1936 onwards. Karakalpakstan has a population of 1.8 million, of whom a third are ethnically Karakalpak, a third are Uzbek, and the rest are Kazakh (300,000) and other minorities. The Karakalpaks are ethnically Turkic, with a language that's close to Kazakh; they're pretty secular, eating pork and supposedly making Uzbekistan's best vodka. There are two reasons to travel out into this Wild West of Uzbekistan: to bear witness to the environmental disaster that is the Aral Sea; and to wonder at how the incredible modern art collection of the Igor Savitsky Museum possibly made it out here.

NUKUS

The capital of Karakalpakstan since 1939, Nukus is also the republic's transport hub. A small, dusty settlement until the 1930s, this planned city grew rapidly after it was chosen as the location for the Soviet Union's Chemical Research Institute. Its remote position made it the ideal terrain for developing and testing chemical weapons, notably Novichok (the institute was dismantled by the United States in 2002).

Today, Nukus is a fairly unattractive grid of tree-lined streets and mainly post-Soviet concrete, visited by few foreigners save NGO workers and environmental campaigners. Oh, and art lovers, as hidden in what is otherwise a desolate cultural wasteland is one of the world's finest collections of early 20th-century Russian avant-garde art: the Igor Savitsky Museum (page 278).

GETTING THERE AND AWAY Reaching Nukus from almost anywhere in Uzbekistan is a trial; it's an unfortunate fact of life. If you are already in Urgench or Khiva it's feasible to travel by road, otherwise look instead at the rail and flight options.

By air There are two flights a day to Tashkent with **Uzbekistan Airways** (1hr 40min; from US$50), with onward connections to domestic and international

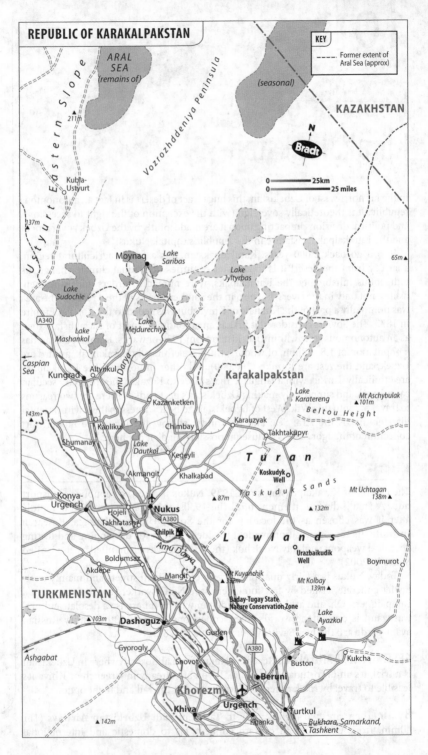

REPUBLIC OF KARAKALPAKSTAN

KEY

--- Former extent of
Aral Sea (approx)

ARAL
SEA
(remains of)

(seasonal)

KAZAKHSTAN

▲ 211m

Vozrozhddeniya Peninsula

N

Bradt

0 ——— 25km
0 ——— 25 miles

Kubla-
Ustyurt

137m

Moynaq

*Lake
Saribas*

*Lake
Jyltyrbas*

65m ▲

*Lake
Sudochie*

*Lake
Mejdurechiye*

A340

*Lake
Mashankol*

Caspian
Sea

Kungrad

Altynkul

Karakalpakstan

*Lake
Karatereng*

Mt Aschybulak
▲ 101m

B e l t o u   H e i g h t

Kazanketken

143m ▲

Kanlikul

Chimbay

Karauzyak

Takhtakupyr

Shumanay

*Lake
Dautkol*

Kegeyli

T u r a n

Akmangit

Khalkabad

**Koskudyk
Well** ○

T a s k u d u k   S a n d s

Mt Uchtagan
138m ▲

Konya-
Urgench

Hojeli

▲ 87m

▲ 132m

Takhtatash

Nukus
A380

Chilpik 🕌

L o w l a n d s

Boldumsaz

Akdepe

Amu Darya

Mangit

**Urazbaikudik
Well** ○

Boymurot

Mt Kuyanchik
▲ 332m

Mt Kolbay
139m ▲

TURKMENISTAN

▲ 103m

Dashoguz

Guren

**Baday-Tugay State
Nature Conservation Zone**

*Lake
Ayazkol*

Gyorogly

Shovot

A380

Buston

Kukcha

Khiva

Urgench

Beruni

Khorezm

Khanka

Turtkul

*Bukhara, Samarkand,
Tashkent*

▲ 142m

Ashgabat

destinations. It is also possible to fly to Moscow with Uzbekistan Airways (twice a week; 3hrs 40min; from US$150). The airport, refurbished and expanded in 2018, is 2km northeast of the city, at the end of Dosnazarov. Bus number 15 runs the length of Dosnazarov from the train station (see below) to the airport.

For airline ticketing, you need the **Uzbekistan Airways** office (43 Pushkin; \ 61 222 8353; e info@uzairways.com) or **Airservis Nukus** (15 Karakalpakstan; \ 61 222 3773).

By rail The railway station is at the southern end of Dosnazarov, 3km from the centre and is reachable on any minibus marked Voksal. Trains run overnight from Nukus via Samarkand to Tashkent (22hrs; from US$12). The new line from Nukus to Navoi bypasses Turkmenistan, thus removing the former need for a transit visa, but there are international services continuing to Saratov and Moscow. Tickets can be purchased at the station or online (w uzrailpass.uz).

By road Nukus lies 140km past Urgench, heading northwest on the A380, a 2-hour drive if you're coming by car. Coming from Khiva and Urgench, there's a fairly new road bridge over the Amu Darya that meets the Nukus road at Beruni (510km west of Bukhara). It's a far shorter drive (40km) across the Turkmen border to Konya-Urgench, though you'll inevitably have time-consuming border formalities to deal with. A taxi from Nukus to the border near Hojeli will cost you around US$12 and take around 30 minutes. On the Turkmen side, you may be lucky and find a taxi, but otherwise you will need to hitchhike with a motorist going in your direction.

The main bus station is the **Yuzhny Avtovokzal** (South Bus Station), beyond the railway station (you'll need a bus or taxi to get from one to the other). From here there are two long-distance buses a day to Urgench (3hrs; US$3), Bukhara (8hrs; US$7) and Samarkand (14hrs; US$10), and more frequent local buses (numbers 1 and 6) to Beruni and Moynaq. **Shared taxis** to Urgench or Khiva via Beruni depart from the same stop (2/2½hrs; US$8/12).

There are two **buses** a day to Tashkent. These depart from the **bus stop** outside Hotel Nukus (4 Lumumba; 22hrs, US$14).

GETTING AROUND The centre of the city is contained within a square roughly 2km across, and the grid layout means it is easy to get around on foot. Most **minibus** routes run from the bazaar and cost US$0.10, the most useful ones being clearly marked Voksal, Autovoksal or Aeroport.

If you prefer to pre-book a taxi, try calling **Taxi Pilot** (\ 61 361 5555), **EST** (m 93 488 4407) or **Avto Vektor** (\ 61 222 0088). You will need to speak Russian or Uzbek to explain when and where to collect you. A ride within the city limits should not cost more than US$2. Bikes may be available at your hotel.

TOUR OPERATORS The following organisations can organise tours of the area.

Ayim Tour 4 Jipek Joli; \ 61 222 1100; e jipek_ hotel@rambler.ru; w ayimtour.com. Karakalpak specialists offering tours of the Khorezm fortresses & the Aral Sea. The same company owns the Jipek Joli hotels & café (page 276) & the House Museum of Amet & Aiymkhan Shamuratov, all at the same address, plus a yurt camp in the desert.

BesQala 29/16 U Yusupov; m 91 377 7729/97 354 0024; w besqala.com. Guided tours to the Aral Sea & a yurt camp; also air tickets.
Sihaya Tours 41 Berdakh; m 93 363 1122/91 383 1122. Guided tours around Nukus, & guides & transport to the Aral Sea.

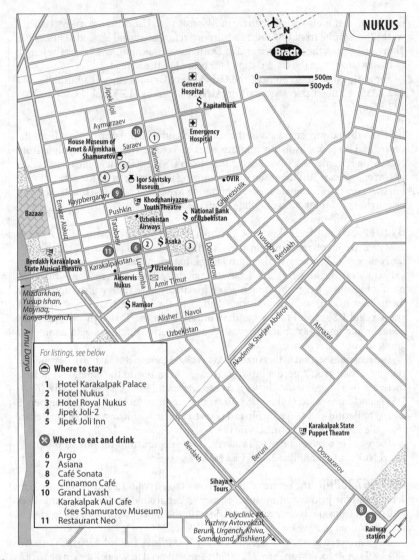

For listings, see below

🏠 Where to stay

1 Hotel Karakalpak Palace
2 Hotel Nukus
3 Hotel Royal Nukus
4 Jipek Joli-2
5 Jipek Joli Inn

🍽 Where to eat and drink

6 Argo
7 Asiana
8 Café Sonata
9 Cinnamon Café
10 Grand Lavash
  Karakalpak Aul Cafe
  (see Shamuratov Museum)
11 Restaurant Neo

🏠 WHERE TO STAY *Map, above*

The accommodation options in Nukus have improved significantly in recent years, and though the hotels are not up to international standards, you'll find the following options clean and conveniently located.

🏠 Hotel Karakalpak Palace (20 rooms) 114 Karimov; ☎ 61 222 5858; m 95 601 5858; e k.palace.hotel@mail.ru; w karakalpak-palace. uz. New in 2018 & just a block north of the central square (the entry is on Saraev, a minor cross-road), this has comfortable AC rooms & free bikes. **$$$**

🏠 Jipek Joli Inn (19 rooms) 4 Jipek Joli; ☎ 61 222 8500; e jipekhotel@gmail.com; w ayimtour. com. The best place to stay in Nukus is owned by Ayim Tour (see oposite). It's in a good location, just north of the Igor Savitsky Museum (page 278), the staff are helpful, & there is a friendly bar (with Wi-Fi) downstairs & in the pleasant courtyard garden. There are a few English satellite TV channels. Request one of the slightly more expensive AC rooms in summer, or head to the newer & slightly better **Jipek Joli-2 Hotel ($$$)** a block west of the museum, which has a restaurant **($$)** & ATM. **$$$**

🏠 **Hotel Nukus** (36 rooms) 4 Lumumba; ☎61 222 8941. Partially renovated & in a good location, this hotel shouldn't be so disappointing, but it is. There is a restaurant **($$)** & bar downstairs, but b/fast is very basic. Haggle, as out of season you can get a dbl for US$25, a third off the advertised rate.

You can pay half that if you share a twin with a stranger, hostel-style. **$$**

🏠 **Hotel Royal Nukus** (13 rooms) 4 Karakalpakstan; ☎61 222 4743; e hotelroyalnukus@mail.ru; w hotelroyalnukus.uz. Opened in 2010 (as the Rahnamo), Nukus's self-professed 4-star hotel is a small establishment with something of the Fawlty Towers about it. It's overpriced for what you get, with erratic electricity & water, but bathrooms are generally clean, staff are helpful & the b/fast isn't bad. B/fast & parking inc. **$$**

✖ WHERE TO EAT AND DRINK *Map, opposite*

✖ **Restaurant Neo** 21 Tatabaev; ◷ 10.00–23.00 daily. We had a perfectly acceptable meal here, with fresh *shashlik*, salads, & beer. **$$$**

✖ **Karakalpak Aul Cafe** 29 Saraev. Decent option at the Shamuratov Museum (page 279), where in summer you can enjoy your *plov* while sitting in a yurt on the patio. **$$–$$$**

✖ **Argo** 6 Karakalpakstan; ◷ 10.00–22.00 daily. Close to the post office, this cheap cafeteria serves decent fresh food at lunchtime & a poorer choice for the rest of the day. **$**

✖ **Grand Lavash** Cnr Aymurzaev & Karimov; ☎61 222 6622. Just north of the central park on

the main boulevard, this large & shiny place serves grilled meats wrapped in lavash flatbread. **$**

🍽 **Café Sonata** 3 Dosnazarov; ☎61 223 3106; ◷ 09.00–22.00 daily. This large Korean-owned café, & the meat-heavy **Asiana** restaurant (◷ 10.00–23.00 daily; **$$**) alongside, are just north of the station on the main drag. **$$**

🍽 **Cinnamon Café** 1–26 Jipek Joli; m 97 789 7789; f cinnamonuz; ◷ 10.00–22.00 daily. Good coffee, pastries, ice cream, burgers & pizza opposite the Igor Savitsky Museum (page 278) – slow service, but they're friendly & speak English. **$$**

ENTERTAINMENT Quite surprisingly for a city that feels like it is on the face of the moon, there are three theatres in Nukus. They all cater to local audiences, performing in Karakalpak, Russian or Uzbek, but regardless of whether or not you understand the words, it can still be a fun experience and tickets are cheap. You will need to contact the individual theatres to find out what is showing, and when.

🎭 **Berdakh Karakalpak State Musical Theatre** 1 Ernazar Alakuz; ☎61 224 0645
🎭 **Karakalpak State Puppet Theatre** 14A Dosnazarov; ☎61 223 7730

🎭 **Khodzhaniyazov Youth Theatre** 47 Kaypberganov; ☎61 222 8457

OTHER PRACTICALITIES
Communications
✉ **Post office** 7 Karakalpakstan; ◷ 07.00–19.00 Mon–Fri. Officially located here, but the public counters are currently a block south at 25 Avezov (◷ 07.00–19.00 Mon–Fri).
Uztelecom telephone office 7 Karakalpakstan; ◷ 24/7

✚ **Emergency Hospital** 100A Dosnazarov; ☎61 222 6005/61 222 6056
✚ **General Hospital** 110 Dosnazarov; ☎61 222 8111
✚ **Polyclinic #6** 1 Ulug Beg; ☎61 224 4196. For less severe complaints.

Medical
Nukus has a surprisingly large number of hospitals, but the 2 most useful to visitors in a sticky situation are included here.

Money
There are just a couple of Kapitalbank ATMs in Nukus, outside the Igor Savitsky Museum & in the Hotel Jipek Joli-2 (see above), but you can change

money at the following banks, some of which can arrange cash advances for Visa card holders.

$ Asaka Bank ☏ 61 222 5030; e qoraqalpoq@asakabank.uz; ☉ 09.00–17.00 Mon–Fri. Advances money to Mastercard holders.
$ Hamkor Bank ☏ 61 222 5340; ☉ 09.00–16.00 Mon–Fri

$ Kapitalbank ☏ 61 141 7190; ☉ 09.00–17.00 Mon–Fri. Advances money to Visa card holders.
$ National Bank of Uzbekistan ☏ 61 780 0020; ☉ 09.00–18.00 Mon–Fri, 09.00–16.00 Sat. Advances money to Visa card holders.

Registration
OVIR 56 Berdakh; ☏ 61 222 8615

WHAT TO SEE AND DO
Igor Savitsky Museum (127 Jipek Joli; ☏ 61 222 2556; e museum_savitsky@mail.ru; w museum.kr.uz/savitskycollection.org; ☉ 09.00–18.00 Tue, Wed & Fri, 09.00–19.00 Thu, 10.00–18.00 Sat, 10.00–17.00 Sun; US$5 for 1 building, US$7 for 2, guided tour US$1.70) Like a ruby in the dust, the Igor Savitsky Museum (also known simply as Nukus Museum) holds the world's second-largest collection of Russian avant-garde paintings after the Russian Museum in St Petersburg. It also has one of the largest exhibitions of archaeological finds and folk art anywhere in central Asia. Two new buildings have recently been added (inconveniently, there's no access to the central one, which houses archives, storage and study rooms). There's a small café in each block. A camera permit costs a stonking US$35, but captions are in three languages (English, Russian and Uzbek).

The museum is currently divided into six sections among two buildings. You enter through the **Archaeology and Ancient Khorezm** gallery, where you will find some of the most significant finds from the various excavations in Khorezm, including from the fortresses. There is some particularly attractive statuary, as well as pots, coins and ceramic pipes from a medieval sewer system that was in use until 1900. This leads into a folk art and ethnography section, with jewellery, ceramic ossuaries and pots, and a terracotta horse from the 7th or 8th century.

The **Applied Arts** gallery is the core of the museum (at least in terms of quantity), with more than 70,000 items from the 19th and 20th centuries, many obtained by Savitsky (see box, opposite) in the 1950s, and it is believed that the relationships and reputation he formed collecting folk art gave him the credibility and network required to later purchase his avant-garde works. The displays include a full-size yurt made of wool, leather, straw and wood, pile rugs, flat weaves, embroidery, appliqué work, printed and stitched leather, carved and inlaid wood and traditional jewellery.

The upper floor starts with **Uzbek Art of the 1920s and 1930s**, a comprehensive survey of schools from realism to avant-garde, including both Uzbek artists and foreign artists painting in Uzbekistan. The works show the important interplay of influences from East and West: architecture and decorative arts are drawn from Uzbekistan's Islamic traditions; artists such as Benkov, Koravay and Kashina depict the region's ancient cities; Nikolayev imaginatively blends the techniques of Italian masters and Russian iconography. There are also works of Impressionism, post-Impressionism and Futurism.

The collection continues with its most famous section, the **20th-century Russian Avant-Garde**, a *smorgasbord* of post-revolutionary works that narrowly survived Stalin's curtailment of creative freedom and prescription of 'Social Realism' as the only acceptable form of Soviet art in 1932. Art that did not conform with Stalin's ideal was repressed and its artists persecuted. Savitsky acquired works by persecuted artists (including M Sokolov, the murdered V Komarovskiy, and the Amaravella group), and paintings by then-unknown artists. The works of artists such as R Mazel, N Tarasov, and K Redko were not recognised, let alone appreciated,

Igor Vitalevich Savitsky (1915–84) was an ethnic Russian from Kiev. He was a painter, archaeologist and, most of all, a collector of art and artefacts. He initially trained as an electrician, but in 1950 he joined the Khorezm Archaeological and Ethnographic Expedition with the renowned Russian archaeologist Sergei Tolstov. Savitsky joined up as the expedition's artist, and the trip was to begin a lifelong love affair with Karakalpakstan.

When the dig was complete, in 1957, Savitsky stayed on in Nukus and began to collect items of anthropological and archaeological interest. He also started buying paintings by Uzbek artists and also a few by Russian artists from the avant-garde school, many of whom had been denounced by the Soviet leadership and were politically and commercially unpopular at home. Savitsky amassed such a large collection that he convinced the authorities of the need for a museum in which to house it all, and the Savitsky Museum was duly opened in 1966 with Savitsky himself as its first curator.

With exhibition space available, and the tacit acceptance of the authorities, Savitsky's acquisitive side was given free rein. Through a network of art dealers, friends and casual acquaintances he bought (or took with the promise of later payment) further works by Russian avant-garde artists including Kliment Redko, Lyubov Popova, Mukhina, Ivan Koudriachov and Robert Falk. These artists were already well-established names, but their work was not widely accepted in Russia. It was therefore a buyer's market, and Savitsky seized the opportunity with both hands, albeit at great personal and professional risk. His purchases made during the late 1960s and 1970s form the core of the museum's 90,000-item collection today.

The story of Savitsky, the museum and some of the artists whose work it displays is told in the excellent 2010 film *Desert of Forbidden Art* and the 2015 book *Homage to Savitsky,* published by The Friends of Nukus Museum.

by anyone else until the late 1960s. Do not, however, expect to see anything by Malevich, Rodchenko or any of the other truly ground-breaking early Soviet artists, with their geometric constructions – there's virtually no abstract art here.

The second building (quieter and rather chillier) starts with art from **Karakalpakstan and early 20th-century Uzbekistan** – some of the same names (Volkov, Tarasov, Redko, Mazel) appear, but there are new painters from Karakalpakstan, notably the innovative Kdyrbay Saipov (1939–72), who produced striking designs for the old Nukus State Theatre. There are even some abstracts!

The **Karakalpakstan Contemporary Culture and Arts gallery** aims to showcase and develop fine art in Karakalpakstan. Among the artists whose work is exhibited here are several of Savitsky's students: J Kuttymuratov, B Serekeev, A Utegenov, E Joldasov and the sculptor D Toreniyazov, who based his style on traditional woodcarving. You can also see some of Savitsky's own oils and watercolours in both buildings: he was a gifted painter in his own right, and indeed first came here as an artist.

The **Museum of Historical Studies** was closed and demolished in 2010. Part of its collection has been relocated here, and the balance was put into storage.

House Museum of Amet and Aiymkhan Shamuratov (29 N Saraev; ☏ 61 222 3452; w shamuratova.uz; ⏲ 09.00–19.00 Tue–Sat (or ask at the Jipek Joli; page 276);

10

US$2) Husband and wife Amet and Aiymkhan Shamuratov must have been the darlings of the Karakalpakstan artistic set: he was a leading poet and dramatist, she a beguiling and beautiful actress and performer in the 1930s and 40s. In addition to their personal papers and photographs, the museum exhibits costumes from Aiymkhan's numerous theatrical roles and also applied arts from Karakalpakstan, which are displayed within a traditional yurt.

AROUND NUKUS If you haven't yet had enough of Uzbekistan's cemeteries and mausoleums, you can drive 15km west of Nukus on the road towards Konya-Urgench, to two sites of interest, Mizdarkhan and Yusup Ishan.

Mizdarkhan was once the second-largest city in Khorezm. It was founded in the 4th century BC and inhabited for around 1,700 years, but then destroyed by Timur. Even after the inhabitants fled, the site was still considered sacred, and so local people returned to build mausoleums and small mosques, some of which have survived almost intact. The most impressive of these is the restored 12th–14th-century Mausoleum of Mazlum Khan Slu. Other Mausoleums of note include the 11th-century tomb of Caliph Yejereb, and the mausoleum of Shamun Nabi, whose 25m sarcophagus is said to grow another inch each year. **Yusup Ishan** was the rival town to Mizdarkhan, and also has a substantially sized cemetery dating back to the medieval period, with a similar range of grand Mausoleums. This is on the western edge of the village of Hojeli (20mins west of Nukus by shared taxi or minibus), from where you can take another shared taxi (heading towards the border) another 2km west to Mizdarkhan.

The Khorezm fortresses (page 270) are most easily visited from Urgench (page 249), but some (including Chilpik) are not far from the Urgench–Nukus road.

MOYNAQ

Moynaq (also written Muynaq) is the harbour without a sea. In just 60 years it has gone from being a wealthy fishing port on the edge of the world's fourth-largest inland sea, to a ghost town where skeleton ships lie broken in the desert. The shrinking of the Aral Sea (see box, page 10) is one of the world's greatest manmade environmental disasters, and nowhere is its impact being felt more poignantly than in Moynaq.

GETTING THERE AND AROUND Regular (but invariably overcrowded) **buses** (4hrs; US$2) make the journey from Nukus's South Bus Station to Moynaq via Kungrad (halfway between Nukus and Moynaq). It's faster to take a **train** or a **shared taxi** (3hrs; US$10) from Nukus to Kungrad, and then pick up a second shared taxi there (1hr; US$2). Direct trains from Tashkent (via Samarkand and Nukus) run as far as Kungrad, some continuing to Kazakhstan and Russia.

If you hire a **taxi** to yourself, it'll cost in the region of US$60–80 return as relatively few drivers want to make the trip of 240km each way. Most people prefer to visit Moynaq as a **day trip** rather than staying the night. A fairly recent alternative is to take an overnight tour including a stay in a yurt camp, arranged through a Nukus-based tour operator (page 275).

A ribbon development less than 2km long, when you get there, you can explore the town **on foot**.

TOUR OPERATORS For guided tours and transport, including helicopter tours out over the sea, you will need to contact Ayim Tour or BesQala in Nukus (page 275).

Although you will have a superb view, taking a helicopter in Uzbekistan is not advised owing to the poor maintenance and safety records of the aircraft used.

WHERE TO STAY, EAT AND DRINK It is not recommended to stay the night in Moynaq unless you really have to. The only hotel in town is the **Hotel Oybek** (\61 322 1868; **$**), also known as the Hotel Muynak, which lies 4km north of the centre, tucked behind the police station. It seems clean enough, and there is hot water in the shared bathroom, but the absence of fans (and often electricity) means it's unpleasantly sticky in summer. There's also the **Mayak Yurt Camp** (book through the tour operators listed on page 275; **$**) next to the reconstructed lighthouse (now a restaurant; **$$**), where you can also camp wild. The hotel can also provide dinner, but you may prefer to bring a picnic from Nukus.

WHAT TO SEE AND DO Coming to Moynaq is, perhaps, what you'd term 'disaster tourism': there are parallels to be drawn with Chernobyl or the 'Polygon' at Semipalatinsk. You come to see where the sea used to be, and the suffering it has left behind. Close to the Hotel Oybek, at the north end of town, is the **Aral Sea Memorial**, and beneath it the **ships' graveyard**, where various rusting hulks of former fishing vessels have been towed from elsewhere in the desert to create a tourist attraction. There were, at one stage, many more, but most have now been sold off for their scrap value in a desperate bid to compensate for the loss of income from fishing. Birdwatchers will want to visit the small brackish pools nearby, still visited by waders.

In September 2018, the first **Stihia festival** (**w** stihia-festival.org/en) of avant-garde electronic music was held here, as a means of raising awareness of the environmental disaster; it was repeated in August 2019, but it remains to be seen whether it has a long-term future.

The **Moynaq Museum** (US$1), halfway along the main street (opposite the old cannery and a fishing boat on a plinth) has photographs and paintings of the town in its heyday, as well as a fully equipped fishing boat, nets and cans of long-out-of-date fish; there's also coverage of other local industries such as fur-farming and rush mat manufacture. Sadly, it's rundown and may well be closed when you visit as it sees few visitors – ask around for the curator.

Tours will take you to the current shoreline, 150km north of Moynaq, and/or to Sudochie Lake, a remnant of the Aral Sea about 50km to the southwest of Moynaq that was turned into a reservoir and still has plenty of birdlife as well as active fishermen. The best **birdwatching** is in a corridor between what was once the western edge of the sea and the *tchink* or limestone cliffs along the eastern edge of the huge Ustyurt Eastern Slope, largely in Kazakhstan. This is still a migratory corridor for birds flying north to Siberia in the spring and back in the autumn. The area's most exciting wildlife, however, are the **saiga antelopes**, with their large bulbous noses that help them to filter dust in summer and to breathe warm air in winter. They are known for migrating in huge numbers, but are now rare. They are also still being hunted, both for meat and because the males' translucent horns are considered valuable in traditional Chinese medicine.

Appendix 1

LANGUAGE

Knowing just phrases of Uzbek and Russian, and being able to read the Cyrillic script, will make your life immeasurably easier when travelling in Uzbekistan, especially given that words are often transliterated into Latin with a confusing variety of spellings: variations such as Tashkent and Toshkent are fairly obvious, things get trickier if you're swapping X and Kh or K and Q, or if more than one word or name are combined. Thus, you might see Amin Khan in one place, and Aminxan in another; Muynak is often written Moynoq and Uzbekistan is often O'zbekiston. You'll have to get used to making some educated guesses. Apostrophes are also added, but you can ignore these.

Though people will always do their best to make themselves understood, English is not widely spoken in Uzbekistan, and you will both help yourself and make a positive impression if you can say a few words. Don't be shy, and don't worry about your pronunciation or grammar. Just go for it.

HELPFUL UZBEK AND RUSSIAN WORDS AND PHRASES In the Russian column of this pronunciation guide, capital letters are used to denote syllables that are stressed.

English	Uzbek	Russian
Hello	*As-salomu alaykum*	Здравствуйте (ZDRAHST-vooy-tyeh)
Goodbye	*Salomat bo'ling*	До свидания (da-svee-DA-nee-ya)
How are you?	*Qalay siz?*	Как дела? (kahg dee-LAH?)
Fine, thank you	*Yakshi, rakhmat*	Хорошо, спасибо (khah-rah-SHOH spah-SEE-buh)
What is your name?	*Sizning ismingiz nima?*	Как вас зовут? (kahk vahs zah-VOOT?)
My name is…	*Mening ismim…*	Меня зовут… (mee-NYAH zah-VOOT…)
Nice to meet you	*Tanishganimdan hursandman*	Очень приятно (OH-cheen' pree-YAHT-nuh)
Please	*Markhamat*	Пожалуйста (pah-ZHAH-luh-stuh)
Thank you	*Rakhmat*	Спасибо (spuh-SEE-buh)
You're welcome	*Arzimaydi*	Не за что (NYEH-zuh-shtoh)
Yes	*Ha*	Да (dah)
No	*Yok*	Нет (nyeht)
Excuse me	*Kechirasiz*	Извините (eez-vee-NEET-yeh)

English	Uzbek	Russian
Is there someone here who speaks English?	Inglizcha gapiradiganlar bormi?	Кто-нибудь здесь говорит по-английски? (КТОН-nee-bood' zdyehs guh-vah-REET pah an-GLEES-kee?)
I don't understand	Tushunmadim	Я не понимаю (ya nee puh-nee-ah-yoo)
Where is the hotel/restaurant/bank/bus station?	Mehmonkhona, restoran, bank, avtobus bekati qaerda?	Где находится гостиница/ресторан/банк/автовокзал? (Gdye nahoditsya gostinitsa/restoran/bank/avtovokzal?)
Where is the toilet?	Hojat'hona qayerda?	Где туалет? (gdyeh too-ah-LYEHT?)
Where can we buy ice cream/spices?	Qaerda muzqaymoq/ziravorlar sotib olsa bo'ladi?	Где можно купить мороженое/специи? (Gdye mojna kupit morojenoye/spetsiyi?)
Cumin, saffron, cardamon	Zira, za'faron, kashnich	тмин, шафран, кардамон (tmin, shafran, kardamon)
Where can we buy natural silk, cotton fabrics?	Qaerda chin shoyi, chin paxta gazmollarini sotib olsa bo'ladi?	Где можно купить натураль ный шелк, хлопчатобумажн ые ткани? (Gdye mojna kupit naturalniy shelk, hlopchatobumajniye tkaniy?)
How long will it take to reach…?	U yerga borish qancha vaqt oladi?	Как долго продолжается путешествие, чтобы доехать туда? (Kak dolga prodoljaetsya puteshestviye shtobiy doyehat tuda?)
How long do we have to wait?	Bunga qancha vaqt ketadi?	Как долго нам надо ждать? (Kak dolga nam nada jdat?)
Where can I exchange foreign currency notes?	Pul almashuvi qaerda?	Где можно обменять иностра нную валюту? (Gdye mojna obmenyat inostrannuyu valyutu?)
How much does it cost?	Buni narhi qancha?	Сколько стоит? (Skolka stoyit?)
It is too expensive	Bu juda qimmat	Это слишком дорого (Eta slishkam doroga)
Do you have this in another size/colour/material?	Sizlarda boshqa razmer/ranglar/material bor mi?	У вас есть это в другом размере?/в другой цвет?/в другом материале? (U vas yest eta v drugom razmerye?/v drugoi tsvyet?/v drugom materialye?)
Please give me the bill	Bizdan qancha	Счёт, пожалуйста (Shyot pajalusta)
I'm sick	Kasaldirman	Я болен (yah-BOH-lyen)/(m)/(f) Я больна (yah-bahl'-NAH)
Help!	Yordam!	Помогите! (puh-mah-GEET-yeh!)

ALPHABETS AND THEIR PRONUNCIATION

LATIN	UZBEK CYRILLIC	IPA (INTERNATIONAL PHONETIC ALPHABET)	ENGLISH SOUND (AS IN)
A a	А а	/a, æ/	ch**ai**
B b	Б б	/b/	**b**at
D d	Д д	/d/	**d**en
E e	Е е	/Э э /e/	sl**eigh**
F f	Ф ф	/ɸ/	**f**ish
G g	Г г	/g/	**g**o
H h	Х х	/h/	**h**oe
I i	И и	/i, ɨ/	m**e**
J j	Ж ж	/dʒ/	**j**oke
K k	К к	/k/	**c**old
L l	Л л	/l/	**l**ist
M m	М м	/m/	**m**an
N n	Н н	/n/	**n**ext
O o	О о	/ɒ, o/	h**o**t
P p	П п	/p/	**p**in
Q q	Қ қ	/q/	Ira**q**
R r	Р р	/r/	**r**at
S s	С с	/s/	**s**ick
T t	Т т	/t/	**t**oe
U u	У у	/u, y/	z**oo**
V v	В в	/v, w/	**w**est
X x	Х х	/χ/	**kh**an
Y y	Й й	/j/	**y**es
Z z	З з	/z/	**z**ebra
O' o'	Ў ў	/o, ø, ɣ/	w**o**rk
G' g'	Ғ ғ	/ʁ/	**g**uest
Sh sh	Ш ш	/ʃ/	**sh**oe
Ch ch	Ч ч	/tʃ/	**ch**ew
	ъ	/ʔ/	(unstressed)
Yo yo	Ё ё	/jo/	**yo**-yo
Yu yu	Ю ю	/ju/	**you**
Ya ya	Я я	/ja/	**ya**wn
Ts ts	Ц ц	/ts/	le**ts**

English	Uzbek	Russian
Where is…?	… *qayerda?*	Как добраться до… ? kahk dah-BRAH-tsuh duh …?) [lit. How do I get to …?)
I am vegetarian	*men vegetarianman*	Я вегетарианец (Ya vegetarianets)
I don't eat meat	*Go'sht emang*	Я не ем мясо (Ya ne yem myaso)
airport	*tayyorgokh*	аэропорта (ah-ehr-ah-POHRT uh)
bus station	*autobiket*	автовокзала (ahf-tuh-vahk-ZAH-luh)

English	Uzbek	Russian
train station	*temir yul vogzali*	вокзала (vah-KZAH-luh)
hotel	*mehmonkhona*	гостиницы (gahs-TEE-neet-syh)
left	*chap*	налево (nah-LYEH-vuh)
right	*ong*	направо (nah-PRAH-vuh)
Do you have any rooms?	*Sizga khona bormi?*	У вас есть свободные комнаты? (oo vash YEHST' svah-BOD-nyh-yeh KOHM-nuh-tyh?)
How much?	*Qancha?*	Сколько? (SKOHL'-kuh?)
cheap	*arzon*	дорого (DOH-ruh-guh)
expensive	*qimmat*	дёшево (DYOH-shyh-vuh)
The bill, please	*Iltimos, xisob-kitob qiling*	Счёт пожалуйста (Schyot pah-ZHA-luh-stuh)
menu	*menyu*	меню (men-YOO)
coffee	*qahva*	кофе (KOF-ye)
black tea	*chorniy chai*	черный чай (CHYOR-niy chai)
green tea	*zilloniy chai*	зеленый чай (zee-LYO-niy chai)
milk	*sut*	молоко (ma-la-KOH)
juice	*shira*	сок (sok)
vodka	*vodka*	водка (VOD-kuh)
beer	*pivo*	пиво (PEE-vuh)
wine	*vino*	вино (vee-NOH)
water	*suv*	вода (vuh-DAH)
1	*bir*	один (ah-DEEN)
2	*ikki*	два (dvah)
3	*uch*	три (tree)
4	*to'rt*	четыре (chee-TYH-ree)
5	*besh*	пять (pyaht')
6	*olti*	шесть (shehst')
7	*yetti*	семь (syeem')
8	*sakkiz*	восемь (VOH-syeem')
9	*to'qqiz*	девять (DYEH-veet')
10	*o'n*	десять (DYEH-suht')
20	*yigirma*	двадцать (DVAHD-zuht')
100	*yuz*	сто (stoh)
1,000	*ming*	тысяча (TYH-see-chuh)
1,000,000	*million*	миллион (mee-lee-OHN)

Appendix 2

GLOSSARY

Aivan Covered veranda with its roof supported by pillars

Ak White

Apteka Pharmacy

Ark Fortified citadel

ASSR Autonomous Soviet Socialist Republic

Aviakassa Airline ticket office

Avtobus Bus

Avtostantsiya Bus stand

Avtovokzal Bus station

Babushka Grandmother or older woman

Bagh Garden

Basmachi Muslim resistance fighters who fought the Bolsheviks

Beg District governor or other wealthy figure

Buz kashi Traditional sport played on horseback, like polo but with a goat carcass in place of a ball

Caravanserai Ancient hostelry for merchants and their animals

Chai Tea

Chaikhana Café or tea house

Chapan Striped coat, as worn by Afghanistan's former president Karzai

Chorsu Crossroads

CIS Commonwealth of Independent States

Cupola Dome

Dacha Holiday home

Daravaza Gate

Darikhona Pharmacy

Darya River

Dom Building or house

FSB Current incarnation of the KGB

FSU Former Soviet Union

GAI Traffic police

Ganch Alabaster carving

Girikh Star-like motif in tiles or plasterwork

Great Game See box, page 19

Hammam Baths

Harem Female living quarters in a household divided by gender

Hauz Pool or reservoir

Hujra Sleeping cell in a madrasa or khanagha

Ibn Son of

Ikat Striped silk

IMU Islamic Movement of Uzbekistan

Ipak Yuli Silk Road

IRP Islamic Renaissance Party

Ismaili Shi'ite sect; followers of the Aga Khan

Iwan (see *aivan*)

Jadid 20th-century Islamic reform movement

Juma Friday

Kara Black

Kassa Cashier or ticket office

Khana House or place

Khanagha Hostel for Sufi holy men

Khoja Descendant of Arabian missionaries; gentleman of high status

Khush Kelibriz! Welcome!

Kino or *Kinoteatr* Cinema

Kishlak Village

Kok Blue

Kolkhoz Collective farm

Ko'cha Street
Kufic Form of stylised Arabic script used in calligraphy
Kum Desert
Kupé Locking railway compartment containing four bunks
Kurgan Burial mound or fort
Kyzyl Red

Laghan Large platter
Lagman Noodle soup
LOI Letter of Invitation

Madrasa Islamic school
Manti Steamed dumplings, usually filled with meat
Marshrutka Minibus
Maydoni Square
Mazar Shrine built around a mausoleum
Mihrab Niche in a mosque that faces towards Mecca
Milliy taomlar National food
Minar/Minor Minaret
Mustakillik Independence

Navruz Persian New Year
Non Round, flat bread

Oblast Administrative region
OVIR Office for visas and registration
Oxus Greek name for the Amu Darya River

Piala Handleless teacup
Pishtak Decorative portico

Platskartny Third- or economy-class train travel, featuring bunks in open compartments
Plov Rice-based dish with meat and carrots
Prospekt Avenue

Qala Fortress

Rabat Caravanserai
Registan Central square

Saroy Palace
Sayyid Descendant of Prophet Muhammad
Shakhristan Inner part of a citadel
Shashlik Skewered lumps of meat cooked over coals
Som Uzbekistan's currency
Somsa Meat-filled pastry
SSR Soviet Socialist Republic
Sufi Mystic Islamic tradition
Suzani Embroidered fabric, usually used as a wall hanging or bedspread

Tash Stone
Teppa Fort
Tim Covered bazaar
TsUM Central department store

Ulitsa Street (Russian)

Viloyat Province

Zindan Prison

Appendix 3

BOOKS
History and archaeology

Boulnois, Luce *Silk Road: Monks, Warriors and Merchants on the Silk Road* Odyssey Guides, 2012. Detailed history of the people and ideas that spread along the Silk Road. Also available in French.

Francopan, Peter *The Silk Roads: A New History of the World* Bloomsbury, 2015. A superb reinterpretation of world history, with the Silk Road rather than Europe as its principal focus.

Hiro, Dilip *Inside Central Asia: A Political and Cultural History of Uzbekistan, Turkmenistan, Kazakhstan, Kyrgyzstan, Tajikistan, Turkey, and Iran* Gerald Duckworth & Co Ltd, 2009. A straightforward introduction to the former Soviet Republics of central Asia, and their immediate neighbours.

Hopkirk, Peter *The Great Game: On Secret Service in High Asia* Oxford University Press, 2001. The seminal work on the Great Game. Lively, scholarly and full of all the excitement of a *Boy's Own* adventure.

Marozzi, Justin *Tamerlane: Sword of Islam, Conqueror of the World* Harper Collins, 2004. Slightly superficial but entertaining account of the most destructive person ever to come out of Uzbekistan.

Soucek, Svat *A History of Inner Asia* Cambridge University Press, 2000. A scholarly account of the history of a complex region.

Tolstov, Sergei *Following the Tracks of Ancient Khorezmian Civilization* UNESCO, 2005. Republished account of the original excavations of the Khorezmian desert fortresses. Translated from the Russian.

Whitfield, Susan *Aurel Stein on the Silk Road* Serindia, 2004. Beautifully illustrated account of Stein's exploration of central Asia and of his archaeological finds.

Wood, Michael *In the Footsteps of Alexander the Great* BBC Books, 2007. A fascinating accompaniment to the television series of the same name.

Post-independence Uzbekistan

Adams, Laura *The Spectacular State: Culture and National Identity in Uzbekistan* Duke University Press, 2010. An accessible discussion of the creation of a new national identity for Uzbekistan in the 1990s. Incorporates both continuity of Soviet traditions and new, government-led cultural and political ideology.

Murray, Craig *Murder in Samarkand: A British Ambassador's Controversial Defiance of Tyranny in the War on Terror* Mainstream Publishing, 2007. Murray lays bare the darker side of the War on Terror and the UK and US support for the Uzbekistan government in spite of its disturbing human rights abuses.

Rand, Robert *Tamerlane's Children: Dispatches from Contemporary Uzbekistan* Ebury Press Oneworld Publications, 2006. Journalist and radio producer Robert Rand draws upon his three years working in Uzbekistan to create this complex picture of a country caught between its history and modernity, unsure of what its cultural and political identity should be.

Central Asian geopolitics

Mullerson, Rein *Central Asia: A Chessboard and Player in the New Great Game* Kegan Paul, 2007. Looks at the geopolitics of the region, with the central Asian republics themselves as players (as against the 19th-century works about the 'Great Game' which tended to regard the region as merely the chessboard across which the 'game' was played out by the great powers).

Whitlock, Monica *Beyond the Oxus: The Central Asians* John Murray, 2003. Vivid account of the last three decades of central Asia's history by the former BBC correspondent to central Asia.

Travellers' accounts

Alexander, Christopher Aslan *Carpet Ride to Khiva* Icon Books Ltd, 2010. Fascinating account of the establishment of the UNESCO-backed carpet workshop in Khiva and Alexander's own travels to discover traditional dyes, patterns and techniques. Well written and highly enjoyable.

Burnes, Alexander *Travels in Bokhara* Oxford University Press, 1973. Classic portrait of Bukhara at the height of the Great Game (see box, page 222). Fascinating.

Krist, Gustav *Alone through the Forbidden Land* Ian Faulkner, 1992. Thrilling account of an Austrian carpet seller travelling incognito in Uzbekistan in the 1930s.

Metcalfe, Daniel *Out of Steppe* Arrow, 2009. Adventurous traveller Metcalfe traverses central Asia in pursuit of distinct ethnic communities disappearing as modernity impinges on their way of life. Features both the Karakalpaks and the Bukharan Jews. A finely written and often moving account.

Moorhouse, Geoffrey *Apples in the Snow: A Journey to Samarkand* Hodder & Stoughton, 1991. Republished by Faber in 2008, this classic from the late 80s contains many insights into late-Soviet life and deeply felt responses to historic buildings.

Omrani, Bijan *Asia Overland: Tales of Travel on the Trans-Siberian and Silk Road* Odyssey Guides, 2010. Beautifully written and heavily illustrated historical travelogue drawing on accounts from Fa Xian to Anton Chekhov, and Marco Polo to Francis Younghusband. Full of humour, *Asia Overland* is an entertaining and informative read for armchair travellers and modern-day explorers alike.

Thubron, Colin *The Lost Heart of Asia* Heinemann, 1994. The author travels through central Asia soon after the emergence of the independent republics. One of a spate of accounts of travels through the region written during this turbulent period. Elegantly written and predominantly focused on Uzbekistan.

Culture, traditions and language

Azimova, Nigora *Uzbek: An Elementary Textbook* Georgetown University Press, 2010. Introductory course to Uzbek that includes a CD with interactive learning exercises.

Eden, Caroline & Ford, Eleanor *Samarkand: Recipes and Stories from Central Asia and Caucasus* Kyle Books (Octopus), 2016. Ambitious account of the foods of the Silk Road cultures.

Harvey, Janet *Traditional Textiles of Central Asia* Thames & Hudson, 1997. Informative introduction to the textiles of the region.

Khakhimov, Akbar *Atlas of Central Asian Artistic Crafts and Trades* Sharq, 1999. The first volume of this series covers Uzbekistan exclusively and has short essays on each craft written by anthropologists and curators. The colour plates are well produced and accompanied by old photographs and maps showing traditional centres for the different crafts.

Visson, Lynn *The Art of Uzbek Cooking* Hippocrene Books, 1999. Authentic recipes for 170 Uzbek dishes, from *plov* to walnut-stuffed quinces.

Art and architecture

Chuvin, Pierre & Degeorge, Gerard *Samarkand, Bukhara, Khiva* Flammarion, 2003. Heavily illustrated with exquisite photographs, this book is a visual journey through the architectural influences of Uzbekistan's three most famous cities.

Knobluch, Edgar *Monuments of Central Asia: A Guide to the Archaeology, Art and Architecture of Turkestan* I B Tauris, 2001. Scholarly overview of artistic styles and influences.

Lukonin, Vladimir & Ivanov, Anatoly *Central Asian Art* Parkstone International, 2012. Architectural tour of central Asia focusing primarily on the influence of Persia and China, Buddhism and Islam. Includes well-produced photographs.

O'Kane, Bernard *Studies in Persian Art and Architecture* Columbia University Press, 1996. Collection of academic articles discussing Uzbek art and architecture in the wider context of the Persian-speaking world.

Literature

Aini, Sadriddin *Bukhara: Reminiscence* Progress Books, 1986. English translation of one of Aini's finest works.

Ferdowsi, Abu 'L-Qasim *Shahnameh: The Persian Book of Kings* Penguin Classics, 2007. Deluxe, three book set of Ferdowsi's epic. Vividly translated and with fine illustrations.

Ismailov, Hamid *The Devil's Dance* Tilted Axis Press, 2017. The masterpiece of the leading contemporary Uzbek novelist, portraying writers from two earlier periods of Uzbek history.

Tabatabai, Sassan *Rudaki and his Poetry* Leiden University Press, 2010. Scholarly biography of the Samanid poet Rudaki, with discussion of many of his poems.

Thackston, Wheeler (trans) *Baburnama* Modern Library Inc, 2002. The finest English translation of the Chagatai Turkic memoirs of the Mughal emperor Babur.

Natural history

Ayé, R, Schweizer, M & Roth, T *The Birds of Central Asia* Christopher Helm, Bloomsbury, 2012. A useful field guide.

OTHER CENTRAL ASIA GUIDES For a full list of Bradt's Asia guides, visit **w** bradtguides. com/shop.

Brummell, Paul *Kazakhstan* Bradt, 2018
Ibbotson, Sophie & Lovell-Hoare, Max *Tajikistan* Bradt, 2017
Mitchell, Laurence *Kyrgyzstan* Bradt, 2019

MAPS The colour country map and regionals produced in this book were based on source material supplied by ITMB Publishing (**w** itmb.com).

Uzbekistan

Uzbekistan 1:1,580,000 ITMB Maps, 2012. New edition in English. Inset city maps of Tashkent and Samarkand.

Uzbekistan 1:1,500,000 Roskartografia, 2001. Large, Cyrillic map. Fergana Valley is shown at a scale of 1:750,000. Inset city map of Tashkent.

Central Asia

Central Asia 1:1,750,000 Gizi Map, 2007. Large, predominantly topographic map with a detailed index of places.

Central Asia 1:1,750,000 Nelles Map, 2011. Combined political and topographical map, including a small city plan of Tashkent.

WEBSITES
Uzbek government sites
w **uzbekembassy.org** Uzbek embassy in London.

Travel advice
w **caravanistan.com** The most comprehensive online guide to travelling the Silk Road.
w **gov.uk/world/organisations/British-embassy-tashkent** Website of the British embassy in Uzbekistan.
w **gov.uk/world/uzbekistan** Foreign and Commonwealth Office travel advice.
w **travel.state.gov** US State Department travel advice.

News and political analysis
w **bbc.co.uk/uzbek** Home of the BBC Uzbek service (in Uzbek).
w **eurasianet.org** News and analysis covering the central Asian region on a site run by the Open Society Institute.
w **novistan.org/fr/ouzbekistan** A wide range of news, mainly in French.
w **orientalarchitecture.com** Detailed and authoritative guide to the country's historical monuments.
w **theconwaybulletin.com** Independent news sheet covering central Asia and the Caucasus, founded in 2010 by the *Daily Telegraph*'s former central Asia correspondent.
w **timesca.com** The Bishkek-based *Times of Central Asia* reports in English on all five central Asian republics, plus Afghanistan.

Culture
w **karakalpak.com** Independent, authoritative encyclopaedia on the history and culture of the Karakalpaks.
w **uzbekcuisine.com** The definitive guide to Uzbek food and cooking.
w **uzfiles.com** An Uzbek YouTube with clips from Uzbek films and tracks from Uzbek singers.

Telephone directories
w **goldenpages.uz**
w **yellowpages.uz**

NOTES

Index

Page numbers in **bold** refer to main entries and those in *italics* to maps.

INDEX OF ADVERTISERS